"*Ecosystem Arabia* is a must read for understanding what actually goes into the making of a robust startup and tech ecosystem. It provides a real-life snapshot into such an evolution in the Arab world. It offers valuable insights from leading global experts on this critical and timely universal topic, as well as a blueprint for how nations can more effectively foster innovation and prosperity."

—**KLAUS SCHWAB,** Founder and Executive Chairman of the World Economic Forum and Author of *The Fourth Industrial Revolution*

"*Ecosystem Arabia* does a remarkable job of enforcing my findings in *Startup Communities* and providing a well-rounded case study of the Middle East and North Africa region or "MENA." It's an invaluable resource to ecosystem participants anywhere."

—**BRAD FELD,** Co-Founder of Techstars and Foundry Group, and Author of *Startup Communities: Building an Entrepreneurial Ecosystem in Your City*

"In an increasingly competitive and globalized world, governments need every tool they can get to revitalize their economies and catch up or stay ahead of the curve. *Ecosystem Arabia* is such a tool."

—**VERA SONGWE,** Executive Secretary, United Nations Economic Commission on Africa

"Hegazi's book is a must read if you are a global investor or want to understand the future flow of capital in and out of the Middle East. It's the next best thing to visiting these countries yourself."

—**KEVIN O'LEARY,** Chairman of O'Shares Investments and television star on *Shark Tank*

"*Ecosystem Arabia* provides a practical blueprint to ecosystem development."

—**TIM DRAPER,** Founder of Draper Associates, DFJ, and Draper University and Author of *The Startup Hero: A Guide and Textbook for Entrepreneurs and Aspiring Entrepreneurs*

"Amir Hegazi has collected the most brilliant thinking on building entrepreneurial ecosystems in one place. This book not only describes the exciting movement happening in the Arab world, but it provides great ideas for people building ecosystems everywhere."

—**VICTOR HWANG,** Vice President of Entrepreneurship at the Kauffman Foundation and Co-Author of *The Rainforest: The Secret to Building the Next Silicon Valley*

"Entrepreneurship and disruptive innovation are the new drivers of economies in the 21st century. In *Ecosystem Arabia*, Amir Hegazi captures the essence of what makes a sustainable ecosystem tick. It's a must read for anyone interested in learning what goes into making an environment that is highly conducive to entrepreneurship and innovation."

—**ADRIAN GARCIA-ARANYOS,** President of Endeavor

"Following early adaptor Dubai, nations throughout the Arab world like Saudi Arabia and Egypt are in a race to the top. *Ecosystem Arabia* offers useful insights for both those leading the charge in these countries and outside observers curious to see whether entrepreneurship can live up to its promise of promoting economic opportunity and stability in emerging economies."

—**JONATHAN ORTMANS,** President of Global Entrepreneurship Network

"Finally, a book that lays out a nuanced and comprehensive view of the Middle East from a business environment perspective. *Ecosystem Arabia* goes well beyond common preconceived notions and stereotypes to talk about the amazing entrepreneurial energy that is forming in this region."

—**SETH LEVINE,** Co-Founder and Partner at Foundry Group, Founder of Pledge 1%, Trustee of Macalester College

"To foster innovation, you need to harness creative minds, creative energies, and creative environments. Surely, it is easier said than done. Amir Hegazi and the countless remarkable individuals featured in his seminal work, *Ecosystem Arabia,* help provide clues and answers on how to do just that."

—**DAVID SHELTERS,** Author of *Building Startup Ecosystems: Introducing The Vibrancy Rating*

"Amir Hegazi has put together an impressive collection of widely diverse views on what entrepreneurship ecosystems are and how we can use the ecosystem metaphor to foster growth entrepreneurship. The ideas in *Ecosystem Arabia* are relevant not just for the Arab world, but for all regions around the world whose leaders want to enrich the soil of the entrepreneurship ecosystem, sow the seeds of growth, and then harvest the benefits."

—**DANIEL ISENBERG,** Professor of Entrepreneurship Practice at Babson College Executive Education and Author of *Worthless, Impossible, and Stupid: How Contrarian Entrepreneurs Create and Capture Extraordinary Value*

"One of the biggest stories in the Middle East—which the media almost never covers—is the world-class tech startups coming into their own and becoming globally competitive. *Ecosystem Arabia* provides a clear and informative guide to understanding the ins and outs of the astounding tech landscape in this region, and inspiring stories of the leaders who are making it so."

    —CHRISTOPHER SCHROEDER, Venture Investor and Author of the bestseller *Startup Rising: The Entrepreneurial Revolution Remaking the Middle East*

"If you're a policy-maker or ecosystem player in MENA or globally focused on developing your local tech community, *Ecosystem Arabia* is the ultimate resource."

    —ANDREW BERKOWITZ, Founder and CEO of Global Startup Media

"*Ecosystem Arabia* provides very useful insights as well as serving as a practical guide for anyone serious about playing a more meaningful role nurturing the Middle Easts' startup community."

    —BADR JAFAR, CEO of Crescent Enterprises and President of Crescent Petroleum

"Building a vibrant tech entrepreneurial ecosystem sits at the heart of our region's discussions on economic development and future prosperity. *Ecosystem Arabia* provides a comprehensive look at the current startup and tech scene in the Middle East, sharing insights on some of the unique opportunities that the market has to offer and the challenges that entrepreneurs have navigated. If you're a MENA ecosystem participant—entrepreneur, investor, mentor, or policy-maker based in the region or internationally—this book is for you."

    —MUDASSIR SHEIKHA, Co-Founder and CEO of Careem

"*Ecosystem Arabia* provides a clear, insightful, and comprehensive guide to understanding the real scoop of the startup and tech landscape in the MENA region."

    —SAMIH TOUKAN, Chairman of Jabbar Internet Group and Co-Founder of Souq.com and Maktoob Group

"The Arab world is experiencing a startup and tech transformation. *Ecosystem Arabia* gathers a wonderful collection of insights from the people in the trenches doing it."

    —AHMED EL ALFI, Chairman of Sawari Ventures, Founder and Chairman of the GrEEK Campus, and Co-Founder of Flat6Labs

"*Ecosystem Arabia* provides an overwhelmingly accurate and deep understanding of the industry that is propelling much of the growth and hope for the future in our region. Amir Hegazi has drawn from his local expertise and network to deliver an insightful perspective on launching and scaling a technology-enabled business in MENA. Through Amir's conversations with leading actors in the startup ecosystem, this book provides invaluable advice for those connected to the industry in any way. I highly recommend it."

—**FARAZ KHALID,** CEO of Noon.com

"*Ecosystem Arabia* provides both a theoretical framework and practical guide for anyone serious about building their own local startup community."

—**AMR AWADALLAH,** Vice President of Developer Relations at Google Cloud and former Co-Founder and Global CTO of Cloudera

"*Ecosystem Arabia* is full of vital scripture for anyone whose helping build an innovation economy in the MENA region and beyond."

—**ANDREW ROMANS,** CEO and General Partner at 7BC, General Partner at Rubicon Venture Capital, and Author of *Masters of Corporate Venture Capital*

"Policy-makers anywhere looking to catalyze ecosystems can benefit from Amir Hegazi's concrete experience and guidance contained in this book."

—**DANNY WARSHAY,** Executive Director of the Nelson Center for Entrepreneurship, Brown University

"MENA is not a mysterious black box. It has common grounds with developed markets and unique aspects that can be understood. *Ecosystem Arabia* offers a leap forward to normalize the way we look at this region."

—**TODD RUPPERT,** Founder and CEO of Ruppert International, former CEO of T. Rowe Price Global, Venture Partner at Greenspring Associates, and Board Member at INSEAD Business School

"Since we started mapping and ranking ecosystems, it was clear that the Arab world has vast innovation potential. We now witness more Arab countries and cities entering the rankings, and *Ecosystem Arabia* is an important resource for understanding the story behind this momentum."

—**ELI DAVID,** Co-Founder and CEO of StartupBlink

"In a time of massive global disruption, this incredible book is literally a playbook for the future of innovation."

—**NICHOLAS J. WEBB,** Author of *The Innovation Mandate*

ECOSYSTEM
ARABIA

ECOSYSTEM
ARABIA

AMIR HEGAZI

TRANSFORMENA
PUBLISHING

Disclaimer: The expressed opinions of each contributor and interviewee in this publication do not represent the opinions or views whatsoever of the author. They also do not purport to reflect the opinions or views whatsoever of other contributors and interviewees. The following material is for informational purposes only. It does not represent legal, investing, or personal advice. The author does not claim or take responsibility for the accuracy of any expressed opinions or views put forth in this publication. The enclosed information is meant for consideration only. It does not constitute advice or recommendation.

Ordering information: Special discounts are available on quantity purchases by governments, NGOs, schools, companies, associations, and others. For details, contact the publisher at www.EcosystemArabia.com.

Hegazi, Amir. *Ecosystem Arabia.*

TRANSFORMENA PUBLISHING, 2020

Hardcover print ISBN: 978-1-7325-4216-7
Paperback print ISBN: 978-1-7325-4214-3
E-book ISBN: 978-1-7325-4215-0

1. Business and Money, International, 2. Business and Money, Entrepreneurship, 3. Business and Money, Management

First Edition

Cover design by Nanne and Dean Adams.
Graphic design by Seham Syed.
Interior design by Andy Meaden.

www.EcosystemArabia.com

*Dedicated to all those working diligently behind the scenes,
making a great impact away from the spotlight.*

CONTENTS

FOREWORD

By Brad Feld

In 2012, I wrote *Startup Communities: Building an Entrepreneurial Ecosystem in Your City* based on my deep personal exposure to and experience with the Colorado startup and tech scene being one of the most vibrant and fastest-growing ecosystems in America. The goal of the book was to identify and break down the building blocks of a vibrant startup community, while highlighting the relationships and interplay of its various parts and providing a practical playbook that can be used by ecosystem builders anywhere.

While I remained hopeful that some of the principles I discussed in *Startup Communities* would resonate with its readers around the globe, little did I know the full extent of how far these ideas would spread. Wherever I went, I seemed to run into like-minded folks who shared some of my findings or practiced them day to day. The same sentiment was commonly passed on to me by members of Techstars, a global accelerator I co-founded in Colorado in 2006, which has grown to support and fund well over 2,000 companies from all over the world.

I have since come to appreciate the similarities between vibrant ecosystems—wherever they are—and it never fails to amaze me how much they actually share in common in terms of basic fundamentals. I learned that while there are universal first principles—founded in the required conditions for commercial creativity and collaborative effort—there is no one-size-fits-all formula. That is to say that, although certain immutable principles apply everywhere, the local context cannot be overlooked, as each ecosystem has unique characteristics. So, while the DNA or components needed to create robust ecosystems are ultimately the same regardless of specific location or environment, how much of and when each ingredient is needed differ substantially from one place to another.

This book, *Ecosystem Arabia*, does a remarkable job of enforcing my findings and providing a well-rounded case study in general of the Middle East and North Africa region or "MENA." As such, it's an invaluable resource to ecosystem participants anywhere. As a reader, not only do you get a driver's seat view into this exciting real-life "under the radar" ecosystem in the Arab world, you get exposed to deep insights and cautionary warnings from a diverse group of local players as well as global subject-matter experts on the topic of ecosystem development.

More broadly, Amir Hegazi recognizes the central importance of ecosystem development to the overall economic health of nations, both in MENA and globally. He crystalizes the key issues involved, leading the way in anticipating the most relevant questions: What are the building blocks of a thriving ecosystem? How can we create regulations that drive, not stifle, entrepreneurial activity and innovation? What policies and programs are needed to further promote regional and international collaboration and essentially "lift the ceiling" for any local startup striving to scale? How can we facilitate conditions that optimize capital flow as well as attract foreign talent and investment? What is the impact of culture on ecosystem development and how do we foster one that is conducive to innovation and entrepreneurial growth?

These are only a few of the questions Amir attempts to shed light on. Additionally, he touches on the key practical aspect of ecosystem development, including the role various participants in a given ecosystem play and how they can maximize their contribution to the overall environment. Meanwhile, he uses the MENA region as a real-life case study for ecosystem development and startup community-building.

In short, *Ecosystem Arabia* provides a unique, multi-lens approach to the topic as seen from very diverse perspectives and views from the greatest thinkers and players in the field, both in MENA and globally. It offers invaluable global and regional lessons on ecosystem development for any community, city, country, or region anywhere, creating both a theoretical framework and a practical guide for anyone serious about building their own local startup community.

I'm delighted to see that many of the principles and the spirit of *Startup Communities* are being carried out across the globe in as geographically remote area from the United States as the Arab world. It's my belief that developing a thriving entrepreneurial ecosystem should be at the center of any debate around economic development and nation revitalization. As such, I'm more optimistic than ever that we are developing much greater awareness and understanding of the best practices and tools available today to create fertile grounds for infinitely great things to come.

—**BRAD FELD,** Co-Founder of Techstars and Foundry Group, and Author of *Startup Communities: Building an Entrepreneurial Ecosystem in Your City*

INTRODUCTION

"A rising tide lifts all boats."

—**JOHN F. KENNEDY** (who frequently used this phrase to underscore that an improved economic environment benefits all participants)

The future of the world depends to a large extent on technology and technological advancements. The promise of up-and-coming innovative technologies that can help solve our most critical problems and significantly enhance our lives cannot be overstated. Some of those groundbreaking innovations are being created as we speak, while others have yet to be conceived. Whether it's artificial intelligence (AI), machine learning (ML), FinTech, autonomous vehicles, 3D printing, genome sequencing, or a host of other digitalization-related disruptions happening across practically every industry, these cutting-edge breakthroughs are bound to unlock massive potential and generate unprecedented benefits to mankind.

Those long-awaited innovations, from both established companies and startups, are expected to come to fruition at a much faster rate than ever before. Moreover, they're expected to come from all kinds of places around the world, even from unlikely ones.

The extent to which these organizations are successful in giving life to those creations largely depends on the environment they operate in, or what is commonly referred to as their "ecosystem." The business and the economic concept of an ecosystem—originally borrowed from ecology and biology, referring to "Something (such as a network of businesses) considered to resemble an ecological ecosystem, especially because of its complex interdependent parts," according to *Merriam-Webster's Collegiate Dictionary*—was first introduced in the early 1990s in James F. Moore's book, *The Death of Competition: Leadership and Strategy in the Age of Business Ecosystems*, in which he defined an ecosystem as:

> An economic community supported by a foundation of interacting organizations and individuals—the organisms of the business world. The economic community produces goods and services of value to customers, who are themselves members of the ecosystem. The member organisms also include suppliers, lead producers, competitors, and other stakeholders. Over time, they co-evolve their capabilities and roles, and tend to align themselves with the directions set by one or more central companies. Those companies holding leadership roles may change over time, but the function of ecosystem leader is valued by the community because it enables members to move toward shared visions to align their investments, and to find mutually supportive roles.

Since then, the term has been widely adopted in the startup and tech community and frequently used by the various participants in those environments—entrepreneurs, investors, incubators, accelerators, educators, policy-makers, and others—who are collectively referred to as "ecosystem builders." It has also been used interchangeably with various loosely related terms, such as "startup communities," "tech hubs," "innovation centers," and others, whether they're actually associated with a defined location or area such as what is referred to as a "cluster," or a more spread out geographic location, like a city, country, sub-region, or region.

That said, it's important to denote the specific differences between an ecosystem and just any business environment. Not every business environment is an ecosystem, no matter how developed it is. An ecosystem is a unique kind of environment that is conducive to the creation and growth of highly scalable and sustainable companies. It contains all, or at least the majority, of the supportive elements required: namely, a defined location, human talent, financial capital, support services, favorable regulations, etc., all dedicated toward a single purpose only—to support highly scalable and sustainable entrepreneurial activities and drive innovation and growth, and consequently maximize job creation, economic development, and quality of life.

An ecosystem also benefits from a certain critical mass of those elements and from a "network effect," whereby an increased number of participants—whether they are individuals or organizations—adds substantial value to the environment and increases the likelihood of it flourishing. As a result, this creates a dynamic where the whole is much greater than the sum of its parts. Ultimately, such a phenomenon bestows tremendous benefits on local economies and societies.

Why I wrote this book

In the summer of 2018, I published *Startup Arabia: Stories and Advice from Top Tech Entrepreneurs in the Arab World*, the first book to cover first-hand accounts from top tech entrepreneurs in the Middle East and North Africa region or "MENA." This was my humble attempt to educate and inspire the next generation of MENA entrepreneurs or, as I like to say, "try to be useful in the community."

Startup Arabia was largely inspired by Souq.com's exit to Amazon a year earlier (Souq.com is a place I am intimately connected with, having helped launch and manage its third-party marketplace platform). Soon after the release of *Startup Arabia*, Careem, a leading MENA ride-hailing provider, was acquired by Uber. This landmark transaction provided further evidence and further reinforced the belief that local tech startups in the Arab world can, in fact, scale and become world-class players. These two remarkable milestones combined with e-payment network Fawry's recent IPO (initial public offering) in Egypt, countless new, exciting local startups coming onto the scene, and many promising government reforms and startup community-building initiatives usher in an environment that is ripe for innovation, growth, and transformation in this region.

Since *Startup Arabia*'s release, I have had the opportunity to interact with hundreds of the most impactful individuals in the MENA tech and startup ecosystem. I also have had the honor to advise entrepreneurs, investors, educators, policy-makers, ministers, and a host of other key regional ecosystem players on the space. Moreover, I got a chance to work closely with dozens of CEOs and executive teams of some of the world's top tech startups, assessing and helping navigate MENA opportunities in terms of both creating and executing their go-to-market strategies for the region.

Through these invaluable experiences, I got the rare chance to gain a 360-degree view of the regional ecosystem, from every angle: top-down, bottom-up, inside-out, and outside-in. Consequently, I increasingly grew fond of the tremendous effort being made by all stakeholders involved in building their local ecosystem brick by brick. Today, I am more excited and energized than ever about the new prospects that lie ahead for the region, which are further accelerated by the advent and power of technology and a creative, young generation of hungry, fearless, tech-savvy local entrepreneurs out to "make it happen" against the odds.

That said, I'm cognizant of the complexity of getting it right. There are, in fact, many moving parts to building an ecosystem and setting up for continued future growth, especially in cases involving a transition from sub-optimal to well-run economies that are capable of competing globally and providing their citizens with jobs and prosperity. Such encouraging early signs in the region are, therefore, by no means a guarantee of long-term success. On the contrary, there is certainly some heavy lifting ahead.

As I began writing *Ecosystem Arabia*, I quickly realized that I was far from having all the answers, nor was there a single regional or global authority or comprehensive resource on the topic. There seemed to be many scattered, seasoned experts in various related areas, each of whom appeared to hold one or several pieces of the puzzle. I thus concluded that—similarly to building an actual ecosystem—the greatest impact lies in mining the best output of the collective. That conclusion led to the specific approach and methodology I decided to follow here.

This book attempts, in effect, to gather those isolated pieces of the puzzle together, hold them up to the light, and assemble them into an organized, cohesive, and meaningful whole. It's not meant to impose one rigid train of thought nor is it meant to push any agenda or ideology, per se. Quite the contrary: it's meant to provide various perspectives and points of view from the carefully selected 100+ diverse contributors featured in this book. Moreover, it brings together the who's who of the region's top ecosystem players and the world's most prominent global thinkers and experts on the topic of ecosystem development. Each contributor provides his or her own individual perspective on what it takes to develop a thriving startup and tech ecosystem, assessment of the current state of the MENA ecosystem, and/or suggestions on how to develop across the globe.

Ecosystem Arabia is, in effect, my second attempt to "be more useful in the community" by lending a hand to the region's ecosystem builders—those very individuals and organizations working diligently behind the scenes, making great impact away from the spotlight. I hope they, and other ecosystem builders around the world, find this book valuable in terms of providing a viable intellectual framework and practical tool that augments their thinking and efforts.

Ultimately, my "moonshot" aim for *Ecosystem Arabia* is to help educate and inspire ecosystem builders—both in the Arab world and beyond—to make the further necessary changes needed to develop their local ecosystems and stimulate their new economies. Meanwhile, I hope to provide an insider view into the current state and inner workings of the MENA ecosystem for globally minded companies and investors interested in doing business there. I strongly believe it's the right time for those players to step back and take a fresh look at the evolving realities of the region and take account of the tremendous opportunities within. I acknowledge that this is not an easy feat in the midst of all the surrounding negative news in the media. It thus takes curious and courageous minds that are willing to let go of their preconceptions about the region and be willing, instead, to put on an entirely new lens and see the MENA ecosystem unfiltered from an entirely different angle.

I invite readers to join me and all of the contributors who collectively made this book possible, and who are as passionate as I am about helping to make a positive change in the MENA ecosystem and beyond. To them, and to the rest of ecosystem builders in the MENA region and worldwide, and to you, I say: thank you for your invaluable attention and efforts. I wish you a rewarding journey ahead.

How this book works

Ecosystem Arabia covers four broad areas: an overview of global ecosystem development, a deep dive into the MENA ecosystem, recommendations for building the local ecosystem, and a scan of best practices in ecosystem development from around the globe.

In chapters I and II, I touch on the macro view of ecosystem development topics. The insights and perspectives presented there are from some of the leading authorities in the field, both from the academic and research side as well as the practical application side. I begin, literally, at the very beginning by defining what's an ecosystem and what it's not, and what purpose it serves.

I then cover the key components of a thriving ecosystem, or what I refer to as "building blocks." You will hear again from a diverse group of global thought leaders and experts who break down the essence and essentials of such an environment. They provide alternative and often complementary views that crystallize the concept and the application more vividly, while presenting the latest thinking around the topic.

Next, I take a detailed look into what's not working in ecosystem development globally. Here I touch on counterproductive practices, misguided efforts, and misallocated resources. I touch on why well-intentioned and well-funded initiatives often fail to deliver their intended results in an effort to warn against some potential pitfalls of ecosystem development.

After establishing the macro or global backdrop, in chapter III, I provide some background for the MENA region in general. I take a brief account of the geographical, demographical, historical, economic, and political backdrop of the region. No ecosystem exists in a vacuum; hence, it's important to get the lay of the land before I proceed to cover the various aspects of the ecosystem. I also make broad stroke assessments of its viability as place for global players to do business and invest in.

In chapters IV, V, and VI, I address the nuts and bolts of the local MENA ecosystem, as viewed from countless stakeholders within it. They include top entrepreneurs, investors, service providers, educators, media professionals, policy-makers, and others. You will hear from some of the leading ecosystem builders in the region, some of whom have been there and witnessed its full transformation from day one, and even played a material role in shaping it to where it is today. Collectively, those remarkable individuals provide a better picture of what happened and what's happening in the region's ecosystem than any single authority can ever provide. They literally have hundreds of years of combined experience in the space. As such, they are by far the most knowledgeable and credible individuals on the topic today. In these three chapters, they generously share their experience and thoughts on the current state of the MENA ecosystem and its evolution over the years. They then break down the most pressing challenges that the ecosystem currently faces, which threaten its prospects for growth. Finally, they share their outlook and expectations on their regional ecosystem.

In chapters VII and VIII, I shift gears by moving from description to prescription. I cover recommendations to further develop the local ecosystem, primarily by addressing the key gaps and challenges discussed earlier. Additionally, I present opposing and non-traditional views and progressive approaches from regional and global contributors. I then explore some of the promising opportunities in the region for startups, in terms of which sectors, technologies, and business models hold the most potential for future impact and commercial success in chapter IX.

No discussion that attempts to provide advice on ecosystem development is complete without also taking a broader view, beyond one ecosystem, into others. Thus, in final chapters X and XI, I examine global lessons in ecosystem development and cover such topics as understanding your own ecosystem's strengths and weaknesses, meanwhile learning from positive international examples of ecosystems that managed to achieve remarkable success in spite of less than ideal circumstances.

All in all, I attempt to provide a full representation of the region's ecosystem from as many angles as possible, via hundreds of hours of one-on-one interviews. My goal being to represent as many facets of the ecosystem as possible, across as many geographies as possible, and covering as many related topics as possible. I was also highly selective and followed strict selection criteria and a process that ensure only "the best of the best" contributors are featured. Similarly, I made sure that only the most insightful and original content is presented. I also placed great emphasis on diversity to make sure all voices are heard, even if the output proved to be contradictory in some cases.

Overall, I adhered to a "blank slate" approach when embarking on this big puzzle, staying open to different outcomes and letting the various pieces fall where they may. Granted, this process is not flawless as it was partially dependent on the access to and availability of the individuals I sought to feature. To offset this, I erred on the side of more contributors (hence, ended with well over 100), in order make sure there's no stone left unturned. Even so, by no means is this book an exhaustive treaty of such a complex, dynamic topic. Thus, there is plenty of room for others to build on this work and/or develop their own unique approach and provide a complementary point of view, or even alternative findings, to ideas and perspectives presented here.

As a bonus, I've included an excerpt from my previous bestselling book, *Startup Arabia*, featuring Mudassir Sheikha, Co-Founder and CEO of Careem, Careem being one of the most successful tech startups in the region, which was recently acquired by Uber for $3.1 billion. Mudassir provides a real-life, in-the-trenches perspective of what it's like to build a leading startup from the ground up in the region and extraordinarily scale.

Essentially, I wrote *Ecosystem Arabia* to help facilitate the creation of an ecosystem that can foster the growth of the next 5, 20, or 100 "Careems," as well as the inception and development of thousands of remarkable startups and entrepreneurial ventures across the region, while employing and serving millions. Some may say such aspirations are too ambitious. I would actually argue that not only are they achievable, they are critical for the region to survive and thrive in the fourth industrial revolution.

As a large portion of the region aims to shift from direct or indirect reliance on an extractive, oil-based economy to a diverse, tech-based economy, and as the world becomes more advanced and competitive, this progression is a must. As such, the topic of innovation and ecosystem development must move front and center in any strategy related to economic development in the MENA region and beyond. Governments and other key stakeholders in the region and the global economy are forewarned to overlook or downplay its role and importance at their own risk.

CONTRIBUTORS

GLOBAL THOUGHT LEADERS AND EXPERTS

DAVID AUDRETSCH—Distinguished Professor and Ameritech Chair of Economic Development at Indiana University and Co-Author of *Entrepreneurial Ecosystems: Place-Based Transformations and Transitions*

BILL AULET—Managing Director of the Martin Trust Center for MIT Entrepreneurship and Author of *Disciplined Entrepreneurship: 24 Steps to a Successful Startup*

MAX BORDERS—Executive Director of Social Evolution and Author of *The Social Singularity*

ERIK BRYNJOLFSSON—Director of the MIT Initiative on Digital Economy, Professor at MIT Sloan School, and Co-Author of *The Second Machine Age: Work, Progress and Prosperity in a Time of Brilliant Technologies*

SANGEET PAUL CHOUDARY—Founder of Platformation Labs and Co-Author of *Platform Revolution* and *Platform Scale*

PETER COHAN—Lecturer of Strategy at Babson College and Author of *Startup Cities: Why Only a Few Cities Dominate the Global Startup Scene and What the Rest Should Do About It*

BRAD FELD—Co-Founder of Techstars and Foundry Group, and Author of *Startup Communities: Building an Entrepreneurial Ecosystem in Your City*

RICHARD FLORIDA— Founder of the Creative Class Group and Author of *The Rise of the Creative Class*

WILL HERMAN—Startup Mentor and Co-Author of *The Startup Playbook: Founder-to-Founder Advice on How to Create and Build Your Startup*

KATE POPE HODEL—Co-Author of *Beyond Collisions: How to Build Your Entrepreneurial Infrastructure*

VICTOR HWANG—Vice President of Entrepreneurship at the Kauffman Foundation and Co-Author of *The Rainforest: The Secret to Building the Next Silicon Valley*

DANIEL ISENBERG—Professor of Entrepreneurship Practice at Babson College Executive Education and Author of *Worthless, Impossible, and Stupid: How Contrarian Entrepreneurs Create and Capture Extraordinary Value*

JOSH LERNER—Chair of the Entrepreneurial Management Unit at Harvard Business School and Author of *Boulevard of Broken Dreams: Why Public Efforts to Boost Entrepreneurship and Venture Capital Have Failed—and What to Do about It*

JOHN MACOMBER—Senior Lecturer at the Finance Unit at Harvard Business School

SAMI MAHROUM—Professor at the Faculty of Social Sciences at Solvay Business School, VUB (Brussels) and Author of *Black Swan Start-ups*

EFOSA OJOMO—Global Prosperity Lead at Clayton Christensen Institute, Co-Founder and President of Poverty Stops Here, and Co-Author of *The Prosperity Paradox: How Innovation Can Lift Nations Out of Poverty*

TIM O'REILLY—Founder and CEO of O'Reilly Media and Author of *What is Web 2.0* and *WTF?: What's the Future and Why It's Up to Us*

ANDREW ROMANS—CEO and General Partner at 7BC, General Partner at Rubicon Venture Capital, and Author of *Masters of Corporate Venture Capital*

ALEC ROSS—Former Senior Adviser for Innovation to the US Secretary of State and Author of *The Industries of the Future*

CHRISTOPHER SCHROEDER—Global Venture Investor, Tech Media CEO, and Author of *Startup Rising: The Entrepreneurial Revolution Remaking the Middle East*

DAVID SHELTERS—Author of *Building Startup Ecosystems: Introducing The Vibrancy Rating*

ERIK STAM—Professor and Dean of the Utrecht University School of Economics and Co-Author of *Entrepreneurial Ecosystems: Place-Based Transformations and Transitions*

GLOBAL ECOSYSTEM BUILDERS

AMR AWADALLAH—Vice President of Developer Relations at Google Cloud and former Co-Founder and Global CTO of Cloudera

ALBERT BRAVO-BIOSCA—Director of Innovation at Growth Lab at Nesta

STEVE CASE—Chairman and CEO of Revolution LLC, Chairman of the Case Foundation, Co-Founder of AOL, and Author of *The Third Wave*

TIM DRAPER—Founder of Draper Associates, DFJ, and Draper University and Author of *The Startup Hero: A Guide and Textbook for Entrepreneurs and Aspiring Entrepreneurs*

ADRIAN GARCIA-ARANYOS—President of Endeavor

JF GAUTHIER—Founder and CEO of Startup Genome

OSSAMA HASSANEIN—Chairman of the Rising Tide Fund and TechWadi and Board Adviser to the Mohammed bin Rashid Innovation Fund (MBRIF)

LAMIA KAMAL-CHAOUI—Director of the Centre for Entrepreneurship, SMEs, Regions and Cities at the Organisation for Economic Co-operation and Development (OECD)

BALA KAMALLAKHARAN—Founder of Startup Iceland and Co-Founder and Managing Director at Iceland Venture Studio

JULIE LENZER—Chief Innovation Officer at the University of Maryland, Board Member of the Center for American Entrepreneurship, and Author of *ParentPreneur Edge*

SETH LEVINE—Co-Founder and Partner at Foundry Group, Founder of Pledge 1%, and Trustee at Macalester College

DAVE MCCLURE—Founder of 500 Startups and Practical Venture Capital

MARC NAGER—Fund Director of the Greater Colorado Venture Fund and former CEO of Startup Weekend

RUBEN NIEUWENHUIS—Managing Director of TechConnect, Managing Partner of TechGrounds, and Co-Author of *StartupCity*

TON VAN 'T NOORDENDE—Founder of PHX

KEVIN O'LEARY—Chairman of O'Shares Investments and television star on *Shark Tank*

JONATHAN ORTMANS—President of the Global Entrepreneurship Network (GEN)

ARUNMA OTEH—Academic Scholar at Oxford University and former Vice President and Treasurer of the World Bank

CHRISTOPHER ROGERS—Partner at Lumia Capital and Co-Founder of Nextel Communications

LINDA ROTTENBERG—Co-Founder and CEO of Endeavor

VERA SONGWE—Executive Secretary of the United Nations Economic Commission on Africa

ENTREPRENEURS AND STARTUPS

JOY AJLOUNY—Co-Founder of Fetchr

EYAD ALKASSAR—CEO of Rocket Internet ME

ABDULAZIZ AL LOUGHANI—CEO of Floward, Managing Partner of Faith Capital, and former Co-Founder and Managing Partner of Talabat

IDRISS AL RIFAI—Co-Founder and CEO of Fetchr

RABEA ATAYA—Co-Founder and CEO of Bayt.com

AMIR BARSOUM—Co-Founder and CEO of Vezeeta

MOHAMMED JAFFAR—CEO of JustClean, Deputy Chairman, and CEO of Faith Capital Holding

FOUAD JERYES—Co-Founder of Alpha Apps Inc.

RONALDO MOUCHAWAR—Co-Founder and CEO of Souq.com and Vice President of Amazon, MENA

AMIRA RASHAD—Founder and CEO of BulkWhiz

ASHRAF SABRY—Founder and CEO of Fawry

RAMI SALMAN—Founder and CEO of Wrappup and Vice President of Growth at Voicea

MUDASSIR SHEIKHA—Co-Founder and CEO of Careem

TEJINDER SINGH—Founder and CEO of Q-Tickets

INVESTORS AND VENTURE CAPITALISTS

ISSA AGHABI—Investment Officer at IFC (International Finance Corporation), MENA and Pakistan

OMAR ALMAJDOUIE—Founding Partner of Raed Ventures

AHMED EL ALFI—Chairman of Sawari Ventures, Founder and Chairman of the GrEEK Campus, and Co-Founder of Flat6Labs

DANY FARHA—Co-Founder and Managing Partner of BECO Capital

ELISSA FREIHA—Founder and Director of Womena

VERA FUTORJANSKI—Innovation Director of 500 Startups

WALID HANNA—Co-Founder and CEO of Middle East Venture Partners (MEVP)

HEATHER HENYON—Founding General Partner of Mindshift Capital

RABIH KHOURY—Partner and Chief Exit Officer of Middle East Venture Partners (MEVP)

WALID MANSOUR—Managing Partner of Middle East Venture Partners (MEVP)

ZIAD MOKHTAR—Managing Partner of Algebra Ventures

NOOR SWEID—Founder of Global Ventures

KHALDOON TABAZA—Founder and Managing Director of iMENA Group

SAMIH TOUKAN—Chairman of Jabbar Internet Group and Co-Founder of Souq.com and Maktoob Group

INCUBATORS AND ACCELERATORS

MAHMOUD ADI—Founding CEO of Hub71

NAJLA AL-MIDFA—CEO of Sharjah Entrepreneurship Center (Sheraa)

AHMAD SUFIAN BAYRAM—Regional Manager of Techstars, MENA and SSA (sub-Saharan Africa)

HANS HENRIK CHRISTENSEN—Vice President of Dubai Technology Entrepreneur Campus (Dtec), a department of Dubai Silicon Oasis Authority (DSOA)

MUHAMMED MEKKI—Founding Partner of AstroLabs

NON-GOVERNMENTAL ORGANIZATIONS AND SERVICE PROVIDERS

ALI ABUKUMAIL—Senior Private Sector Specialist at the World Bank

DEEMAH ALYAHYA—Founder of Womenspark

DINA EL-MOFTY—CEO of Injaz Egypt

YOUSEF HAMZA—Partner at V7 Group

AIMAN KABLI—Co-Founder and COO of eleva8or

EYAD LATIF—Counsel for Emerging Companies at Latham and Watkins, Middle East

SAMIA MELHEM—Lead Digital Development Policy Specialist at the World Bank

TAMMER QADDUMI—Founding Partner at VentureSouq

CORPORATIONS AND CORPORATE VENTURES

PATRICK CHALHOUB—CEO of the Chalhoub Group

ROBERTO CROCI—Managing Director of Microsoft for Startups, MEA (Middle East and Africa)

BADR JAFAR—CEO of Crescent Enterprises and President of Crescent Petroleum

NED JAROUDI—Startup Business Development Lead at Amazon Web Services, MENA

MUHAMMAD NABIL—Partner and Startup Strategy Lead at Microsoft 4Afrika

RAMEZ SHEHADI—Managing Director of Facebook, MENA

OSMAN SULTAN—Founding CEO of Emirates Integrated Telecomm-unications Company PJSC (du)

MEDIA AND EVENT ORGANIZERS

PHILIP BAHOSHY—Founder and CEO of MAGNiTT

ANDREW BERKOWITZ—Founder and CEO of Global Startup Media

OMAR CHRISTIDIS—Founder and CEO of ArabNet

MUHAMMAD MANSOUR—Co-Founder of RiseUp Summit

ZUBAIR NAEEM PARACHA—Founder of MENAbytes and Qraar

ALISÉE DE TONNAC—Co-Founder and CEO of Seedstars World

EDUCATORS AND UNIVERSITIES

OMAR AYYASH—Ambassador of the UAE Innovation and Entrepreneurship Program at Higher Colleges of Technology

BIJAN AZAD—Director of the Center for Innovation Management and Entrepreneurship at the American University of Beirut (AUB)

SHADI BANNA—Founder and CEO of Potential.com

ANAND CHOPRA-MCGOWAN—Vice President and Managing Director of General Assembly, Europe, the Middle East and Africa, and Asia Pacific

HISHAM ELARABY—Regional Director of Udacity, MENA

RAMESH JAGANNATHAN—Managing Director of New York University Abu Dhabi (startAD)

SHERIF KAMEL—Dean of the School of Business at the American University in Cairo (AUC)

POLICY-MAKERS AND GOVERNMENT AGENCIES

ABDUL BASET AL JANAHI—CEO of Mohammed Bin Rashid Establishment for SMEs Development (Dubai SME)

AMMAR AL MALIK—Managing Director of Dubai Internet City and Dubai Outsource City, and Tech Lead at in5

MARYAM EID ALMHEIRI—Vice Chair of twofour54

AREIJE AL SHAKAR—Senior Vice President of Bahrain Development Bank and Director of the Al Waha Venture Capital Fund of Funds

YASMEEN AL SHARAF—Head of the FinTech and Innovation Unit at the Central Bank of Bahrain (CBB)

MAZIN AL ZAIDI—Director of Innovation and Entrepreneurship of Saudi Arabian General Investment Authority (SAGIA)

NABEEL KOSHAK—CEO of Saudi Venture Capital Company (SVC)

MOHAMED ANOUAR MAAROUF—Minister of Communication Technologies and Digital Economy, Tunisia

Chapter I

WHAT IS AN "ECOSYSTEM" AND WHY DOES IT MATTER

The phenomenon of ecosystems—in the business, not the ecological or biological, sense—as referred to throughout this book, is not new (neither are any of its commonly interchangeable variations or derivatives, such as "entrepreneurship ecosystems," "startup ecosystems," "tech ecosystems," and "startup communities"). It's nearly as old as mankind.

As long as humans have inhibited this planet and had basic needs, desires, and fears, we have needed to constantly learn and adapt simply to meet the sheer challenge of survival. We had no choice but to solve problems, be resourceful, and stay resilient. As we started congregating in organized cities, we also needed to learn to interact and trade with others, and to group together around common goals to provide for our own needs and those of our families and communities. Hence, we needed a system that governed our behavior both individually and within a group.

Hundreds and thousands of years ago—well before there were large corporations, boards of directors, IPOs, and "unicorns" (privately held companies valued at over $1 billion)—every one of those groups was, in effect, a startup commonly led by a founder or an entrepreneur. Of course, they were never differentiated and identified initially as such; the startup phenomenon has only been studied and understood very recently, at which point the concept was comprehended and crystallized, and ultimately labeled. Nevertheless, these groups were exactly that: startups led by entrepreneurs, organized around a shared purpose, and operating within a specific environment with its own defined rules or system—what we refer to today as an "ecosystem."

The fact that these past entrepreneurs and startups had relatively simple endeavors, and did not have the luxury of relying on the advanced technology we have today, is no reason to classify them, their activities, and their environment any differently than their modern-day counterparts. They, too, were "entrepreneurs" running "startups" and driving "innovations" within an "ecosystem." It just happens that their operations and environments were much less complex and intricate than those we associate with such terms in our modern-day world.

In other words, just because people grouped around, say, the task of finding and transporting clean water to a small community does not make them any less entrepreneurial than a modern multimillion-dollar startup on the verge of disrupting the water sanitation and water supply industries. The difference is, of course, a matter of complexity and scale.

Likewise, we're no less entrepreneurial in our societies and no less participatory within an ecosystem as people will be hundreds or thousands of years from now, when humans will likely have transformed beyond anything we could fathom today, and will perhaps look back on us as "primitive." Once again, it's only a matter of complexity and scale, not of classification or terminology.

The same is true for other key aspects of ecosystems—from fundraising, to policy-making, to supportive services. Those, too, existed historically, although they didn't have fancy names back then. There were no "mentors" or "accelerators" in the distant past. Perhaps they were all recognized as apprenticeships, where knowledge was mainly passed on generationally, typically within the family. There were also no "angel investors" or "venture capitalists" (VCs) back then, yet investing and lending in exchange for a share of profits or accrued interest are as old as trade itself. Traders, by definition, need a significant amount of cash flow to stock up their inventory and pay for physical space and labor well before they can sell their inventory and reap a full return on their investment. Therefore, they have always needed substantial investment and capital; otherwise they could never have survived. It's clear that angel investors and VCs were around a long while back as well, even if they weren't labeled or professionalized as such.

By the same token, there were no government-run backing organizations or "funds of funds" in those days, yet it was common practice for kings, queens, and governments to fund private endeavors and projects they felt were necessary for their countries. These included infrastructure-related projects: structures, roads, bridges, water supply systems, schools, and other endeavors they typically stood a chance to profit from, either as governments or on a personal basis as monarchs.

One notable example is King Ferdinand and Queen Isabella of Spain sponsoring Christopher Columbus on his voyage to sail west to reach the Indies, which ultimately resulted in his landing on San Salvador island in what is now the Bahamas during his first expedition (or what is commonly known as his "discovery" of America). At the time, it was believed that a shorter route to Asia existed. Meanwhile, Spain had a strong interest in trading with Asia, so the monarchs decided to finance Columbus, believing that they would ultimately benefit from the discoveries that resulted from his expedition. There are countless other similar examples from history, some dating as far back as ancient Egypt and even earlier.

As this shows, entrepreneurs, startups, investors, and ecosystems have existed for ages. In their most primitive contexts, they were assembled by groups using simple tools or manual machinery, or what we consider today to be very low-level technology. Nevertheless, at the time these were innovations in their own right. In fact, some of those low-level technologies remain as commonly used as any new, massively disruptive technology we have today—case in point: the wheel.

That said, the concepts of entrepreneurship, innovation, and ecosystems as we know them today have advanced light years beyond those early days—especially in the last 40 years or so. With the emergence of new and transformative technologies, we have come to understand and appreciate many of the underlying forces at work, not to mention their wide-ranging effects on practically every facet of our lives. Moreover, this trend is not going away anytime soon. As technology evolves, we will learn by trial and error and by reverse-engineering successful outcomes. We will be in an increasingly better position to distill what works and what doesn't. Ultimately, we will be able to more consistently and predictably create optimal conditions for innovation, value creation, and prosperity.

I anticipate, as we become more advanced in our societies, that there will be even greater interest in the topic of ecosystem development. It is even likely that it will become a specialized academic field of study, perhaps known as "ecosystemology," "ecosystem-thinking," "ecodev," "innovironments," or whatever variation. It might even become just as separate and recognized as other well-established areas of study in business and economics.

Today, when we speak about ecosystems and their definition, characteristics, and principles, we're obviously associating them with a defined dynamic. Daniel Isenberg, Professor of Entrepreneurship Practice at Babson College, and Brad Feld, Co-Founder of Techstars and Foundry Group and Author of *Startup Communities,* are two of the most prolific experts on the topic. They shed light on the nature of an ecosystem in this chapter, especially underscoring the complexity and organic nature of the phenomenon. Additionally, Sangeet Paul Choudary, Co-Author of *Platform Revolution*, makes a great distinction between three types or models of ecosystems in the world today, and highlights their relevance to emerging economies, such as the MENA region. Other contributors describe their views on the purpose and various applications of ecosystems, which always boil down to driving innovation in its different forms (as insightfully illustrated by Efosa Ojomo, Co-Author of *The Prosperity Paradox*).

Just as universities are organized to provide an efficient structure to accelerate learning, and hospitals are organized to accelerate healing, so ecosystems are developed for the purpose of accelerating problem-solving and innovation. Granted, unlike universities and hospitals, ecosystems are not defined physical structures or even defined geographic territories (as Will Herman, Co-Author of *The Startup Playbook*, points out). Nevertheless, the operative attributes in all of those examples are speed and efficiency. How effective an ecosystem is at accelerating the pace of problem-solving and innovation from within depends on how efficient it is in doing so using the least amount of resources. It's the delta of those two factors, speed of innovation and use of resources, that drives value and wealth creation and, ultimately, economic development, growth, and prosperity.

Without further ado, I refer you to the remarkable global thought leaders and experts in this chapter and their points of view on what an ecosystem is and why it matters. As with each subsequent chapter in this book, you will have to proactively decide what makes sense to you from both a conceptual organization and practical application standpoint. My purpose here is merely to present the various points of view of some of the best minds and most experienced individuals in the field, both globally and regionally, and highlight how they think and approach various topics related to ecosystem development. It's up to you, the reader, to use this content to distill valuable takeaway lessons or trigger new ways of thinking or seeing the world, so that you may ultimately play a more impactful role in shaping your own ecosystem.

1. Definitions, Nomenclature, and Models

DANIEL ISENBERG: I'm probably to be somewhat blamed for having popularized the term "entrepreneurship ecosystem" a decade ago in my *Harvard Business Review* feature article called "How to Start an Entrepreneurial Revolution." Fast forward to today: although the two terms are often used interchangeably, technically speaking I don't think it's as useful to use the term "startup ecosystem" as much as "entrepreneurship ecosystem." That's because entrepreneurship is not defined by the age of the companies or the age of the assets; entrepreneurship is defined by the extraordinary economic value that the entrepreneur infuses into the asset, though I realize that "startup ecosystem" is a simpler term to use.

Further, the term "ecosystem" itself is also often misused. The vast majority of references to entrepreneurship ecosystems refer to one or more of the following: incubators, accelerators, co-working spaces, angel networks, angel funds, mentoring, and pitch competitions. The problem with that identification is that it overlooks a number of critical elements of an ecosystem. Culture, social norms, and society's values are just a few of the intangible aspects that hardly anyone associates with an ecosystem, but their roles are essential.

I also think the term "technology" in the context of a "technology ecosystem" is often misused. Back in the 1970s and 1980s, we talked about science-based industry and high-technology enterprise and it was pretty well defined that there had to be some IP (intellectual property), patents of some kind that defined novelty, defined innovation, etc. Today, it's unclear what people mean by technology companies, since technology is used across the board for any company that wants to be competitive, even in traditional industries such as retail, manufacturing, energy, natural resources, logistics, real estate, banking, insurance, and transportation. Technology per se is no longer a differentiator, and so the term "technology ecosystem" has lost a lot of its usefulness.

Furthermore, "entrepreneurship" is often viewed as a new

phenomenon that was created by tech companies in Silicon Valley or Boston, but a historical analysis shows clearly that entrepreneurship has been around for ages. Speaking of the Middle East, I actually did a research project on the Phoenicians, who lived roughly 3,000 years ago, and it's remarkable how entrepreneurial they were. When you examine all the innovative work that they did—all the discoveries, the proliferation of their ideas and their know-how—you realize how much they have in common with our modern-day view of entrepreneurship. Sure, the context is vastly different, but you would be surprised to learn how much is the same—much more than people fathom. Angel investing existed centuries ago as well, in the era of maritime exploration.

Personally, I prefer the term "scaleup ecosystem," to be precise. It encompasses all of the key conditions that need to exist in order for local companies to grow very rapidly, as opposed to "startup ecosystem," "technology ecosystem," or even "entrepreneurship ecosystem." "Scaleup," which is just a catchy substitute term for "growth," connotes only the kind of entrepreneurship that is associated with real growth of the business activity in terms of customers, sales, profits, and productivity. Shareholder value is often a byproduct of these outcomes, but it is not front and center, and if it is not based on real business growth, it can be societally detrimental.

BRAD FELD: When I initially wrote my book, *Startup Communities*, the phrase "startup communities" didn't exist. This phenomenon was referred to as "entrepreneurial ecosystems" or "innovation clusters." There was a lot of academic literature about it, but there wasn't much in terms of actual practical lessons or examples outside of Silicon Valley and beyond just saying, "Look at how amazing Silicon Valley is. You should copy Silicon Valley," which I didn't think was a logical construct. There were also a handful of popular writers, and one in particular, Richard Florida, who had written a very powerful book in the early 2000s called *The Rise of the Creative Class*. The book highlighted the beginning of a new kind of urbanism with the greater concentration of people in cities, and the idea of getting lots of diversity and different types of experiences in a tight geographic area. Before that, there was another important book by AnnaLee Saxenian in the mid-1990s called *Regional Advantage*, which compared Silicon Valley to Route 128 and the Boston technology area in terms of the strengths and weaknesses of each. She also shed light on what caused Silicon Valley to have a much more robust, durable, and vibrant startup-conducive environment.

I used some of this thinking to form the way I approached the subject. In *Startup Communities*, which was a very practical book, I didn't try to write an academic treatise; I didn't try to make quantitative, research-driven arguments. Rather I tried to generate an anecdotal understanding, from an entrepreneur's perspective, of this phenomenon. What it really created was a catalyst for talking about and describing startup communities in 2012, and over the last eight years it has become part of the language of how entrepreneurship works. Fast forward to today: entrepreneurship is now a real global phenomenon that's reasonably well understood. The idea of building a startup community in any city in the world that has at least 100,000 people is now a believable and understandable construct, which is powerful and having a lot of impact around the world.

Historically, people use the word "ecosystem" as a description for many types of systems. One of the types of systems was this dynamic within a geographic region of how entrepreneurial activity occurred. Most entrepreneurial ecosystem-thinking prior to *Startup Communities*, and even since then in terms of academic writing and consulting frameworks around it, says that most systems are designed as a top-down phenomenon. They lay out what we like to call "actors and factors," where the "actors" are the people in organizations and the "factors" are all the things that occur within the ecosystem. Interestingly, most startup communities or startup ecosystems are very heavily oriented toward the organizations alongside the entrepreneurs. You end up with these frameworks that say these actors need to interact with factors in this way, and these other actors need to engage with factors in this way, and that's how an ecosystem works. It's very much a top-down construct that is defining, or more declarative, about what plays out over time in such environments.

The reality is a startup community is a complex system and a complex system is one that you can't, in advance, define or control. That's the key framing here. What you're doing with the startup community is you're allowing the startup community as a complex system to evolve over time, where you end up with something that evolves in ways that are not predetermined. The inputs generate outputs that become inputs. Those new inputs generate more outputs that become new inputs. As time passes, it evolves in a model in a way that is non-deterministic, which means that you can't say "here's what the outcome is going to be" when you start. As a startup community becomes more evolved, and as it grows and develops, ecosystem-thinking can start to be helpful. That's also when you start to put some frameworks around how different pieces of this startup community can help positively reinforce each other, but you still need that complex system to continue to move forward, even against the backdrop of the ecosystem.

SANGEET PAUL CHOUDARY: If you look around the world today, there are three different classifications or models of technology ecosystems. All three have different components. The problem is that very often one of them, being Silicon Valley, is seen as the poster child, and everybody tries to copy that model and it does not really work. Depending on where you are in the world, a different template may apply to you.

The first template is the Silicon Valley tech ecosystem, which has taken at least four decades, if not more, to develop. It started with Fairchild Semiconductors in the 1970s. Other successful companies, like Sun Microsystems and others, have grown organically from its alumni and the funds it generated. Then, over time, there have been numerous breakout firms. Fairchild was the first one, then came Netscape, then Google, then PayPal, then there was Facebook. Every time we had a breakout firm, the alumni of that firm would then create the next set of startups and that's how the whole ecosystem regenerates itself, leveraging a massive pool of talent and mentorship going back to the 1970s.

The combination of talent and mentorship attracted capital. Then capital, talent, and mentorship combined attracted a lot of IP, whether it was IP that was developed in the Valley or from other companies around the world that came in and set up their offices there. These were the key components that worked well for Silicon Valley. The problem is that, within the last seven years or so, many countries around the world have tried, and are still trying, to copy the Silicon Valley ecosystem, and because they could not copy talent and mentorship, they started by copying capital. That resulted in waste because people would just spend a lot of capital that would go nowhere without the fundamental ingredients: talent and mentorship.

There were and still are many governments around the world spending a lot of money to spark the next Silicon Valley in their countries. The problem with that is that governments typically spend money on sparking innovation, but there is no follow-on institutional commitment to capital from VCs. As such, there are a lot of bad ideas entering the funnel, but not enough capital to support good ideas to expand. That model of copying Silicon Valley does not work.

The second ecosystem model that we've seen has been the China model, where it's been the government coming in and retroactively helping the private sector build out its tech ecosystem. This happened not solely because the government wanted to build a thriving tech ecosystem, but also because the government wanted to prevent external tech companies from coming in. The Chinese firewall and regulation enabled the creation of companies like Alibaba and Tencent, which are very powerful today but which may not have succeeded if the Chinese firewall had not existed. On the other hand, companies like eBay and Google had to exit China.

If you look at that model, there's an unfair advantage that the government creates. The same thing is happening in AI. A lot of leading Chinese startups in AI today are in some way enabling or helping the government with its AI agenda. That's a second model where the government is very heavily involved, protection-wise. Again, that's not something that can be easily replicated, and most governments have not attempted to do so.

The third model, which I believe is the most successful one and most relevant and applicable to developing countries and countries in the Middle East, is the Singapore model. Singapore initially tried to copy the Silicon Valley model by starting with capital and startups, setting up a lot of funding programs, and all of that failed. Then Singapore realized that if it couldn't attract talent and mentorship, it wouldn't be able to solve this gap with just capital, and it would have to solve it with IP. So, it changed its strategies completely and as a result has been massively successful.

WILL HERMAN: We have moved greatly in the direction of having virtual ecosystems, or non-geographically-rooted ecosystems, but I don't think we'll ever move away from the importance of geographically local resources to really make a successful company. Not completely anyway. What it does mean is you can actually have a smaller team located in a central geography, and that makes more geographic locations good for potential startup ecosystems. Instead of needing, for example, several hundred engineers locally, it's certainly possible now to have 50 engineers locally with some distribution of the effort. Almost all of the companies that I've worked with that generate $25 million in annual revenue or less are looking at securing resources, especially engineering, in such places as Eastern Europe and parts of Central America that have become excellent outsourcing locations for engineering talent.

That takes a level of management skill that most startups don't have. A lot of VCs take an all-or-nothing approach when it comes to physical versus virtual ecosystem preference. They either want everybody local or everybody remote. I don't know if there is a right or wrong hybrid model; it really comes back to the ability of the leaders of the startup and whether they are able to manage remotely. It is much harder to manage a virtual team than it is to manage a physically located team. So, there's still a bias toward a somewhat centralized team to make things work. Where there are resources in specific geographies, there also tends to be money. Those two aren't completely unrelated, although they could potentially be. Often, you'll get good ecosystems built around major universities or clusters of universities. Therefore, you can get around location and geography a bit, but never completely away from it. If you look in the US, of course, you have the Bay Area, which is clustered around Berkeley and Stanford. In the Boston area you have MIT and Harvard and a dozen other schools. In New York you have NYU and several schools that are really the basis for the very quickly growing ecosystem there. In Austin, Texas, we see the same dynamic. You have UT (University of Texas) which has become a stronghold for entrepreneurship. These environments also attract venture capital or at least angel investors who can help start companies.

2. A Key Driver for Innovation and Economic Development

EFOSA OJOMO: When I initially started the research for Professor Clayton Christensen's and my book, *The Prosperity Paradox: How Innovation Can Lift Nations Out of Poverty*, I was not quite sure where it would lead because I had my own preconceived views. I didn't see how any innovation could happen in a country that was poor or that didn't have well-developed institutions, universities, governments, and infrastructure. My thinking then was that innovation is a byproduct of society developing.

Then, the more we learned about how today's rich countries have developed, the more we found that we have the equation backwards— that innovation was in fact the trigger or the prime mover by which nations developed. Infrastructure and institutions essentially build themselves around innovations in a society. It does not happen the other way around, contrary to widespread belief. That was an interesting insight for us and it became the central thesis of the book.

So how do we define innovation? Chapter 2 of our book is titled "Not All Innovations are Created Equal," and that's where we dissect what we mean by innovation. We identify three types of innovations. The first type we call "efficiency innovations," which essentially allow companies to do more with less. When a company outsources operations to a region with cheaper labor, invests in automation to reduce cost, or extracts resources from the ground that are more cost-effective, these are all efficiency innovation plays. What they're doing, in effect, is freeing up cash flow as a result of automating or streamlining processes in order to reduce the cost of operations. This new freed-up cash can then be allocated to shareholders or reinvested back in the company. Efficiency innovations in and of themselves don't really create development. If anything, they may actually eliminate jobs and lead to negative development of a given region, perhaps to a lower-cost, more competitive one. They are not harmful per se; they are actually a prerequisite for every successful organization and region. As such, every organization and region need to invest in efficiency innovations to stay competitive in the local and global marketplace.

The second type of innovations are what we call "sustaining innovations." These are innovations that make good products better. Sustaining innovations help companies increase margins and stay vibrant. Examples of such innovations include heated car seats, adaptive cruise control, and higher resolution cameras or more memory on smartphones. Sustaining innovations are also important; they help organizations stay relevant and keep their customers and employees engaged. They increase margins because they enable companies to sell their products and services for a little bit more money, in spite of the fact that they don't really create growth and development. These are merely substitutes or enhancements. When a smartphone maker manufactures a new, higher resolution camera or adds more memory to its devices, it doesn't need entirely new manufacturing plants or distribution and sales channels. It can use the existing infrastructure that's already set up.

The third type of innovations, and the most impactful, are "market-creating innovations," also referred to as "disruptive innovations." These innovations transform complicated and expensive products into products that are significantly simpler and more affordable. As a result, a massive segment of society starts using them. Thus, these innovations can have a truly transformative impact on the development of a nation. A simple example would be the evolution of computing. Sixty years ago, computers were really quite complicated. We needed technical people to operate them, and they were incredibly expensive. Only the largest organizations in the world could actually afford them. Today, the smartphones we have in our pockets are more powerful than the largest mainframe machine back then. They are also available at a fraction of the cost and usable by the layman without the need for technical skills. Every time the computer went from one evolution to the next, the innovators had to create an entirely new, what we call, "value network." A new value network is essentially an entirely new way to make the machines, sell the machines, distribute the machines, write software for the machines, and educate people to use the machines. That created a solid foundation for growth and development to occur, which created an entirely new industry and a massive number of new jobs.

If you look closely, you'll find that regulations oftentimes actually often follow innovation, not the other way around. You first create innovation and then the regulation tries to catch up with it, which is what we're seeing now happening in social media, for example. How do governments regulate privacy, data protection, etc.? There are examples of this dynamic virtually everywhere where there is disruptive innovation. A similar cycle happened historically in the car industry, which, as a result, triggered infrastructure buildout around the car. Then, new traffic laws sprang up to regulate this innovation. We then started paying for the infrastructure—the roads that the cars were being driven on. You begin to see this beautiful cause and effect relationship between innovation, infrastructure, and regulations. It's not to say that a society has to put a halt on all of the infrastructure they're building or regulations they're developing until full innovation takes place. That's not really the case. But we're trying to clarify the relationship between innovation, infrastructure, and regulation, to develop good polices that can help create sustainable innovation ecosystems.

ERIK BRYNJOLFSSON: The purpose of any ecosystem is, ultimately, to facilitate technological innovations that will enhance our economies and our lives. The argument has been raised for quite some time now that with greater innovation, most particularly in terms of automation and robotics, there will be a lack of jobs. Now, I don't think that there's any shortage of jobs that humans can do, so I'm not too concerned about job creation—but I am concerned about the transition and about income inequality as a result of such fundamental changes in society. If people don't have the right skills for the new jobs, they're going to be left behind and stuck in lower-paying jobs. It's really the responsibility of governments to invest in people so that they can make that transition. It's a huge opportunity going forward, and ultimately it will lead to much higher productivity and higher wealth for countries if they embrace it.

DANIEL ISENBERG: While innovation can certainly be transformative in our economies and lives in a very positive way, if we look at the evidence, it does not always come without a significant cost or investment, at least initially. It's not a straight upside proposition, as it is commonly perceived. Historically, along with providing immense value to mankind, innovation can contribute to inequality of income and wealth. More recently, serious issues have developed regarding the impact of innovation on privacy, along with a host of other newly surfaced issues.

In some ways, the problem for society is that the explosive

growth of innovation has exceeded society's ability to anticipate its ramifications. Slowing down the innovation, as some have tried to do with facial recognition, for example, is a bad answer. Instead, we should be speeding up our ability to use the discipline of ethics in decision-making in this increasingly complex environment.

The facts show that innovations and disruptions can trigger, directly or indirectly, some negative externalities or side effects in addition to great social and economic value. They often drive real estate prices way up, make the cost of living much higher, and reduce access for the broad base of the population to goods and services. I'm not saying let's ban it, even if we could. I'm just being realistic about the pros and cons of innovation and stressing the need for innovative companies to use disciplined ethical processes from the get-go as they expand their markets and apply their innovations.

I believe there's naturally always going to be a huge tension between our ability to make new things and our ability to foresee their implications. Surely, a lot of that is self-corrective. Take the introduction of the automobile, for example. While it provided great mobility and all the benefits that resulted from greater mobility, it also caused environmental pollution, led to dangerous accidents road fatalities, and invited misuse as with drunk driving. Over time, however, a combination of new safety innovations and safety and traffic regulations caught up to minimize, though not entirely eliminate, the damage in terms of the personal injury and death toll. Meanwhile, self-driving vehicles promise to significantly improve safety eventually, but again not without introducing a host of negative externalities, certainly in the short run. We need to learn how to manage those without slowing down progress.

There is a groundbreaking invention in biology called CRISPR-Cas9, which is an enzyme that was discovered just few years ago and has taken the scientific world by storm. It acts like a scissor, if you will, precisely clipping and replacing small segments of DNA. It's obviously a potentially great tool for preventing genetic disorders, but it also has huge ethical and social implications, because it has given people new power in an amazingly short period of time. It's really the nature of innovation, it solves something big in one dimension, but then problems arise that need further thinking and innovations to solve, and so on and so forth. So, every innovation comes with a phase of correction, regulation, and oversight. It's a never-ending cycle, but the cycle needs to happen more rapidly. Hence, in that sense, the antidote to the downside of innovation is more innovation, as well as more rapid-response and greater social responsibility in general.

Chapter II

MACRO VIEWS ON ECOSYSTEM DEVELOPMENT

So far, we have identified what defines an ecosystem and, just as importantly, made clear what it's not, according to top global thought leaders and experts on the topic. In doing so, we've identified current usage of the term that is too broad. This is the case for the term "technology ecosystem," for example, which practically subsumes any organization today (commercial or otherwise) that uses technology as a means to gain efficiency and productivity. On the other hand, we've implicitly differentiated our usage from those having too specific an application, such as a "financial ecosystem" or "software ecosystem," and countless other uses of the term in various industries for various purposes. Most notably, Daniel Isenberg, Professor of Entrepreneurship Practice at Babson College, illustrated the concept quite vividly and pointed out common misuses of the term.

Additionally, Brad Feld, Author of *Startup Communities*, provided some historical context on how his own thinking has evolved on the topic. He stressed one key underlying similarity with the term's root in ecology and biology: its organic, non-hierarchical nature. An ecosystem—as Brad Feld explained—is a complex system with no locus of control. Hence, it doesn't function with a single operator, just as no living creature can survive or function by relying on a single organ. In essence, an ecosystem is the sum of its parts, with none of its components exuding power over the entire system. In other words, it's the interactions within this environment that are responsible for its output. In fact, by implication, no component can fulfill its own purpose without involvement from at least some, if not all, of the other components.

By analogy—to borrow again from ecology—living organisms cannot survive without water any more than water can serve any meaningful function if it cannot be consumed by living organisms to aid biological processes. Similarly, in an entrepreneurship ecosystem, there's also that element of interdependency between the various entities involved. Customers need new products and services, which are created by startups and entrepreneurial ventures. Meanwhile, startups need funding, but investors themselves need to see, or at least project, the flow of customers to provide critical funding for startups. Both startups and investors need to be governed by laws, otherwise such relationships will be fragile. The rule of law and regulations lay out the rules of the game for all the players. But the rules themselves are useless if there are no players involved, or not much in the way of a game to begin with. Thus, the fundamental nature of an ecosystem is interactivity and interdependence; none of the elements that make up a given ecosystem are valuable or sustainable on a standalone basis.

Chapter I also highlighted the direct impact of ecosystem development on innovation and, ultimately, economic development. Several views were put forward on the value of an ecosystem and how it contributes to creating prosperity for nations. We now proceed to ask: What are the building blocks of a thriving ecosystem?

This is the next natural and fundamental question at the heart of any attempt to catalyze or actually develop an ecosystem, regardless of its stage of development. Granted, there is no sure-fire recipe or one-size-fits-all formula across all geographies. Nevertheless, the components are the same, though they may be classified or articulated differently from a mental mapping and communication standpoint. As an analogy, you may think of various recipes for the same type of dish. They all use the same set of ingredients, yet vary in terms of amount, timing, cooking procedure, and presentation. Obviously, the outcome will be different for different recipes, in spite of the fact they all share the same, or at least most of the same, ingredients.

Similarly, various ecosystems will require the same components, but entirely different levels of each at various stages of their development. In this chapter, we first look into those essential components that go into the making of an ecosystem. An ecosystem may survive in the absence of any one, or even a few, of those components; however, it will ultimately be handicapped and stifled or, at a minimum, never reach its true potential. As such, we attempt here to make sure that, first and foremost, we identify the various key components of an ecosystem, recognizing that some may be tangible and obvious while others may not. We distinguish between two main groups by classifying them as "hard" and "soft." Hard components are quantitative by nature and therefore can be objectively measured. Soft components are qualitative and can only be assessed subjectively. Yet, both are foundational to any study of ecosystem development.

We then attempt to break down each of those components and illustrate how they interact with the overall system. We next identify the key players and influences in any given ecosystem, or what Brad Feld has coined "actors and factors." Steve Case, Co-Founder of AOL and Author of *The Third Wave* touches on this as well, along with others.

Next, we shed light on some of the principles at work in a thriving ecosystem, particularly its needs at various stages. Julie Lenzer, Chief Innovation Officer at the University of Maryland, Board Member for the Center for American Entrepreneurship and Author of *ParentPreneur Edge* illustrated this with her "hierarchy of needs in economic development." Jonathan Ortmans, President of Global Entrepreneurship Network, and Kate Pope Hodel, Co-Author of *Beyond Collisions: How to Build Your Entrepreneurial Infrastructure*, also provide their own roadmaps. They each describe—from their point of view—the stages of ecosystem development and its changing needs at each stage.

It is interesting to note that there's no one way or view put forward by a single contributor or expert that is universally applicable across all geographies and timelines, or that can predictably and consistently produce desired results. As such, the ideas presented here, as in the rest of the book, are meant to be guidelines or tools for thought and action—they are neutral on their own. Their application or execution will ultimately determine whether or not they achieve their intended outcome.

Finally, we discuss what does *not* work in ecosystem development globally. There are a lot of great intentions and great effort being made across almost every corner of the globe, often with significant backing and support from the right decision-makers and stakeholders. Nonetheless, not all of those initiatives—whether public policies or private programs—achieve their objectives. This chapter attempts to provide an explanation as to why this happens.

As such, we then take an in-depth look at three foundational areas: regulations, capital, and culture. More specifically, we look into how counterproductive approaches, poor execution, misperceptions, or misguided viewpoints can adversely affect the growth of an ecosystem. We provide clues and insights as to what to avoid from these "worst practices," so to speak. More often than not, half the battle is just to minimize, if not entirely avoid, landmines and pitfalls. This is as great a priority as undertaking the right initiatives.

1. The Building Blocks of a Thriving Ecosystem

Foundational "soft" and "hard" components

BRAD FELD: I started thinking about the topic of entrepreneurial ecosystems in 2010. At that point, entrepreneurship was still not all that trendy outside of Silicon Valley and a couple of other places. That was post Web 2.0, in 2004-2008, and the iPhone had just come out.

Around 2010, I came across a very interesting article that made the case for entrepreneurship being the path forward out of the global financial crisis, which was obviously an extremely difficult time that triggered enormous structural challenges around business, governments, banking, capital flow, and a massive retrenchment of lots of organizations because of the revaluation of lots of assets and debt.

Entrepreneurship clicked along through this phase and a number of companies got created that are household names today. Facebook, LinkedIn, and Twitter are three that are probably front and center that all started in the 2004-2008 time period. This article talked about how entrepreneurship was really starting to become very visible again in the Bay Area, New York, Boston, and Boulder. What really caught my attention was Boulder being mentioned side by side with the other three very large cities. Boulder is a very small city by comparison. So, what was it about Boulder that made it special? For one, the density of entrepreneurial activity in Boulder was incredible. This realization got me thinking about the reasons behind such phenomena, which led me to come up with what I called, "the Boulder thesis." It entailed four principles that I detailed in my book, which were really the essence of what creates a startup community.

The first principle is that the entrepreneurs have to be the leaders of the startup community, and viewed as such, while everyone else is a participant. Government, academia, non-governmental organizations, large companies, service providers, and other participants are what I call "feeders" into the startup community. Feeders are important to startup communities and employees of feeders can play a leadership role, but the organizations themselves cannot.

The second principle is that the leaders have to have a very long-term view: they have to be looking at least 20 years into the future. That dynamic is a really important one, because many of the feeders run on much shorter time cycles—quarterly, annual, maybe multi-year time cycles—whereas the startup community is one that evolves and grows over a very long-time horizon.

The third principle, which is increasingly important, not just in the

US but globally, is this notion of inclusivity. You want to be inclusive of anyone who wants to engage in the startup community, regardless of their background, gender, ethnicity, educational background, and so forth. You want to basically create this startup community that involves, engages, and welcomes anyone who wants to participate either as an entrepreneur or working for a startup.

The fourth principle is that you have to have activities and events that engage everyone in the process of entrepreneurship. The mistake that's made so many times is that you end up in this world where you have lots of people celebrating and talking about entrepreneurship, but not really practicing entrepreneurship in a functional and structural way. There's an important distinction between a startup community that's healthy and one that's not. Where you have a bunch of people who are talking about entrepreneurship but not creating companies, not actually doing things that engage in entrepreneurial activity, it's not a healthy community.

DANIEL ISENBERG: There are a number of components that make up an ecosystem, some of which are obvious while others are not, and some of which are tangible while others are not. I have tried to illustrate this in "The Domains of the Scaleup Ecosystem" diagram I created.

Historically speaking, if we look at places that people associate with intense entrepreneurial activity—Silicon Valley, Boston, Bangalore, Boulder—none of those environments would have flourished as much without the existence of large corporations. That's an aspect that often gets overlooked. I wrote a *Harvard Business Review* piece called "When Big Companies Fall, Entrepreneurship Rises." It borrows an analogy from biology, a phenomenon called "whale fall" that refers to when a whale dies and sinks to the bottom of the ocean.

It actually becomes the wellspring of a complex new microcosm of seabed flora that can thrive for over half a century. It forms an aquatic ecosystem of its own, with different organisms and different colonies that actually feed on it.

DOMAINS OF THE SCALEUP ECOSYSTEM

LEADERSHIP

Unequivocal support, social legitimacy, open door for advocate, entrepreneurship strategy, urgency, crisis and challenge

GOVERNMENT

Institutions e.g. investment, support, financial support e.g. for R&D, jump start funds, regulatory frameworks incentives e.g. tax benefits, research institutes, venture-friendly legislation e.g. bankruptcy, contract enforcement, property rights, and labor

EARLY CUSTOMERS

Early adopters for proof-of-concept, expertise in productizing, reference customer, first reviews, distribution channels

FINANCIAL CAPITAL

Micro-loans, angel investors, friends and family, zero-stage venture capital, venture capital funds, private equity, public capital markets, debts

POLICY

MARKETS

FINANCE

NETWORKS

Entrepreneur's networks, diaspora networks, multinational corporations

SUCCESS STORES

Visible successes, wealth generation for founders, international reputation

HUMAN CAPITAL

CULTURE

LABOR

Skilled and unskilled, serial entrepreneurs, later generation family

SOCIETAL NORMS

Tolerance of risk, mistakes, failure, innovation, creativity, experimentation, social status of entrepreneur, wealth creation, ambition, drive, hunger

SUPPORT

EDUCATIONAL INSTITUTIONS

General degrees (professional and academic) specific entrepreneurship training

SUPPORT PROFESSIONS

Legal, accounting, investment bankers, technical experts, advisors

INFRASTRUCTURE

Telecommunications, transportation & logistics, energy zones, incubators, co-working, clusters

NON-GOVERNMENT INSTITUTIONS

Entrepreneurship promotion in non-profits, innovation, creativity, experimentation, business plan contests, conferences, entrepreneur-friendly associations

Source: Daniel Isenberg, Babson College

Similarly, large corporations are essential to building a thriving ecosystem, because they feed the growth of micro organizations or, in this case, startups. Boulder, Colorado, for example, the startup community that Brad Feld eloquently talks about, could never have existed without the adjacent IBM facilities developing and attracting talent. That talent was seeping into the ecosystem by undergoing several waves of layoffs from IBM for decades. The same is true of NORAD, StorageTek, and several large telecommunications and media firms. In addition, the beautiful landscape, friendly people, and top-notch winter sports served as additional factors in retaining that talent.

ALEC ROSS: A lot of the focus today has been on such areas as centers for R&D, high-end university students and graduates to do basic research, ability to do technology transfer and commercialize research, and access to high-risk early-stage capital including the networks around that: accountants, lawyers, mentors, business executives, technical talent, etc. This is the common formula applied today everywhere people are trying to build a thriving ecosystem. Certainly, these are all critical pieces of the puzzle.

However, I would like to emphasize one area that doesn't get as much attention as it deserves, and it is what I consider to be the principal political and economic binary of the 21st century. Looking back, the principal political and economic binary of the 20th century was left versus right when it comes to political orientation. In the 21st century, it's much more accurate to characterize the principal political and economic binary as open versus closed.

One thing that is almost indispensable to the creation of a successful ecosystem is openness. If you look at places like San Francisco and Boston and many others that have been successful, the cost of labor, goods, services, and real estate are all incredibly high. Nevertheless, there's an open culture that enables entrepreneurship to flourish. Meanwhile, a lot of the most interesting entrepreneurship has taken place outside the US over the last 10-plus years. Many of those environments can be characterized by their openness. They have diverse workforces; they have men and women and other diverse groups working alongside each other.

On the other hand, I find entrepreneurship lacking or debilitated in more closed societies. They may have the money, the talent, and the research; they can have a lot of these things and still be unable to create robust entrepreneurial environments. This is why Russia's attempt at creating its own Silicon Valley has failed. This is also why there have been disappointments in other parts of the world. So, a lot of attention goes into specific initiatives, legislation, programs, or funding that is meant to ignite a local ecosystem, whereas much less attention is placed on creating the right kind of open society that sets the stage for entrepreneurial and economic development.

When I talk about openness, I'm referring to three elements. First, it refers to economic and social mobility being available to non-elites. That means upward economic and social mobility is not constrained to the least. It doesn't matter who your daddy is, it doesn't matter who your uncle is, it doesn't matter if you come from a lower caste, literally or figuratively—you have the ability to achieve upward economic and social mobility.

Second, it refers to respecting rights of racial minorities, religious minorities, ethnic minorities, sexual minorities, and women. This means that religious and cultural norms are not set by law or by a central authority.

Third, it refers to religious and social norms that are not set by law, by a central authority. Ultimately, people want to be able to live and learn and worship as they choose, and think as they choose, without having a central authority say that something is state sanctioned or against the law. Those are some of the key characteristics of openness that I would define, which are critical to optimizing ecosystems and which are often overlooked. Additionally, things like the mobility of capital and the mobility of people into and out of the workforce are also quite essential.

The question often arises about how to reconcile this view with China. Surely, China is not entirely open, but it's not entirely closed either. I think there are aspects of it being closed, but there are other aspects where it's completely open. For example, regarding women, there is a big difference between the role of women in China and Japan. In Japan, even though by age 22 Japanese women are the most highly educated women of all the 36 OECD nations, Japanese business environments are historically very antagonistic to them. In Chinese business environments, however, one out of every three people in the

C-suite is female.

China is actually in the mid-range on the openness scale, if you will. There is a fair amount of free-flowing capital there. It is not always accepting of American capital, but often it is. It is a hybrid case. I do think that the comparative lack of openness of China, in particular its market, keeps it from doing real innovation. Most of the innovation that I've seen come out of China is derivative. It is based on the research and the creativity coming from somewhere else in the world. I find that there has been a fundamental lack of creativity in Chinese business. So, it's a mixed story for China on the question of open versus closed society. There's certainly room for improvement there.

We have two models in the world today. There's an American model and there's a Chinese model. The Chinese model is authoritarian. If you're a company, all of your data, all of your customer data, all of your business data, is shared with the state. The distinction between company and country doesn't exist. Then, there's the American cowboy model, which is where the companies act like countries—they act like their own sovereign nation-states.

I don't predict much regulation is going to come soon in the US because of the dysfunction of the American Congress. In order for there to be regulations in new areas like data privacy, they need to be passed by Congress and then signed into law by the president. These guys can't agree on what time of day it is, whether the sun rises in the east and sets in the west, much less on something complex like data privacy. So, I don't think we're going to see much come out of the US anytime soon. I also think we're going to continue to see an authoritarian "the state owns the data" approach in China. And then what's left is everybody else in the middle.

There are 196 countries on Earth, with less than 194 countries that are independent of China and the US, that have to make choices about what their own models of growth in governance will be. I am waiting to see what alternative models to the American cowboy model and the Chinese authoritarian model emerge. Meanwhile, Europe reminds me of a football match with both the Chinese and American teams on the pitch. The Europeans haven't actually put a team on the pitch, yet they have a referee running up and down the field, blowing the whistle and handing out yellow cards.

There needs to be some original thought given to what facilitates business and economic growth, while also protecting the basic rights and values of individuals. I'm curious to see if any other model emerges that strikes the right balance. In order for it to emerge, it would have to connect Europe with other parts of the world—for example, the Middle East, South America, or South Asia. It would have to prove to be something more than just regional. I don't think a Middle Eastern model, a European model, a South American model, or an Indian model can work on its own. In order to compete against the American model or the Chinese model, it's got to be much larger.

ERIK BRYNJOLFSSON: There are a number of building blocks of a thriving ecosystem. At a foundational level, education and human capital are critical components. As societies invest in basic educational skills, like reading and writing, more advanced skills such as critical thinking, engineering, science, and technology are needed as well in order to enable people to apply technologies in new and entrepreneurial ways. We're finding that as machine learning automates a lot of routine tasks, the role of humans increasingly shifts to being more creative by learning to ask the right questions and not simply work through solutions to existing questions.

I definitely put investment in human capital at the top of the list, not just in more education, but also in new kinds of education that are more focused on creativity and problem-solving. That's something that individuals need to invest in. Also, it's something that governments need to invest in because education is a public good that the private sector won't invest efficiently in on its own. So, we also need public investment on that front to make it worthwhile.

Another building block is making it easy for entrepreneurs to thrive and encouraging entrepreneurship by reducing the kinds of regulations that protect big companies from startups. Having a culture that embraces these kinds of challenges, reducing occupational licensing and other policies like that, allows for more dynamism and economic change over time. Too many governments are invested in trying to preserve and hang on to existing industries, existing companies, existing jobs, when what they should really be doing is embracing what Joseph Schumpeter called "creative destruction": the idea that new technologies enable new goods, new services, and new ways of doing business. These new ways can create new jobs and new opportunities for their citizens, even as the old ones get replaced. Those are two of the pillars that I would identify.

A third building block would be investment in infrastructure. That includes basics like good roads, water, electricity, and also, increasingly, digital infrastructure, internet access, satellite, and mobile telephony that allow people to communicate and connect with each other more easily.

ARUNMA OTEH: A major building block of any ecosystem is education, which is a topic I'm very passionate about and speak on quite frequently. First and foremost, you need a society that is digitally literate. I often say to people that if I was a president of a country, I would teach people to be digital. I would also teach them finance. Then I would just let them grow, because digital education gives you access in ways that you would not have if you were not digitally literate. Of course, finance gives you the discipline and the background to do so. Education, for me, is key for the average person. Great education doesn't come without a cost, however, because you need a significant investment in experts if you're serious about focusing on technology and building a startup culture.

Second, governments need to fully appreciate the value of a startup ecosystem and create initiatives that encourage and support startups. These can take the form of tax breaks, incentives for research and development, and a focus on creating a regulatory environment that is entrepreneur- and startup-friendly. The top leadership stance on entrepreneurship is also critical. You need champions at every level of government and in society at large, whether they're policy-makers, bureaucrats, educators, etc. This is more likely to permeate across society if the leaders of the country themselves are publicly vocal about the importance of entrepreneurship and the development of their local ecosystem.

When you look across Africa, as an example of a developing region, you see that some of the nations that have moved faster on technology adoption and encouraging startups have been the ones where their leaders promoted it. For example, the President of Rwanda, Paul Kagame, and the President of Kenya, Uhuru Kenyatta, have both been very much at the forefront, actively promoting technology and a startup culture. You have a small country like Rwanda setting a great example, in terms of ease of doing business. Rwanda completely re-engineered its whole process to make it seamless to start and operate a business, thereby further encouraging and supporting entrepreneurs. Government and top leadership promotion of entrepreneurship, in effect, sets the tone for the country and influences the culture in that regard. The message needs to be perceived—whether via public communication or regulation—as one that encourages, rather than one that prevents or slows down, entrepreneurship. Most governments and regulators tend to focus on preventing what might go wrong rather than focusing on facilitating positive change.

Finally, finance is essential. Without sufficient capital and liquidity in the ecosystem, great intentions and efforts will stop dead in their tracks. Government's role is not just to provide seed money, but also to encourage other players to invest. They also need to learn from local players what their needs are, and even invite entrepreneurs to be involved in designing the requirements of a fund, and setting some guidelines as to how it functions.

Developing a robust telecom and technology infrastructure is also absolutely essential for tech startups. Without proper investment in this public utility, governments are disadvantaging their local startups against other global startups in places with better infrastructure. Other areas include, for example, laying out a proper address system or enabling solutions around the lack of one, which has historically posed a big challenge for e-commerce growth and the delivery of physical goods and food. Those are examples of areas that governments are responsible for, at bare minimum, if they are serious about supporting their local ecosystem.

LAMIA KAMAL-CHAOUI: At the OECD, we analyze a country's or a region's entrepreneurship ecosystem, which we see as a combination of institutional conditions and access-to-resources conditions for startups to scale and transition into new industries. As such, the key to good ecosystem policy is to look at the specific sets of these conditions in each place and understand both the enablers and the barriers. From this analysis we can understand what is not working and share information among national and local leaders across the world on how policy already applied in various places can help to address the types of local failures we find elsewhere.

One of the key institutional conditions for a thriving ecosystem is supportive formal institutions. This means simple but effective business regulations. Government has an important role to play here by "thinking small first" in its regulatory policies.

Another critical institutional condition, one that is harder for a government to affect directly, is a positive entrepreneurship culture. This means a local culture that recognizes and rewards the contribution that entrepreneurs make to society and in which entrepreneurship is seen as accessible.

A further key institutional condition is dense networks offering entrepreneurs access to ideas, information, and connections with supplier, customer, and collaborative businesses. Such networks also need to include research organizations and higher education institutions, business service suppliers and consultants, and financial investors.

Some places suffer from weak trust and social capital, but governments can address this gradually with initiatives that bring together actors working on collaborative innovation projects, where the government acts as an honest broker. We have found this approach in a number of our case studies on local entrepreneurship ecosystems and emerging industries, including a recent one on Malopolskie, Poland.

Sufficient access to vital resources is important to a thriving startup ecosystem. A gap in any one of them can create a bottleneck that can prevent the whole ecosystem from taking off. The conditions we examine include access to entrepreneurial finance, access to talented people, access to knowledge and research, and access to business development services like mentorship and consultancy. We also see a key role for place leadership, such as serial entrepreneurs and public sector bodies that can make strategic investments and build networks in cooperation with other stakeholders. A final key condition is connectivity—in terms of road, rail, and air links, but also in terms of widespread high-quality broadband access for businesses.

When identifying the institutional conditions and access to resources conditions that may be acting as bottlenecks, it is crucial to take a local as well as national view. Both the scale and the details of the policy measures needed to promote entrepreneurship vary between big cities and rural areas. As we show in *The Geography of Firm Dynamics*, urban regions are the strongest in business creation and this boosts their employment-generation rates. They tend to have strong assets to build on, such as local research facilities, sophisticated demand, highly developed infrastructure, and dense networks. The job of policy is to make connections and to fill a few gaps. In contrast, remote rural areas often need a more intensive dual effort to create better links to actors in more dynamic areas while strengthening the rural area's internal assets.

JOHN MACOMBER: Simply put, to build an entrepreneurial ecosystem, you need what I call the five Cs: customers, capital, capability, competition, and contracts.

The first requirement is customers, there has to be some economic tailwind. It's really hard to be an entrepreneur in an economy that's going nowhere, where society is going sideways. If there's no money and nobody to buy, it doesn't make a difference how much one wants to build an ecosystem.

The second requirement is capital to bridge this yawning chasm between starting your own two-person sandwich stand on the side of the road and being ready to attract $40 million in venture capital when small private equity capital is less available. Where's that growth capital? In a lot of emerging markets, that is hard to find, partly because people don't really understand the businesses and partly because the investors don't know what the return is going to be. There's not really a step forward in that regard.

The third requirement is capability—not just the capability of the technology, but of the entrepreneur to deliver on the business plan. Secondarily, the ecosystem must have the adjacent capability: you need marketing people, programming people, finance people, accounting people, human resources people, delivery people, and logistics people, all those other capabilities to build on each other to build a true ecosystem.

The fourth requirement is competition, meaning that policy-makers are not picking favorites or allowing non-competitive decision processes to gum up the good ideas of entrepreneurs. There needs to be transparency and competition based on merits. It's really hard for entrepreneurs to create their own ecosystem if, say, the banking system and the political system are really hard to figure out and policy favors certain industries or companies. Investors also prefer places that have competition, clarity, and enforceable contracts.

The fifth and final requirement is contracts: the way around the property—legal property and intellectual property—and the ability to get paid for commercial work or to resolve commercial disputes through the courts.

LINDA ROTTENBERG: From our point of view, at Endeavor, the main elements of a healthy, thriving, entrepreneur-friendly startup ecosystem are regulations, infrastructure, capital markets, education, media, and culture. We believe in a world where anyone, from anywhere, can hatch an idea; access the networks, talent, and capital to take it scale; achieve success; and pay it forward to inspire and enable the next generation.

Today, we're seeing ecosystems building fueled by local entrepreneurial leaders taking place in scores of emerging and developing markets globally. The MENA region is a perfect example of that. While broadening the job market and bringing in outside investment are a crucial part of the equation, building networks that encourage the open exchange of ideas and value reinvestment are what create sustainable ecosystems of entrepreneurship. That's why paying it forward is a key part of Endeavor's model for economic change, and an important criterion for how we select entrepreneurs. Economies—and even the most successful businesses—cannot thrive if the "big fish" don't feed the "little fish."

RICHARD FLORIDA: Some of the basic ingredients of ecosystems that are commonly discussed are access to venture capital and proximity to top tier research universities. Less discussed, but increasingly important, are urban environments themselves. The tech industry has seen a monumental shift in recent decades from suburban office parks to bustling downtowns: Amazon in downtown Seattle, Twitter and Uber in downtown San Francisco, and Google in downtown San Jose and New York City, to name just a few. Urban environments are valuable for tech companies because of the convenience and creative friction they afford. Chance encounters between colleagues from different companies can spark new business partnerships, legal and financial services are convenient and nearby, as are amenities like housing, transportation, and world class cultural offerings. The young, talented workers these companies are competing for want to live in cities and they'd prefer to have a reasonable commute.

I like to talk about the "four Ts" of urban economic development.

They all relate to one another. The first is talent: how to attract and retain the best and brightest workers. This means providing housing, transportation, and amenities, as well as a strong, diversified local economy. The second is technology: hosting top tier research—whether in the private, public, or academic sector—that stimulates innovation and company formation. The third is tolerance of all people regardless of race, gender, sexual orientation, religion, or nationality. A tolerant culture is one that is open to new ideas. It also opens its arms to the smartest and most ambitious people, no matter who they are. The fourth T, which I've been focusing on more recently, is territorial assets: deeply rooted institutions or natural or man-made features that make a place attractive. Universities are the most obvious, along with longstanding companies and civic organizations. This also includes natural amenities, like access to the ocean or the mountains, which so many west coast cities in America, including the Silicon Valley area, enjoy.

Key actors and factors

ERIK STAM: I define an entrepreneurial ecosystem as a set of interdependent "actors and factors" coordinated in such a way that they enable productive entrepreneurship within a particular territory. Key elements of thriving entrepreneurial ecosystems can be seen in two layers. The framework conditions include the social—being formal and informal institutions—and physical conditions enabling or constraining human interaction. In addition, access to demand for new goods and services is also of great importance.

These conditions might be regarded as the fundamental causes of value creation in the entrepreneurial ecosystem. However, in order to fully understand how these fundamental causes lead to this outcome, we need to gain insight into how systemic conditions lead to entrepreneurial activity. Systemic conditions are the heart of the ecosystem: networks of entrepreneurs, leadership, finance, talent, knowledge, and support services. The presence of these elements and the interaction between them are crucial for the success of the ecosystem.

BILL AULET: As I mention in my book, *Disciplined Entrepreneurship*, there is a single necessary and sufficient condition for a business. If you have this condition, you'll have a business, and if you don't, you won't have a business—and that condition is a paying customer. Once you understand that and define the business that way, a lot of the complications that come about in describing a business go away. A business is about getting customers.

Likewise, the single necessary and sufficient condition for an entrepreneurial ecosystem is entrepreneurs. Not policy, not funding, not infrastructure, not how many PhDs you have, but entrepreneurs. Certainly, the others are supportive factors. To make a great entrepreneurial ecosystem, you need to have more entrepreneurs, better skilled entrepreneurs, and entrepreneurs that are connected together so that they can achieve a network effect. In that sense, entrepreneurs are the prime movers or the engine that drives the ecosystem. Meanwhile, everything surrounding them, such as capital, education, policy, infrastructure, etc., serve as important catalysts or accelerators.

Similarly, to borrow an analogy from the sports world, entrepreneurs are much like athletes. They are the players on the field responsible for winning and losing. Meanwhile, there's an entire organization and environment that is, by design, meant to support and help them perform at their best. It includes coaches, trainers, physical therapists, organizers, promoters, managers, etc., along with other aspects such as funding and physical facilities that contribute to the recruitment and development of great athletes. It's a micro-ecosystem in that sense, geared for the purpose of helping teams to win and clubs to profit, while entertaining and retaining teams' fan loyalty. The customers in this scenario are the fans. As such, everything in this environment is geared toward the athletes' need to be at their best and produce the best output for their teams so those teams can win. Likewise, an entrepreneurial ecosystem needs to have entrepreneurs front and center to ensure that everything is tailored for their companies to succeed.

STEVE CASE: Through the "Rise of the Rest Road Trip," we've visited over 40 cities, experiencing first-hand the successes and challenges of each ecosystem. Every city is different, but we've found there are at least seven entities that help to fuel the rise of startup ecosystems: local governments, universities, investors, startup support organizations, corporations, local media, and the startups themselves. These groups use a variety of levers to help connect, convene, and support startups. These efforts, in turn, inspire an environment that is conducive to innovation and entrepreneurship.

We've also found that many successful ecosystems take advantage of legacy industries. For example, Minneapolis is home to many health care startups, given its proximity to Epic Systems and the Mayo Clinic. Pittsburgh is a hub for robotics and AI because it is the home of one of the most well-regarded research universities, Carnegie Melon, and the community embraces its history of powering the industrial revolution. Playing to its strengths and knowing its comparative advantage can help to push an ecosystem to the next level. This is also true on a global scale, as you see ecosystems thriving in places like London, Barcelona, Nairobi, Tel Aviv, and Abu Dhabi, to name just a few.

ANDREW ROMANS: It's important to map out the building blocks or elements in an ecosystem. Then, examine and audit your own unique resources and capabilities and figure out which areas you can amplify or establish, and which ones will be harder to amplify or establish. The primary player or "actor" in any ecosystem is the entrepreneur. Granted, some countries are more likely to have more entrepreneurs than others, for whatever reason, but successful entrepreneurs can now come from anywhere.

I believe that an entrepreneur can be born in Casablanca or Beirut just as easily as Palo Alto. It does require some inspiration, like Amir Hegazi provides with his book, *Startup Arabia*, which features stories of top tech entrepreneurs in the Arab world. It can also come from events or even TV content, YouTube videos, and movies that people are watching. The media and content that people are consuming play a big role in shaping their thoughts and fueling their motivation, and even influencing a culture.

The second player or actor in an ecosystem is investors. In an ideal world, you would have a large choice of investors for the entrepreneur to go to for funding at every stage: pre-seed, seed, accelerators, post seed, pre-A, A, B, C, and growth stages.

Another mission-critical actor in an ecosystem is the big balance-sheet buyer. These are the large corporations that will purchase and acquire startups. If you don't have a thriving set of M&A buyers, then you have to seek to get acquired from outside your ecosystem. This is the hardest thing to replicate. Even the east coast of the United States hasn't replicated it. The only place where it has been replicated outside of Silicon Valley, in my opinion, is China. Now you start to see Tencent, Baidu, Alibaba, and Huawei. There are quite a few large, high-tech companies that have managed to get publicly traded on the stock exchange, which is normally required. Outside the United States, maybe this doesn't need to be a requirement. This is something that the government or people involved in the planning and fabrication of a real startup ecosystem are overlooking to a large extent.

The large corporations need to work closely with the startups. It needs to be communicated to the large corporations that if they don't access startup innovation, they will die. If they're not going to embrace digitalization, instant settlement with payments, using blockchain for their supply chain, using smart contracts, and be more AI- and data-driven, they simply have no chance of surviving.

The other key actor is the service provider. These include mentors, advisers, accountants, bankers, headhunters, and lawyers who are experienced in working with investment bankers and have well developed contact networks. The service providers' role is often overlooked, as they are typically behind the scenes and not in the spotlight like entrepreneurs and investors. Nevertheless, no ecosystem can function optimally without a minimal supply of service providers with the right expertise, experience, and network. Well-versed lawyers in an ecosystem, for example, are exposed to more deals than entrepreneurs or even investors. As such, they can bring a lot to the table and often provide the connective tissue of a given ecosystem. It's also important these days to have many accelerators. Often, good accelerators have a fund and they will fund startups to get through the accelerator. Then, they perform a role of aggregating lots of angels and pre-seed funds to further support the growth of those startups, both during the accelerator, at demo day, and beyond.

Policy-makers obviously play a big role in ecosystem development. It's important that they prioritize innovation and have a program like Saudi Vision 2030, especially in the centrally planned economies that I've experienced in the GCC (Gulf Cooperation Council). Getting them to come up with sensible policies that drive ecosystem growth is crucial. Tax incentives should be extended to large corporations. The large corporation should be told, "Listen, you're paying all this tax. If you deploy funds into CVC (corporate venture capital) funds or other active VCs that are investing locally, you will get tax exemptions." The government should offer to match at least 40% of the capital raised by VCs. Tax incentives to high net worth individuals, family offices, and corporates can also help provide the matching funds and establish a critical mass of investors across sectors and stages in the region. Once this becomes operational progress on establishing VCs will happen, but again the difficult part is to get the big balance sheet buyers locally that buy startups and provide exits for the investors and entrepreneurs.

Another important actor in ecosystems is the universities or educational institutions and programs in general. We're seeing that in the Middle East with universities that have accelerator programs; they're real hubs of the startup communities developing in the Arab world.

Finally, another actor in the ecosystem can be the military, which can foster technology development and entrepreneurship. Some countries do a great job of transferring the technical, management, and leadership skills acquired in the military into commercial activities. You see a lot of successful founders and entrepreneurs, especially in tech-related sectors, who have military backgrounds. That's one area that gets overlooked and might be useful, at least in some countries, to emphasize via some kind of transitional programs that bridge between military experience and entrepreneurial ventures. I have even seen VC funds that focus on backing startups led by military veterans perform quite well.

BADR JAFAR: When you consider what is actually required to build a robust and resilient ecosystem, corporate governance is one key factor that is often viewed as only being applicable to large, late-stage companies. In reality, it is just as important to embed good governance principles, standards, and practices early on. In fact, it's vital when you're structuring a new business to utilize the right governance tools to ensure that you are building the strongest foundation that you possibly can.

Corporate governance is an area that often gets overlooked early on and thus gets left behind until very late, and in some cases too late, especially when it comes to the fast-growth tech companies of today. Some companies grow exponentially and, a couple of years later, before they've even figured out what a shareholder agreement looks like, they've already got a significant burn rate. At that point, it can be overwhelming and complex to instill good corporate governance practices and standards retroactively, especially with VCs involved. We need to be more proactive about creating a culture of good governance, including identifying and articulating the business case for corporate governance to startups and SMEs (small and medium-sized enterprises).

The Pearl Initiative is an initiative that I co-founded—in cooperation with the United Nations Office for Partnerships—to help promote higher standards in corporate governance, accountability, and transparency as key drivers of competitiveness and sustainable economic growth across the MENA region's private sector. We launched in 2010 with a group of like-minded business people who believed in the business case behind corporate governance, and have been actively pursuing programs, convening roundtables and events, conducting advocacy and publishing reports and research since then. The original programs were initially focused on issues such as anti-corruption and corporate governance in family businesses in particular, which have been estimated to generate 80% of non-oil GDP in the region. However, we eventually realized that we were missing a huge opportunity by not tailoring our programs to accommodate small businesses, startups, entrepreneurs and even non-profits and we have therefore placed a lot of effort on these areas in the last couple of years.

DAVID AUDRETSCH: It's common to view the building blocks of a thriving ecosystem in terms of forms, when the focus should be on functions. What I mean is that all too often the research and literature about ecosystems say, "An ecosystem is comprised of entrepreneurs, investors, universities, government, and other types of organizations and institutions."

The mistake in this way of thinking is that it confines a particular function to one form. For example, it may confine education to universities. It may also confine the function of funding to investors, commonly viewed as angel investors and VCs. By focusing too narrowly on specific forms, or embodiments, of a given function, it's easy to miss the broader spectrum of options available and limit our thinking to much narrower options.

On the other hand, by identifying and focusing on the underlying functions of a robust ecosystem—irrespective of specific groups and organizations that carry out such functions—we acknowledge that there can be a lot more flexibility and improvisation in any ecosystem. Hence, it can develop in its own way, leveraging its own strength and unique context.

For example, if we take the function of funding, we realize that there are all kinds of options available for companies to get financial backing, other than just angel investors and VCs. These may include bank loans, research grants, government funding, crowdfunding, and other non-traditional funding options. Obviously, some are more available and more suited than others to any particular company.

Similarly, when it comes to education, there are plenty of non-university options, many of which are virtual so they don't need to be present geographically within any given ecosystem to make a contribution to that ecosystem. In Germany, for example, they commonly have Fraunhofer institutions and Max Planck institutes, which provide basic academic research. Thus, not every ecosystem that is trying to be "the next Silicon Valley" needs a Stanford University. As long as the functions that are needed to build the ecosystem are supplied, it can thrive without any particular organization or institution.

The other mistake this kind of thinking leads to is this notion that you have to copy the ecosystem you like. This approach is typically taken in regard to Silicon Valley, but it could also be Boston, London, or Singapore. As a result, we see various stakeholders in ecosystems around the world preoccupied with wholesale emulation of a particular ecosystem they admire. Of course, this rarely works in terms of being an effective or efficient approach. They would be better off putting their efforts into understanding their own ecosystem's strengths and weaknesses, using some kind of local ecosystem functions assessment or gap analysis. Meanwhile, they can learn from others and adapt what they learn to their own context to fill gaps in the functions of their ecosystem.

Needs at different stages of an ecosystem life cycle

JONATHAN ORTMANS: Ecosystem development is all about evidence-based startup ecosystem diagnosis, setting clear priorities, and developing effective strategies. We learned from the Global Startup Ecosystem Reports (GSERs), that startup ecosystems go through a life cycle.

At the early-activation phase of the ecosystem life cycle, when there is a relatively small population of startups, a smart approach might focus on local resource activation—drawing existing talent from corporations, small businesses, and universities into the ecosystem. As ecosystems grow and progress through the ecosystem life cycle, they need to move from activating organic, local resources to attracting and connecting with resources from other ecosystems. At these later stages, high-profile exits (IPOs and acquisitions) act as triggers for ecosystem growth because they help draw in additional resources from elsewhere.

Ultimately, what matters most—regardless of which stage a given ecosystem is at in its life cycle—is well captured in the Kauffman Foundation's recently released *America's New Business Plan*. Entrepreneurs need a level playing field, less red tape, equal access to the right kind of capital, and relevant knowledge. They also need support from their society in mitigating the risks of being one of the nation's risk takers in terms of health care and retirement security. This is why the Global Entrepreneurship Network is focused on building communities to foster healthier ecosystems that engage both entrepreneurs and policy-makers.

JULIE LENZER: One of the things that I created when I was in the US Department of Commerce is called the "hierarchy of needs in economic development." It's inspired by Maslow's hierarchy of needs pyramid, but more tailored to economic and ecosystem development. It focuses on what's needed to build resilient communities, centered on startups. The most basic needs, such as infrastructure (reliable power, roads, water, etc.), are at the foundation. Then, as you move up the pyramid, the next level is technology infrastructure, such as broadband, access to reliable WiFi, and other basic connectivity needs. Then, we move to higher-up needs with business support and professional services, such as access to lawyers, accountants, marketing professionals, and talent recruiters. Talent, in particular, is paramount at this level. So, where does the talent come from? Academia, workforce development programs, specialty training agencies, community colleges, and apprenticeships are all great contributors to filling the talent gap in an ecosystem.

As you move up the hierarchy, next come the engines of innovation. Engines of innovation are often universities, through their research. It could be corporate innovation, it could also be government-funded innovation, but you have to have something funding that innovation generation. Along those lines are also favorable policies to entrepreneurial activity. Capital is also one of those key resources entrepreneurs need to have access to.

We then have, at the very top of the hierarchy, connecting people to the ecosystem and bringing like-minded folks together to drive the results. People have referred to these encounters as "collisions." I also heard somebody call it "bumpability." Can you bump into somebody who can help you with your business? What are the events and programs that act as connective tissue within the community to bring people together?

Then, along the mortar of the pyramid of the hierarchy of needs is having a culture that's innovation-oriented. Many international communities I've seen lack the mechanisms and the tolerance for failure that are needed. That can stifle innovation greatly because it is such a risky deal and you do have failures. If you can't afford to fail, or there's a negative social stigma associated with it and you become a social pariah, that will deter risk takers and stifle creativity and innovation.

At the heart of it all is the people. You have to have the entrepreneurs, the mentors, the advisers, and the investors. Having said that, there's no real prescription because it's different in every community. It's more like getting the ingredients together and seeing how to best utilize and connect them and build on regional assets that you already have.

HIERARCHY OF NEEDS IN ECONOMIC DEVELOPMENT PYRAMID

Connected Ecosystem
(e.g., clusters/hubs, matchmaking venues, events, networks, etc.)

Engines of Innovation
(e.g., universities, research, corporate innovation, government-funded innovation, etc.)

Business Support
(e.g., professional services: lawyers, accountants, marketing professionals, and talent recruiters; access to capital; entrepreneurial activity friendly regulation; etc.)

Technology Infrastructure
(e.g., broadband, access to reliable Wi-Fi, and other basic connectivity needs, etc.)

Basic Infrastructure
(e.g., reliable power, roads, water, etc.)

Source: Illustration of Julie Lenzer's Ecosystem Development Model

Certainly, from an economic development community perspective, it's difficult to not start at the very bottom and work up, especially if you're talking about a physical place, because the foundational infrastructure is needed. If it's a digital community, on the other hand, you have to have access to reliable technology. You need different elements in different situations and at different times; but the process is not necessarily sequential, though all the ingredients are required at some point.

KATE POPE HODEL: In working with communities all across the United States to help them build what we refer to as their "entrepreneurial infrastructure," we've found that it's not really individual programs but processes that drive forward motion. Maria Meyers, the founder of SourceLink, has come up with four steps—identify, connect, empower, and measure—which she covers extensively in great detail in our book, *Beyond Collisions: How to Build*

Your Entrepreneurial Infrastructure.

The first step is "identify." This step is about taking account of and organizing resources that are already there. Then, what we found to be very successful is connecting those resources through a central hub. We developed a technology that we call our "Resource Navigator." This is simply a "smart" search engine that organizes those resources and is easy for people to just come in and use to find the resources most relevant to their needs. If I'm a restaurant owner in the north part of town and I need help with a business of financial plan, then I can search those criteria and find, say, three resources that are going to be a good fit for me, versus having to look at a list of hundreds of different resources. We also recommend creating a hotline. People love having a place to call and talk to a live person. If you're talking to 3,000 entrepreneurs every year on the phone, you start to get a real picture of what's going on in the community.

The second step is "connect." This step involves linking the various resources together. In any community, there are resources that are helping entrepreneurs and SMEs. Frequently, they are invisible and not very accessible. That's usually because those resources are not-for-profit, government, or educational organizations, and they have no money for marketing. The first thing we do when we work with a community is start to map these assets. We have a taxonomy that we use when we go into a community. We actually have a form that we ask these resource organizations to fill out that says what kinds of services they offer. We also ask them what kinds of entrepreneurs they work with, because one of the things we found was critical is the need to get the right person to the right resource at the right time. If you are an innovation-based entrepreneur, you do not want to be talking to someone who has all their expertise in the restaurant industry, or vice versa.

One of the things we try to understand in any community is who all these resources are, what they do best, and with whom they do it by industry and by stage of business. We also ask them questions about audiences that they specifically focus on. Do you have a specific expertise in working with women? This way, we can get a picture of who is doing what, so that we can make those resources more visible and more accessible to entrepreneurs and small business owners.

The third step is "empower." This step focuses on engaging, listening, responding, and collaborating to solve problems and fill gaps in the community. The goal here is to create a network of resources within a community. You're going to have a wide variety of organizations, some of which will spend all of their time working with entrepreneurs and small business owners. Meanwhile, others will only offer one little program that might be useful, but they do have this one thing that's useful to entrepreneurs and small business owners.

What we try to do is create a sense of community, and a lot of that has to do with identifying these organizations—not the entrepreneurs themselves but the resource organizations, the entrepreneurial support organizations. They can then get to know each other, understand what the person next to them offers, and recommend people to them or get referrals from and so forth. At that point, you begin to see the gaps where the opportunity for additional programming becomes obvious. It's not a top-down command-and-control kind of planned economy. It's the community figuring out, "How can we get a microlending program or some proof-of-concept funding?"

The fourth step is "measure." This step is where you gauge the progress and impact made, based on your entrepreneurial ecosystem's stage of development. There's a continuum of measurement. If what you're trying to do is build infrastructure, the first thing you may want to measure is the infrastructure itself and not the results of building it. At the beginning of the process, you will not be able to measure those things because you're not working directly with the business owners; you're working a step back with the organization that supports them. What you're probably going to be measuring at that point is what your entrepreneurial infrastructure looks like, and how many organizations are part of the network and are using it. One of the things we recommend is a community calendar. How many events are on that calendar? You're very much counting things, which doesn't feel like measurement, but it can be very important to see what's happening. Is the network getting bigger? Is it getting stronger?

Then, in the second phase, we talk about things like how effective the network is, and how effective this infrastructure is. That's where you start to look at that whole empowerment piece. Who's collaborating with whom? What kinds of gaps are being identified and what kinds of gaps are being filled?

TIM DRAPER: There are six key initiatives to any healthy ecosystem. They could occur sequentially or in parallel. First, educate engineers and entrepreneurs to become what we refer to as "heroes," which is an area we focus on at Draper University of Heroes. At Draper University, we understand what it takes to overcome frustration and ridicule to create something that has never been done before and seems impossible to most people. Entrepreneurs need to be "battle hardened" before venturing out to start a global transformation.

Second, encourage industry leadership (e.g., what BoostVC has done with Bitcoin, VR, and OceanTech). The best entrepreneurs are those who see things that the rest of us don't see and they have the passion to show us what's missing. To become an industry leader, an entrepreneur usually needs to define his or her own industry to lead.

Third, build a network of suppliers to the industry who are well versed in supporting the ecosystem. As companies get started, they may need lawyers, accountants, headhunters, real estate professionals, or other consultants who know the startup landscape and can save them time by pointing them in the right direction.

Fourth, create events and venues that encourage collisions, with investors and entrepreneurs mingling. Entrepreneurs need to randomly run into people, if for no other reason than to create informal focus groups on their product or service. These serendipitous events often connect entrepreneurs to customers, investors, and other supporters who get on board.

Fifth, build a connection to the rest of the world so entrepreneurs can be connected to corporate partners, customers, joint venture partners, etc. No entrepreneur has the kind of network they will need to run their business globally. For global partners, global hires, and other global connections, some leverage into a new region is critical.

Sixth, fund companies and have a vehicle for those companies to get noticed. Distribution is critical for the startup to achieve greatness. Some can achieve it by making the customer into their sales force through viral marketing or some other word-of-mouth system. Others need air cover in the form of marketing and PR for their sales team. Media presence is very powerful for a young startup.

DAVID SHELTERS: Startups need vital financial, relational and knowledge-based resources. The efficacy of a startup ecosystem should be judged on the level of availability of these resources to entrepreneurs. The efficiency of the ecosystem can be measured by how well the various stakeholders collaborate in the provision of such resources.

Ecosystem development occurs in stages and thus requires an iterative approach. In too many instances, stakeholders in an ecosystem try to determine the amount of resources they need to go from their fledging startup ecosystem to Silicon Valley status. This is the wrong approach and ultimately leads to failure and frustration.

The better approach is to identify stages of development and determine how the stakeholders can work together to acquire the necessary resources to reach the next development stage. Once the next stage is reached, additional resources have likely been attracted or generated in the process and can now be utilized for the attainment of the following stage. The optimal role for each stakeholder also varies by stage.

2. What Is Not Working in Ecosystem Development Globally

Excessive, inefficient, and untimely regulations

ALEC ROSS: If you ask any entrepreneur, they will tell you that the more regulated an environment is, the less they want to operate in it. I do think that it is reasonable for certain regulations to be in place, but often the government's hand is too heavy and entrepreneurs just leave or choose to stay away in the first place. There's a reason why many great Italian entrepreneurs start their companies in London or in California versus Rome or Milan. It's because Italy is too heavily regulated, which keeps it from being able to create the kind of ecosystem it is capable of and retaining some of its best.

When in doubt, I would say don't regulate. If you do regulate in order to appropriately steward the values or the interests of a society, that is your right, but understand that it tends to come with a corresponding loss in terms of people wanting to invest there.

WILL HERMAN: If you look at regulations in the US, there really aren't a lot. We have very flexible legal entities and companies and very low barriers to entry. For example, the state of Delaware might possibly have the best corporate law in the world. Anybody anywhere in the US can incorporate their company in Delaware and get all the benefits of being a Delaware company. That's a huge advantage, but that doesn't bias anyone in particular because very few companies are actually in Delaware.

Taxation would seem to be an issue because tax laws throughout the US vary widely. It turns out that California, including Silicon Valley, has some of the nastiest capital gains taxes in the US. Clearly, that's not keeping people away. There are some areas throughout the US where local governments give some tax incentives to SMEs to start, but those are not substantial since federal tax law allows net operating losses to be held against future earnings, So, all in all, there's no tax issue that poses a barrier to startups. The bottom line is regulation in the US is not a particular driver of ecosystem development. Again, it really comes down to the environment, the people, the capital, and the culture.

TIM DRAPER: Governments that recognize that they are in competition for the startups of the world realize that regulation is the death of innovation. Those governments that embrace new technology, rather than trying to control it, will be the winning ecosystems of the next four decades and beyond. Innovations to be embraced include AI, Bitcoin, blockchain, smart contracts, airdrops, CRISPR, autonomous vehicles, drones, etc.

ERIK STAM: One of the worst practices for policy-makers is to pursue ecosystem-related policies that directly affect entrepreneurs and the entrepreneurial ecosystem at large without involving entrepreneurs. That two-way dialogue between policy-makers and entrepreneurs on issues affecting the ecosystem is vital for both sides. For policy-makers, it helps them gather feedback and input, which they can, in turn, incorporate when initiating new policies (including subsidies, laws, and regulations). For entrepreneurs, it gives them the opportunity to flag any concerns and offer recommendations and ideas, and become more proactive and influential in contributing to adequate policies.

Often, policy-makers draft policy in a vacuum without actually talking with entrepreneurs. Granted, it's difficult to find seasoned entrepreneurs who are well versed and have valuable perspectives and insights on the ecosystem. Nevertheless, that should not stop policy-makers from seeking them out. Not involving entrepreneurs, especially in the early stages of policy creation, is almost always a guarantee of policy-making failure.

So, policy-makers also have to open up communication channels with entrepreneurs and other key stakeholders in the ecosystem, and get their feedback well before actually rolling out new policies. This will help them anticipate and avoid potential problem areas ahead of time, as well as deal with any unavoidable issues down the road. Preferably, this dialogue starts with a relatively objective diagnosis of the current strengths and weaknesses of the local or the national entrepreneurial economy. Key elements that need to be in place are formal institutions, culture, networks, demand, physical infrastructure, finance, talent, knowledge, intermediate services, and leadership.

This dialogue between public and private parties needs to be an ongoing process, both before and after policy implementation. Before policy-makers implement any new policy, they need to open a conversation with a group of entrepreneurs and leaders or their representatives and listen to their experiences and concerns. Policy-makers can never please everyone, nor should that be their goal, so naturally some of that feedback might not be relevant or useful and policy-makers may choose to dismiss it. Nevertheless, going through that exercise is critical. The closer policy-makers are to the ground, in terms of having their fingers on the pulse of what's actually happening in the space, the greater chance that policy will be aligned with improved market realities and beneficial to the overall development of the ecosystem.

Having those conversations, as well as opening up communication channels and other feedback loops, is a must. I cannot stress this enough. What happens often is we see governments draft law behind closed doors and suddenly roll it out, to everyone's dismay. Other times, governments are well intentioned and try to engage the private sector but do so ineffectively. For example, they may just post an announcement on their website without making an effort to publicize it and get word out in order to engage key stakeholders in the discussion. Or they announce the framework of upcoming policy in the country's native language only and thus fail to engage local expats who may not speak that language. They should, for example, also make announcements in English to make it more inclusive to key international players. Otherwise, they never really get that dialogue going and end up having a low level of engagement. They need a wide, ongoing effort to engage the key stakeholders on the key issues, and incorporate that feedback into the creation and subsequent revision of policies.

If policy-makers don't engage entrepreneurs enough, they won't know what real pain points and bottlenecks they face in the ecosystem. Additionally, if the entrepreneurs are left in the dark and don't know what is happening, they will not perceive an improvement and thus lack confidence in the ecosystem.

Obviously, this engagement is not easy. It necessitates a government that is able both to talk with entrepreneurs and also to find the entrepreneurs that represent the business world. It also demands that entrepreneurs step outside their comfort zone, think beyond their own situation, and look at the broader ecosystem. Also, the entrepreneurial communities need to organize themselves, especially in big countries like Egypt or Saudi Arabia where you cannot mobilize the thousands of entrepreneurs that are working in the economy at once. You need some kind of organized entrepreneurs' circle that is more or less representative of the larger community.

VICTOR HWANG: Ecosystem development doesn't work when efforts to shape policy or build programs or subsidies do not take into account long-term sustainability, which almost always requires some kind of culture shift. If a government allocates subsidized capital for investing in startup companies, are they seeking to grow fund managers who are respected and have the credibility to raise future capital for the second, third, and fourth funds? If a university wants to host a talent recruitment program for startups, are they changing the way their placement offices value the importance of startup jobs versus large corporate jobs? If a school wants to develop a program to expose students to the startup world, are they shifting the way that teachers think about the importance of skills like design-thinking and project-based learning? These are some of the questions that regulators and bureaucrats need to take into account when developing policies and programs to boost the local ecosystem.

JONATHAN ORTMANS: One key barrier to entrepreneurship and innovation rests with how our governments are organized. While most governments organize around small and big business, it is not the size but rather the age of a business the matters. For example, in the United States, according to Labor Bureau statistics, almost all net new jobs come from firms less than five years old. Governments need to codify the distinction between age and size if scarce resources are to be more wisely deployed to foster new generations of job creators.

MAX BORDERS: From my perspective, regulatory environments often stifle innovation. That is because most laws, to the extent that they are helpful at all, are only appropriate to the time and context in which they are passed.

In an increasingly fast-paced and dynamic world, the law ends up protecting and preserving the status quo over time. In other words, many laws are obsolete after a time, but don't change or at least get updated soon enough. They tend to hang around and create barriers that prevent new entrants from competing. Regulations rarely change because special interests come to depend on them. Incumbent firms will therefore fight regulatory reform. When we consider the hostility that most countries have toward distributed ledger technologies and cryptocurrencies, for example, we can only imagine that the innovations in these areas will really stifle.

DAVID SHELTERS: While residing in Southeast Asia, I have seen first-hand how unpredictable and continuously changing regulatory regimes have doomed many promising startups. This kind of "regulatory fluidity" introduces an additional element of uncertainty, that is detrimental to the local ecosystem. This is particularly clear in the FinTech space, where startups are not able to secure independent banking licenses, or institutional investors are scared off because they require a greater degree of rule of law before making commitments in support of the FinTech ventures. Many of the successful "Singaporean" startups are not Singaporean at all. Investment-grade startups from neighboring countries have discovered that registering a Singapore entity offers better IP protection, lower taxes, and a better opportunity to raise investment funds because investors prefer investing in a Singapore entity, where the rule of law is the strongest.

Misperception, misallocation, and lack of capital

JULIE LENZER: One area that I see that doesn't work is overreliance on venture capital. Certainly, capital is crucial, especially in capital-intensive industries or development-intensive industries, but so many places just focus exclusively attaining capital from VCs when really the best capital for any company is a paying customer. That relationship with customers is something that more entrepreneurs need to pay attention to. That's definitely something that often gets overlooked in favor of overdependence on outside capital. Part of that is just educating entrepreneurs. They often see the hype around venture capital but, in reality, only a very small percentage of companies actually get funded. Instead, they need to focus on how to build capital-efficient startups, how to use non-diluted capital whenever possible, and building self-reliant companies.

TIM O'REILLY: I find it depressing when you ask an entrepreneur, "How are you doing?" and they respond "Great. We just raised our Series C." They don't say, "We just reached some revenue target or we've served this many customers," or anything about their actual business. This illustrates that funding and valuation is what those entrepreneurs are optimizing for, not creating actual and lasting business value. Meanwhile, the investors are doing the same. Then, the entire game becomes about marking up funds based on each successive round of financing.

The media will often jump into this frenzy and celebrate those investments as if they were real business milestones and indicators of success. That's what we see happening with companies like WeWork: the investors were bidding up the asset because they were going,

"Well, we can eventually pass this off to public market investors at this inflated valuation, or we can pass it off to a large financial institution or sovereign wealth fund."

I think we need to go back to basics and infuse a culture of realism and discipline versus one of hubris and hype. We need to go back and look at the fundamentals of the business—irrespective of valuation—and ask: Is this a real business? Does the technology actually work? Are customers happy with the product and the experience? Does it make money? Is it sustainable over the long haul?

We need to stop this culture where our real goal is to simply grow the valuation, often by convincing everybody that we have a future monopoly that will be super-profitable someday. Meanwhile, all we have to do is grow, grow, grow, and we'll figure out a sustainable business model that makes make money later.

We should go back to having a reality-based, fact-based ecosystem comprised of companies that are pioneering new areas and making real impact. That's why the most interesting startup ecosystems for me were during the early web or open source, where it wasn't about trying to get as much money as you can. I personally believe that Silicon Valley has lost some of its soul in that regard, and I'd love to see other ecosystems not make that mistake and go down what I think is essentially a wrong path.

RABEA ATAYA: Obviously, Souq and Careem, recent acquisitions by Amazon and Uber, respectively, in MENA are a very encouraging signs for the region. Having said that, what I want to discourage is this thinking of many local entrepreneurs who say, "I want to build this fast and sell really quickly at high valuation and become rich." The challenge with that mentality is it's not valuable for building sustainable, institutional businesses.

What is not ideal is an entrepreneur who builds a business for sale, and then within a year of the sale, the buyer shuts down the entire business—which has happened now several times—and the whole economic value for the region immediately disappears. As a result, the golden opportunities disappear, the investment in R&D disappears, and everything else disappears. Rather, we need a culture of building successful, sustainable businesses. If those successful, sustainable businesses result in exits, great. But if they also result in businesses that operate for decades, if not centuries, that's also great.

I think too often people view entrepreneurship with a short-term, trading mentality: "I want to build something to sell it." That's not the right way to view entrepreneurship, and it's not the best way to build long-term positive value in our region. This is true in the MENA region, as it is with ecosystems anywhere.

ANDREW ROMANS: It's often a mistake for a government official or appointed bureaucrat to make an investment decision on a technology startup or even on a venture capital fund. That worries me because the stakes are too high to not go with a professional, seasoned investor who has the best credentials, has an industry background, and knows technology, not to mention not to mention a large network and a 20-plus year relationship with the various stakeholders involved. Instead, governments should provide that same capital to someone that has the qualifications, credentials, and experience to be a venture capitalist and make that investor decision.

Another issue is wasting money on pointless conferences and events, since many don't add much in terms of ecosystem development. There are some conferences and events that are worthwhile and impactful, but there are many that are not. As such, I would rather see that money go to a startup. Give them 18 months of runway and give them the opportunity to build the kind of product that their customers would want. So much money is spent there. A fraction of that money, for example, could literally go to buying copies of Amir Hegazi's book, *Startup Arabia,* or other entrepreneurs' education-focused publications and distributing them, physically or electronically, to thousands and thousands of aspiring entrepreneurs in the Arab world, who are hungry for learning and getting inspiration from relatable, local successful entrepreneurs. Such content can also be added to schools and universities' curriculums or as supplementary material and case studies. Such investment could help educate and inspire the new generation of entrepreneurs in the region. I would also like to see some of that money go to help create seed funds, new Series A funds, and growth funds. So, there is often a lot better use of funds to elicit impact on the ecosystem than funding another conferences or event.

After all, government policy in developing startup ecosystems can truly make all of the difference. If you accept the fact that practically every corporation in every industry is now a tech company and you observe that the largest companies on the US stock market are all relatively new technology companies, you cannot overstate the importance of getting this right. It is literally a matter of war for survival for countries and current regimes in power in the Middle East and beyond.

TON VAN 'T NOORDENDE: One big thing that's actually missing in many ecosystems is legislation around capital gains, stock options, and employee stock option plans. There's a bit of a blind spot on the role of capital, equity, and incentive. If you can't provide equity through the company to employees or other co-founders, then they have to commit to paying taxes based on the valuation of funds, which is, of course, something that most of these individuals don't have.

It's not enough to have sufficient capital within an ecosystem, it's also critical to have the right mechanism to ensure the right incentives are in place for stakeholders, so that capital can flow to the right channels.

BADR JAFAR: One thing that we see that doesn't work in MENA, and I'm sure other parts of the world, is the propensity for well-intentioned governments to provide generous funding programs to startups that may not have demonstrated a compelling proposition from an investment opportunity standpoint, or to fund failing projects. We need to be careful here. It is a bit like bringing up a child, in the sense that help and assistance and support are great, but there is a point at which you can actually go too far and get diminishing returns. You might not be doing your children a favor by doing absolutely everything for them, because they might not learn on their own and be prepared to fall.

JONATHAN ORTMANS: Our 2019 global survey of barriers for entrepreneurs revealed that, across the development spectrum, leaders of entrepreneur support organizations perceive insufficient access to capital as a major constraint on entrepreneurship. Digging into this issue, we found that in a number of countries, government intervention to address this challenge has failed to elicit private sector participation. As a result, entrepreneurs in many places have access to seed capital in the form of government grants and prize money, but then hit a wall and struggle to find growth capital.

The Startup Chile program, for example, has been grappling with this issue. Its successful accelerator graduates have had to look overseas for funding for global expansion. The government detected this issue and has been working to address this barrier.

The key with financing gaps is to think of the longer-term entrepreneurial pipeline. Addressing gaps in terms of seed capital may not automatically generate investment for the later stages of startup development. When governments intervene, they must be mindful that some financing instruments may crowd out private investment.

Also, capital is not flowing to enough of the deserving founders, whether by geography, nationality, and/or gender. In the United States, women, Black, and Latino entrepreneurs are an untapped economic power and when you leave people out, the economy suffers. Further, while there is plenty of venture capital, it is not a good fit for most startups, not to mention the fact that 75% of venture money in the US goes to California, New York, and Massachusetts. There remains a big gap in terms of sufficient access and efficient allocation of capital across various groups and geographies within the ecosystem.

LAMIA KAMAL-CHAOUI: Access to finance for startups and scaleups remains a major obstacle across a wide range of countries in the MENA region and globally. This obstacle exists despite governments introducing initiatives to help bridge the gap before an innovation-based startup business experiences steady revenue.

Whereas governments have generally been successful in strengthening access to credit, innovative startups and scaleups are more suited to equity and hybrid debt-equity finance inputs. There remain significant gaps in the availability of equity and mezzanine finance in many countries and regions, which is always one of the main complaints of potential high-growth entrepreneurs.

More can be done with policies that facilitate finance sources such as crowdfunding, business angel networks, and access to venture capital networks, as we stress in the *G20/OECD High-Level Principles on SME Financing.*

One of the concerns we commonly come across is that the most promising startups in an ecosystem, unable to find local venture capital, may only find the finance they need in US-based venture capital funds. However, these funds do not have the networks to reach out to all businesses and places, and they can also lead to an eventual transfer of the key innovation-based value to the US. This is why it is important to develop local finance solutions and take a spatial perspective in access to finance programs.

Counter-productive beliefs and approaches

ERIK BRYNJOLFSSON: When it comes to ecosystem development, the worst strategy would be to try to slow down new innovation technologies in the name of protecting particular local companies or industries. The opposite should happen; namely, go full speed ahead with the technology, but push on the accelerator with organizational change. In short, the answer is not to slow down the technology. The answer is to speed the adaptation and the investment in human capital.

The countries that will be successful in the 2020s and 2030s are the ones that embrace the future and make those complementary investments. In my research, we found that for every dollar of technology investment, you need up to $10 of investment in human-capitalized education and organizational capital for business process change. Most organizations and most nations aren't making those complementary investments to the extent that they should be, but the ones that do are going to come out ahead for their people and lead going forward.

BRAD FELD: One of the biggest mistakes I see early on is trying to control what's going on. Somebody or some entity shows up from the outside, and says, "If you want to build a vibrant startup community in Istanbul, New Delhi, or Abu Dhabi, here's how you do it." The problems arise because of the lack of familiarity and intimacy with the local community, city, or country, and its context, history, and all the nuances involved. They can do the research on a particular environment or geography, but they haven't lived and worked within it. I see this mistake happen over and over again. The passive version of it is, "You should just do it like they did it over there. You should go do the things that they did in Silicon Valley or in city X."

Another mistake is this notion that there is a specific deterministic outcome. Irrespective of who the ecosystem participant might be, whether it's entrepreneurs, organizations, governments, or academia, when they say, "If you want to be successful, then we need to create this or we need to have this happen," that's not very healthy either, because, again, you're dealing with a complex system where you're focusing way more on the inputs and the activities than you are on the outputs, because the outputs just become inputs to the next cycle.

Another common mistake is what I like to call a "measurement mistake," which is that you get obsessed about measuring everything because you view the measurements as the definition of progress. That's another problem in the cycle: the measurements are not really the essence of what you're trying to create. The measurements are simply outputs at various points in time, which are certainly worth tracking, but they are not the determinants of whether you're successful enough.

Also, on the regulation side, there is a philosophy that has emerged in the last five years—you certainly see it in lots of different types of businesses that operate around regulatory systems. It involves initially ignoring the current legal or regulatory framework, creating something new, and then challenging the regulatory framework when you have something that users like. Only then do you leverage your success to try to lobby or change the regulatory framework.

A good example of this is the ride-sharing business. We read lots and lots of articles written not just about Uber, but also about how different companies around the world would simply ignore the existing regulatory environment. It wasn't even that they'd ask for forgiveness later; they just blatantly ignored it and created conflict, which then generated change in the regulatory environment. Sometimes the change was constructive and sometimes not.

One of the things that's starting to build a backlash against that approach—we're seeing it in Europe and in the US—is the dynamics around consumer privacy, information privacy, data privacy, and regulations like Europe's GDPR (General Data Protection Regulation), where there wasn't a really good understanding of the issues. There were privacy laws and privacy frameworks prior, but they just weren't well defined in the context of digital data.

Rather than companies proactively trying to define them in a way that was good for consumers, they went about their business as usual. They proceeded to build super-powerful and significant businesses, ignoring those issues or putting them on the back burner. It wasn't until they felt pressure to do something that they finally reacted. Some of those companies are still incredibly successful businesses, and there's now a steady and growing backlash against them, certainly on the dimension of trust. Probably Facebook is the most front and center in this right now, but there are plenty of others that struggle with this.

It's hard to see how it resolves, because what it does is cause governments to feel like they need to take a more active role in doing something, because the companies themselves are not being proactive. The very large incumbent companies are the ones that tend to have the resources to be able to respond to it. The unintended consequence of this approach is that it tends to cause smaller entrepreneurial companies much more distress and stress.

ANDREW ROMANS: Governments should not try to keep all the control by figuring out everything on their own, within their own geographic walls. Rather, they should engage the right international experts and advisers to help. They need such professionals to examine their ecosystems with fresh eyes and to develop unique, customized policies for them. Some policies from other countries can be examined, from the government side, to help decide which of those policies would work for them. Saudi Arabia, Kuwait, Egypt, and Jordan are different from the UK and Singapore; what works in France and Singapore might not work in the Middle East.

That said, there are a number of things that are ecosystem-agnostic and are safe to replicate. The Middle East can benefit by replicating things like Temasek in Singapore, which is owned by the government of Singapore and focus on transforming economies, growing middle income populations, deepening comparative advantages and emerging champions. They could also replicate R&D tax incentives from Canada, which has done a great job on that front. They should also be replicating the tax incentives that you get in France, Germany, and the UK for investing. These are obvious ones that can make an impact and don't need a whole lot of time to figure out.

MARC NAGER: I'll give two examples of potential areas for wrong approaches or missteps that I've seen many places struggling with for over a decade now. First is how to balance top-down and bottom-up approaches to building a startup ecosystem. Governments, especially, can prioritize entrepreneurship in a great way; however, heavy-handed efforts can often become disingenuous and turn away the highest-potential founders. Even worse, it has never been so trendy to be an "entrepreneur." It is easy to romanticize startups and the path of entrepreneurship. I often tell folks that being an entrepreneur is the hardest and lowest paying career you might ever choose.

As large organizations and institutions seek to promote entrepreneurship, they also have to be very mindful about the bleak statistics around everything from failure and mental health to the impact on the overall workforce. The reality is that successful entrepreneurial ecosystems will be led by entrepreneurs and limited in size by the nature of the challenge. These grassroots communities have to have incredibly strong values and integrated support structures, yet they can be controlled by no single person or entity. The relationships and health between these elements govern the potential size and velocity of any given ecosystem.

A second big challenge is around data and tracking. Too often, government bodies, corporations, and program leaders focus on startups as the primary unit of measure and success. The reality is that we have great statistics on the high failure rates, and the value of the skills that founders learn (even through their failures), yet we place a huge emphasis on the short-term success metrics of startups.

The reality is that the gestation period for most entrepreneurs spans decades. From classes in primary school and university to accelerators and incubator programs, our lens of data and tracking is unable to incorporate the reality of this incredibly long-time horizon. Practically, the data doesn't really exist anywhere yet. The holy grail would be to track their trajectory over decades, and see the impact of key programs on their journey. For example, a young woman takes an entrepreneurship class, gets a job at a big company, and quits after five years because she attended a startup weekend and was inspired to start her own business. She attends several other local programs, then gets accepted to an accelerator, gets investment, and the startup fails. She gets a job with another startup, eventually launches another startup, raises venture capital, and goes on to achieve big success. So, the data available today doesn't capture this progression.

Chapter III

CONTEXTUAL OVERVIEW OF THE MENA LANDSCAPE

For many people, the term "Middle East," unfortunately, often evokes images of violence and conflict. International media has historically painted a picture of a region that is synonymous with instability, terrorism, and wars. Granted, some of that coverage is warranted and driven by honest journalism and reporting. However, some of the reporting is biased by outside influences or is at a minimum lacking context. That is to be expected with any media coverage, some journalists will get the story right and some will not. Naturally, a certain portion of that coverage will be untrue, exaggerated, or taken out of context. That's nothing to be alarmed about. This dynamic occurs everywhere, and it's up to consumers to filter media and news stories for themselves and critically reach their own conclusions.

That said, what's alarming is the lack of balance in international media coverage of the Arab world. There is a historical tendency to focus on negative stories, which end up dominating and obscuring positive ones. Typically, international journalists are assigned to follow the most dramatic headlines of the day, which more often than not tend to be negative. Hence, international media coverage is disproportionately negative when it comes to this part of the world. Meanwhile, positive, uplifting stories coming out of the region receive little, if any, mainstream coverage internationally. Naturally, this skews the global perception of the region.

Beyond this bleak external portrayal lies a very different reality—one that is dramatically more promising than common international perception. That's the other side of the story few outsiders are ever exposed to. For those relatively few who have the opportunity to lift that curtain, more often than not—by simply getting on a plane and experiencing the region firsthand for themselves—they will discover an alternative universe. They will discover a young, dynamic, fast-growing, and tech-savvy population. They will discover a region that is full of commercial opportunities. They will also discover an ecosystem that is pulling from every corner—from entrepreneurs, to investors, to corporations, to universities, to governments, in a concerted effort to catch up with or even surpass the rest of the world.

This book aims neither to warn of a doom-and-gloom scenario for the region at one extreme, nor to paint a utopia at the other. Rather, it aims to help present a more balanced view by relying on a comprehensive, multi-lens approach from the 100+ featured contributors. The goal is to present an unfiltered, realistic, and intelligent prism through which to view the region's economic reality and prospects. Ultimately, the aim is to help unpack this part of the world, which is frequently presented as one sprawling, mysterious "black box."

Initially, I will take a step back and provide a bit of context on the region in terms of geography, history, and demographics. No ecosystem exists in a vacuum, hence having a basic understanding of the region is essential going forward. I will then attempt to provide my own assessment of the region as a place to do business and invest in. I utilize a model that I developed, namely the Market Attractiveness Index (MAI), which I cover in detail in this chapter. The MAI is meant to provide a dynamic, snapshot assessment framework that's subject to change depending on the specific time and place. Yet, for the sake of simplicity, I took a holistic approach in assessing the region, as a unified whole, in terms of commercial opportunities. In short, the

MAI provides a quick reference and back-of-the-envelope method to assess a given region, country, or industry for international players considering market entry. Obviously, to the extent that these players are serious about exploring local opportunities, they will certainly need to do their homework and more thoroughly investigate the specific countries and industries that are most relevant to them.

1. Geography, History, and Demographics

The Arab world, also sometimes referred to as "Arabia," is composed of 22 countries that are official members of the Arab League. They are: Algeria, Bahrain, Comoros, Djibouti, Egypt, Iraq, Jordan, Kuwait, Lebanon, Libya, Mauritania, Morocco, Oman, Palestine, Qatar, Saudi Arabia, Somalia, Sudan, Syria, Tunisia, the United Arab Emirates, and Yemen. This region is also often referred to as the "Middle East and North Africa," "the MENA region," or simply "MENA." All of the above labels are used interchangeably throughout this book and in common literature. The MENA acronym, in particular, is often used in formal and professional literature, including academia and business, and in some media contexts.

Geographically, a few countries that are part of the MENA region are not part of the Arab League. For the purpose of this book, we focus only on the 22 members of the Arab League which comprise the bulk of the region. In terms of territory size, MENA covers approximately 15 million square kilometers (50% larger than the US or Europe). Saudi Arabia, which is the largest country in the region, is approximately 2 million square kilometers (or the combined size of the UK, France, Germany, Spain, Italy, the Netherlands, Ireland, Sweden, Denmark, and Switzerland).

ARAB WORLD: GEOGRAPHY

The Arab world, also referred to as "Arabia", is comprised of 22 countries

MENA has three main sub-regions, though not all MENA countries are included within those sub-regions. They are:

(1) The Gulf Cooperation Council (GCC): Bahrain, Kuwait, Oman, Kingdom of Saudi Arabia (KSA), Qatar, and the United Arab Emirates (UAE).

(2) The Levant: Jordan, Iraq, Lebanon, Palestine, and Syria.

(3)   North Africa: Algeria, Egypt, Libya, Morocco, Sudan, and Tunisia.

Occasionally, the "Maghreb" sub-region is used to describe Algeria, Tunisia, and Morocco.

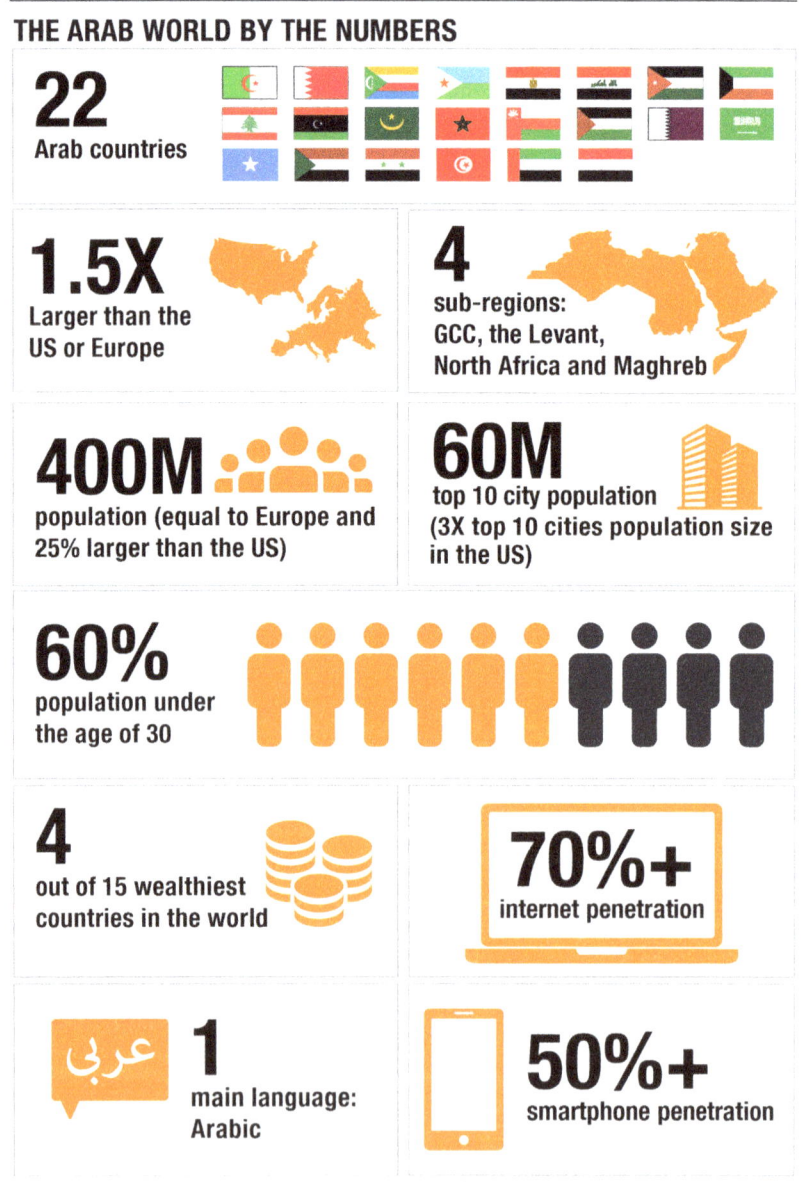

The common link between all of these Arab countries is the Arabic language. While English, French, Kurdish, Berber, and a few tribal languages are spoken in small parts of the region, Arabic is by far the dominant language. By comparison, Europe has over 200 spoken languages, Africa has over 1,000 spoken languages, and Asia has over 2,300 spoken languages. Therefore, this is a fundamental attribute that differentiates the MENA region from other regions worldwide. While there are many dialects of Arabic, which vary by country or territory, formal standard Arabic is understood across the region. This is also the version often used in professional communication contexts (e.g., news coverage, legal writing, business and mass publications, and formal public announcements).

Other foundational commonalities among all Arab countries include elements of shared culture, history, religion, and media. Combine these commonalities with a shared sentiment of patriotism on a regional level, and a sense of identity and pride in being an Arab, and these countries have a lot more in common with one another than differences. Granted, there are vast differences in the physical geography, climate, and environment of each country, as well as intangible differences, such as levels of openness and local customs. Nevertheless, there's always an underlying cultural bond that unites the region. This creates what is referred to as the "pan-Arab" dynamic, which is associated with a common collective mindset as much as it is with a defined physical geography. This makes it relatively easier to communicate with and engage the region's mass population than practically any other region in the world.

The population of MENA as of 2020 is estimated to be well over 400 million (the equivalent of the population of Europe and 25% larger than that of the US). This constitutes about 6% of the world's population. Egypt and Saudi Arabia are the two most populous countries in the region, with approximately 100 million and 30 million-plus people, respectively. MENA also hosts relatively dense cities. For example, Cairo is the ninth most populated city in the world, with over 16 million people. In fact, the top 10 cities in MENA have a combined population size (approximately 60 million) that is three times that of the top 10 cities in the US. MENA's population is also projected to reach over 600 million by 2050.

MENA POPULATION GROWTH (2005-2050 IN MILLIONS)

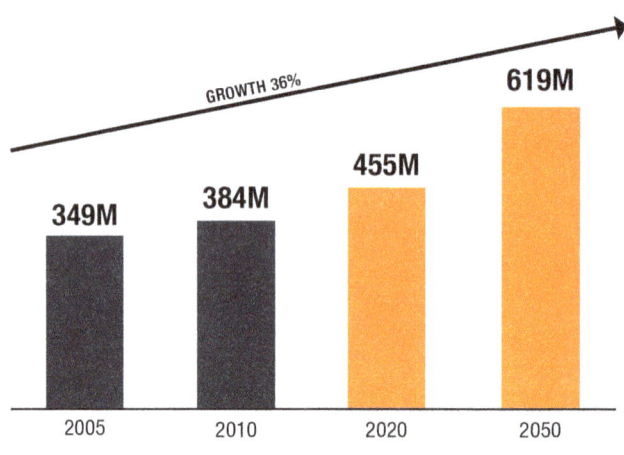

Source: United Nation Population Division

MENA has the second-youngest population in the world after sub-Saharan Africa. More than 60% of its population is under the age of 30, while its median age is 26.

POPULATION DISTRIBUTION BY AGE

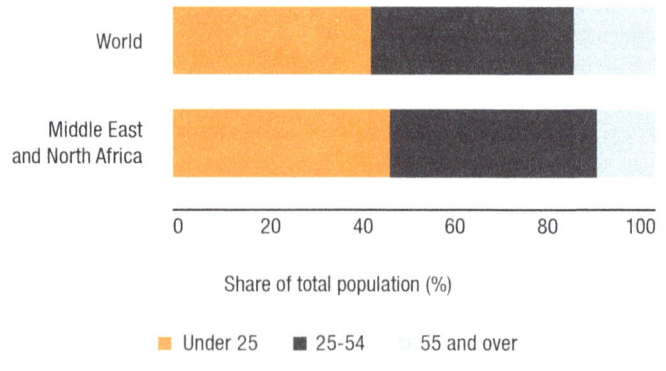

Source: United Nation Population Division

MENA DEMOGRAPHIC STRUCTURE

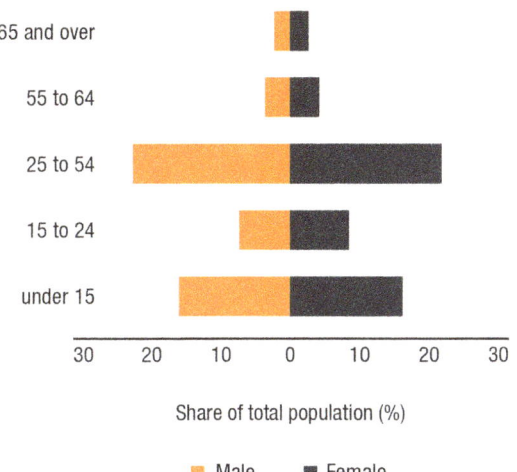

Share of total population (%)

■ Male   ■ Female

Source: United Nation Population Division

MENA POPULATION AGE STRUCTURE

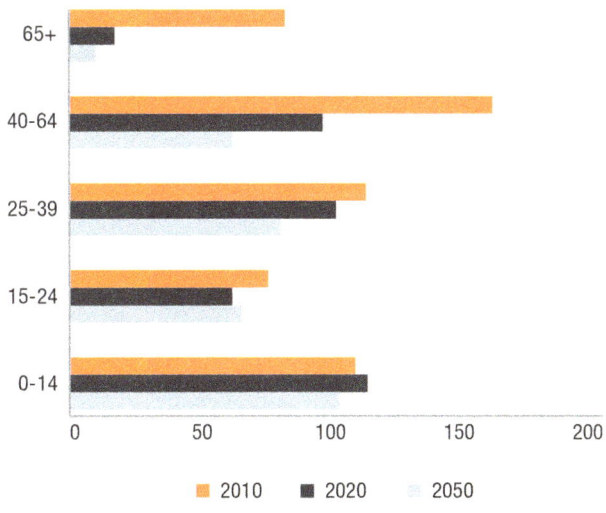

■ 2010   ■ 2020   2050

Source: United Nation Population Division

Because of its young population, the MENA region has relatively high internet and mobile penetration, as well as some of the highest social media usage in the world. Internet penetration, for example, is at around 65% across the region and closer to 80% in the GCC. Meanwhile, mobile penetration is over 70% for most of the region, and as high as 80% in the GCC.

INTERNET PENETRATION RATE IN THE MIDDLE EAST VS. THE GLOBAL INTERNET PENETRATION RATE FROM 2009 TO 2019

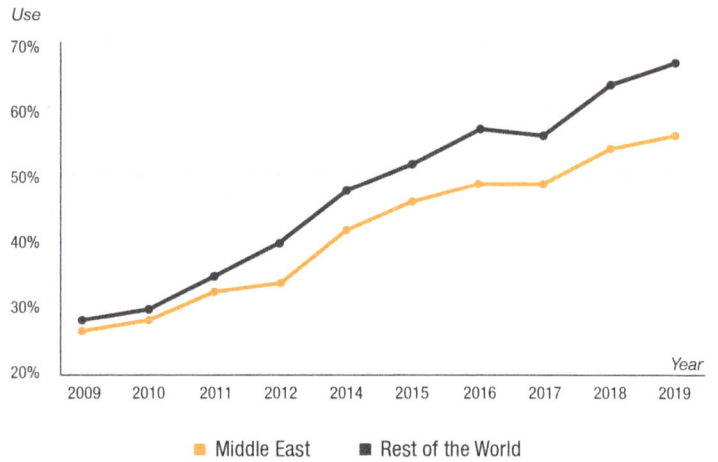

Source: Statista Internet World Stats 2019 (www.statista.com)

Four of the fifteen wealthiest countries in the world are in the MENA region: Qatar, Kuwait, the UAE, and Saudi Arabia. As such, the region has some of the highest per capita income levels in the world, especially in the oil-rich sub-region, the GCC. Additionally, this sub-region has vast reserves of petroleum and natural gas that make it a vital source of global economic stability. According to the Oil and Gas Journal, the MENA region has approximately 50% of the world's oil and natural gas reserves.

The region, particularly the GCC, hosts a significant percentage of expats, most notably from Southeast Asia and Europe. This brings significant diversity in terms of being multinational, multicultural, and multireligious. In fact, in some countries, such as the UAE, expats comprise as much as 80% of the total population.

Finally, it is worth mentioning that Dubai, a focal point and business and tourism hub of the region, is one of seven emirates that make up the UAE, and not a standalone country as it is sometimes perceived to be.

MENA MOBILE SUBSCRIBER PENETRATION BY COUNTRY

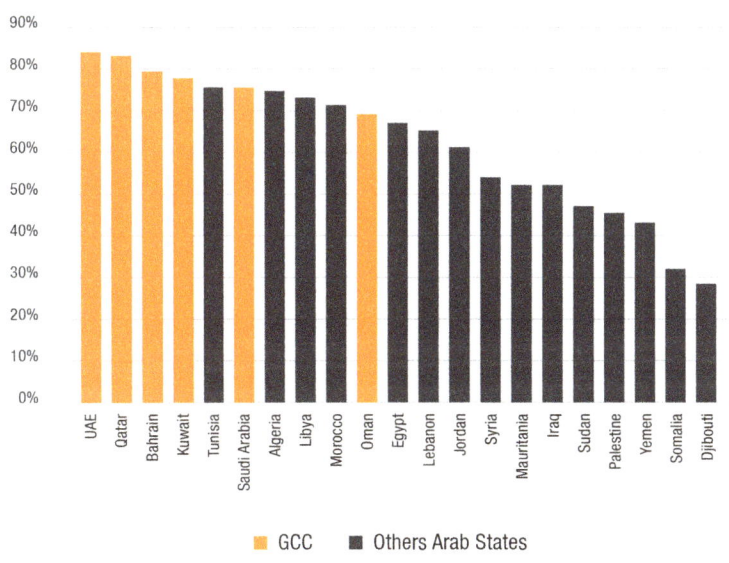

Source: GSMA Intelligence 2018 (www.gsmaintelligence.com)

2. The Case for Doing Business in MENA

In addition to some of the favorable demographics mentioned above—such as the presence of a large, young, tech-savvy population with relatively high levels of per capita income and purchasing power—a number of other factors make MENA a particularly ripe environment to do business in. When evaluating the level of attractiveness of a given country or region in terms of both available economic opportunities and prospects for growth, 10 metrics can help with this assessment (which I collectively refer to as the "Market Attractiveness Index" or "MAI"):

(1) Fertility

(2) Readiness

(3) Scalability

(4) Traction

(5) Transferability

(6) Saturation

(7) Smoothness

(8) Resourcefulness

(9) Transparency

(10) Stability

The following section examines each of these metrics as it pertains to MENA to see how the region stacks up. For all practical purposes, the following assessment is rough and quite broad. Perhaps a more rigorous, scientific approach that utilizes this methodology, but relies on measurable data and comparative analytics, could be the subject of a follow-up publication or study.

Additionally, this assessment is by no means final since it represents a constantly changing environment. Also, for the purposes of this book, I do not assess the metrics country by country or industry by industry. Instead, I provide a simple framework to make a generalized assessment of the state of the region and its level of attractiveness for market entry by international players. In effect, this approach is inspired by the old adage popularized by economist John Maynard Keynes, which states: "It's better to be roughly right than precisely wrong." With that, let's take a closer look at each of the 10 metrics in the context of the MENA region.

(1) "Fertility" refers to the extent of sizable opportunities available within a given geography. This is often a reflection of untapped markets and market segments, and/or significant unmet needs in the local population. With the exception of traditional industries in MENA, such as oil and gas and real estate, huge gaps exist across the board in practically every sector—education, infrastructure, logistics, healthcare, etc. Even developed sectors such as banking and hospitality have significant room to digitally transform. So, there are plenty of opportunities to fill those gaps and bring the region up to par with more developed places such as the US, Western Europe, China, Japan, and South Korea. Granted, the gaps vary significantly from country to country within MENA. For example, infrastructure is much more developed in oil-rich countries than non-oil-rich countries. Nevertheless, those gaps uniformly exist across the region and thus create tremendous opportunities for innovation and upside.

The region's assessment in the fertility category: High.

(2) "Readiness" refers to the presence of macro and micro trends that increase the likelihood of adoption of a given product, service, or technology. Certainly, the region's population is relatively young and tech savvy. Its youth population is a hungry adopter of innovation and all things digital and mobile. This is evident since MENA's population is one of the most engaged users of technologies like smartphones and social media platforms like Instagram, Snapchat, and YouTube. Both smartphone penetration and internet connectivity rates continue to climb rapidly as a new, young generation come of age and better digital products and services lure additional market segments

into using them. All in all, the timing and conditions in the region are conducive to future growth, as the region is significantly accelerating in terms of technology adoption. It is approaching what seems to be an inflection point in that regard, which is likely to alter its course indefinitely.

The region's assessment in the readiness category: High.

(3) "Scalability," in this context, refers to the size of the addressable market of any given product, service, or technology. Relying on some of the data shared earlier around population size, age, income, tech use, etc., the region is large enough to provide an attractive opportunity for international companies considering doing business there. It's not as large as some of the other more populated countries and regions in the world, such as China and India, or Asia in general. It's also more fragmented politically, thus simultaneous expansion across the region is not that straightforward (more on this topic in later chapters). For those companies willing to tackle the challenges posed by these hurdles, to cross borders and penetrate new markets in the region, those same hurdles provide a bit of a shield against regional and international competitors. So, while scale is there on a regional basis, cross-border expansion within the region carries an entry price. That said, these challenges are by no means prohibitive to regional expansion, as many local and multinational companies have already demonstrated for quite some time.

The region's assessment in the scalability category: Medium.

(4) "Traction" refers to how much proven success a given product, service, or technology has in a particular geographic region. To the extent that a consumer product or offering is truly innovative, the likelihood that it will have a well-defined track record or history of any kind

in the region is going to be limited. There may have been some trials and early steps by local or even international players, but they most likely have been insufficient to accurately project an entire region's prospects. In fact, the more footsteps left behind on the track, the more likely it's too late to enter a market (or the more challenging entry becomes), given the presence of entrenched competitors. A narrow method of assessment looking only at historical accounts of similar companies in a given space is not always the most effective in gauging market potential. On the other hand, a broader approach that looks into similar dynamics for international companies penetrating the same market and achieving great success might be required. The region provides a promising outlook in that regard, since literally hundreds of multinationals have built very successful divisions in MENA across practically every sector.

The region's assessment in the traction category: High.

(5) "Transferability" refers to how adaptive a given product, service, or technology is to the local environment—in other words, how much customization, in the form of localization, is required to fit with local market needs. Localization goes well beyond translation (or what is referred to as "Arabization" in this case) and varies significantly from one industry to another and one consumer segment to another. The question that always arises is whether an international company's offering can readily plug-and-play in the region, or whether it needs to be, in effect, reinvented. If the answer is the latter, then the follow-up questions one needs to ask are what kind and degree of reinvention are required, and how much time and resources will be consumed by that process. Answers to such questions can sometimes be found with

preliminary research. More often, though, it comes from actual experience launching an offering in the market and testing it firsthand. That's the case for new business models and new business practices, as well as particular niche-oriented products or services. As such, new international entrants need to allow enough lead time for the initial learning curve and cannot expect to simply utilize exactly the same formulas successfully used elsewhere and get identical results. Transferability varies in the region depending on many factors, mainly being market- and sector-driven, but ultimately depends on the ability to combine the best of both worlds: original innovation and local adaptation.

The region's assessment in the transferability category: Medium.

(6) "Saturation" refers to how crowded a given market or industry is. The more established players involved in a given space, the greater the competition and the greater the challenge to differentiate and win customers. From that perspective, MENA provides a relatively green field in terms of no or low direct competition across many cutting-edge sectors. Certainly, the level of competition is significantly lower in any given space than its counterpart in the US, Western Europe, and most of Asia. Thus, the regional environment is quite favorable for both local and international companies to "disrupt" many sectors and gain significant market share by being an early mover.

The region's assessment in the saturation category: High.

(7) "Smoothness" refers to the ease of doing business and how "frictionless" a given environment is. This applies in terms of both setting up and operating a business, especially a foreign one. Obviously, the more vague, complex, restrictive, and unstable the legislation, the more

challenging, time-consuming, and costly it is to navigate. How business-friendly the legislation is, especially for startups and SMEs, plays a big role in how smooth such businesses' experiences will be getting off the ground. Similarly, this is true of international entrants looking to access a particular market, and in need of a "soft landing." Increasingly, there's a big push by governments in the region to improve the ease of doing business there. Some jurisdictions are actually improving by leaps and bounds in this area, while others remain behind. Deciding where to place your foot first, as an international newcomer, is key.

The region's assessment in the smoothness category: Medium.

WORLD BANK EASE OF DOING BUSINESS 2019

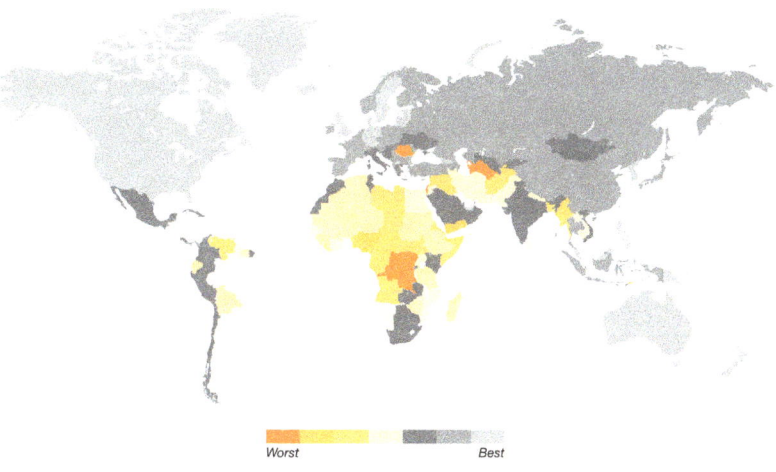

Worst   Best

Source: World Bank Ease of Doing Business 2019 (www.worldbank.org)

(8) "Resourcefulness" refers to access to local talent, capital, and other facilities needed to conduct business effectively. How readily available the so-called "factors of production" are plays a big role in determining how attractive an environment is to international companies. These factors

include the state of the talent pool, especially in senior-level positions in new fields, the abundance of high-growth-oriented investors, and the presence of a centralized venue or hub (for operational and networking purposes). All of these factors make it faster and easier for international companies to get up and running, and ultimately to scale.

The region's assessment in the resourcefulness category: Medium.

(9) "Transparency" refers to the availability of valuable information and data that can be utilized for commercial purposes. This is one area that often gets overlooked, yet its role in providing accurate visibility to both international and local players into the markets where they operate (or intend to operate) cannot be overstated. It also aids their commercial decision-making. Outside of traditional industries in the region (e.g., banking, insurance, food and beverage, retail) this is an area that the region struggles with, especially in new sectors with a minimal historical track record. Furthermore, there's often a lack of uniform, agreed-upon definitions or units of measure for certain aspects of a given sector. Another corollary to this factor is how readily available, accessible, and affordable information and data are. Obviously, data availability is not particularly useful if they sit in the hands of a few—be it with the public sector, consulting groups, or large corporations—and are not shared publicly. This is a fundamental gap in the region, which obviously creates discrepancies in evaluations of market conditions and introduces an additional layer of uncertainty that is counterproductive to good commercial and economic decision-making across many sectors.

The region's assessment in the transparency category: Low.

(10) "Stability" refers to the volatility of a given environment

insofar as it has an economic impact. Obviously, geopolitical instability can have such an effect, but so do other variables, from social unrest (as was the case with the so-called Arab Spring), to currency fluctuations, to changing regulations. While certain parts of the region are very unstable, others are very stable, historically speaking. In that regard, there are certainly some issues with uncertainties in the region, depending on location. Hopefully, those issues can work themselves out over time. Meanwhile, there's plenty of space within the region where such issues don't exist at all, or at least are contained enough to no longer pose a threat so they can be worked around or avoided altogether.

The region's assessment in the stability category: Medium.

WORLD RISK MAP

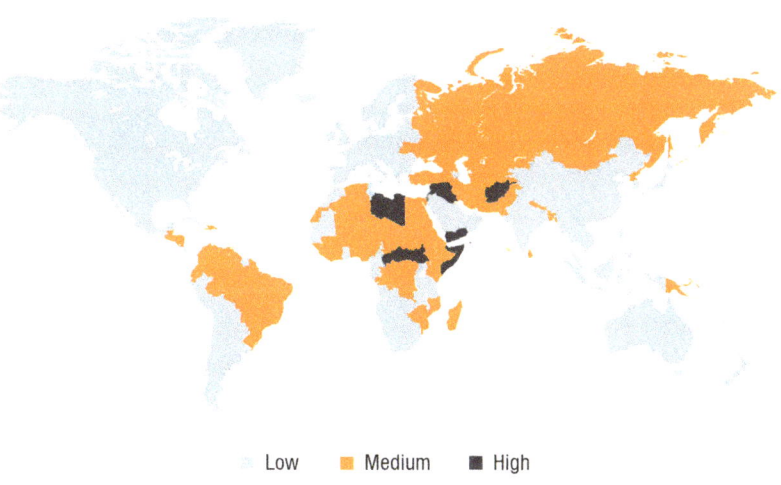

Low   Medium   High

Source: Drum Cussac World Risk Map (www.drum-cussac.com)

Based on the foregoing broad assessment, doing business in MENA clearly presents a substantial opportunity for international players. Furthermore, it's ripe to grow significantly across different areas. That said, there are some challenges to this growth (which we touch on further in upcoming chapters). There are some infrastructure gaps, economic volatility, political instability, and various difficulties around doing business in general.

Despite these challenges, the potential is there for international entrants to achieve extraordinary growth and profitability provided they get their go-to-market strategy and execution right. As such, they will need to chart a clear path to entry and a roadmap to growth that entails at minimum the following steps:

- Prioritize which markets to enter or focus on first.

- Leverage the strengths of various countries.

- Understand local nuances, especially as they relate to consumer or client behavior within their industry.

- Forge the right relationships with key potential local advisers, partners, and stakeholders within their industry.

- Differentiate their offering against the competition.

- Account for all-in costs and available resources up front.

- Fully leverage past success and lessons learned from their own experience in the region and elsewhere.

- Adapt their business model and execution based on local conditions utilizing a try-and-test approach.

- Attempt to be on the ground as much as possible to form a well-rounded picture of the space, and engage with and elicit trust from local potential customers, partners, and/or investors.

There are plenty of examples of international companies that have done exactly just that and pressed ahead to achieve great success in the region.

MARKET ATTRACTIVENESS INDEX (MAI) ASSESSMENT FOR THE MENA REGION

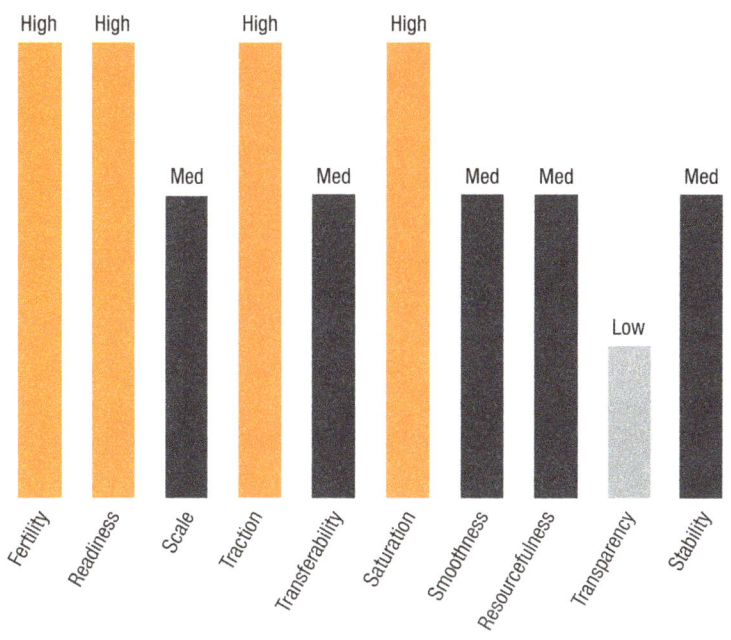

Source: Ecosystem Arabia, Amir Hegazi, 2020

Chapter IV

STATE OF THE
MENA ECOSYSTEM

The consensus among the vast majority of the contributors I interviewed—both from within the region and from outside—is that material progress has been made in improving and advancing the MENA ecosystem recently. In fact, most pointed out that just a dozen or so years ago, there was hardly any ecosystem to speak of. Fast forward to today and there's more of everything—not just more entrepreneurs, startups, and tech-based companies, but more investors, service providers, incubators, accelerators, and mentors— you name it. All of those entities work as the supporting cast in the background helping companies succeed. Combine this with the countless number of recent government policies, initiatives, and programs dedicated to encouraging this growth and the overall improvement in quality and sophistication of the various stake-holders involved, and you end up with an environment that is substantially more conducive to entrepreneurial activity than before. Accordingly, the MENA ecosystem is undergoing some major developments and transformations as we speak.

Obviously, when you're starting an ecosystem from a small base in a relatively nascent environment, a great head start is not uncommon and neither is significant early growth. The question remains, however, as to how much of that early momentum can be leveraged to further accelerate growth, and whether it's sustainable both in the medium and long term. We also have to ask which unique attributes or gaps in the ecosystem are bound to pose a risk to the whole. Even worse, could these gaps be taken advantage of through illegitimate or fraudulent activities that will ultimately harm the consumer, the market, and/ or public opinion? It's easy to be seduced by the growth, the hype, and all the smoke and mirrors; it's much more difficult to take a cold, hard look at the state of the region's ecosystem, assess its shortfalls objectively, and thoroughly examine what is needed to take it to the next level.

As with any ecosystem, including but not limited to MENA, every stage of development comes with its own challenges. And it's often the case that "what got us here, won't get us there." Naturally, a certain level of continuous progression is needed, combined with additional safeguards. To put it metaphorically, the question is, "How can we feed and grow a bigger fire and not get burned in the process?" A bigger fire needs more wood and more fuel to burn bigger and longer, but additional safety precautions are needed to ensure that the fire is contained and used without any material harm. Those are some of the key issues that ecosystem builders grapple with, and which, hopefully, this book can at least raise and get us thinking and talking about. Hopefully, it can provide some useful clues for, or even an actual roadmap of, how to tackle those issues.

Finally, we must not rely on the great progress made recently as a guarantee of continued progress. A fast start is no more indicative of a long-term utopia than a slow start is indicative of long-term collapse. As history has demonstrated, ecosystems, much like startups, can hit the ground running with all the buzz, noise, and hype surrounding them, only to stagnate or flame out altogether just a few years later. Meanwhile, other kinds of startups are slow right out of the gate but grow incrementally and consistently, and eventually appear on the radar to everyone's astonishment. Similarly, ecosystems and companies can steadily bloom as much as they can flash and burn.

As a matter of fact, there are plenty of inspiring and cautionary tales of both dynamics reflected in global ecosystem development case studies available in the research literature, including some key examples covered later in this book.

1. Historical Evolution and Progression

AHMED EL ALFI: If we step back and ask, "What is an ecosystem?", it's a complex network of interacting organisms, jostling for balance. Like in a rainforest, you may have too much rain one year or too much sun another year. Some years you may have too many tall trees or too much underbrush. Eventually, it adjusts and starts to reach equilibrium and every step feeds the next one.

We are in the growth phase of the entrepreneurial ecosystem across MENA. It's quite a dynamic environment. So, naturally, different parts will develop at different rates, in different places. For example, at different points in the growth cycle there may be too many startups. Later there may be too many VCs or too many angels. Of course, these are all judgment calls from different perspectives, but the good news is that all the parts of the ecosystem are developing.

Taking only snapshots is therefore not really an accurate way of examining the evolution and growth of an ecosystem, which is full of nuance and complexity, without taking a full historical and contextual account. We need to take a look at the different components of the ecosystem and evaluate the role they play in the overall environment, how the various pieces fit together, and how they evolved historically over time. Are all the components growing and getting better? Is one area growing so exponentially that it creates an imbalance in the rest of the ecosystem that could possibly be harmful to the whole? So, while it's important to look at each component individually, it's also important to evaluate how each contributes to the overall ecosystem and not assume that any development in one area automatically translates to better results for the environment as a whole.

That said, I am happy with the health of the ecosystem in Egypt and in the region and how it has evolved, especially over the past nine years since the Egyptian revolution in 2011. Barring social unrest, every year has been better than the year before. Of course, one can point out some areas for improvement, but if we take an objective, high-level overview, we are clearly moving in the right direction.

SAMIA MELHEM: The region is obviously not all the same across all the various countries. We have amazing things going on presently in the GCC countries. The UAE, Qatar, Bahrain, Oman, and KSA (Kingdom of Saudi Arabia) are leading in digital government adoption and in improving the skills of their policy-makers and their people. They have the financial means to make the large capital investments needed, and their leaders are willing to change and to make reforms.

The rest of the MENA countries are going at various speeds, depending on their geopolitical situation. The Maghreb countries, for example, are doing well under the strong influence of the EU, while benefiting from peace and stability and their spillover benefits, such as tourism, trade, and foreign direct investment (FDI). Meanwhile, specific territories in the region are facing conflict, violence, displacement, and destabilization. It's very difficult to focus on digital economy development under such circumstances.

Over the last 10 years, the private sector grew very quickly in MENA, but the public sector was very slow, except in the Gulf. A few countries are trying to catch up now, like Jordan, Tunisia, and Morocco. Meanwhile, countries like Egypt, Lebanon, Iraq, and Syria have had a lot of setbacks, but the private sector hasn't stopped. You see in Egypt, for instance, a resurgence of private sector investments in services like offshoring and outsourcing after a short pause due to the Arab Spring. Notice that the Arab Spring took a toll on digital government, as evidenced by the fact that all these countries were doing OK according to the E-Government Development Index, what we call EGDI, but they all went backward during the Arab Spring. Egypt is a good illustration of that fact.

Meanwhile, the countries that are moving the fastest are those that have the highest rate of online adoption, as illustrated by an increase in their Online Adoption Index, which means that their government is making online transactions possible. The GCC countries are a good illustration of this. The GCC countries are also witnessing a large increase in private sector investment and venture capital in technology companies, and the creation of new venture capital funds to invest in technology startups, some backed by public sector/sovereign funds.

Some MENA countries also have pressing priorities—such as displacement, a refugee influx, and conflict—such as Yemen, Syria, Iraq, and to some extent West Bank and Gaza. In these places, most investments in digitalization are donor-driven. The rest of MENA, except perhaps the Maghreb region, is also struggling to bring in private capital because of the instability and lack of trust in the macro situation, and the brain drain of highly skilled youth. Look at Lebanon, for example, which has an outside diaspora that's three times the size of its current local population.

SAMIH TOUKAN: I've been in this startup and tech ecosystem in the region since day one, since 2000 or even before, when there was no ecosystem to speak of. Things were just getting started. You can say that was the birth of the ecosystem in the region. Obviously, we have a much different environment today than what we experienced back then. In those days, our main challenge was that we didn't have enough internet users and connectivity in the region. Today, that's no longer a pressing issue. Today's ecosystem has evolved quite a bit, yet it's still relatively small compared to other regions of the world. When we started Maktoob, there were probably a dozen or so tech startups in the region. Now, there are thousands of startups. You can also see the formative signs of the ecosystem through the proliferation of VCs, service providers, funding programs, and government support. The ecosystem is developing as we speak. Even in countries that are experiencing a slowdown in traditional economic activity, there is growth in e-commerce, the internet, and the technology sector in general.

RABEA ATAYA: I've seen tremendous change in the 20 years since the internet/tech industry started in the region. The "internet switch" in the region was turned on in 2000, around the same time I founded Bayt. So, I've obviously seen quite a bit of an evolution. In the early days, everything was quite challenging. Capital for this type of digital business was rare to find. The legal structures were very challenging due to the complexity around business incorporation and also due to foreign investment being limited across the region. Movement of talent was also very difficult because the visa laws were restrictive back then, and so were a host of other things—everything from online payment methodologies to infrastructure.

Fast forward to today's environment: What's changed? Every one of these areas has changed—for the better. The legal structures for incorporation have become less complex. Foreign investment into private companies has become easier. Talent today moves around a lot more freely. Capital is also much more readily available. The infrastructure is much more developed and a lot more people now have access to digital and online technologies. The combination of these things has meant that there is a lot more startup activity than ever before, including a lot more successful startups that have managed to scale faster and grow larger than ever before.

ABDULAZIZ AL LOUGHANI: If we look at the historical evolution of the ecosystem in the past 10 years, we witness a huge change in the entrepreneurial mindset in the region. There is big, positive change happening with many young adults in college studying to create their own future, rather than waiting to get a "normal" job, so to speak.

In terms of startup community-building, we see that a lot more locally grown, organic communities have sprouted, that draw like-minded people together. I'm not just referring to bigger conferences, but even smaller sub-technology groups. We see coders having their own community and events, especially in places like Egypt, Kuwait, and Saudi Arabia. These are all remarkable improvements recently.

Infrastructure-wise, if we look back 10 or 15 years, internet penetration has really gone through the roof. On a MENA level, we're probably at 65%, but when you zoom into the GCC, Egypt, Levant, Lebanon, we're probably even higher, close to 80% internet penetration in the GCC specifically. Infrastructure has improved significantly. We still see some variations in cost for internet bandwidth across the region, but it has gone down compared to 10 years ago.

Education-wise, specifically in computer science, software development, and engineering, we are still lagging behind. We really need to invest more in that segment when it comes to talent.

From a startup success stories perspective, the rate and frequency of unlocking value have also increased significantly. For example, there was a seven-year period between the Maktoob exit to Yahoo! and Talabat's to Rocket Internet, whereas today exits happen a lot faster.

NED JAROUDI: The regional ecosystem has seen a huge leap forward in the last decade, certainly in the last five years, in every dimension. I remember when I first moved to the region over 20 years ago, there was practically no startup activity, except for a handful of enterprise software companies out of Egypt and Lebanon that were involved in areas such as core banking or retail solutions.

Then, the whole startup scene evolved to other places like the GCC and Jordan, primarily due to the dotcom boom in the West. A lot of Arabs in Silicon Valley, Route 128 in Boston, and Europe were excited to come back to the region and replicate what they saw or worked on there. This ultimately gave rise to the second wave of internet startups such as AME Info, Arabia.com, Bayt.com, Maktoob, and Zawya.com. But they were a handful of isolated ventures and there was not much of an ecosystem to speak of. Back then, you didn't see any kind of government support, corporate sponsors, VCs, incubators, accelerators, etc. Recognizing the increasing technological momentum, and the opportunity it created to grow the knowledge economy, the Dubai government established Internet City free zone in 1999. This led all major tech multinationals and most of the startups I mentioned to set up their regional headquarters there. Thus, the ecosystem was established with Dubai as the startups' window to the region and the world.

Next, the smartphone revolution exploded on the scene around 2011-2012, making it very easy to develop apps for iOS or Android. A new generation of regional startups was born, mostly copying other proven solutions that existed in the West and Asia. Major events at that time in Dubai, such as the Celebration of Entrepreneurship and the Global Entrepreneurship Summit, with government support, cemented this coming of age for the regional startup scene. In parallel, different countries across the region started embracing the knowledge economy with initiatives like Oasis 500 in Jordan, Circular 331 in Lebanon, and national innovation and SME initiatives in the UAE, Saudi Arabia, Bahrain, Kuwait, and other countries, leading to funds, incubators, and accelerators mushrooming everywhere.

Specifically on funding, new VCs are being set up every day, attracting limited partners (LPs) from family offices. These investors have started to diversify their portfolios, especially with their second- and third-generation leadership becoming more in tune with technology. So, we've reached a point where there's a pretty vibrant startup ecosystem in the region, with the level of maturity obviously varying from country to country.

NABEEL KOSHAK: For the MENA startup ecosystem, many things have definitely evolved. I remember nine years ago when I started Wadi Makkah, everyone was complaining about the environment, the equity funding gaps, the risk capital availability, and the enabling programs in the ecosystem. Things have evolved quite a bit on all those fronts if you fast forward to today's environment.

Back then, there were a lot of events and celebrations, but no substance on the ground in terms of quality deals and investments. Now we see more quality deals and more maturity overall. We are seeing more professional angel investors, angel groups, and VCs. Granted, it's still a nascent market, but we do see a healthy increase in risk capital and better overall quality entrepreneurs and startups.

My view is that the key players in the ecosystem are the founders and the funders. Meanwhile, the government sometimes plays an enabling role in the background—not to interfere, but to help catalyze and support, and to debug the regulations and facilitate local startups' growth.

COUNTRY WHERE STARTUP IS REGISTERED OR INCORPORATED

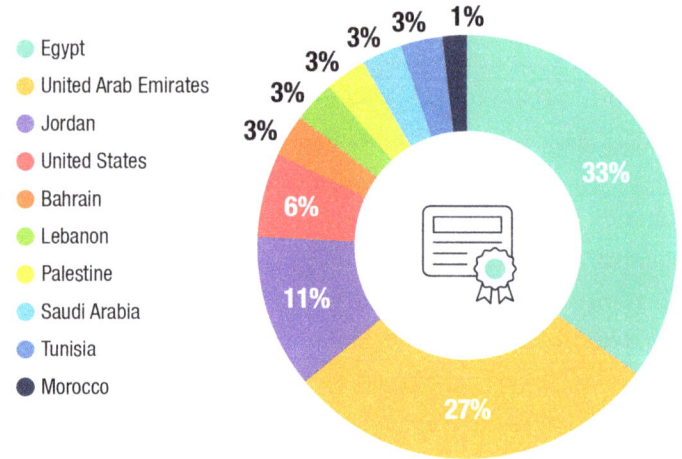

- Egypt
- United Arab Emirates
- Jordan
- United States
- Bahrain
- Lebanon
- Palestine
- Saudi Arabia
- Tunisia
- Morocco

Data was collected from the applications of Wamda X programme and complimentary research from STEP Conference

Source: The State of Pre-Seed Startups in MENA (www.wamda.com & www.stepconference.com)

OSMAN SULTAN: Seven or eight years ago, there were many more obstacles for startups than we have today. Today, the ecosystem has evolved significantly, in multiple dimensions, including the startup culture. The mindset driving more and more young entrepreneurs to take risks is becoming more common. People are beginning to see that it's possible to have an idea, work hard, and create significant value in a relatively short time, which is encouraging youth to pursue similar aspirations in the hope that they, too, will have a great success story.

This is also stimulating the appetite of global investors to tap into other big opportunities in the region or acquire successful local startups. More recently, however, some key figures are asking why we always need to wait for an exit offer from the Western world. Why rely on the appetite of a global North American or European player? Actually, that's the theme raised and voiced by Mr. Mohammad Alabbar saying, "We can have our own large and global companies. We can create them here. We can be partners in these and we can try to keep the value more in the region." That's an interesting angle to look at the issue from and an interesting discussion to have.

The jury is still out on how things will play out. Mr. Alabbar mentioned this as it relates to his e-commerce venture, Noon, as well as his Chinese partnerships, and how we should focus on a more home-grown, local business model.

2. Recent Success Stories

WALID HANNA: One recent event with a great impact on this region is Uber's acquisition of Careem for $3.1 billion, as well as Amazon's acquisition of Souq before that for around $600 million. Earlier, we also had Rocket Internet's acquisition of Talabat and Yahoo!'s of Maktoob for around $170 million each, and many smaller exits in between. These exits are the best way to put the region on the international map, as well as to inspire the region's entrepreneurs to dream big. These deals represented great milestones for the region and, in effect, unlocked significant barriers for many others to follow suit, from both a psychological and financial standpoint.

CHRISTOPHER SCHROEDER: Clearly, what has happened with Ronaldo Mouchawar, Co-Founder and CEO of Souq, and the Careem team, says a ton about what is achievable. Their success has created an unprecedented model for entrepreneurs across the region to emulate and, in effect, showed them how it can be done. The leaders at BECO, MEVP, Wamda, Sawari Ventures, Algebra, and Leap Ventures, among others, also remain an enormous influence within the ecosystem.

Keep an eye on Abdulrahman Tarabzouni at STV and Sharif El-Badawi and his colleague Hasan Haider at 500 Startups, bringing experience from places like Google to the Middle East. There is also an enormous and wonderful rise in women building great companies, such as Mona Ataya at Mumzworld and Amira Rashad at BulkWhiz, among others. They are providing real inspiration for all.

OSMAN SULTAN: You have some individuals who are showing passion and support around the entrepreneurship ecosystem. You cannot talk about the ecosystem in this region without mentioning Ronaldo Mouchawar and his commitment and effort over the years to build Souq. What he managed to accomplish is remarkable and demands respect and admiration. Mudassir Sheikha and Magnus Olsson from Careem are also key figures and contributors in the ecosystem. I had the opportunity to sit down with Mudassir, and I was impressed with his strategic vision for Careem, in terms of the type of evolution he had in mind for the company. It has obviously turned out to be an amazing success story for the region.

Others include the founders of Talabat. One has to mention Huda Kattan and what she's doing in the beauty sector. Another individual that comes to mind is Michael Lahyani from Property Finder. Other individuals and institutions that are having a great impact on the ecosystem are BECO Capital with Dany Farha and Amir Farha, Walid Hanna and the team at MEVP, and the UTURN team. These are some random names that come to mind. I apologize if I forget to mention some, as there are too many to mention.

Overall, I'm optimistic when I see the maturity level of some of the young entrepreneurs I come across. What's equally impressive is the people in top leadership roles who are now supporting these young entrepreneurs. My dear friend, Patrick Chalhoub, is an exemplary model on this front, as well as Badr Jafar, Muna Al Gurg, Khalfan Belhoul, and Najla Al-Midfa. These are people involved in large institutions but are well integrated in the startup ecosystem.

MENA EXIT EVOLUTION

The MENA region saw its first unicorn exit with Careem's $3.1B acquisition
- 27 startup exits take place in MENA, the highest on record
- Total disclosed exit value amounted to $3.6B, another all-time high

Yearly Number of Exits and Exit Value of MENA-Based Startups

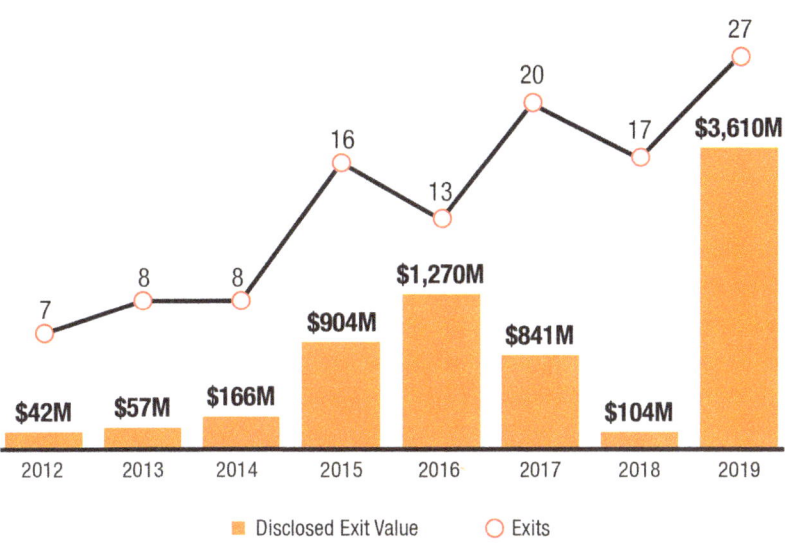

Source: MAGNiTT MENA Venture Investment Summary 2019 (www.magnitt.com)

OMAR ALMAJDOUIE: There are a number of exciting startups making great impact. Noon Academy, founded by Mohammad AlDhala'an and Abdulaziz Alsaeed, is one of the most impactful EdTech startups in the region. It socializes the learning experience in a way that is not only more engaging, but also much more effective and results-oriented. It has more than 2.5 million students in Saudi Arabia and hundreds of thousands in Egypt after just a few months of operation.

There are a few examples of outstanding startups that come to mind. Swvl is one of the fastest-growing startups in Egypt and in the region. Co-founded and led by Mostafa Kandil, Swvl provides an affordable alternative to Uber and Careem in the emerging markets for more than 100,000 passengers daily. It uses the huge number of underutilized buses to provide smart routes to users in high-density cities, including Cairo, Alexandria, Nairobi, Karachi, and many more.

Salla has onboarded thousands of new merchants that are trying their luck in the e-commerce arena every month, using a very smart and convenient way of making a shop online through Salla.sa. Founded by Nawaf Hariri and Salman Butt, this Shopify-like service provider is a true enabler for the merchants to have a reliable and modern gateway to online customers. Mrsool is a delivery platform that is one of the fastest-growing apps in the Saudi market. It performs large numbers of deliveries to the end users every day by enabling the 200,000 crowdsourced drivers to deliver anything anywhere in the country. It's by far the most extensive drivers' network in Saudi Arabia.

MENA UNDERLYING FUNDING EVOLUTION

Record year for total funding when excluding the investments of Souq & Careem
- 2019 saw an increase of 12% in total underlying funding
- This reflects a 33% 5-year CAGR as the ecosystem grows and matures

Yearly Startup Funding Excluding Souq & Careem

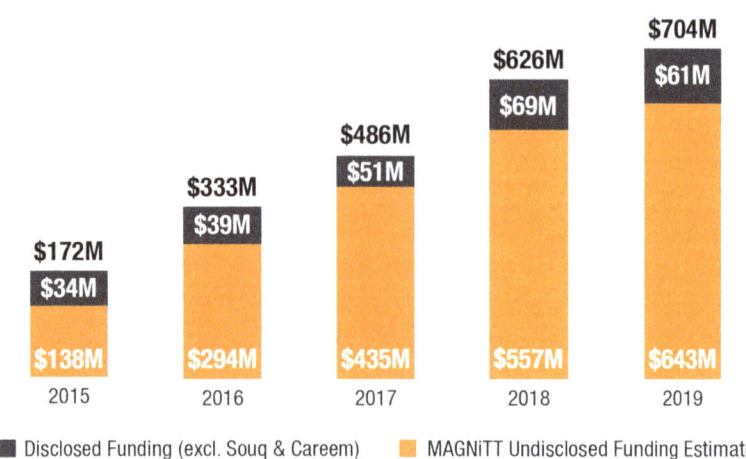

Disclosed Funding (excl. Souq & Careem)   MAGNiTT Undisclosed Funding Estimate

Source: MAGNiTT MENA Venture Investment Summary 2019 (www.magnitt.com)

3. Funding is at an All-Time High

ABDULAZIZ AL LOUGHANI: Funding has increased significantly in the region. We're starting to see deeper pockets entering from the private sector, and developmental money has started becoming more available. Today, even on a sovereign level, the asset class is finally treated commercially, rather than viewed as a developmental kind of tool to create jobs and solve cultural problems, or migrate public servants to the private sector. Saudi Arabia, Bahrain, Qatar, and Oman are examples of sovereign funds that basically decided to establish different kinds of fund of funds (FoF) programs. In these programs, managers are being selected on their merits to deploy capital into this part of the world, hopefully with the best standards. However, we still don't see the asset class having players focused on different stages. I feel that the startup founders' pipeline is still too thin for us to be focused on horizontally different stages or on different verticals in this part of the world.

MAHMOUD ADI: When it comes to the state of funding in MENA, we have made a significant improvement and we continue to accelerate at a very rapid rate. It's exciting to share some figures from the MAGNiTT report, which suggests that roughly $900 million went into the ecosystem. Four years ago, it was around $100 million. It's still below the level of developed markets. In the US, for example, roughly $100 billion went into the industry. We are sitting roughly at 1% of that market, but we are growing really fast from a very small base.

If you look at our evolution across the region, the oil and gas industry got us off the ground; that was our first wave of economic stability. Then came the second wave, defined by a lot of construction, a lot of superstructures were built—residential, hospital, educational, and so forth. Then a third wave emerged, which is starting to get into some services like retail, tourism, major financial sectors, and so forth. Now, moving forward, there's a global consensus that the next wave is a technology wave. This is being driven by millennials to some extent. This generation is entering the workforce, and they are used to consuming a lot of technology and are not necessarily satisfied with traditional types of work. They're figuring, "Why don't I go invent something?" They are also inspired by global success stories.

On the capital side, the second- and third-generation family offices are starting to realize this has been done in the US, and some of them actually have exposure to some of this asset class. They say, "I'm seeing that the government is backing this sector and I see folks with great jobs leaving to start something new, while other entrepreneurs have become wildly successful. Why don't I get my hands dirty and get into this space?"

INVESTMENTS IN MENA BY MENA INVESTORS

This map is a snapshot of the value and number of deals across the MENA region. Map breaks down total value of investments across top markets in region.

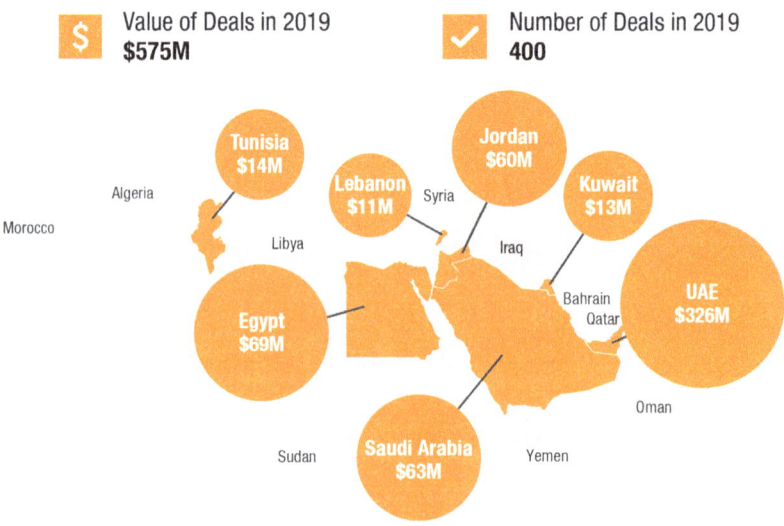

| $ | Value of Deals in 2019 **$575M** | ✓ | Number of Deals in 2019 **400** |

Source: ArabNet Business Intelligence Investment Report 2019 (www.arabnet.me)

AMMAR AL MALIK: There is no doubt that the local and regional startup and tech ecosystem is thriving, with the UAE far ahead. There's a significant and continuous increase in regional VC investment activity; in the number of companies starting up; in the number of ecosystem enablers, incubators, and accelerators; and in the number of global investors and institutions investing here.

According to MAGNiTT's "H1 2019 MENA Venture Investment Report," 238 startups raised $471 million in the first half of 2019 alone, a 66% increase from the same period in 2018. In 2018, we saw a more than 30% increase in investment activity over 2017, even excluding the $200 million in new funding that Careem secured from existing investors.

MENA FUNDING SHARE BY COUNTRY

The UAE still accounts for the lion's share of total funding
- The United Arab Emirates (UAE) accounted for 60% of total funding
- Saudi Arabia's share of total funding increased by 3%, moving to 3rd place

MENA's Top 5 Countries by Total Funding in 2019

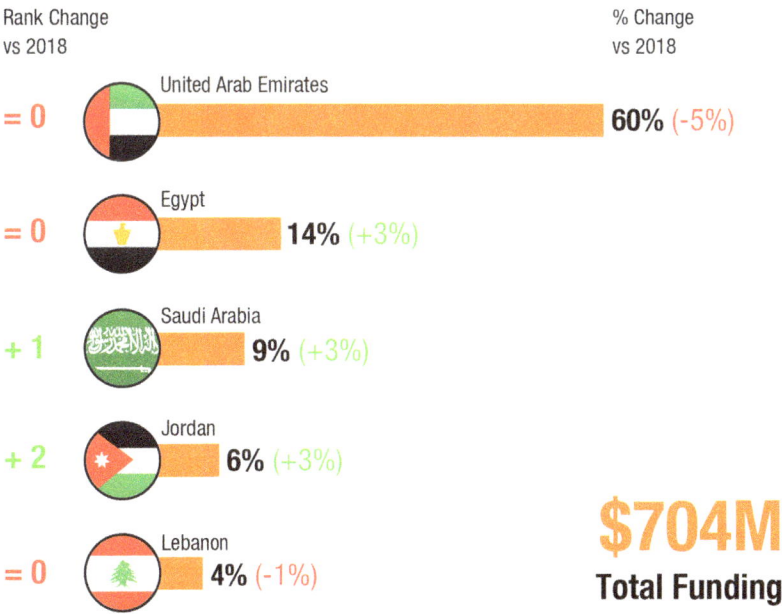

Rank Change vs 2018	Country	% Change vs 2018
= 0	United Arab Emirates	**60%** (-5%)
= 0	Egypt	**14%** (+3%)
+ 1	Saudi Arabia	**9%** (+3%)
+ 2	Jordan	**6%** (+3%)
= 0	Lebanon	**4%** (-1%)

$704M
Total Funding

Source: MAGNiTT MENA Venture Investment Summary 2019 (www.magnitt.com)

4. More Proactive Governments

RONALDO MOUCHAWAR: Over the past decade or so, governments across the region have increased the level of support available to nurture the growth of technology startups. This support has had a major impact on the development of local ventures, capabilities, and consumer offerings in the e-commerce sector. Additionally, governments are increasingly focusing on developing a few key ingredients that help drive the growth and adoption of technology. First, policies that are forward-looking and embrace change go a long way toward encouraging entrepreneurs to take bold risks. Second, a region-wide focus on innovation has helped to provide opportunities and space for entrepreneurs to operate in. Third, encouraging a competitive business landscape and operating environment always helps drive growth, and we see this across many parts of the region.

As a result, e-commerce is now an increasingly mainstream part of companies' omni-channel offerings across MENA. It's no longer limited to the early adopters and tech-savvy enthusiasts—everyone is using it. This is being felt across all sectors, with bespoke fashion and food and beverage offerings becoming available, in addition to more generalist e-commerce players. Ultimately, government support throughout the region was a factor that enabled the journey of Souq. In general, any initiatives or projects that enhance people's connectivity, help unlock new technologies, and see active engagement with the private sector will contribute to the development of e-commerce in the region going forward.

BADR JAFAR: One thing that is working is that there is a clear imperative at the government level to see entrepreneurship flourish as an essential source of job creation and innovation. Governments are becoming more active in encouraging the region's youth to consider this pursuit as a valid and viable career path, providing funding where required, and even creating venues for the community to get together and pitch and discuss ideas. Sharjah is a great example of a local government that nurtures SMEs and small businesses and supports innovation in a way that genuinely encourages a level playing field. The UAE government is serious about developing conducive regulatory and policy frameworks that allow viable businesses to compete and grow.

VALUE OF INVESTMENTS BY STARTUP INDUSTRY IN MENA

Lifestyle startups not only capture the biggest proportion of deals (19%) but also the largest share of investments (29%). The biggest investments in lifestyle-focused companies include Wadi ($30 million) and Mumzworld ($20 million). Value by industry continues to be swayed by growth-stage deals; thus, while transportation businesses only make up 3% of all deals, Careem's $200 million and Swvl's $30 million rounds mean that the transportation sector consistently captures the second largest proportion of dollars invested (27%).

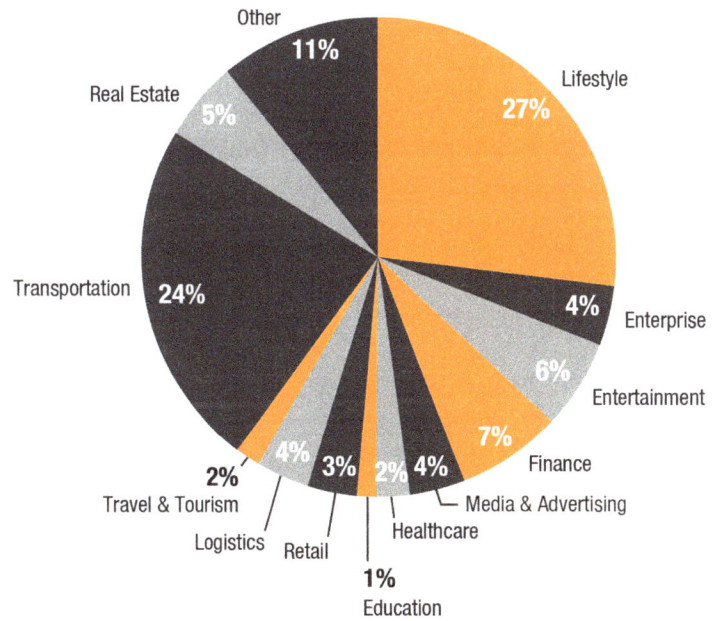

Cumulative years: 2013-2018

Source: ArabNet Business Intelligence Investment Report 2019 (www.arabnet.me)

AMMAR AL MALIK: The UAE government has been and continues to be proactive in promoting startups and SMEs. One very good example, and something that I am personally excited about, is part of the "50 Year Charter" initiative by His Highness Sheikh Mohammed bin Rashid Al Maktoum that allows students in universities to start businesses, get trade licenses, and study a curriculum that will actually help them get into entrepreneurship.

This is extremely important for the ecosystem and for the whole region because entrepreneurship is a fundamental pillar of the future growth and sustainability of the region. That's why you see governments across the GCC and MENA setting up funds and investment schemes for entrepreneurship. We have to support the growth of the SME sector and we have to create more jobs in the private sector. This will happen by supporting entrepreneurs and startups from a very early stage and helping them grow into the mindset. We need to tutor and mentor them about things like: this is how you start a company, these are the connections you need, these are the laws you have to follow, these are the regulations and support the government sorted out for you, this is how you get funding, this is how you do your balance sheets, this is how you can think like an entrepreneur, and this is how you develop an MVP (minimum viable product).

VERA FUTORJANSKI: Nowhere else have I experienced a place that has such an open and supportive government culture than in the UAE. I remember traveling to the US on behalf of the Dubai government and speaking to the local ecosystem players, startups, VCs, various institutions; they were all saying they do not want government involvement since it would always slow them down. Here in the UAE, my view is different. We want government involvement because it speeds up the process.

Speaking from first-hand experience, the government of the UAE fosters and pushes innovation. It's a top-down approach. It's inspirational and educational. When I worked for the Dubai Future Foundation, we launched a project called "10X". Every government entity was mandated to participate in the project and embrace disruptive innovation. 10X aims to propel the city of Dubai 10 years ahead of any other city in the world by coming up with new, innovative ideas and adopting exponential technologies. This effect ripples down through the people who live in Dubai. The government entities need startups to support them in their innovation endeavors.

5. Examples of Local Startup Community Champions

ALI ABUKUMAIL: I would like to acknowledge the role of two individuals who have contributed significantly to supporting the ecosystem in the region. The first is Fadi Ghandour, whom I have personally learned a lot from over the last 10 years. His role was key in building Wamda as the catalyst for entrepreneurship ecosystems in the region and building the culture of entrepreneurship, as well as inspiring, advising, and investing in entrepreneurs and startups. Most recently, Fadi has also been supporting underserved communities with Ruwwad Al-Tanmeya in such places as Jordan, Palestine, Lebanon, and Egypt. This organization has really been helping educate and inspire aspiring entrepreneurs and teaching 21st-century skills.

The second is Ahmed El Alfi, whose contribution to the ecosystem cannot be overstated, has been an accelerator, incubator, investor, and adviser on so many fronts across the region. His work with Flat6Labs alone, which he expanded to other countries beyond Egypt, and all the impact he made on the ecosystem over many years has been nothing short of remarkable. The support he provided and continues to provide to youth and his overall contribution is strongly felt. I salute both as inspirational and impactful leaders in our community.

DINA EL-MOFTY: RiseUp Summit is a great example of a local startup community champion. It's been really amazing to see it develop from an idea, from when Abdelhameed Sharara was working with us as a consultant at Injaz, that evolved into this thriving startup community. We supported him initially in starting his very first event by getting some partners from the private sector involved. This was shortly after the revolution, with all the heightened sense of change. Fast forward to today, and the impact RiseUp Summit has had on gathering entrepreneurs and investors from the whole region is quite remarkable. It really created a sense of community, not only in Egypt but across the region, where everybody looks forward to their annual event, bringing people together, bringing speakers, and so on. It's really inspiring to see. They also recently created the *RiseUp Manifesto* to help improve policies and governance for entrepreneurs and startups, which is also a great tool for the local ecosystem.

NED JAROUDI: The proliferation of startup community-building programs, including more investors, incubators, and accelerators, as well as government initiatives such as Ghadan, Khalifa Fund, Dubai Future Economy, and Dubai SME in the UAE, and Jada, Badir, Monshaat, and MiSK in Saudi, are also contributing greatly to this momentum. I also had the privilege of being associated with such an initiative when I was at the UAE Prime Minister's Office, where we worked closely with Stanford University and the Ministry of Higher Education to co-design an innovation and entrepreneurship course that has been taught for three years in 43 UAE universities by 104 professors trained by Stanford. As a result, thousands of students have gained skills and knowledge that will allow them to seriously consider entrepreneurship as a career path, which is commendable.

Chapter V

OUTLOOK OF
THE MENA ECOSYSTEM

There is no denying that, when it comes to ecosystem development, most of the region is heading in the right direction, according to all the tested indicators. Certainly, there are gaps and imbalances here and there, but that's expected at this stage of the game. Ecosystems, by nature, will eventually adjust themselves and find some kind of balanced equilibrium, as Ahmed El Alfi, Chairman of Sawari Ventures, the GrEEK Campus, and Flat6Labs explains in this chapter. It's quite normal that there might be too much of one component and not enough of another initially. Eventually, organic forces will correct most of the imbalances, assuming the presence of a healthy environment that is conducive to growth to begin with. That is the natural course of ecosystem development. Much like supply and demand in economics, a similar dynamic takes hold in any ecosystem. The real question is, how fast and how wide can such changes occur?

The MENA ecosystem today presents greater access to capital and talent, better infrastructure and policies, and more support and events. Funding, both from local and international players, is at an all-time high. Governments across the board are acknowledging the power of the new economy and are being more proactive to try to stimulate and harness that power. In addition, there's a greater level of urgency than ever before to attempt to achieve economic diversification. These top-down strategies and mandates have certainly helped improve the ease of doing business for both local and foreign companies, and made some parts of the region more attractive for international talent, companies, and investments.

The ecosystem is also being further carried by strong winds, in terms of powerful forces both locally, such as growing markets and a young population, as well as globally, with the emergence of new technologies. We're starting to see sizable exits from world-class companies (e.g., the Uber/Careem and Amazon/Souq acquisitions) and the first IPO of a locally grown, Egypt-based e-payment network (Fawry), plus countless promising startups popping up everywhere. We even see sandboxes 1 and other innovation-oriented environments being introduced in an effort to remove barriers to and boost innovation. Even more corporations are integrating startups into their open innovation and R&D programs and budgets. The Tunisian government has formally issued its Startup Act, designed to explicitly nurture the space in a concerted effort to listen to its young population's needs, meet the demands of the new economy, and create its own innovation hub. Meanwhile, Bahrain is implementing innovative pilot programs in FinTech to catalyze more local and international entrepreneurs and startups to emerge in that space. Positive examples are, in fact, everywhere.

All in all, looking at every metric, the ecosystem is developing at every level and spreading geographically, beyond just Dubai and a few other places where early growth occurred, to many other cities and countries across the region. There is plenty of hard data to back individuals' views and insights. Some key findings are highlighted in this chapter and elsewhere in this book to provide a more rounded view of the landscape.

1. Current Positive Trends

RABIH KHOURY: There are many positive trends and indicators for the ecosystem, especially in the last three years. Governments have been focusing on funding, incubation, and acceleration because they have to answer the question of high youth unemployment. However, former asset managers in the region who are global investors have not really looked at investing in local technology VC funds.

Mubadala finally announced about three or four months ago the Abu Dhabi Catalyst Partners fund, which is a $1 billion umbrella. That's going to cover incubation, acceleration, and a fund of funds platform. They're going to also see some new managers. In Lebanon, we had a program in 2014 called Circular 331, where the Central Bank stepped in and gave a subsidy to banks investing in technology. This made $400 million available to the technology sector in Lebanon, which was a lot of money for a small country like that. It also created a whole wave of entrepreneurs. We were the first fund that got approved by the Central Bank, and the largest fund in Lebanon, so that's also an encouraging sign.

WALID HANNA: The MENA technology startup ecosystem is maturing and the startup community has been receiving a considerable amount of attention over the past couple of years: larger VC funds, larger equity rounds beating every record, and larger exits. Progress may have been slow in the past, but the pace has accelerated considerably, especially in the past two years.

The number and the quality of startups have multiplied by 10 times over the past three years. In our deal pipeline we now evaluate more than 1,000 investment opportunities every year, up from 200 five years ago. The number of incubators, accelerators, tech co-working spaces, government initiatives, and entrepreneurship-related NGOs has also multiplied by 10 over the past five years. There is still a long way for us to go in developing a deep tech ecosystem, but the region is on the right track.

ISSA AGHABI: One noticeable trend over the past 12 months is the role of governments. They are realizing that this is a relevant asset class that requires proper focus and attention. This is also the case for family offices and retail investors who are now becoming a lot more aggressive and interested in this space. I believe this positive trend will be confined in the short run, with a large burst over the next 12-18 months. Careem and Souq employees will be concluding their vesting periods for stock options and looking to invest or launch businesses in this space. I really think we're at a pivotal point in the ecosystem.

The landscape is changing very quickly. The UAE continues to be the core hub and a true force to be reckoned with. Saudi Arabia, right now, is increasingly becoming a big player with a lot of positive support and investment taking place. It's now becoming a lot more home-grown in terms of local startups, which is quite promising over the long term once the infrastructure is more developed. We're also seeing better quality entrepreneurs coming out of North Africa; Morocco and Tunisia are certainly up-and-coming. Egypt, with massive outflows of entrepreneurs, was not even a contender two years ago. Bahrain has been a pioneer in how governments should be looking at supporting the ecosystem. Jordan and Lebanon are seeing a big portion of its diaspora returning to leverage the lower cost of operation at home than in the GCC.

SAMI MAHROUM: What I see as a very positive event, for instance, is the introduction of an entrepreneur visa in the UAE. If you set up a business in the UAE and make a certain level of investment, you are entitled to five years on an entrepreneur visa that's renewable. Before, you could set up a company in the free zone area and get a two-year visa, maybe a three-year visa, and you'd have to pay quite a bit to renew. Now it's easier and less expensive. This kind of initiative sends a positive signal to foreign entrepreneurs to consider setting up in the UAE.

This program also links the entrepreneurs and startups with large companies and government departments. If the government department has a problem, there is a mechanism to engage with startups and entrepreneurs and to try to find a solution for this problem, and then the government acts as the first client or the main client for those startups. There are also a number of catalyst and matchmaking initiatives, where the government helps create potential markets and business fraternities for startups to help them grow. This level of awareness and understanding of what it takes to support startups is quite positive.

ABDUL BASET AL JANAHI: Economic diversification and government-led initiatives to strengthen the entrepreneurial ecosystem are promoting SME activity across MENA, much to the benefit of the overall economy in the region. MENA has the world's second-largest youth population after sub-Saharan Africa; 60% of the population are aged below 30, and startups are increasingly seen as the best course for creating more opportunities for them.

The proliferation of smart technologies and rising internet penetration are particularly favoring digital startups in the region. In 2018, $674 million was invested in 255 digital investment deals across MENA, according to ArabNet's "State of Digital Investments in MENA, 2013-2018" report.

Persistent efforts to accelerate the transition toward a knowledge economy and attract talent and capital have led to Dubai and the UAE dominating digital investment activity across MENA. It has the highest share of investors, number of deals, and value of deals. In fact, Dubai accounted for $459 million (AED 1.68 billion) of the overall digital investment deals in 2018, the highest in the region and six times above second-place Egypt ($66 million). Dubai also hosts the largest number of operational startups (192) in the MENA digital domain. Undoubtedly, bold initiatives such as Dubai Internet City and enhancing investor confidence through corporate governance practices, as well as a strong commitment to innovation, are all attracting digital entrepreneurs and new asset classes to Dubai.

NABEEL KOSHAK: Today, there are more enabling programs, in terms of private accelerators, incubators, and investors, than ever before. Previously these were led by the government, which wasn't sustainable or scalable because they have no skin in the game, so to speak. Recently, we've seen the rise of investor-backed accelerators and incubators, where the investors are vested and have a lot more skin in the game. They are keen to protect these startups because they are investing in them. That is actually happening worldwide. It's not something new. These programs could be co-sponsored by the government, but they should be backed by investors as well in order to make them more sustainable and scalable.

On the funding front, the role of VCs has certainly evolved. Seven or ten years ago, we had a handful of VCs in Saudi Arabia and the region. Now we have a dozen or so local VCs, as well as others from outside Saudi Arabia who have joined us, thus bringing more benefits and an exchange of ideas and experiences to entrepreneurs and the overall ecosystem. We're seeing startups starting in Egypt or Dubai and scaling to Saudi Arabia, as well as ones starting in Saudi Arabia and scaling to Egypt. So, there's a lot more regional orientation and regional play for startups than previously had been the case, which further incentivizes investors and VCs as they recognize the full potential of the region.

We are also seeing agencies in Saudi Arabia continuously updating their bylaws and regulations in terms of funds. We now have valuable professional organizations, like Venture Capital and Private Equity Association (VCPE), which provide professional educational programs and platforms for VCs to voice their pain points, in order to enhance governmental support. All in all, the funding landscape has been evolving, though it's not at the pace of entrepreneurs and the VCs yet. I think the government needs to continue to catch up to what's happening in terms of the startups and the investments in the industry.

2. Promising Government Policies and Initiatives

OMAR CHRISTIDIS: There are just so many initiatives within the Saudi Arabian government, through Monshaat, which is trying to tackle everything from training and capacity building through entrepreneurial culture and funding mechanisms. The Ministry of Commerce and Investment (MCI) has also helped, along with the investment promotion and attraction that the Saudi Arabian General Investment Authority (SAGIA) has been doing. The way they make the licensing for entrepreneurs really easy to enter the Kingdom, I would say this is one of the top initiatives that is going to really have an impact. I see entrepreneurs going there, really excited, and having a path to entering the region's top market.

The E-commerce Council Committee (ECC) is also working diligently on developing a strategy for boosting e-commerce in the Kingdom, which will permeate to the entire digital sector. There's a lot of infrastructure-building taking place in terms of co-working spaces, which is also exciting for me. That's now the minimum requirement—Beirut Digital District (BDD), Dubai Internet City (DIC)—everyone is now building these hubs, but that's not where the differentiation really is. The real differentiation is going to be able who's able to attract the best talent, and in many ways the startups are going to be attracted to strong, progressive regulatory regimes.

AMIRA RASHAD: I think some government entities are putting their money where their mouth is. For example, we've recently been preparing to launch BulkWhiz in Saudi Arabia, starting with the process of getting a license, and I've started interacting with SAGIA. I can tell you, so far, I have had a very positive experience there. If anything, they actually have more of a consulting-sales mentality there. I was sitting in a room with five SAGIA colleagues explaining the benefits of getting a SAGIA license. I was pleasantly surprised that they followed up with all the support I needed. This is what they call their "one-stop-shop service" model, which is very encouraging. At the end of the setup process, we got our license in under a month. I would say, overall, it was a really positive experience. Sure, some issues could be better addressed. However, when I discuss this with people, the reaction is quite positive. People ask me, "What do you mean you got a license to operate in Saudi Arabia within a month?" That was just unheard of just two years ago. This is great example of what happens when deliverables mandates are put into government organizations as such, and they're able to produce tangible, on the ground results.

OMAR ALMAJDOUIE: As part of the private sector support initiative, the Saudi government initiated Saudi Venture Capital Company to work as a development fund for the innovation ecosystem in Saudi Arabia. This includes a $750 million fund of funds to support fund managers from anywhere in the world to invest in Saudi startups. Another ambitious initiative is the Public Investment Fund (PIF) fund of funds. This is by far the largest fund of funds initiative in the region, with an additional $1.1 billion of support for fund managers to invest in Saudi-related startups. Another initiative that the SME Authority ("Monshaat") took recently was the establishment of the Private Equity and Venture Capital Association (PEVC). This step is important because it will unify investors of this asset class to work together, standardize deal documents, and create studies in order to support government entities to form policies that support this type of investment.

Today, almost every country in the region has initiatives to support the innovation ecosystem. Mubadala just created its fund of funds, in addition to the ambitious Hub71, aiming to attract the best startups globally and setting up development offices in Abu Dhabi. Bahrain established its fund of funds to enable VCs and startups to establish a presence in Bahrain. Other similar initiatives are also happening in Jordan, Egypt, and other MENA countries.

ABDUL BASET AL JANAHI: The exemplary entrepreneurial ecosystem that Dubai has created is much owed to the vision and leadership of His Highness Sheikh Mohammed bin Rashid Al Maktoum. From establishing Dubai SME to launching a series of initiatives to inculcate entrepreneurship as a culture and an engine of sustainable development, His Highness has accorded utmost priority to nurturing ideas, innovation, and startups.

In 2014, Dubai SME announced the launch of the Hamdan Innovation Incubator (Hi2), a complete support environment to stimulate and foster innovative entrepreneurial projects among the nation's youth, under the patronage of Sheikh Hamdan bin Mohammad bin Rashid Al Maktoum, Crown Prince of Dubai and Chairman of the Executive Council. The goal of Hi2 is to incubate and develop more innovative startups into new businesses of the future. Hi2 is the first and the largest hub of its kind; it provides knowledge, guidance, and support to ensure the uninterrupted growth of an entrepreneurial idea into a successful business.

The public-private partnership model that Dubai has created is another significant asset to entrepreneurship development initiatives. The government is collaborative and responsive to the private sector, which brings unique flexibility to the business environment and policy framework in Dubai. Two years ago, Dubai SME announced new regulations for incubators and business accelerators to draw in further support for innovative entrepreneurs, particularly in monitoring and mentoring their business growth. The initiative is aimed at providing greater opportunities for investment. It is developing business leaders across varied industry sectors through business incubators, accelerators, and shared workspaces, thus advancing economic growth and the fourth industrial revolution (Industry 4.0) in Dubai. Subsequently, Dubai has seen a number of business incubators and accelerators being set up across the emirate, opening a new investment avenue and offering varied opportunities for entrepreneurs and SMEs to develop their innovations. The fastest-growing segment of startup investments in MENA has been these accelerators, displaying 32% growth between 2013 and 2018.

MAHMOUD ADI: Hub71 is built in the financial sector, a regulated environment, in ADGM (Abu Dhabi Global Market). Of course, that gives us a significant boost in terms of the standard of our jurisdiction and regulation. The positive story here is we have regulation that is quite sophisticated. I think they were one of the first, globally, to issue a world-class, thought-leader type of framework when it comes to cryptocurrencies, the crypto regulation, and so forth. They are at par with their global counterparts.

That definitely gives us a significant advantage that today, at ADGM, you can incorporate different types of businesses, including venture capital funds. You no longer need to have the Cayman Islands structure. I would say that prior to Emirates Development Bank (EDB) and the framework around VCs, probably Cayman was a lot more attractive.

ADGM is quite attractive as well. We see a lot of entrepreneurs and investors are becoming interested in recently. There are discussions around economic substance and the jurisdictions that you incorporate your funds in, which is relevant for people who are going to set up Cayman patches, and so forth. That's on the regulated side, whether it's a fund, whether it is a sophisticated business, like crypto, or these money managers, and so forth.

Now, on the unregulated side, where you have, let's say learning, logistics, tech, and software companies, among others, the licensing assessment is quite affordable. It's probably one of the cheapest in the entire region. Also, it has the ability to give you enough leeway to structure your company so that you can have holding structures, operating structures, and so forth. Those are all the great stuff that we want to have more of in the region. Those are all taken care of now.

When it comes to other regulations, for attracting talent, one of the things that we have been working closely with the government of the UAE on is entrepreneurship visas. This was announced a few months ago. The exciting piece around this is, of course, a longer-term visa and a visa that is granted based on merit. It gives entrepreneurs the ability to build their companies for the long haul. If they say they can move on, they don't need to be tethered to a sponsorship from another company. This would allow entrepreneurs to take greater risks. That is a significant advantage for the new type of visa that we are working with the government on as we speak.

MAZIN AL ZAIDI: Streamlining and simplifying the licensing system in KSA is an important reform to help it achieve the goals set out in Saudi Vision 2030 to boost SMEs' contribution to GDP from 20 to 35%. SAGIA currently leads the National Licensing Reform Program (NLRP), which has accomplished a lot recently. In two years, the NLRP has completed a comprehensive inventory of licenses and permits for business operations and requirements to obtain a license. Then we conducted a step-by-step review of all requirements, licenses, and permits to identify potential inefficiencies and challenges, which impact the growth of startups and SMEs doing business in KSA. Finally, SAGIA and the NLRP oversaw the development of a legislative and institutional framework for a new licensing and permit system that is consistent, fair, and easy to navigate.

Every government entity in Saudi Arabia is now tasked with promoting investment opportunities. These entities offer a compelling incentive program to attract foreign investors, including land subsidies, tariff exemptions, and project financing schemes. As the first "port of call" for many international companies looking to set up in the Kingdom, SAGIA serves as a central hub, directing investors toward the most beneficial and applicable incentive scheme available to empower their growth, while also benefiting the continued economic diversification of Saudi Arabia.

Additionally, the primary, overriding challenge that entrepreneurs face is securing capital. This is where Saudi Arabia is really setting new best practices. In July 2019, MiSK Innovation announced its growth accelerator program to support technology startups across the region that are looking to scale their operations. MiSK Innovation will run the program in partnership with two entities: Seedstars, a private group of companies from Switzerland, and Vision Ventures, a Saudi-based venture capital firm.

YASMEEN AL SHARAF: There have been a number of recent initiatives within the Kingdom of Bahrain that have made it quite appealing for startups to approach Bahrain, especially in the past two years. The whole of Bahrain is open for business. Unlike other jurisdictions in the region, we do not have to resort to free zone areas within Bahrain, which helps to create business-friendly conditions throughout the Kingdom. This makes it easier for startups to set up operations in Bahrain, allowing them the flexibility and freedom to deal with both residents and non-residents. Another enabling factor is that we do not have any laws that restrict foreign ownership in Bahraini entities and assets. Additionally, we invest a lot in the education of our people, providing businesses with access to highly skilled human capital in Bahrain. This is despite the fact that our laws do not restrict foreign employees. Another important law is the bankruptcy law recently passed in Bahrain, which makes it easier for startups to be able to get going without the fear of what happens if they were to have liquidity issues. In such an event, the law would enable them to reorganize and restructure their plans and continue operation through bankruptcy court proceedings.

Bahrain has also established an efficient ecosystem that supports startups. This approach has worked quite well under what we like to call the "Team Bahrain" approach. It involves private companies and government entities working together to make it more efficient for startups—in terms of dealing with both private and government agencies—to set up their businesses in Bahrain.

Back in 2017, the Central Bank of Bahrain (CBB) also launched its regulatory sandbox. Basically, this sandbox allows startups focusing on FinTech solutions to be able to test their ideas in a controlled environment without being subject to the full regulatory requirements. We accept startups and very early-stage companies and there are no prerequisites for pre-technical testing for an applicant to be admitted into the sandbox. For example, we can have a startup that just has an idea it wants to develop or a concept it wants to test. It can actually approach us and just apply for the sandbox, and use it to build prototypes and test out solutions with real volunteer customers in a controlled environment.

The regulatory sandbox in Bahrain is similar to sandboxes in other renowned jurisdictions, such as the UK. In fact, our sandbox is open to any company or startup, at any stage of their business cycle. Those applicant startups that enter the regulatory sandbox will then have a period of up to one year to test out their solutions in a live environment. I like to think of the sandbox as an enabler for startups—it enables them to understand the country's regulations, business environment, and the market forces, without having to apply for a full-fledged license right from the start. The sandbox also enables the sharing of ideas and innovations between regulators and startups, which is important for implementing the necessary regulatory reforms to accommodate these entities once they exit or graduate from the regulatory sandbox. So far, our regulatory sandbox has proven to be very successful. We currently have 35 companies operating within the sandbox, and we have graduated three companies. And we're expecting many more in the months and years to come.

SHERIF KAMEL: There are several initiatives and projects across the MENA region. One of them is Egypt's government initiative with the Central Bank of Egypt (CBE) issuing guidelines to incentivize banks to participate in a massive four-year nationwide comprehensive program to help finance both SMEs and startups. Its objective is to help create job opportunities and support economic growth. The program, which started three years ago, involved the injection of $25 billion into supporting small businesses across the nation. The initial objective of the program was to finance 350,000 small businesses and help create around 4 million new job opportunities. In addition, multiple projects in the works are addressing the notion of financial inclusion as an attempt to migrate a large portion of people taking part in the "informal economy," which is neither monitored nor taxed by government.

MOHAMED ANOUAR MAAROUF: In 2018, Tunisia issued the Startup Act. The law is built on a number of ideas that were generated through discussions with the youth, for the purpose of removing the obstacles that hinder their ability to initiate projects and access the ecosystem. We thought through what we could possibly do to help those individuals develop their ideas and help them take risks and overcome fear of failure. We decided to provide a number of incentives that encourage the youth to access the ecosystem, among which a few were particularly important. One states that people who are currently employed can benefit from a leave, meaning that they can establish their startups and if their projects fail, they can return to work in their previous roles. Another incentive is the provision of a grant that is almost equal to their previous job's pay. These two benefits allow individuals who are currently employed to take an initiative to start their own business.

As for university graduates who are unemployed, the state provides a number of benefits to help facilitate them working in startups. We wanted to encourage this category of people to focus on developing startups instead of focusing on becoming wage earners. We therefore allowed these first-time job seekers to still receive state benefits following their unsuccessful attempts to develop startups and once they are employed—that way they would have nothing to lose. We also thought about IP (intellectual property) and decided that the state will assume the costs for IP registration for startups.

Additionally, the law states that all administrative procedures concerning startups are to be made available online, and we therefore stated in the text of the law that these procedures will be conducted through a dedicated portal for entrepreneurs and startups. This is to facilitate operations with administrations, allowing them to run smoothly, and to mitigate the risks of bureaucracy and administrative hurdles.

The law also covers fiscal benefits to ensure that investors focus on developing and running startup projects and not on administrative procedures. We also ensured that startups are exempt from corporate tax and from contributing to what we call the social security scheme, which are social taxes that the state requires. These resources would instead be covered by the state's funds. Investors in startups are personally exempt from individual income tax upon withdrawal of their investments. We also incorporated a number of other procedures that make investment in startups as secure, cost effective, and profitable as possible. For example, we have set up a security fund that represents some guarantees to those investors.

One of the core issues in Tunisia is the restriction on obtaining foreign currency accounts. We agreed on the need to help startups enter the global market by allowing entities that have obtained a startup label to manage exchanges in foreign currency without going through the Central Bank. This is a reform from the Tunisian regulations that dictated that individuals and companies need to go through the Central Bank for every transaction in foreign currency. We lightened this burden because we believe that startups need to enter global markets and operate rapidly, and therefore they should be able to manage foreign currency in a rapid manner. As such, we removed the obstacle of having to go through the Central Bank and made it easier than ever for startups to enter the global market.

3. Additional Exciting Programs

MUHAMMED MEKKI: An unexpected and very welcome change in policy over the last couple of years has been Saudi Arabia's opening of its local market, streamlining of its company establishment regulations for foreigners, and deciding to pour support into the small but growing startup sector. For the first time ever, we are seeing some international companies and founders jump straight into Saudi Arabia instead of setting up a base in Dubai first. What used to literally take between one and two years to achieve can now be completed in one to two weeks. This is an incredible reform that opens up one of the most interesting markets in terms of size, wealth, and relative lack of competition in the tech sector. The change in policy creates a massive opportunity for entrepreneurs and startups that had previously assumed that there was no way to directly access the Saudi market without a local partner. We're seeing a lot of exciting policies and programs in the works in the Kingdom today.

HEATHER HENYON: Some of the newer steps around insolvency, such as bankruptcy laws and the ability to enter jurisdictions, such as the DFSA (Dubai Financial Services Authority) and ADGM, are positive developments in the UAE. Governments are becoming more engaged in diversification away from oil and toward entrepreneurship, which is a very positive step.

I especially like roles where governments serve as passive investors, so I am therefore supportive of matching programs like the ones by Saudi Venture Capital Company, Al Waha in Bahrain, and the Abu Dhabi Investment Office's Ghadan Fund. The sandboxes for FinTech and RegTech in the DIFC (Dubai International Finance Centre), ADGM, and Bahrain Economic Development Bank are effective ways for startups to test and iterate without undertaking lengthy, costly regulatory approvals. Meanwhile, the investment in new accelerator and incubator programs like Hub71 in Abu Dhabi, Badir in Riyadh, and Sheraa in Sharjah are necessary to build the next wave of startups and talent in the region.

SAMI MAHROUM: Dubai Future Foundation is a great example of an organization making a great impact in the ecosystem. It developed Area 2071, which is a place where companies can also use spaces and interact with designers and with other companies. It's a hub space for entrepreneurship and innovation. The government also launched Dubai Future Accelerators, which is an area where they link government needs with entrepreneurs and choose paid projects to work on together. It also has an initiative called "One Million Arab Coders," whereby the goal is to train one million coders across the

Arab world, which will have a very positive trickle-down effect on entrepreneurship and startups.

NAJLA AL-MIDFA: With the number of startups growing in MENA, the entrepreneurship ecosystem has seen rapid growth. It has been remarkable to witness the transformation since 2010, particularly with entrepreneurship becoming a more viable career option. At the time, based on GEM (Global Entrepreneurship Monitor) reports, only about 2% of the population had any intention of starting a business. Last year, it grew to almost 40%.

Sharjah is a great example of a city working to enhance support for entrepreneurship and the innovation ecosystem. Drawing on the critical mass of 30,000+ students and 35,000+ alumni from University City to empower future entrepreneurs, educational institutions such as the American University of Sharjah (AUS), Higher Colleges of Technology, and University of Sharjah are beginning to incorporate entrepreneurship into their curriculums. Universities are also becoming more research-based, as evidenced by the focus on R&D, research commercialization, and knowledge-intensive businesses at the upcoming Sharjah Research, Technology and Innovation Park (SRTIP). The private sector is playing its part as well and is starting to see startups as a real source of innovation rather than mere corporate social responsibility projects. Sheraa is proud to be partnered with corporates such as Bee'ah, Air Arabia, and Crescent Enterprises, as well as government entities such as Sharjah Media City (Shams), for example, to facilitate interactions between startups in their respective industries. In fact, Bee'ah has been working with Sheraa startup BluePhin, which has developed an automated vehicle that clears debris from water bodies, to help develop their prototype and provide proof of concept for their product.

MARYAM EID ALMHEIRI: At twofour54, we've implemented a number of initiatives in line with the UAE government's vision. Our dual licensing initiative now enables our partners to work with onshore entities. We recently announced an extension to our entrepreneurship scheme to enable people running small businesses to work from home.

From the beginning, we have understood how long it can take for small businesses to grow and develop a network. That's why we have regular Connect networking events where partners meet, share and collaborate. They can also access the twofour54 Briefing Room, a unique portal where clients, partners, and affiliated entities post requests for proposals for our community to respond to. We also created a dedicated freelance relations team to assist partners and freelancers and connect them with each other and with government entities. We take care of everything in the process from the initial sourcing to the paperwork and billing.

MUHAMMAD NABIL: The government of Morocco has launched the Innov Invest Fund as part of its Caisse Centrale de Garantie strategy, with financial assistance from the World Bank. The fund will support companies in seed stage, and pre-seed companies will benefit from interest-free loans in the near future.

Also, LaFactory in Morocco is doing fantastic work in building a startup community. It helps accelerate collaborations between tech startups and big corporates in Africa. The company was founded by a young Moroccan entrepreneur, Mehdi Alaoui, who knows about creating fertile ground for startups. Microsoft is fortunate to be working with LaFactory, where we're collaborating on introducing next-gen technologies, including information architecture, machine learning, and cloud computing.

4. Future Prospects and Expectations

AHMED EL ALFI: Countries are like people; people who talk about their present and the future, no matter what their age is, stay young. On the other hand, people who are stuck in the past, and that's all they talk about, age fast and fall behind the times. The same applies to countries. Our region has seen a massive shift in leadership; throughout, the region is now focused on the future. Additionally, we often talk about an event from the past and wonder what would be different had it happened differently. Or if someone goes to the past as if it was a movie and changes one thing and that has an enormous ripple effect on our present. We say, "If only this happened this way or that way." Instead, we need to look ahead and focus on small things that we can change today that will have a major positive impact on our future. So, we need to focus on the present and the future first and foremost.

SETH LEVINE: The Middle East startup ecosystem has certainly developed quite a bit over the last few years I've been working in the region. That evolution continues to this day. The fundamental question remains, especially for the Gulf countries, how will they be able to transition from a primarily extractive oil-based economy to an economy that's more diversified? Some of that might be tourism; some of that, clearly, should be in other kinds of industries. We've seen that in a number of different markets, either with projects already on the ground that governments are working on or projects that are under discussion.

A great example is the work we're doing through Techstars, with Foundry Group being Techstars' largest investor. Techstars is building out several programs in the region that were encouraged by government and local business leaders. I think those are signs that, perhaps, there is or should be a closer partnership between government and the entrepreneurial sector than, say, in the US, where government has been kept more or less at arm's length from the startup world.

DAVE MCCLURE: The ecosystem is going in the right direction, though it is fairly early to tell conclusively. There has been quite a bit of change in the MENA ecosystem over the last five years particularly.

We started investing in the region around 2012 and did about 30 investments between 2013 and 2016. We have over 100 investments in the region to date, most of which were done in the last three years by our MENA fund, 500 Falcons. When we started in the region, a very small number of VCs were operating at the time, maybe just three or four. Now it seems like there are 30 or 40, both large and small funds. Many new VCs have launched across the region, including veterans like BECO, MEVP, and Wamda operating at the Series A stage. There are a few MENA investors at later stages, like the Saudi PIF and the UAE-based Mubadala; however, I expect more will launch over the next several years.

A number of government organizations are also operating, some of which are deploying capital and some of which are providing services. There is a lot going on in the GCC as well as, in the last few years, in Cairo and in Amman. Generally speaking, there are developments in the right direction as far as ecosystem growth is concerned.

Although there is potentially quite a lot of money available to invest, I would still say the region is mostly undercapitalized. Different people may have a different take on that. There might be occasional discrepancies in what's actually being deployed, or sometimes what's being deployed to startups as opposed to what's being deployed in real estate, or whatever gets framed as innovation. All in all, I would say that the Middle East is still somewhat underdeveloped as far as its ecosystem goes and so has plenty of room to grow.

RAMI SALMAN: We're still in the early growth phases of the MENA startup and tech ecosystem. We've had a few really great top-line unicorn exits that prove the liquidity and value of the market, but those exits remain in business models that were somewhat paved by other international startups before them, basically mimicking the Uber or Amazon models for example. The Careems and Souqs of the region have shown a tremendous amount of innovation and entrepreneurship in taking those Western startup concepts and really adapting them to their full capacity in the region. Lots of kudos to them for having done that at such a fast pace and on such a large scale.

However, if we compare the Arab world to arguably the most developed startup and tech ecosystem per capita in the world, just next door, we're ways away from being at the same level when it comes to cutting-edge innovation. There you've got people at the leading edge of research in almost every technical field, a massive fundraising ecosystem to power their startups to higher limits, and an incredible bridge to the US and Europe that has been paved for quite some time.

At this stage, the MENA startup ecosystem is capitalizing on the opportunities of a young and growing population underserved by tech compared to East Asia and the Western world. Startups here aren't out-innovating anyone in terms of R&D or hyper-scalable concepts that take the rest of the world by storm, and that's perfectly fine. At this stage, both the startup and investor ecosystems are still figuring out what the biggest potential projects are; what concepts will lead to the greatest returns for founders, investors, and employees; and what types of startup stories can get the best talent world-wide to rally around and move into the region.

If you take a historical perspective, where we are today is an incredible leap forward compared to where we used to be in the ecosystem, just looking at the last 10 to 20 years. It's a complete shift: what seed-stage startups are able to raise and do today is mind-boggling for some of the former founders of just 10 years ago. Some of the latest seed-stage valuations are starting to almost come in line with Silicon Valley standards, which is extremely impressive.

However, not enough of those deals are happening on a per capita basis. Being in the early stages of the ecosystem, the value remains in the investors' hands. We haven't even begun to create enough excitement to generate a "fundraising bubble," which is OK. There is more than enough value to be generated and captured by startups over the next decade. That overexcitement will naturally build with more exits. What we need to be working on is core infrastructure and talent development and retention, rather than higher valuations.

PHILIP BAHOSHY: I believe we're at somewhat of an inflection point for the region where we've seen an acceleration in the number of investments that have been taking place and the amount invested in startups in the region, even when we strip out the outliers like Souq and Careem. We're seeing more investors than ever before and more funding activities—whether it's VC, CVC, private equity (PE), or angels—investing in Middle East-based startups, with a higher percentage coming from international players. There are certainly more ecosystem-building government initiatives, more ecosystem platforms, such as incubators, accelerators, and co-working spaces, than ever before. However, let's put that into context. These numbers pale in significance compared to the US or Europe, which are not comparable benchmarks, but they are also only a fraction of the numbers in other emerging markets such as Southeast Asia or South America. So, while we are seeing an acceleration of interest in the region, there's still a long way to grow to become a hub for tech-enabled startups.

KHALDOON TABAZA: I think we're at a tipping point that enables scalability for many business models in the ecosystem. We are also at a stage where we have talent that could build global businesses. Having said that and while we've seen some exits that will encourage people to invest, I still believe that we're at a relatively early stage of the development of the ecosystem. The ecosystem has not been through a full cycle yet. My view is that the vast majority of organizations in the ecosystem have not been through full cycles from seed to exit. This means that we haven't gotten to a stage where the majority of the capital is coming from long-term investors—such as pension funds, insurance companies, sovereign wealth funds, foundations, and trusts—that can take the long-term view across full cycles.

The biggest risk that the ecosystem is facing today is that there are a lot of investors who got excited by the exit stories that they've seen in the market and got excited by the global boom in technology and the stories that they're hearing. Hence, they went ahead and made one, two, maybe three investments, with the hope that they were going to see returns on all of them within a few years, similar to flipping real estate or a piece of land in times of boom.

I'm also concerned that there are founders who might have the same impression: that it takes two, three years, and they'll always be able to raise money. We're already seeing difficulties in the market, especially in the growth and late-stage startups in various countries. My concern is that those people won't continue forward, and then we're going to have, basically, funding crunches, maybe in Series A, maybe in Series B or later.

We're not yet at a stage where we have several waves of successful founders that have become investors, several waves of companies that graduate founders that go and start other companies, several waves of funding that get the market into a steady state, regardless of the economic cycle. Therefore, I still see that as a big risk. Another double-edged sword in the ecosystem is the geography-specific view that many of the investors are taking. It's great on one hand, because it's resulting in the availability of significant amounts of capital in countries like Saudi Arabia and in places like Abu Dhabi and Egypt, with the country's specific initiatives that will match the money invested in local startups. On the other hand, this could lead to a suboptimal deal flow and could lead to people establishing businesses only to be able to tap into those sources of capital, rather than to build sustainable businesses.

MOHAMED ANOUAR MAAROUF: As far as future outlook, there is one point that I would like to emphasize, and that is the fact that Tunisia is now a democratic country. When we talk about a democratic country, that entails it being a state of rights and law. All investors in Tunisia are protected by the law. We have set up a number of regulations that ensure the protection of investors' and economic players' rights. These include laws for the protection of personal data and privacy, and the new Investment Law that protects investors, in addition to other regulations that help set up this climate of trust that is required for investment development.

I aspire to see a unicorn built in Tunisia. This will require great deal of effort, perseverance, and hard work to make this a reality. In addition, we want to continue to support hundreds, if not thousands, of startups to flourish in Tunisia. My second aspiration is to see this dynamic not only covering startups, but generating a real change in the national economy as well. We aim to change the economic pattern from its current state, which relies on cheap labor and on investments in traditional sectors such as energy, mines, and agriculture, into one that is based on high added value, on creativity and innovation, on export and intellectual capacity. These are essential assets that Tunisia has—namely, its intellectual capacity and human resources. I'm optimistic about what lies ahead.

Chapter VI

CHALLENGES IN
THE MENA ECOSYSTEM

Ecosystems, by definition, are not perfect economic environments. While they are meant to provide a conducive environment for businesses to seamlessly start and grow rapidly, they are by no means flawless or perfectly organized. This is the case no matter how mature a given ecosystem is. As technology advances, and the world becomes more complex, ecosystems have to keep up. Hence, there will always be some kind of lag between what ecosystem players—most notably entrepreneurs and startups—need and what an ecosystem can provide.

Some of what are commonly perceived as the challenges or shortcomings of any ecosystem are inevitable and intrinsic to such an environment. Of course, it's the job of the ecosystem builders to help bridge those gaps: to remove business friction and prevent any significant bottlenecks or barriers that can slow down local entrepreneurs and startups and make them less competitive in an increasingly global market.

Similarly, the MENA ecosystem is full of challenges, mainly as a result of the ecosystem being relatively new. Some gaps, therefore, will sort themselves out naturally as the environment develops. Others will close as entrepreneurial activity flourishes around the region. Meanwhile, other gaps are the result of regulations falling behind in certain areas or certain countries and failing to meet the requirements of the modern world fast enough. Obviously, the more the stakeholders involved (whether entrepreneurs, investors, service providers, policy-makers, or other ecosystem builders) are aware of those issues and their effects and are actively working toward resolving them, the greater the likelihood that they will find solutions to such challenges sooner rather than later.

This chapter highlights some of the most common challenges regional entrepreneurs and startups face, some of which are distinguished as "pain points," given the magnitude of the challenges and the fact that they are too time- or resource-consuming to deal with. Meanwhile, others are more growth-related. As such, the former are basic operational challenges and the latter are more scalability-related challenges. Obviously, every company needs to be concerned with both because a business that cannot grow ultimately dies.

One antidote to such challenges is for stakeholders to play a more proactive role, as many have done in this book, by articulating any ecosystem-related difficulties or inefficiencies they face relating to infrastructure, capital, regulation, or other areas. Obviously, the more they can make their voices heard, be constructive, suggest solutions, and be more of a change agent in general, the more likely it is that the appropriate authorities will listen. After all, both groups are two sides of the same coin if we operate on the assumption that they are aligned in terms of objectives and incentives. Theoretically, they are both interested in moving toward a healthier, more vibrant ecosystem and domestic economy—one that positively impacts all of their respective constituents.

The other method, seemingly used by clever, adaptive entrepreneurs, is often referred to as "regulatory hacking," though it can apply outside of regulations as well. It involves simply using workarounds to help either create or influence change, and often involves collaboration with regulators. After all, the role of the entrepreneur is to find solutions to economic problems and serve customers in spite of such challenges, or perhaps because such problems exist in the first place. Case in point, if credit card penetration in a given ecosystem is lacking, a clever e-commerce entrepreneur introduces cash on delivery to meet the demands of the local market. Granted, such patch-up solutions like these may not be ideal, efficient, or sustainable in the long term. They are, however, critical to deal with the current reality of the market. These creative workarounds ultimately keep the economic rhythm going until infrastructure or regulation, or whatever is missing, catches up.

All in all, an entrepreneur should not wait for the ecosystem to repair itself, any more than a policy-maker should wait for entrepreneurs to complain, to be proactive. Both should anticipate the needs of their respective constituents and work diligently to develop long-term solutions. Meanwhile, they should aim to provide short-term shortcuts as needed—within the rule of law and ethical standards, obviously—to neutralize any immediate inefficiencies or dysfunctions. All the while, they should cooperate as much as possible with other stakeholders in the ecosystem to create a more conducive environment that serves the needs and protect the rights of all stakeholders.

The following represents some of the common problems in the ecosystem. Some of these have been pointed out by others, loud and clear, for some time now, so they are no surprise to local players. Others may be more subtle or have slipped under the radar. Obviously, not all of these issues are created equal or are uniformly present across the entire region. Whether we're talking about access to talent or access to capital, setup and licensing challenges, broadband affordability or ease of doing business-related issues, operational cost or cost of failure (such as proper bankruptcy laws or lack thereof across many jurisdictions), flow of goods and people, or a host of other issues, different countries have made varying strides and levels of progress in addressing those issues.

One notable challenge that uniformly cuts across all portions of the region, however, is market fragmentation. With the exception of Egypt and Saudi Arabia, all MENA countries have small populations.

Hence, for the rest of the 20 or so countries in the region, it's virtually impossible for a company to reach true scale—one that's comparable to global standards—if it is confined within national borders. For the region to be able to support world-class startups and be truly competitive on a global basis, the limitations that exist due to these physical and figurative boundaries can no longer be ignored.

To the extent that a truly cooperative commercial relationship between the various countries in the region can be established, significant benefits are likely to follow for all players involved. The concept, in short, is to create a one-stop incorporation program that is accepted across multiple, if not all, jurisdictions in the region; then, supplement that program with collaboration-oriented regulations and initiatives that make it easier to simultaneously do business across borders. Other regions have used these tactics elsewhere, perhaps not flawlessly, but effectively. There's a lot of room for learning and an impetus to take action on this front. The sooner we can link the ecosystems of the MENA region together, the more each ecosystem stands to benefit on its own (more on this topic in subsequent chapters).

Finally, we must touch on the "elephant in the room"—namely, geopolitical instability in the region and its real impact. Whether it's actual or perceived, it's definitely hurting the ecosystem, if not always tangibly and measurably, certainly invisibly and indirectly. The business world, especially the realm of tech startups, already carries a high level of uncertainty. However, this is what I refer to as "predictable uncertainty." That's because—as an entrepreneur— while you cannot anticipate the nature and development of any given variable, you're relatively clear on what the variables are and how their variability may affect your venture and your prospects for success. In other words, you're typically clear on what the rules of the game are even if you're unsure of the decision-making or fairness of the referee, so to speak.

On the other hand, geopolitical instability, even if it never turns into any direct harm in the form of anti-trade regulations or military confrontations, creates a cloud of all-around fogginess in the ecosystem. It becomes difficult to even identify the variables involved, let alone to chart appropriate responses to different scenarios. Granted, those who operate within the region often develop a sort of "psychological callus" and in effect are immune to it in everyday life. This may be an effective defense mechanism from a psychological standpoint, but it's by no means an effective strategy for building a visionary or successful company or economy in the long term. Moreover, such numbness to the geopolitical backdrop is merely a local psychological defense mechanism, as it does not apply to foreigners and international players at large, especially ones who originate from environments without such issues, like the US, Canada, and Western Europe. And since a majority of the most impactful companies and investors in the world come from such places, these uncertainties create a further unhealthy effect of isolation that often haunts the local ecosystem and the region at large. To the extent that those issues are addressed, the international media and international business community will be more engaged with the region in a positive and collaborative way.

The lesson here is that ecosystems don't exist in a vacuum. The geopolitical health of a country or a region is a big factor in it actualizing its full potential. Granted, there are a couple of examples of ecosystems and economies that flourished in spite of geopolitical instability. I would argue that those are the exception to the rule, that perhaps other factors were at play that are not so easily replicated elsewhere, and such ecosystems might have flourished to a much greater extent had their government-related problems not existed in the first place.

The geopolitical future of MENA is obviously a much different and bigger topic that is clearly outside the scope of this book. Nevertheless, it's worth taking a closer look at how these geopolitical issues are navigated at a local level and the real impacts of these forces on the MENA ecosystem, by hearing from those individuals on the ground who regularly face them, as well as from outsiders looking at and assessing the region from a distance.

1. Common Startup Pain Points

AMIRA RASHAD: The regional ecosystem is obviously quite complex and involves many variables. It's therefore difficult to pinpoint all the issues, yet there are a few adversely impactful ones that I would like to point out. For example, if you take one variable, such as payment methods and credit cards, it's easy to say that most people who have access to credit cards can use them, and that could boom online businesses. However, a lot of the banks here in the UAE are either underdeveloped or have purposefully refrained from connecting to new technologies when it comes to payment, such as accepting triple tokenization as a technology or as card systems.

Talent is another issue—finding the right talent with the right skill sets to actually walk into a startup. It's a complete pain in this part of the world. Just being able to find someone who can think on their feet, who has a sense of ownership and that mentality of being empowered to do what it takes to get something done and develop as the business grows, is very challenging.

The other issue is licensing. When we first started, I went to obtain a permit from DMCC (Dubai Multi Commodities Centre) here in Dubai. Technically, you can get a license for about AED 20,000 (approximately $5,450) to operate any e-commerce business. Then when I told them that I'm actually looking at owning my last-mile delivery operation, they said, "Wait, that's a different license. You also have to get a home delivery license. And since you will have two licenses, you need to have two offices. Here are the square footage requirements for this license, and here are the square footage requirements for that other license." I was like, "That doesn't make sense. I can barely afford the two licenses." Basically, one would go bankrupt if they do not consider the idea that there is one company with two licenses that needs to operate from one office. I escalated the issue with DMCC management and, to their credit, they saw the issue and proceeded to resolve it immediately for us.

The same thing happened with my visas. We run an e-commerce

business. I actually have a warehouse and staff at the warehouse and drivers, and so forth. But the number of visas you get is based on the square footage of your office space in that free zone, so I couldn't get visas for my warehouse staff. Once again, I had to escalate this issue until I got a special visa allocation for my warehouse. I guess what I'm trying to say is that the system isn't always structured to address the needs of startups, even though there might be some workarounds. The challenge, of course, is if you can't get to the right person or you can't build your case, then you find yourself at the mercy of a system that is still learning and adapting to the needs and business models of startups. The good news is that, by and large, there is an entrepreneurial mindset at the top of government entities here in the UAE. If it makes business sense, decision-makers will listen and make it happen.

IDRISS AL RIFAI: While there has been a lot of positive movement in many countries in the region in terms of development of the startup ecosystem on all fronts, a lot of things are still fundamentally wrong with regard to enabling startups to launch and thrive in this part of the world. For example, in logistics, technically you need to have a core license, and there are only seven core licenses permitted in Saudi Arabia, our largest market opportunity. So, that option is out. You also have tons of regulations that actually limit your growth, even if your solution is better than that of the core-license-holding companies'.

On the funding side, you have a massive funding drop in the availability of Series B and Series C funding. It's very difficult in the region to raise capital of around $50 to $100 million. No on-the-ground investors that fund tech companies currently fill this gap. It is also extremely difficult to get a loan if you're a startup that's not profitable, even if you provide collateral. This was a situation we faced in the past year; even a 100% collateralized loan is not possible. I think any regulations that would force a bank to put a percentage of their funds into startups, at least in the form of a loan, could really decrease the financial pressures that startups face.

For example, new regulations in Germany, and to some extent in France and a few other countries in Europe, ensure that banks are doing actually what they're meant to—namely, re-injecting the money into the economy and creating jobs. After all, 90% or so of businesses in the economy are operating startups and SMEs rather than big corporates. Banks are sitting on massive piles of cash with very limited incentive to inject any into SMEs. Obviously, if they don't have the incentive, they're not going to do it. But if the incentive were offered by government or high-level leadership, it would be an entirely different story.

I wish the sovereign funds were more bullish on their own region and allocating more funding toward their local, new economy, rather than literally having their mandate be to invest away from the region. I find it mind-boggling that to get big money, you have to go seek it outside the region, rather than from local players within the region.

We obviously still have many issues with regard to visas in the region. It's very expensive to bring a new hire here, especially since not all new hires will work out. Some will drop out within the first couple of months or get recruited by another company. It's extremely expensive for a company to actually bring somebody from abroad if that person is not going to stick around for some time. I would love to see some kind of exemption, where companies get back a full or partial refund on visas, or at least some kind of credit, if their hire does not work out—especially in the initial six-month probation period. Combine this with the difficulties around firing someone and we have no choice but to think twice before recruiting and adding staff, which ultimately hurts our growth and job creation more broadly.

Additionally, the number of visas allowable, in the free zone especially, is related to how big your office is. That makes sense if you're a traditional company. We are a courier and technology company, which means that we're forced to have a big office just to make sure that we can hire more drivers. This doesn't make any sense. We actually face roadblocks based on this and we have to ask for exceptions, and it's only because we have a good relationship with

Dubai South that they managed to alleviate those constraints.

The other issue, which is specific to Dubai, is the cost of living. Even though housing rates now is going down and the cost of living is becoming more affordable, Dubai is still in the top 20 most expensive cities in the world. I also find it incredibly damaging from a cash flow standpoint to have to pay rents in advance on a full-year basis. I don't really know any other country that does that. That needs to change.

It's also very difficult to open bank accounts when you're dealing with cash on delivery (CoD). I understand that banks are regulated and they need to be careful with money laundering and other fraud-related issues. But for us, not being able to acquire such a basic service at our current stage is ludicrous. We had three or four banks that actually turned us down, and we could not open a new bank account for a few months. They know that 80% of transactions in this part of the world are cash on delivery and this has been the case for many, many years, yet they have yet to adapt to this reality. There is definitely an outdated, unnecessary mismatch between regulations and reality on that front.

FOUAD JERYES: One issue, which my e-commerce company, CashBasha, unfortunately has been a victim of, is the unsettling and sudden changes of laws and policies at times. Mark Zuckerberg's notorious work mantra, "Move fast and break things" is only good when startups do it. It's not so much the case for governments because when they move fast, they actually break things.

For instance, CashBasha suffered a nearly fatal blow in August 2019 due to a surprise change in customs tariffs and clearance policies. Although regulating e-commerce is something that we are generally for, our reservations on the change are because the alteration was announced and put into effect in a matter of only four days. The new policy requires shoppers to go through an extensive process to declare packages prior to their arrival, which is outside of standard e-commerce procedure. The new tariffs also had significant adverse effects on market size. We actually protested this instability and new crippling policies by shutting down the CashBasha website and service in Jordan for two full weeks and setting up a page to highlight the objections we had to this move and our proposed solutions. We also set up a petition with almost 10,000 signatures to influence course correction through civil channels. As members of the industry, we want to be part of a thriving digital economy that is moving forward incorporating proven world-class practices, not one that's moving backward.

As we've seen with ride sharing apps and the censorship of internet media in the past, governments sometimes act against innovative business models to protect large, traditional incumbent groups. Instead of playing offense, governments at times prefer playing defense to save themselves from the headaches of incumbents' uproar, which is not healthy for the advancement and evolution of a fair, competitive business environment. Having a national strategy to seed and enable new industries as well as convert traditional ones, even at the very bottom of the pyramid, is crucial for sustained economic growth.

JOY AJLOUNY: I'm speaking first-hand from founding and funding two companies: one in the US and one in the Middle East. I have had the unique and rare experience to know and understand the real differences. The cost of setting up a company in the Middle East is truly astronomical. I've set up my first company in the US and I can tell you that the setup and legal costs are so much less expensive and easier to understand than the legal and setup costs in the Middle East.

The US has a population of over 300 million people, so when you enter the market, whatever the cost, which is not a lot, it makes sense because you immediately have room to grow and potential to scale. When you enter the Middle East, in order to scale, you must set up in multiple countries. You can't be limited to just one or two markets. Every time you expand, you have to get a lawyer for each subsequent market you want to expand into and pay setup costs all over again, each and every time. Not to mention needing to understand the laws and idiosyncrasies of each country, which are ever-changing. The one thing startups don't have is money, so the cost of setting up and having to re-set up can be crippling. The biggest advice I give to startups is, I realize it is costly, but please set up your legal structure correctly from the beginning or it will be a big problem in the future.

The funny part is that it is very unclear what is needed legally, and sometimes if you don't just enter a market, you will never get started because you're waiting for all the details to pan out. The challenge I have found in some instances is that often the law itself is not solidified or is too slow to change or get implemented. For example, it was announced at the World Economic Forum that as founders of one of the top 100 startups, we could now get a 10-year visa in Dubai. So, I went to apply for it and I was told, "It is not ready yet." Certainly, the positive intentions and resolve are there, but the question is how fast can those reforms get implemented? I would argue that in the fast world we live in, speed is the name of the game—whether in terms of startups looking to scale or reforms that are critical to developing the ecosystem—especially if our aspiration is not just not to fall behind but to actually be world-class.

Another area that has been challenging is the cost of hiring people. As example, in the US, when you hire someone and it's not working out, you simply let him or her go. In startups, the saying is, "If you fail, fail fast." If it isn't working you must change it fast, since time and money are available only in limited supply. The longer you wait, the more damage you incur. A lot of times, in the Middle East, you're forced to keep an employee who is not performing simply because of the cost it took to hire them and the painful, costly process of replacing them, if you can find someone at all.

Good talent is hard to find and it's a huge challenge for startups in the region. The costs and time incurred to get visas is tough. Sometimes you find great talent in other countries and it takes months to bring them on board. Then if you had to bring them over from another country and decide to let them go, you have to wind up keeping them because it is so time-consuming and disruptive to a business to replace them. So, you end up with mediocrity, simply because of all the hurdles and costs in the system around recruiting from abroad and hiring in general. That's the whole thing with startups; startups don't have time to wait. Corporations do, because they have lots of money. Startups, on the other hand, by definition, are operating against a time-bomb, namely running out of cash. That's the reality of the startup world or as Reid Hoffman pointed out, "An entrepreneur is someone who will jump off a cliff and assemble an airplane on the way down." So here you are being scrappy, operating on a tight budget, trying to get your company off the ground and building something amazing, and then on top of it all you are fighting all these external administrative things and dealing with all this red tape.

KEY MILESTONES FOUNDERS ARE HOPING TO ACHIEVE

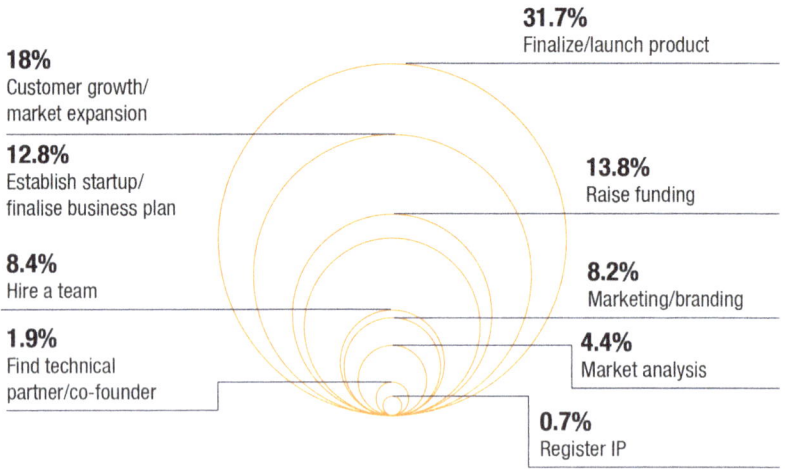

31.7%
Finalize/launch product

18%
Customer growth/
market expansion

12.8%
Establish startup/
finalise business plan

13.8%
Raise funding

8.4%
Hire a team

8.2%
Marketing/branding

1.9%
Find technical
partner/co-founder

4.4%
Market analysis

0.7%
Register IP

Data was collected from the applications of Wamda X programme and complimentary research from STEP Conference

Source: The State of Pre-Seed Startups in MENA (www.wamda.com & www.stepconference.com)

Traditionally, the cost of doing business in the Middle East is quite high. Whenever someone responds to me making this claim by saying, "Sure it's expensive, but there are no taxes in the Middle East," I smile.

What they do not understand is that in the US, you only pay taxes on profit, and since startups are not typically profitable for years, there is zero tax. In the Middle East, however, whether you make money or lose money, you have to pay. For example, every time you ship a package you must pay a per package fee. Whether you make money or lose money there is a per package fee. It's not a tax, but it's hard when you are trying to get on your feet and every dollar counts. When you are trying to walk before you can run, all these fees add up. I give credit to every entrepreneur in the Middle East, because they are some of the toughest people on the planet who are choosing to stay and go through all these hoops.

AIMAN KABLI: Entrepreneurs face a number of challenges in this region. Perhaps the most prominent one is related to recruitment and finding talent, especially technical talent, since there's a big shortage on that front. Another obstacle is finding professional support services at a reasonable cost. The market is not used to having startups traditionally, so many affordable, startup-friendly support services are still lacking. For example, companies that provide social media services or SEO (search engine optimization), or ones that provide design, marketing, legal, or finance support set their package and rate card for larger corporate players. Thus, it's quite a challenge for local startups, especially pre-funding ones, to attain the support they need utilizing available options that are more suitable for them. This is not the case in other developed ecosystems, where such options typically exist in abundance, thereby making it feasible for startups to more feasibly develop.

Another key challenge is funding. The culture in MENA is very risk-averse, perhaps due in part to the geopolitical situation in the region. Not a lot of people have an appetite for risk with their money, especially toward early-stage startups. Thus, the sources of funding in that stage or for new technology sectors in general are very limited. Funding is more readily available for traditional startups, which are already proven—for example, non-tech, physical businesses like hotels, shops, cafes, and restaurants or technology startups that are already tried and tested, like ride sharing and e-commerce models, which have already been proven in other regions. There's much lower proclivity toward truly innovative technologies and business models. This perception ultimately stifles locally-grown innovation because any new innovation will typically be seen as too risky, and thus less likely to get funded.

Finally, on regulation, in some of the countries in the MENA region, regulations are not very clear, which hinders foreign investment coming into the region. Investors, both local and foreign, are more drawn to clear regulatory environments, where the rule of law is defined and the rules of the game are not vague or ambiguous, especially in such areas as shareholder rights, liquidation preferences, and bankruptcy laws.

DANY FARHA: One of the biggest remaining bottlenecks to ecosystem development in the region is talent. There are short-term and long-term fixes and they differ from one place to another. Take Egypt, for example: Egypt needs to celebrate and decorate its technology winners. Fawry just got listed on the exchange in what is the region's first tech IPO. Meanwhile, it barely made the headlines. The founders of Fawry need to be given a medal of the highest order and celebrated in the media. Role models create hope and incentive for the next wave of bold founders to come forth. Egypt has by far the greatest talent pool of tech and deep tech professionals. Egypt and the Levant should red-carpet the return of tech professionals from abroad to commence the reverse brain drain that the region has suffered from to date. We cannot develop into a world-class ecosystem without addressing the talent challenge head on via massive action on many fronts beyond just traditional methods.

ROBERTO CROCI: When it comes to challenges around entrepreneurship in the region, a lack of funding or access to capital tends to dominate the discussion. Of course, funding is crucial to getting any business off the ground, but I believe that entrepreneurs need access to six core things in equal measure to succeed: technology, finance, markets, information, skills, and services. Skills are particularly important. Entrepreneurs often have a great idea for a product or service but lack the business skills to take the solution to market, or the financial skills to manage cash flow once they start generating a profit.

Additionally, for entrepreneurs to remain competitive in today's technology-driven age, there's an added need for more advanced digital competency—especially in emerging markets where digital literacy has historically been lower. This includes the ability to manage and draw actionable insights from digital data or build new revenue streams using digital services. Fortunately, many of today's technology platforms make it easier on entrepreneurs. Cloud services take away a lot of the upfront capital and skills investment, reducing the in-house IT requirements of an entrepreneur. Tools like Microsoft Power Platform also make it easier for anyone, even with limited technical ability, to build an application for their business. There is still, however, a significant need to develop foundational digital skills among entrepreneurs, and this should begin as early as school level. By introducing young children to computer science, coding, problem-solving, and other skills of the future, they'll be better equipped to one day start businesses that champion digital. Because of the exponential pace of change driven by technology, it's also important to sustain this early training through continual learning and upskilling, through university and beyond.

Technical and business skills development for entrepreneurs is a core focus of our work at Microsoft. Through initiatives like Microsoft for Startups, we work directly alongside startups and SMEs across the Middle East and Africa (MEA), supporting everything from business development strategies to cloud migration and partner strategy. We also partner with startup enablers—from governments to banks, telecommunications companies, and accelerators—to ensure that technology is part of any startup offering.

As I mentioned, skills are only one part of the game. To provide the full range of services, we need an enabling ecosystem of service providers who bundle their resources to provide entrepreneurs with everything they need in one smart package. And the benefit is shared: entrepreneurs access best-in-class resources, and service providers attract a large and influential consumer base. Just as it takes a village to raise a child, so it takes an ecosystem to nurture an entrepreneur. The final and maybe most important element is access to market. For this, Microsoft empowers startups by broadening their access to market via partner-to-partner access or using Microsoft's massive customer base. So these are some of the key challenges, I observed, entrepreneurs and startups face in the region, and which we're actively working on addressing and help resolving.

HANS HENRIK CHRISTENSEN: Entrepreneurs in the Arab world face a number of challenges. One of the biggest challenges they face is finding mentors, accelerators, incubators, and investors that will support them. The second challenge, and one that accelerators are getting more and more attuned to, is how to gain traction in market. Most markets are still fragmented and there's quite a shortage of data, information, and online resources. So, it's often difficult to search for and find potential clients.

In some countries in the region, the business ethic leaves much to be desired in terms of delivering on contractual terms, paying on time, and making it easy for startups to do business in general. Many prospective clients overburden startups with unnecessary bureaucratic due diligence, which makes the sale cycles slower, longer, and more costly—all negative issues startups encounter. Even government institutions that, on one side, foster entrepreneurship in the region are often insensitive on this procurement side.

EASE OF DOING BUSINESS IN MENA

For MENA policy-makers and other ecosystem participants, knowing where their economy stands in the aggregate ranking on the ease of doing business is useful. Also useful is to know how it ranks compared with other economies in the region and compared with the regional average. Another perspective is provided by the regional average rankings on the topics included in the ease of doing business ranking and the ease of doing business score.

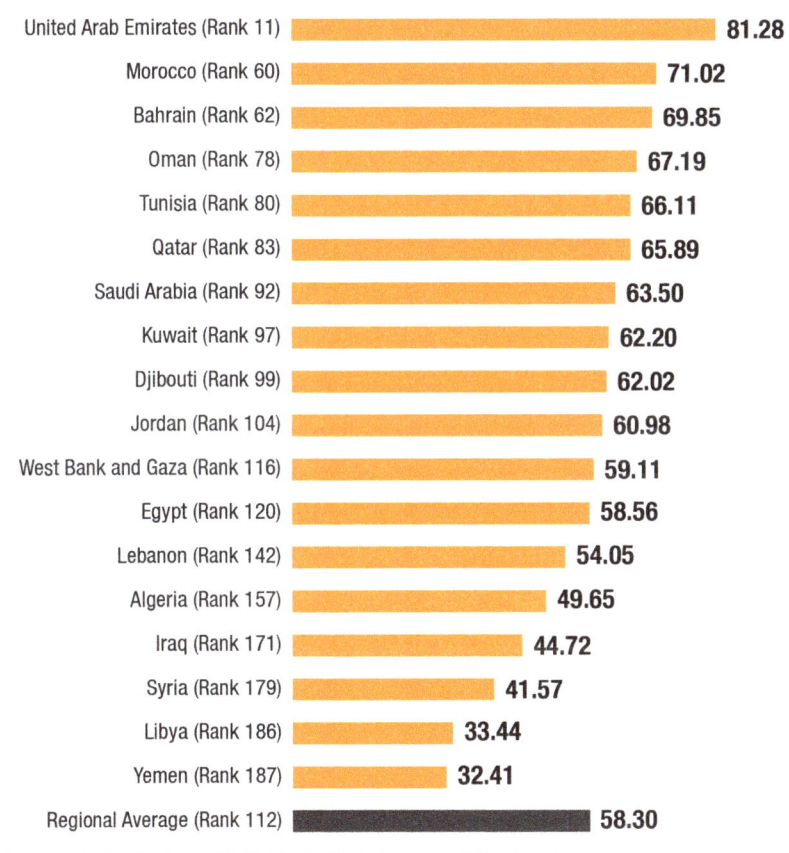

Economy	Score
United Arab Emirates (Rank 11)	81.28
Morocco (Rank 60)	71.02
Bahrain (Rank 62)	69.85
Oman (Rank 78)	67.19
Tunisia (Rank 80)	66.11
Qatar (Rank 83)	65.89
Saudi Arabia (Rank 92)	63.50
Kuwait (Rank 97)	62.20
Djibouti (Rank 99)	62.02
Jordan (Rank 104)	60.98
West Bank and Gaza (Rank 116)	59.11
Egypt (Rank 120)	58.56
Lebanon (Rank 142)	54.05
Algeria (Rank 157)	49.65
Iraq (Rank 171)	44.72
Syria (Rank 179)	41.57
Libya (Rank 186)	33.44
Yemen (Rank 187)	32.41
Regional Average (Rank 112)	58.30

Source: Doing Business 2019, World Bank (www.worldbank.org)

BADR JAFAR: One of the biggest challenges entrepreneurs face in the region is that they can often find themselves in the awkward situation of competing with governments or government-owned enterprises. I'm sure that isn't the intention of governments, but it has unfortunately been the reality in certain industries. This can certainly be harmful to the growth and health of the private sector, which is accepted by all as critical to the urgent need for the creation of tens of millions of meaningful jobs and opportunities for our youth.

SAMIH TOUKAN: One area that often gets overlooked is data. It has always been scarce in the Arab world and continues to be so. There is more data and more research than before, but it's still something that needs to be worked on and developed, whether by governments or by the private sector. We still have a lack of data in practically all aspects and across all sectors.

2. Shortage of Local Scaleup Capital

AHMED EL ALFI: A number of areas need improvement across the region. One major current bottleneck for the success of local startups is post-accelerator funding. Startups are typically loss-making right after they've undergone accelerator and may not have perfected their business model or their product yet. Hence, they will require additional several funding rounds before reaching profitability. Too many good startups still face difficulty raising funds after graduating from accelerators, and there are only a few local investors who are active at this stage. Some individual investors with pre-Series A focus tend to be overly risk-averse. They either wait for a larger fund to participate, which negates their importance in the ecosystem in the first place, or they impose excessively harsh terms on the startup that end up either turning off the company or deterring investors in later rounds. We need more awareness for the angels and individual investors to grasp the needs of companies at this stage and the associated risks.

Some people still think that one can fund startups with debt capital. Startups can only be funded with equity so that they can take risks and innovate. The traditional, debt-heavy financing approach is not suitable for high-growth startups. Debt doesn't match the equity financing they need, since the speed of their growth outpaces the stable historical track records banks look for when making lending decisions, and they don't have assets to present as collateral.

DANY FARHA: While the region's funding landscape has improved dramatically over the last five years, we are working from a small base five years ago. And we are still one of the most underfunded regions in the world. In the US, $300 per capita is invested in venture; in China, it's around $30 per capita; and in MENA, its closer to $3. We also need a technology bellwether listed on an exchange. Fawry has recently gone public, and it seems to have been very well received by investors, but at $100 million in market cap, it's still small. We need a Careem-sized company to be listed on an exchange, preferably a regional exchange. This will create public role models and set public metrics for wealth creation and enterprise value. It will also spur a vibrant M&A scene, with such public companies being acquisitive with their balance sheets and using cheap stock as currency to fund M&A. This will accelerate the flywheel of liquidity events, distributions to investors, and the commensurate returns, with technology and venture as an asset class.

NOOR SWEID: When comparing the region with the rest of the world, and particularly the amount of capital deployed into venture as a percentage of GDP, the role of venture in the economy becomes apparent. In the region, this oscillates between 0.01% and 0.03% for Saudi Arabia and 0.03% and 0.1% for the UAE from 2016 to 2018. For comparison purposes, these contrast with approximately just 0.4% for the US, Singapore, and China, where venture plays a major economic role, and approximately 0.1% for Brazil, France, and many European countries. Closing this gap would lead to an estimated increase of $500 million in annual investment for the venture capital industry in Saudi Arabia and $200 million in the UAE.

PHILIP BAHOSHY: I believe there is a complete mismatch in the demand and supply of capital for startups at every single level. The continued debate has been, "It's more acute at this startup stage versus it's more acute at this stage." My opinion is that they're completely mismatched at all levels. The problem is that as the ecosystem continues to mature, you're seeing more startups enter. Where there are early-stage investors, more angel investors, and more seed funds that are beginning to pop up and invest at the early stage, there are also, like any pyramid or pipeline funnel, more startups entering because of the success of other startups at the early stage. Therefore, there continues to be a mismatch at early-stage investment even though there is more capital being deployed than ever before.

As you go up the chain, more startups are evolving and becoming successful in raising Series A and B, although you continue to see a valley of death of startups funding at later stages. As they go further and seek more funding, there are fewer institutions in the region, and hence the need to seek capital internationally to continue fund them. So, while there is a constant growing risk appetite to invest in MENA-based startups compared to traditional assets like real estate, banking, and construction, there is still some apprehension. Specifically, this applies to MENA-based VC funds as LPs (limited partnerships) or ones directly investing in startups, and that is only natural, but we're seeing an acceleration of that as the ecosystem develops.

HEATHER HENYON: In 2018, $120 billion in venture capital was invested in the US while only about $1 billion was invested in MENA, which has a population roughly equivalent to that of the US. There is still a major shortage of capital, especially growth and scaleup capital (Series B+). Growth-stage capital is primarily coming from outside the region and is difficult to access without the right networks.

I also see a significant shortage of smart money at the early stage. Many of the early-stage investors don't have the bandwidth to engage actively with the startups to help founders build their business. There is a shortage of strong mentoring, coaching, and adding value that a startup can't hire due to resource constraints. In markets like the US, the angels and advisers play this role. Because so many of the angels are new to startup investing and because so few of them have actually been entrepreneurs, they are limited. The VC funds invest in both seed and Series A rounds but the two or three partners also have limited bandwidth. Investors like 500 Startups, for example, have large portfolios that prevent them from actively supporting the founders operationally.

TOTAL AMOUNT RAISED SINCE THE START

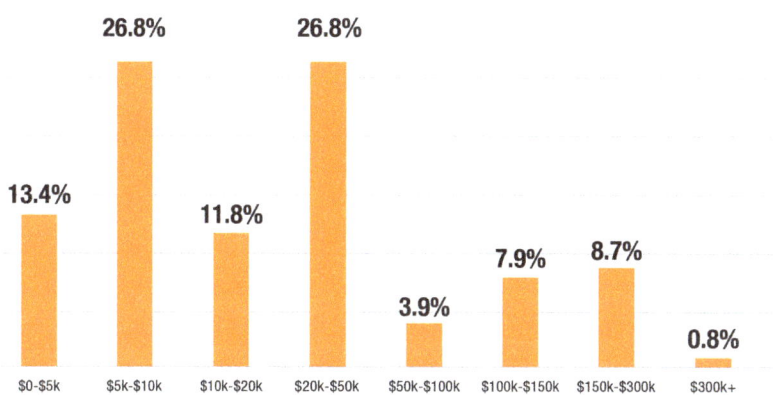

Data was collected from the applications of Wamda X programme and complimentary research from STEP Conference

Source: The State of Pre-Seed Startups in MENA (www.wamda.com & www.stepconference.com)

DAVE MCCLURE: Given the lack of sufficient capital to optimize ecosystem development in MENA, I really believe providing liquidity for investors in the region is very important because venture capital and startups take a long time, 10 years or more sometimes, to return capital. It tends to be a challenging asset class without providing some other incentive structures there. Thus, a focus is needed on not just providing upfront capital to companies, but providing upfront capital to investor organizations and VCs, and providing liquidity incentives and structures that may or may not just be public markets. That might mean developing a secondary market, venture debt markets, or fund of funds capitalization.

As concerns government-backed funding, if you look at Lebanon's Circular 331 as an example, nearly half a billion dollars was subsidized by Lebanon's Central Bank to go to Lebanese entrepreneurs. It was just way too much capital for such a small geography. It was actually inflating prices in the region, and not taking advantage of talent outside the region. That probably wasn't the right way to implement a program. I've seen similar issues with capital that's allocated to SMEs without any consequences of loss, where you're basically funding small businesses that aren't really set up for innovation or scale. It might be great for job creation, but it's a questionable allocation of resources and unsustainable nevertheless. You have to emphasize risk capital combined with the possibility to lose money as part of the equation, but you also want to encourage people to take risks and not just invest in profitable businesses that are already there. That sounds like a contradiction in terms, but you need to strike the right balance there for it to work.

It's important to encourage access to capital, but still acknowledge the consequences of loss, and encourage that capital to be allocated at earlier stages to businesses that are running on a negative cash flow. Emphasize scale and profitability in the long run. In other words, investors are not rewarded by those investments unless they get to scale and unless they get to profitability or maybe acquisition. Meanwhile, they must still provide capital at the early stages and not wait for it to be too easy, and not reward businesses that are not going to get to scale or that are unprofitable forever, just because they're creating jobs.

I don't know the specific reasons why Circular 331 didn't fully work. On a high level, I'd say that they were restricting that capital only to Lebanese entrepreneurs, and with a country of only six million people, that's a small population to provide that much capital to. That resulted in inflating prices, because being Lebanese was a requirement for the capital to be deployed. Some of it was also being decided by banks, and maybe you don't want bankers to be making equity-risk investment decisions, generally speaking.

MENA FUNDING VS. OTHER GEOGRAPHIES (2019 VS. 2018)

MENA funding is just 1% of the total funding in the US, despite accounting for roughly 10% of all deals. The same goes for other ecosystems. Asia saw $81B of investment in 2018, roughly 90 times the amount in MENA, and Europe saw $21B, about 23 times that of MENA.

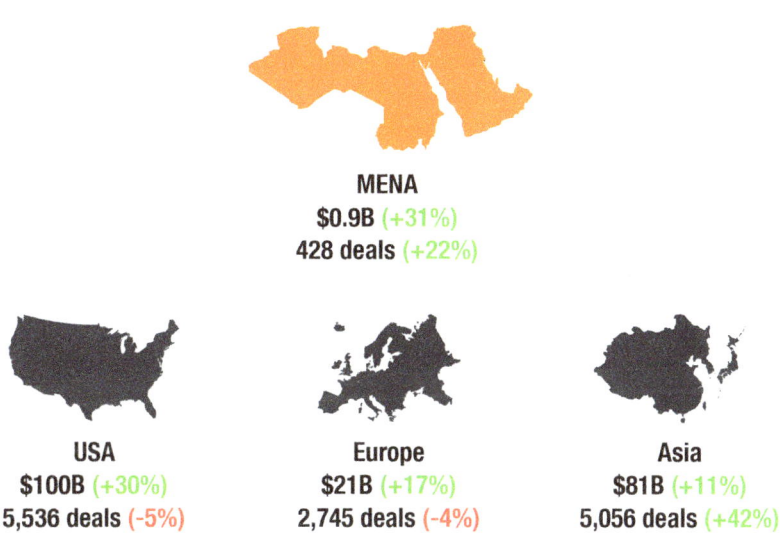

MENA
$0.9B (+31%)
428 deals (+22%)

USA	**Europe**	**Asia**
$100B (+30%)	**$21B** (+17%)	**$81B** (+11%)
5,536 deals (-5%)	**2,745 deals** (-4%)	**5,056 deals** (+42%)

Source: CB Insights Venture Capital Funding Report 2019 (www.cbinsights.com)

OSSAMA HASSANEIN: According to ArabNet's "State of Digital Investments in MENA, 2018" report, there has been significant growth in the last five years; 2018 was a record year: $674 million was invested in 255 deals. Investors, which have tripled in the last five years, include angels, VCs, corporate, and growth capital. Meanwhile, exits have exceeded $3 billion in the same period. So, all in all, the funding environment in the region has evolved nicely more recently. Investments have tripled and the number of investors has multiplied by a factor of 10 in the last five years alone across MENA countries, especially the top five markets—UAE, KSA, Egypt, Lebanon, and Jordan—which account for 80% of the funding. But the question we must ask: is this funding enough? And the answer is: perhaps not. In countries like Canada, China, and Korea, the governments bridge the gap based on priorities: applications of AI across disciplines in Canada ($300 million), EVs and scooters to reduce carbon emissions in China ($60 billion), and sustainability in Korea ($9 billion).

A few months ago, I actually received a proposal from an Israeli VC to collaborate by bringing entrepreneurs from Israel and the Arab world to a new incubator in Berlin. His argument was that the Arab entrepreneurs need support. He cited the following statistics: while the Israeli population is 2% of the Arab world (8 million versus 430 million), in 2018, $6.5 billion (almost 10X the Arab world's total) was invested across 623 deals in Israel. Return on investment between 2013 and 2017 reached $56 billion in 540 Israeli startup exits, or close to 20X the Arab world. While such statistics can be quite annoying, they evidently show us that we have our work cut out for us and the best is yet to come.

EYAD LATIF: While the funding environment in the region has certainly evolved over the years, there are still some glaring gaps. I recommend focusing on the pre-revenue proof-of-concept stage: seed stage, pre-seed stage, and so forth. We would encourage sources of financing to write more $50,000 checks, write more $100,000 checks. It's a good problem that we have a critical mass of people who want to write $5 million checks, but to create more $5 million Series A opportunities, the Middle East as an ecosystem needs to be writing more $50,000 checks across the region. That isn't to say that people are not already doing this, they are. We just need to encourage more of it.

We see people investing more in North Africa and in the Levant, and the biggest issues are lack of legal advice and consistent VC investment documents that apply equally across the region. In Egypt, there's been a unique phenomenon with startups using Dutch structures for tax purposes, which is a product of M&A deals and large cross-border transactions historically using Dutch structures for tax efficiencies. This mistaken belief that a Dutch structure is the most optimal option for a startup domiciled in Egypt has created issues because Dutch structures are more involved than a typical structure. They have more bespoke aspects that make closing the financing take longer and make attracting sources of capital that are unfamiliar with Dutch structures more difficult. Meanwhile, in places like Lebanon, having to use local structures to get Central Bank money has made it difficult for a Lebanese-based startup to evolve into a startup that has a holding structure that is consistent with international standard market practices, and one that would lend itself to a typical VC financing structure.

The irony is that of all the jurisdictions, the ecosystem in Palestine ended up with corporate structures that you would most expect to see with an international model of standard VC financing. Because they don't have any other options, they've used Delaware structures, which fit in perfectly with the NVCA (National Venture Capital Association) and other sophisticated structures.

There still aren't enough venture-capital-focused legal providers, though that's changing, slowly but surely. We are doing three dozen VC financings at the moment in the Middle East. We did over five dozen last year just in the region. That is a massive spike in activity. People are taking notice of that, so that's an issue that will solve itself, quite frankly. Now that you see the demand for this service, the supply of the VC lawyers will catch up; inevitably free-market economics will solve this issue.

I wouldn't be surprised if our peer legal firms that operate in this space in Europe and in the US were to start to do more work like this in the region, because it's not that there's a lack of VC legal practitioners globally. There are fantastic firms that do this all over the world. Prior to the Souq and Careem deals, the Middle East ecosystem was not on as many radars as it should have been outside the region. Given that what happened has been nothing short of revolutionary in terms of transaction values, new investors, new money in the region, new ideas in the region, and government support, there's a significant shift globally in how people are viewing this ecosystem.

3. Regional Collaboration and Fragmentation

SAMI MAHROUM: When I look at the MENA region, I see that there has been a division of labor happening between the countries within, where from the beginning many startups are operating at a regional level. They might open an office in Dubai to raise funds; they might open an office in Egypt or Jordan for technical talent; they might also open another office in Beirut. So, they draw on what I sometimes coin the "ABCD ecosystem" (Amman, Beirut, Cairo, and Dubai). It's like a regional network or a system of entrepreneurship, whereby if you were to start a company in, say, just Amman, Cairo, or Beirut and be exclusively immersed in that local ecosystem, you are less likely to succeed than if you created a multiple-site ecosystem from the outset. You won't have access to global networks as you might have in Dubai. On the other hand, you could base your company in Beirut, but set up an office in Dubai for marketing, PR, business development, and/or fundraising. You might also have a technical team in Beirut and another in Amman, and so on.

This dynamic seems to be characteristic of the emerging MENA entrepreneurship ecosystem. It leverages the surpluses, the strengths that exist across different multiple localities, as opposed to being very locally grounded. The resources are there, the ideas are there, the talent is there, but the matchmaking is often missing. Thus, such activities as networking events are incredibly crucial to making things happen and filling this gap, and making the resources flow from one place and one country to another, resulting in a cumulative positive effect.

SAMIH TOUKAN: Free access to markets and the free movement of goods and services across borders are still major problems in the region. The beauty of the internet is that it democratizes access to everyone. We started Maktoob in Jordan and were able to create a pan-Arab product that had users across the entire Arab world, from Morocco to the UAE. We even had Arab diaspora users in the US and Europe as well. The beauty of the internet is that it breaks all geographical barriers. Unfortunately, this is not the case offline.

We like to think of the Arab world as one unified market, but we remain fragmented markets. The internet has certainly helped bring it together, but more work on the ground is still needed. Entrepreneurs still face many challenges today due to the lack of free movement of goods, services, and people. There are different legal setup requirements and regulations across countries. When it comes to e-commerce, there is restricted movement of goods due to complicated and outdated customs regulations. Each market also has its own difficulties, challenges, and particularities. We sell the Arab world to the world as one homogenous, powerful market with 400 million people, just like, say, India with a billion people. This is not entirely true. While we share many commonalities—language, culture, and history—when it comes to business, not so much. As a result, entrepreneurs face many challenges when they try to expand and execute across the region, given its fragmentation.

Whether an economic union of this kind needs to happen on the Arab League level or on a country-by-country level, this could have great impact. Saudi Arabia, Egypt, and the UAE, for example, are the three biggest markets in the region for entrepreneurs and startups. If these three countries were to cooperate in creating a single market for these startups, that would solve 50% of the problem across the region, given the size of those markets. This would make things much easier for entrepreneurs, not only in terms of setting up and registering their companies, but in terms of operations as well. It would help remove a lot of friction and break down many unnecessary restrictions and mandates, whether regarding employee loans, employing non-locals, employing locals, setting up offices, and so forth. We need to lobby the governments in our region to cooperate with each other and to try to create more of an open market. It's definitely to the benefit of everyone.

RABEA ATAYA: One of the biggest issues is the fragmentation of regulations. In any single country, such as the United Arab Emirates, in order to conduct business, you might have to incorporate multiple times. Even within the same emirate, you might have to acquire multiple incorporations in order to do business with all the parties that matter. Moreover, with each incorporation comes significant upfront expense, but also significant ongoing expense for each legal entity to maintain tax files, audit files, personnel files, and various other jurisdictional items. Not to mention, in most cases in this part of the world, if you're going to incorporate you are also required to have a physical space. This is typically unnecessary, particularly when you are in the technology space. As such, there are significant legal obstacles to scaling, which either prevent individuals from attempting altogether or make it very expensive to scale to address a more sizable market.

The whole point of being in the tech business is that you want to achieve very large scale very quickly. The regulatory environment still significantly negatively affects the time, cost, and overall potential to scale. The hope is that government regulations operating across the region are increasingly made easier: where a single incorporation serves you throughout the region and you can deal with both government and non-government entities with just that one incorporation, and governments continually engineer ways to bring down the regulatory costs required to operate across borders.

EYAD ALKASSAR: The biggest issue MENA-based startups face as they try to scale is simply the fragmentation of markets in the region. Looking at the Arab world, you see nearly 400 million people, a huge market that has a lot of similarities in terms of language, culture, history, and consumption of the same media. However, if you want to tackle this region, you have to open a dozen different operations with different legal setups and so on for each market. It's the opposite of Europe, where you have a lot of countries that are very diverse, very different in terms of language, in terms of culture, and media consumption, but then you have one kind of legal framework and basically the same kind of regulations across all of Europe.

This is such a pity because the Middle East is one of the largest untapped markets globally, especially the GCC where you have high income and high purchasing power markets. If this fragmentation can be resolved and the region becomes more unified—via, let's say, some kind of startup framework so we have entities with the same kind of structure all over the region—this would lead to an incredible boom in terms of companies scaling across borders and outside capital flowing into the region.

HEATHER HENYON: One of the largest challenges in MENA is that the markets are not monolithic. Each country is bespoke—with its own regulatory requirements, currency, and market. The markets, with the exception of Saudi Arabia and Egypt, and a couple of other countries are small—typically less than 5-10 million people—and highly fragmented. On a macro level, inter-regional trade is tiny; on a micro level, getting a travel visa for a Tunisian to go to the UAE is very difficult. Founders have been tackling this issue by starting in their home market (e.g., Lebanon) and then moving to the UAE and then expanding into Saudi Arabia, and so on. Unfortunately, this is expensive and relies on the founder and his or her team to be willing to relocate. Many of the successful Jordanian, Egyptian, and Lebanese startups have opened sales and fundraising offices in the UAE (e.g., Little Thinking Minds has a nine-person office base in Dubai since 70% of their revenues come from the UAE). So, overall, any measure to make the region less fragmented is a step in the right direction for the ecosystem.

MOHAMMED JAFFAR: One fundamental challenge in the region is that we simply don't work and collaborate together enough together enough. We're too segregated by what nationality we are, what country we are from, and what religious background we have. All of which doesn't help business a bit for many reasons.

For example, it's still not easy for Arab nationalities to travel across different Arab countries, because of either visa restrictions or nationality restrictions, which hinders cross-border collaboration. We need to address this issue head on once and for all if we want to excel faster.

We still have some outdated rules and regulations when it comes to a number of Arab countries. I know first-hand because I worked in Talabat across six different countries and came across regulations that have yet to catch up to the requirements of the new economy.

Hiring certain talent in some of our countries in the region remains extremely difficult, simply because certain nationalities are banned from entering that country. That obviously depends on which countries we're talking about; some countries are much more business-friendly than others. For example, our company, JustClean, operates in five countries and employs around 150 people at the moment, and sometimes we need to have some people travel from one place to another for training purposes and special assignments. Unfortunately, not everyone can attend, as certain nationalities are completely banned. Recently, one staff member who is very talented, who I critically needed to travel to one of our offices, simply couldn't go there just because of his nationality. We have encountered countless other similar examples and continue to do so on a regular basis.

DANY FARHA: We need a common market at least between the three largest economies in MENA, at least for licensing and people flow. Imagine if a startup was issued a trade license in Egypt, Saudi Arabia (through SAGIA), or Dubai (through TECOM) and these three countries collaborated on the know your customer/anti-money laundering (KYC/AML) database—which is used for anti-money laundering purposes—such that a trade license in any one of these countries automatically extends to the other two with a fast-tracked process and reduced fees. Imagine if the staff of these companies would be given fast-track entry on arrival at the airports of all three countries just because they are working in the tech startup ecosystem.

The beautiful thing about this type of arrangement is that

the technology sector is, for the most part, subject to "increasing economics" (as opposed to diminishing returns at scale, which traditional business are subject to) because of attributes such as network effects and AI, machine learning, and predictive technologies. This means that technology offerings require scale, and with scale they become much better, are more valuable for all stakeholders, and remain competitive. This scale is required throughout the region, especially within the largest economies. Enabling, say, a successful Egyptian company to scale into Saudi Arabia and the UAE, and vice versa, creates FDI (foreign direct investment), jobs, and digitalized GDP all around.

Governments could also remove red tape and reduce the high costs associated with setting up a startup in the region, especially in the largest economies—Egypt, Saudi Arabia, and the UAE. We live in a very unique time where the leaders of those countries (President Sisi, HH's MBZ and MBR, and HRH MBS; the rulers of Egypt, UAE, Dubai, and Saudi Arabia respectively) have a very good, friendly, and supportive relationship. As such, we can achieve an unprecedent economic cooperation of this kind that would be a game-changer and history-making, setting the region on a course to participate in the fourth industrial revolution.

AMIRA RASHAD: I think there should also be an exchange program that could help move people around the region. Today, I'm sitting here in the UAE and, theoretically, I have a business that could span the region. I don't have access to anybody except people sitting here in the UAE, which obviously hurts my prospects for expansion and growth. There is no organization that I can reach out to and say, "I'm looking for some marketing folks," and they would say, "Great, here's a great talent pool in Amman or here is one from Casablanca." That kind of network doesn't exist.

Also, the ability to facilitate mobility across the region for talent doesn't exist. Our youth is much more likely to jump from Tunisia to Paris than to Cairo or Amman. The immigration structure needs to be able to effectively and quickly separate the ones who are really desired from those who pose national threats. Otherwise, we're going to lose valuable talent and encounter a further brain drain across the region.

4. Outdated and Restrictive Legislation

PHILIP BAHOSHY: The biggest challenges facing entrepreneurs in the region boil down to basic regulatory and infrastructure-related challenges—things as basic as how to get a license, how to set up a holding company and the associated costs, and how to do so across multiple jurisdictions. Currently, there is a lack of clarity on how to do that as a tech company and the cost associated with setting up and operating across all countries.

The second part is, if you are looking for investment from large international entities, especially the US-based entities, they are not typically comfortable investing in MENA-based companies unless they have offshore or international holding companies. Therefore, there is the regulatory burden of being able to connect. Operational licenses are required for the holding company to receive international investment. Until governments acknowledge that this is the model that needs to operate for successful tech companies and make it easier for them, it becomes challenging for entrepreneurs to scale.

One of the biggest challenges I see is the need for a clear, unified definition of what constitutes a high-growth tech, VC-backed startup compared to other kinds of SMEs (typically being offline and non-tech focused businesses). Certainly, SMEs can also be very successful companies, but they do not require the same scalability, funding, and growth. Until governments address the fact that they are two different types of entities, it is very difficult to have one policy that fits all. To a bank considering approving a loan, a company that plans to provide dividends and become cash flow positive within one or two years is very different to a Careem, a Fetchr, a Luxury Closet, or a MAGNiTT that operates an online platform and expects to generate revenue online, and that is looking to expand into multiple geographies very quickly. A tech startup is very different than an offline retail shop or a bank.

Acknowledging those differences is critical and reflecting them in differentiated policies is key. You would define upfront what type of companies you are looking to promote. Then you put certain policies in place that provide incentives for those companies. Thus, if the goal is encouraging high-growth startups, which by definition have the greater potential for impact and job creation, then you would offer that group meaningful incentives. Incentives could include special exemptions for licensing, visas, audits, and banking requirements. On the other hand, if you do not acknowledge that there is a difference between the two types of companies, then you're effectively lumping both types together and it becomes increasingly more challenging for high-growth tech entrepreneurs to operate within the environment.

So, how do you define a high-growth startup? I have a crude definition, "A high-growth startup is one that VCs invest in." The simple reason for that is VCs are not in it for charity or even for modest, incremental success; they only invest in companies that they believe have a chance of achieving exponential growth. If a given company does not meet this criterion and is addressing a real-life, scalable, and monetizable opportunity, it is in effect un-investable, and no VC will touch it. That's certainly not a high-growth startup.

BADR JAFAR: One thing we haven't yet managed to sort out in the region is the development of regulatory and legal frameworks that make it seamless for someone with a great idea to get to a stage where they're able to test their ideas in a safe, institutionalized capacity, by creating a company, employing people, and growing their operations in accordance with local laws and regulations. Doing that today in this part of the world still consumes far too much effort, stress, and tears. Something that probably should not even consume 5% of an entrepreneur's focus, time, and energy is, unfortunately, taking up closer to 50%. It's time and energy that should be spent on creativity and growth. The challenge we have in the region is that most of our systems were set up to regulate traditional business models and industries, and have not caught up to accommodate the different needs of today's entrepreneurs and startups.

AMIR BARSOUM: One of the biggest problems in the healthcare sector in the region is you don't know if, when, or how you will find yourself competing with the public sector. This puts a lot of restraints on innovative companies for investing in growth as well as capitalizing on public-private partnerships. There is quite a bit of uncertainty in the region since no one knows exactly which position governments will take with regards to the majority of emerging sectors. Most of our governments in the region are still not decisive on that front, except for maybe what you hear from Saudi Arabia, that they're going private.

How is this impacting healthcare as a sector in the region? A lot of the investment is going to the infrastructure and to the less risky, less progressive channels, given all the uncertainty and perceived risks around any new space. As a digital healthcare startup, I would prefer to know what the public sector plans are in this space and the anticipated regulation that might follow as a result, so I can allocate my focus and resources accordingly and position myself to avoid competing with the public sector or wasting valuable resources having to correct course and strategies.

BIJAN AZAD: Regulations remain one of the most fundamental challenges to startups and to the overall short- and long-term growth of the ecosystem. Many regulations, for example, concerning business establishment and particularly business closure are still outdated. For example, the equivalent of the American S corporation is still missing in many countries in the region. For the ecosystem to flourish, regulation has to be updated or overhauled altogether as needed to support the requirements of today's startups and the ecosystem at large.

MOHAMED ANOUAR MAAROUF: Among the most common challenges in any ecosystem is company setup. Although startups are small companies, they typically undergo the same establishment process as large corporations. We are currently working in Tunisia on digitizing this process, including the investors' process and the life cycle of startups. The objective is to digitalize these processes, which would make the setup of such ventures and the various administrative procedures associated with them happen much more seamlessly and quickly. We're actually trying to resolve this difficulty for all companies and not just startups.

The second challenge we're working on overcoming, which is a major one, is the administration's bureaucratic mentality. Despite all the facilitation and the positive dynamic that we have created, and all the simplification of processes concerning customs, for instance, this area still requires great effort. Administrators don't necessarily adapt to these procedures easily or immediately. We therefore formed a support team to assist whichever startups needs support, and I personally sometimes intervene to assist those companies with minor administrative procedures. We're using this approach to further support startups. We need to change the administrative mentality from a disabling and prohibitive one to one that favors enabling and support.

ASHRAF SABRY: Red tape remains a big challenge for entrepreneurs in the region. That said, entrepreneurs cannot just sit back and wait until the bottlenecks go away. They have to understand that red tape will not disappear; it will always be there to some extent or another, for a good reason or not. That will always be the case whether we're talking about Egypt, the Middle East, or anywhere in the world. The expectation that a regulator will not regulate just to make your job, as an entrepreneur, easier is a fantasy. So, the real question then is how to work with the system rather than against it.

As an entrepreneur, you have to understand the way regulators think. You have to understand their concerns and have people who can speak with them using their own language, and to help educate them as needed. Otherwise, you are just dreaming and screaming. The good news is that you can, in fact, have an influence on changing certain regulations or enacting certain reforms, but there is a right and wrong way to go about it and it takes time and patience. If you can show the regulators that you are mature enough to understand and convey your concerns coherently and constructively, no matter how much you disagree with them, then you have a chance of earning credibility and their respect. They might even approach you to ask for your opinion or professional advice. On the other hand, if you dismiss their concerns as negligible and not important, or worse being ill-intentioned, then they will likewise ignore your demands.

EYAD LATIF: The more that we—as members of the ecosystem—are engaging with the regulators and providing consultation when they put out policies, the faster these reforms can take place. We address this problem by having people in the ecosystem take up their civic duty by speaking to the regulators, accessing the regulators, and helping the regulators to navigate the space. It's incumbent on us as members of the ecosystem, as practitioners of VC, whether it's on the service side or the investment side or the entrepreneur side, to take up our civic duty to educate people in the ecosystem, to advocate, and to be involved and proactive in the process of reform. That opportunity does not exist in every ecosystem in the world, so we're fortunate in this respect. Thus, it's incumbent on us as members of this ecosystem to participate and to be the change that we want to see in the region.

5. Other Gaps Undermining Growth

RAMEZ SHEHADI: There are a number of structural gaps that frankly have been talked about ad nauseam by many people. I'm not quite sure what it's going to take for these issues to unlock, but they must be unlocked. For example, we continue to talk about bankruptcy laws, and while we have seen traction over the past year in markets including the UAE and KSA, the need for this is region-wide, as is the need for any law to take into account specific market and industry nuances. In the tech world, companies will be born and die frequently, and we can't apply the bankruptcy laws of the traditional brick and mortar space to these types of companies. We need to be much more agile and flexible in light of how these companies are ignited, how they scale, and how they survive.

We need to improve the reach of funding in the SME space in general and try to help onboard more and more companies into the digital economy. Not only is there an opportunity for them to plug in and gain access to meaningful audiences in their immediate, regional, or even global communities, there is also the much broader opportunity of impacting the overall economy. It is an economic fact that SMEs employing more and more people and scaling more efficiently are the greatest source of economic growth for any given economy—it's not the large corporates employing more people, and it's not the governments making everyone a pseudo-government employee.

The birth and growth of SMEs is the name of the game. That's the ticket to sustained economic growth. We've got to get them better funding and we've got to help them survive. We've also got to be forgiving and flexible when they don't. We have to give the entrepreneurs a chance to come back at it when they fail, and we've got to help plug them into the digital economy.

Another remaining major bottleneck is cross-border trade and the movement of goods. Consider for a moment that it can be cheaper and faster to ship a package from New York to Dubai than it is to send that same package from Dubai to Riyadh, or somewhere else similarly in the region. It's just got to become more efficient.

We've also got to work toward bringing the region in line with the behaviors, the expectations, and the critical attributes of digital economies when it comes to cash and cash transactions. We have been far too tolerant of cash on delivery and we've been far too tolerant of payment schemes that are stuck in the past. When you look at the percentage of e-commerce in the region, we're just getting started. It's got amazing growth rates and growth potential, but we still have ways to go if you look at what's happening in other regions not too distant from us, in Europe especially.

Finally, another issue, which is a bit thorny, is VoIP (voice over internet protocol) block. The region has been rightly positioning itself as a beacon of technological advancement and economic excellence for years, and yet the ban on a service as essential as VoIP harks back to less forward-thinking times. There is room enough for all parties to grow and prosper with VoIP in play, and while the time to implement the change was yesterday, it can, and needs, to happen.

OMAR CHRISTIDIS: In our Insights Division, we do research we call an "Innovation Ecosystem Assessment." We use a six-pillar model and we go in and do a survey of tech startups across the region. We ask them questions about access to funding, access to talent, access to markets, regulations, infrastructure, and support services. Now, in each country the challenges are slightly different. I can provide the following highlights based on our research findings and the answers we've received.

In Lebanon, the number one challenge was regulation. In Saudi Arabia, the number one challenge our research revealed was funding. In Kuwait, the number one challenge was talent. Now, this is if you just look at the number one challenge. Talent is a recurring theme that cuts across all markets. It's also the number two challenge in both Lebanon and Saudi Arabia. Everywhere we go, there is a talent crunch. There is a talent crunch on what I call "the practical skills for the digital economy." We're talking about coding, certainly, and that differs in different markets. Only 40% of startups in Lebanon said that they could find the coders they need, meanwhile only 11% of startups in Saudi Arabia said that they could find the coders they need. Finding sufficient coding talent is a major challenge.

There are also other practical skills for the digital economy, like digital marketing skills, usability, UX/UI (user experience/user interface) skills, data and analytic skills, product development skills, and product design skills. There's a gap in all these skillsets as well, between demand and supply, so I would say that talent shortage is the overall number one problem across the region.

There are also too many outdated regulations at the national level in many countries. In many places, doing business is still very difficult: shutting down a company, establishing a company, tax regimes, etc. So many challenges to the regulations have yet to be resolved. But, one in particular is a top priority: we cannot succeed in the tech industry today if we don't operate at a regional level and if the Arab market is not really a unified market—400 million people and billions of dollars in GDP.

SAMIA MELHEM: The first and most basic need for all Arab countries is to increase access to affordable, available, secure broadband. This can have tremendous economic impact. In fact, the latest International Telecommunication Union (ITU) study shows that even a 10% increase in mobile broadband adoption will cause an increase of 1.5 to 2.5% in GDP.

So why do countries need to adopt broadband? For one, broadband is necessary for access to online education content. Education is such a promising area. Imagine kids in public schools accessing their courses online and being able to enjoy education apps designed and built to entice their curiosity—call it the gamification of education. Actually, education is one of the ideal areas to bring online. Imagine if you digitalize all of it in the cloud for the region, and every school and academic institution can reuse what they need. First of all, imagine the impact on job creation that it will bring. Who should do it? It's going to have to be people from the MENA region who are fluent in Arabic. Second, imagine the amazing impact it will have to provide all that curriculum in an agile way on a regional education cloud, open and online for all.

Education doesn't have to be just for schools. It could be for youth—some of the educated youth who are not finding jobs and who could benefit from reskilling. It could also be for people who are employed but need upskilling. Imagine procurement officers who now need to work on e-procurement and the challenges around that unless they are properly trained and onboarded on the relevant digital skills needed to properly operate an e-procurement system.

The same applies to building capabilities for politicians and policy-makers through a common offering to all of the Arab world—through The Arab League—to help them further understand what it means to live in a digital world and create policies that will take our youth in the right direction. This could cover cybersecurity and cyber ethics, as well as how to create mobile apps, games, etc., all of which is completely missing in our region.

I would focus on these two needs first: broadband access and education on a digital scale. They shouldn't take too long. We're taking way too long to do that. We need to really reform our laws, and we can even copy things like what the Europeans are doing, which is quite advanced for digital signatures, data protection, cybersecurity, and what we call a digital single market, so countries can exchange data safely and it's easier for services to cross borders without red tape.

RABIH KHOURY: By and large, the regulation across the region affecting startups and investors is quite difficult. Every country has a different set of laws. There are limitations on foreign ownership in the Gulf. In Lebanon, for example, if you want to close the company because it's not doing well or because of issues with taxes, it takes seven to eight years to close the company. That's a real damper on VCs, where naturally some companies they invest in might die. That's a risk VCs understand and are willing to take, so long as the overall return on their investment portfolio as whole offsets those losses and provide a significant return.

We also still don't have a go-to IPO market, which is super important. In fact, you cannot find one public company in MENA that's a technology company, with the exception of Fawry in Egypt, which just went public. Before Fawry, there wasn't even a public multiple we could look at in technology to be able to gauge valuations. This all makes it riskier for early-stage investors: exit multiples are held back by a ceiling because there is no IPO market that can push them. Thus, we need better financial infrastructure that helps facilitate startups to do IPOs. We also could use a bit more funding from the sovereigns to invest in later-stage deals, because right now there's not enough Series B and Series C capital to do so.

I actually have my own theory about why Careem sold to Uber, and it's up for debate. Ride-hailing companies tend to burn lots of cash. If Careem wanted to raise their next round, they would've needed to raise $500 or $600 million. Now, if you take regional funds, even all of us put together wouldn't be enough to finance Careem. Hence, Uber came in, good arbitrage, with a liquidity event in New York at a premium price, and solved their funding requirements.

If you remember when Souq sold to Amazon, a few months earlier right before they sold, it did a round at a $1 billion valuation, and nevertheless ended up selling the whole company at less than $600 million. Again, I believe that it was also a capital scarcity issue that forced Souq to sell at a lowered valuation price.

For the large transactions, we simply don't have enough money in the region. Then for the exits, if you cannot show that you have an IPO option or some multiple you can see in a public market, it doesn't give you a lot of leverage when you're negotiating a trade sale, because a trade sale becomes your only opportunity. The capital markets have to mature. Meanwhile, it's difficult for them to mature because they're not one unified market.

The country with the most advanced capital market infrastructure is Egypt. In Lebanon, we don't really have a public market. In the UAE, in the last year, we had three large IPOs coming out of the region. You have the Finablr, which is the UAE exchange. You had the companies that Abraaj put money into, which came out of the banks. They also held IPOs in the UK: you had Jumia for example, which operated throughout Egypt, Morocco, and many African countries. All the large IPOs ended up listing internationally except for Fawry. Also, why would you want to list in markets that don't have liquidity? Even in Dubai, there's not enough volume. That's also a big problem from the public market perspective.

The other issue is bankruptcy law, which is way overdue. Most governments in the region are still fearful that if you're looking to shut down a company, you're trying to escape from social security liabilities, taxes, value-added tax, etc. The bigger risk is that you will stunt the overall growth of companies by multiplying their risk profile by a significant factor. We lack bankruptcy laws that provide a fail-safe mechanism. The UAE has recently made some positive strides on that front, while some governments are working on it as we speak. Lebanon is working on something related, which hopefully will be available soon, so that's promising.

Unfortunately, Lebanon has some bigger issues right now than just the bankruptcy law. When we created our fund in Lebanon, along with the IMPACT fund for Lebanon in 2014, it was basically the largest fund in the Middle East. We could not create a GP/LP (general partner/limited partner) structure because a lot of key components were missing. We had to create the holding company and bring in the investments of the LPs through a convertible, which was quite complicated and time-consuming. You also create some tax burden because the interest on the convertible is taxed. When you're trying to actually mimic an LP commitment and other capital related issues over investment deals, it becomes very complicated. They finally have a draft law for a financial company that somewhat looks like it's a GP/LP structure, but it hasn't been approved yet. Saudi Arabia has advanced in that area quite a lot. Bahrain has also done it quite well.

ABDULAZIZ AL LOUGHANI: If you look at any big, international conference or summit in the world, whether it's the G20 summit, Davos, the UN, or the GCC summit, the same theme comes up: unemployment is a ticking bomb this region is facing. The numbers vary, but possibly up to 100 million jobs need to be created within the next 10 years, which represents one of the highest unemployment rates per region in the world and a massive challenge indeed. A lot of governments mean well in trying to solve this, but many stakeholders are conflicted over participating in the design and architecture to solve this problem.

Visas remain a huge issue in this part of the world. We even have our differences when it comes to visas among Arabs ourselves. You'll see many Arab nationalities that don't really have the freedom to move between different geographies across the Arab world. Moreover, if you're not from the Arab world, it's a lot more expensive and difficult to move there. So, visa laws really need to open up for others and specifically be more welcoming and internationally business-friendly. There are free zone jurisdictions, but in practice that's still quite limiting. Opening up our economy and focusing more on the economy as a whole rather than on a particular nationality is a shift we have to undertake. You'll see a lot of policy-making and legislation that puts nationalism-favored law ahead of the overall country's economy. I think we really need to open up our economy for foreigners to come in, and set up better visa laws.

Many local laws are still outdated for the digital world. For example, if I want to run a promotion in Saudi Arabia, Kuwait, or the UAE, I'm required by law to ask for permission from the regulators, usually the Ministry of Commerce, to run the promotion. If I want to run a campaign, say, within the next month, September, corresponding with the National Day of Saudi Arabia, then I need to get permission from the regulators well in advance. This extra red tape step puts me at a disadvantage in terms of efficiency and responsiveness to market needs versus an international e-commerce player who doesn't have local presence in Saudi Arabia, who can run a promotion every day without needing to ask permission from the local regulators. As such, they can be more agile and flexible, whereas as a local player I'm actually disadvantaged. So, opening up our laws and updating our thinking to serve the economy, and updating our laws to align with the needs of the new economy, are things we really need to work on.

COMPARISON IN PERCENTAGES OF YOUTH UNEMPLOYMENT RATES BY REGION

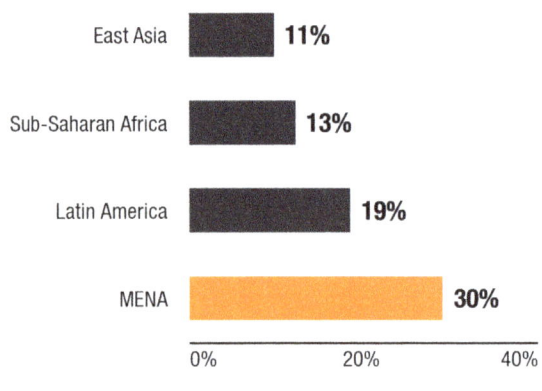

Share of unemployment rate (%)

Source: The World Bank, International Labour Organization 2017 (www.worldbank.org)

ABDUL BASET AL JANAHI: When it comes to funding, the level of bank credit to SMEs in the UAE leaves much to be desired. We need a better understanding among banks regarding the SME business model and a stronger commitment and longer-term strategic plan from them to support SME growth.

For growing SMEs, the challenges are mainly in expanding capacity and capabilities to match growth. One such challenge is corporate governance, especially financial governance and risk management for growing SMEs. Not enough SME owners realize the need to have properly audited financial accounts as they grow and expand internationally until it affects the growth and reputation of the business. The other challenge among growth SMEs is that the owner-entrepreneur fails to build an adequate management team that can be delegated some authority in the absence of the owner. Such a "one-man show" risk devalues the SME in the eyes of investors.

SMEs also face issues related to attracting good human resources, and the overall skills for executing a business. The Dubai

Entrepreneurship Academy in Dubai SME seeks to address this challenge through custom-made educational programs for diverse business sectors and disciplines to educate owners about managing a business.

JOHN MACOMBER : First and foremost, ease of setting up and doing business is key. In a lot of environments globally, including many in MENA, it can take months to years to incorporate, to have a license to operate, to get an address—things like that. That really slows things down. Second, there are a lot of environments where it's thought that having multiple viewers or regulators protects the public interest, which it might, but the flip side is it leads to redundancy and inefficiency. By contrast, governments need to streamline the process by, say, having a single window where businesses can get licenses, building and property permits, tax registrations, and employee permissions, and all those things from one window rather than having to go through all these government agencies.

The incumbents in this situation are the regulators who very accurately feel that their responsibility is to make sure that every piece of paper is correct. Those incumbents don't want to be displaced. I personally don't bother about environmental regulations when it comes to startups. It's more about overlapping regulations around how you actually do business. There are places that certainly say they're going to provide extraordinary approval for all. It's hard to do and it's very hard for a local, state, or national governments to say, "Okay, we will give up some of these regulatory controls because we think it's going to make business grow." This is not how most of the other regulators think. Perhaps that's how the nations' leaders think if they are pro-business, but more often than not that outlook does not trickle down to the regulators, and it needs to.

ZIAD MOKHTAR: One area that is not working in the ecosystem as well as it should is stock options. Employees expect them but don't value them that much. You can't fault employees. This is driven by the relatively long time it takes to exit and cash out, while there's no active secondary market. Both are slowly improving as the market has seen some exits, but a more vibrant market is still needed where the stock options that employees get are more frequently validated. Startups and their investors need to encourage the rise of a secondary market with reasonable controls from the side of startups.

Another area I would highlight is the limited adoption of digital authorization and digital payments. Wider adoption is central to eliminating friction from digital experiences, which would allow for fast scaling. A big part of this can be attributed to cautious regulators and some part to cultural norms. The sooner regulators embrace the digital world, the quicker we will see a big uptake in innovation. The good thing is that governments are starting to move in the right direction. Digital transformation that leads to wider financial inclusion and also more security has become a priority in many countries in the region.

SHADI BANNA: The major spenders in the MENA region are still the governments. Some governments have put in laws where they would purchase a certain amount from startups, or digital businesses, for their procurement needs. Those kinds of policies that encourage government entities to buy from local startups or local tech companies, as in local e-commerce companies for example, are quite helpful.

That said, one problem we still have is delays in payments from governments to the private sector, which affects the whole market. It affects the larger companies, which in turn trickles down to the smaller ones. Some of the bigger companies can survive, but many small companies can't when their payments are delayed for 180 days or sometimes even a year. That's a big drain on all of the energy at these startups and puts their survival at risk. This issue needs to be addressed once and for all.

MUHAMMAD MANSOUR: There's still the challenge of corruption here in Egypt, which poses a threat to startups that want to scale. I see many startups leaving Egypt recently. They're going to Dubai for a more business-friendly environment, greater access to investors and talent, more government support, less corruption, and a better legal environment in general. It's time we change and become more open and get rid of corruption to pave the way for those startups to find success within Egypt and reverse much of the brain drain that has plagued us historically.

It's also time to become more accepting of differences and encourage more freedom of expression. When you look around the world, you see liberal, democratic economies outperforming their counterparts. Clearly, there is a strong case to be made that those factors help contribute to better economies, not to mention better societies.

The government has been supportive on many fronts, but it also remains a hurdle in a number of ways. It is relatively bureaucratic and slow, specifically when it comes to legalizing a lot of the new technologies like blockchain, implementing cybersecurity as well as privacy and data protection regulations. It has also been slow in developing high-speed internet and other hard infrastructure, which is so critical for businesses and startups.

Government involvement in startups—either direct or indirect, as in the case of publicly or public-private funded entities like universities or incubators—is not necessarily a healthy or sustainable dynamic. Having government owning or controlling a private venture gives it a certain unfair advantage that is likely to tamper with the organic nature of the market. It also creates an element of uncertainty, and a concern that the government can step in anytime and be a competitor. This can't be healthy to the ecosystem in the long run.

IDRISS AL RIFAI: The key issue that foreign investors are concerned about is regional stability, not just in terms of the geopolitical situation, but the stability of the regulations. They start looking into this and right off the bat they realize that 51% of the company is given to someone who is only involved on paper, and in the case of a judicial dispute it's not clear who the judge will ultimately side with. Not to mention, financial structures are not exit-friendly. Then the investor tries to call in via VoIP, only to find out that it's blocked, unlike in the rest of the world. All of these things create a ton of real and perceived hurdles that deter foreign investors, especially when they look at global markets at large and decide where is best to allocate their resources. They consider the opportunity cost in sorting out all those issues in the region when they can hit the ground running— executing from day one—elsewhere. As a result, they place the region to, say, priority market number five or six instead of being number two or three. This means that as a region, we lose that foreign investment for two or three years, if not forever, in which case we don't just miss the boat, we actually destroy the boat.

6. The Real Impact of Geopolitical Instability

KEVIN O'LEARY: The biggest challenge the Middle East has right now to attract international players and foreign investment is the misconception by both American and European investors that it is a war-torn, unstable, politically risky, and unsafe environment—and that's simply not true. Yes, there are local tensions and geopolitical instability in a number of pockets, some of which have been there for a long time. Meanwhile, vast geographies are relatively stable environments. So, it's important to make that distinction between the various territories. That often gets overlooked when outsiders view the region as one lump-sum place. Let's take Saudi Arabia for example. That is probably the most misunderstood country in the region because it was closed off for a long time. It was very difficult to get a visa to visit until just even two months ago. Now they have the electronic visa for tourists, which actually made it much easier for businesspeople to travel there.

The Saudi administration has now decided they want to be more open and communicate a little bit more about their culture and their society to the rest of the world. Unfortunately, they had some serious issues in the last couple of years that didn't reflect so well in the media and negatively affected international perception. On the other hand, we see greater access and transparency is now starting to happen. The biggest challenge remains getting the Western press and European press to go there and cover the country, so they can get a fuller picture of what's really happening in the country. It's easy to take one headline narrative and see an entire nation or region from such a limited lens or view. It's much more challenging to roll up your sleeves and experience first-hand what's actually happening on the ground. That's how a lot of people overlook the massive opportunities there.

The Saudi population is one of the youngest in the world. About 70% of the people are under 30 years old. That means there's a whole generation of people that want entertainment, hotels, education, sports, etc., and are going to need all kinds of new infrastructure and digital services. The investment opportunities there are plentiful and very interesting. People don't realize that Riyadh has nearly 8 million people. That's a world-class city, and yet for a long time the city didn't allow anybody to build towers, so you got these really strange, very low-density buildings. This turns out to be a massive opportunity to go now and build apartments, hotels, and industrial and recreational facilities.

When I was in Riyadh, I was asking local partners, "Wait a second, everybody's flying to Abu Dhabi on the weekends. Why aren't they staying at home? Why go to Bahrain and Dubai? Why not build the things that they have there right here in Riyadh or in the suburbs so people spend their money staying home?" That's the kind of massive opportunities I'm referring to, which will catalyze a whole new world and all kinds of new opportunities in time.

From the Middle East countries' standpoint, they have to make an extra effort to open up and allow Western—American and European—press to come in and cover the story of the country and highlight some of the real market opportunities there. That is actually how you get foreign capital allocation—when people start to feel comfortable, and when they start to do risk-adjusted investments, and it's all because they started to feel they understand the culture and the country. It comes down to demystifying the region and uncovering the black box stigma that surrounded it for a long time. Nobody has an issue investing in England, Germany, or France because they've been there multiple times and they understand how these countries work, and those are big markets that have been open for a long time. The Middle East has to do the same.

The good news is that today, with the advent of social media, it's easier and faster than ever before to influence mass perception. On the other hand, the opposite is also true. Any small negative story coming from the region, and they're bound to come out, will have an adverse outcome. Even the narrative of any attempt to control or block social media is in itself very damaging perception-wise for foreigners considering investing or doing business in the region, perhaps even more damaging than the story being sought to cover itself. Social media makes it so that you can't hide anything from anybody anymore, even if you try. If you're a government, you have to assume that everybody's watching, and they are. It's impossible to censor out communications, virtually impossible, so you might as well capitalize on your virtues and be transparent, and make an effort to create a reality that is consistent with the image you're trying to present.

SAMI MAHROUM: What clearly is not working in the region is politics: the discriminatory aspect of the region, the constant tension and threat of terrible wars, the political hiatus in Lebanon and sometimes in Egypt and Jordan, and of course the civil wars in Syria, Iraq, and Yemen. This is really a major distinguishing factor when you talk about MENA compared with other regions in the world. As such, it's not fair to compare entrepreneurs in MENA to entrepreneurs in Asia, Africa, Europe, North America, or Latin America. It's just not fair to compare them because they don't have to deal with the extra challenges that we need to deal with.

In this region, every time we make progress, some progress, something bad happens and we are sabotaged. Often it is something that is beyond our control. Some sort of geopolitical crisis happens, which sets us back. For me, the successful entrepreneurs in this region are real heroes. They have made a strong commitment to this region. They have stayed in it. They are resilient despite all these subtexts and continued subtext. They continue to work against the odds. Politics don't work, and have never worked across the region. Regulations are also not so great in general across the region. They're not particularly great in Lebanon, in Egypt, and in many other places.

JOY AJLOUNY: The unstable political climate in the region unfortunately negatively impacts international investors' appetite for the region. If you're a big VC sitting in Silicon Valley, and possibly have never been to the Middle East, and you have two comparable companies, one in Riyadh or in Cairo, and another in the Netherlands. Where are you likely going to put your money? The interesting thing is that Silicon Valley-based VCs' jobs are on the line if they bet on the wrong company. VCs are typically partners in the fund. It's not a job; you get judged and financially rewarded on the winning bets you make with companies. There is a real incentive to hunt for great startups. So, I believe the political instability is definitely harming the ecosystem and, unfortunately, often can overshadow any great commercial opportunities or reforms happening in the region.

SETH LEVINE: The Middle East has often been seen as a black box. Historically, there has been a bit of fear of the unknown for outsiders looking into the region. Given some of the political situations in the region, it can seem daunting.

For example, Saudi Arabia was making great strides and was starting to be perceived as an international finance destination and even a place for startups. Then suddenly Saudi was all over mainstream US and international news in a very negative light. Almost instantly it has become somewhat taboo in the US to be working with Saudi

Arabia. These types of incidents anywhere in the region cause investors to be cautious across the region unfortunately, not just in the countries specifically involved in any given issue.

Overall, the region can be more open to investment, travel, etc., from global entrepreneurs, and be more welcoming from a regulatory and cost of doing business perspective. It can try to encourage more people to come over and spend more time and explore opportunities. I think those global connections are really helpful to local entrepreneurs because they can meet people who have gone through similar businesses before, and those people will become resources to them and, hopefully, cheerleaders for the work that they're doing.

ANDREW BERKOWITZ: With regard to geopolitical instability in the MENA region, one question is how local governments can help create an ideal growth-conducive environment, whether that's through tax credits, or whatever, in order to calm international investors' fears regarding geopolitical risks. That's one of the toughest challenges emerging-market startups face generally when they're fundraising, especially when they take a trip to New York or London to find investors for instance. The issue investors are likely to raise is, "If I invest my money in this country, tell me about the geopolitical risks," and a lot of times it's heartbreaking if that is the piece that actually kills the deal. Governments need to be able to implement a mature tax and regulatory framework that supports their entrepreneurs by getting out of the way.

Chapter VII

RECOMMENDATIONS FOR DEVELOPING THE MENA ECOSYSTEM

This chapter addresses some of the most common recommendations and suggestions put forward by both global experts and regional practitioners to better develop the MENA ecosystem. What's particularly interesting is how applicable this advice is to any ecosystem in the world, wherever it may be. Every ecosystem is unique—geographically, economically, politically, culturally, and historically, among a host of other variables—so naturally no one formula for success exactly fits all when it comes to ecosystem development. That said, certain high-level, fundamental principles do apply across all commercial environments because the critical elements required for any population to function optimally, from a productivity and commercial standpoint, are universal and eternal. This is, in effect, what allows us to learn and borrow practices from one ecosystem and adapt them to another ecosystem (as covered extensively in a subsequent chapter that highlights international best practices and case studies in ecosystem development).

However, some ecosystems may stand to benefit more from greater emphasis on certain elements of ecosystem development than others.

For example, some parts of the region have been historically more inclusive and diverse from a gender, culture, and religious standpoint, while others need to catch up. As such, inclusivity and diversity would be a higher priority for those ecosystems. Even within the MENA region, countries measure up differently in terms of where they stand in such key areas as talent, education, capital, policy, and culture.

To stay competitive in today's increasingly global world, attracting the right foreign talent is key. This is especially true in small countries, where there is intrinsically a much smaller talent pool to draw from than in larger countries. This is exaggerated by the fact that—with respect to new technologies, new industries, and new business models—it's particularly difficult to find local people with academic credentials in advanced technology fields, let alone practitioners with sufficient depth of career experience in those fields. This is the case in such advanced areas as AI, data science, and blockchain to name a few, but also in relatively older sectors as well, such as e-commerce, cybersecurity, and ride-sharing. So, the question becomes: What are some of the best practices to attract and retain international talent and investment to further optimize improvements in these areas locally?

Certain obvious basic conditions attract talent, and people in general, to a particular environment—namely, good living and working conditions, and a reasonable cost of living. There is no way around such factors. Talent and money typically flow to places where quality of life is great and living expenses are not too prohibitive. After all, humans are not robots; they have personal needs and seek out environments that help them grow and develop, not just professionally, but personally and socially as well.

Furthermore, it's not enough just to attract such talent. Retaining talent in the region on a long-term basis poses a larger challenge, but it is critical for sustaining the success of an ecosystem in the long haul. Losing talent to overseas jobs after they have acclimated to the particular environment in MENA and become functional and productive members of society is a waste. This phenomenon has been labeled as "brain drain." It commonly refers to losing local people who migrate to foreign countries, but it applies equally to expatriates moving back to their countries of origin or somewhere else. In both cases, talent is moving away from an ecosystem rather than into it. So retaining talent in ecosystems and societies at large is crucial, similarly to a business where the departure of a great staff member is a great loss to the organization. The lost know-how, skills, and relationships of individuals cannot always be replaced quickly and cost-effectively. Hence, it's a cardinal tenet in business practice to try to retain great staff as long as possible.

The question then becomes how best to retain talent. Certainly, in addition to living and working conditions and the cost of living, some of the most significant factors include the ease and cost of doing business: simple licensing procedures, residency visa requirements, property and IP rights, language, and connectivity with the outside world.

Beyond retention, a bigger challenge in ecosystems is how to create a sense of connectedness and self-identification with a given place. It's one thing to attract people physically to a particular environment; it's another to help them develop an emotional connection with that environment so they feel welcomed and valued as equals with locals. They should feel that they belong in a given place, versus feeling like transients or outsiders, and that they have a long-term stake in the place flourishing. This way, immigrants become more "vested" in their new environment and more reluctant to move away.

Historically, some Western societies have set a great example for this. The US, in particular, has set the tone for the rest of the world in attracting immigrants and infusing a sense of "Americanism" in them. The "American dream," defined by the notion that America is a free, equal-opportunity place where anyone can work hard and succeed, has been a great selling point for the US for decades. Granted, it's never been this rosy or flawless in practice, and tension does often arise between the various racial groups. Certain types or groups of people may remain unable to be assimilated into American society. That said, all in all, America has benefited much more than it has lost as a result of promoting this dream and its culture of openness over countless generations. The MENA region—and the rest of the world—can learn much from the US in this area specifically. Perhaps MENA leaders will even develop or adopt a new, improved version of the American model, which potentially has its upside without much of its downside.

When it comes to engaging women in the workplace and inspiring and supporting them to pursue their own career ambitions—whether those ambitions include high-level executive jobs, entrepreneurial pursuits, or a host of other diverse career choices—the MENA region has historically underestimated the capabilities and potential of women. Only recently has it awoken to the valuable role they play in the economy and society in general. The signs on that horizon are certainly encouraging, and will hopefully continue to move forward and spread across the region.

Education also plays a big part in engaging women, as well as youth and society at large, in the new economy. While schools and universities no longer have a monopoly on learning in increasingly knowledge-based economies, they still play a vital foundational role in the education system. All kinds of options powered by technology and countless innovative online models today were not available just a few years ago. It is up to each individual to complement their own formal education using other available channels. In that sense, individuals are now more in charge of where to go to find what they need to learn. They can thus capitalize on a more democratized educational environment than ever before, and not always rely exclusively on traditional academic institutions to provide for all their educational needs.

That said, formal reskilling and upskilling programs are required to help acclimate a large portion of the working class to meeting the demands of the 21st century. One notable example is MiSK Academy in Saudi Arabia, which is attempting to graduate thousands of students in such future-oriented areas as data science, software development, UX design, product management, and others, utilizing some of the most innovative educational practices and partnerships available in the world today.

In the meantime, educators must commit to modernizing their curriculums, in terms of both content and teaching methodologies. There needs to be greater emphasis on project-based STEM (science, technology, engineering, and mathematics) learning and more exposure to industries, industry leaders, and role models in general. Conversely, both companies and business leaders need to make themselves more available for internship programs and other youth mentorship opportunities. Historically, there has been a disconnect between the academic world and the business world, on both the student and administration levels. Greater collaboration is thus needed between universities and companies to bridge this gap today. Similarly, greater collaboration is needed between local universities and world-class educational institutions to borrow and implement the latest and greatest teaching tools and curriculum in the field.

In terms of educational methodologies, the world is becoming more complex and dynamic, with most basic information across many fields available online at our fingertips. Hence, the knowledge of facts will no longer be a differentiator. A greater emphasis on comprehension and creativity, and less on rote memorization, is paramount. This is a vastly different approach from how curriculums have been taught in most of the region and many parts of the world. Also, a greater emphasis on teaching self-learning skills and techniques, and infusing young people with resilience, will go a long way to help them adapt quickly to their ever-changing world and turn them into lifelong learners. This needs to happen at an early age to be most effective.

In this chapter, Julie Lenzer, Chief Innovation Officer at the University of Maryland, Board Member for the Center for American Entrepreneurship, and Author of *ParentPreneur Edge*, goes one step further to address the role parents play in their children's education. She explains that instilling an entrepreneurial foundation early on will serve youngsters well in their lives, whether they choose to start a company or not. The virtues and disciplines of integrity, organization, and a strong work ethic, as well as basic business and project management skills, will go a long way in shaping who they become and their prospects for success.

Exposure to success stories and role models can also provide inspiration and "fuel the fire" in a way that is as valuable as knowledge transfer. Greater opportunities on that front, what I refer to as the "local success narrative," are critical. This can take shape in many forms and channels—whether physically in schools and company environments or virtually via media and online channels. Mainly, it's about helping match youth with, and exposing them to, aspirational and insightful local, successful entrepreneurs and business leaders.

When it comes to regulation and policy, both "hard policy" and "soft policy" are equally instrumental in developing a thriving entrepreneurship ecosystem. Daniel Isenberg , Professor of Entrepreneurship Practice at Babson College Executive Education, clearly makes the distinction between the two. He stresses the importance of the soft policy, which often gets underestimated. He says, "Hard policy is the laws, regulations, and financial systems. Soft policy is the roles that the policy-makers can play in convening the other stakeholders from the other sectors, aligning them, encouraging growth, celebrating growth, cheerleading when growth occurs, and recognizing it in many different ways. Soft policy encompasses all the initiatives that governments do that do not have a legal dimension, but nevertheless help catalyze and facilitate more and more local firms growing more and more rapidly." He goes on to emphasize that, "Soft policy is much more important than hard policy when it comes to fostering entrepreneurship ecosystems. When it comes to innovation, on the other hand, hard policy is probably more important. I don't think providing subsidized loans or other incentives on their own can be effective unless they're accompanied by a lot of other things. In fact, on their own they can be harmful because they prevent market discipline."

From that perspective, it's important for governments to know when to step forward to aid ecosystem development, how much aid to provide, and when to strategically hold aid back. There have been ample historical cases of too much or too little, or too early or too late government involvement, and countless examples and case studies to learn from. One big challenge governments all over the world are tasked with is how to strike that balance between ensuring the right catalysts and protection mechanisms are present without tampering with the organic nature of the ecosystem and throwing off that natural balance with artificial initiatives and policies. That said, fundamental to any ecosystem development effort is a foundation of property and IP rights protection, conflict-resolution, fail-safe-related legislation, and mechanisms to promote ease of doing business.

Some of the most progressive practices when it comes to government involvement in an ecosystem revolve around greater understanding and collaboration between the policy-makers and the ecosystem players. Sangeet Paul Choudary, Co-Author of *Platform Revolution and Platform Scale* and Founder of Platformation Labs, underscores this point using the following example: "The best way for regulation to help catalyze innovation is by creating collaboration models. If you take Singapore, for example, they created a FinTech regulatory sandbox where banks can share data and startups can come and work with that data, but the startups cannot just take off and work on a business on their own. They still need the banks to continue to partner with them even after the innovation has been created within the sandbox. That creates more of a sustainable partnership between the larger incumbents and smaller companies, which encourages the incumbents to participate and open up their data, but also ensures that they do not miss out on the advantages of the innovation. That is where you can really have sustainable innovation and create a truly innovative ecosystem, not just from startups but also leveraging the assets that the incumbents have in a given geography."

The above approach is particularly valuable in an environment like the MENA region. Other forms of public-private collaboration can take place around local infrastructure development or other large-scale local problems, which the government cannot always solve alone due to limited bandwidth or know-how. That's when open-innovation models can be a great tool. This is where governments would define in detail a problem they're trying to solve, provide the necessary data and historical context, give some indication of their budget and criteria for success, and even provide attractive incentives and rewards. Then they would publicize the challenge to the private sector, addressing both local and international industry players, who could then step forward and propose solutions to such critical problems. The public-private relationship needs to involve a two-way communication dynamic. Clearly, each side has its own defined domain and should not attempt to diminish the role of the other party. Nevertheless, behind-the-scenes dialogue and collaboration following a publicized campaign for assistance can help synergize the efforts of both sides to speed progress on solving those large-scale local problems.

Also, with respect to regulation, I touch briefly on protectionism and nationalism in this chapter and examine their pros and cons, both in terms of intended outcomes and potential downsides. We hear ideas and opinions on the topic from various contributors; more specifically, we explore how to maximize the upside of protectionist and nationalist policies and minimize their potential side effects. The views on these types of government policies are certainly mixed, so it's not clear-cut, as we learn from many featured contributors, including both global and regional ecosystem experts and practitioners. Readers may process the various viewpoints presented here and then form their own opinions. The debate on these two issues has persisted for some time and continues to do so; the discussion presented in this book is by no means new. Nevertheless, I hope that evaluating the topic in a different context sheds some new light and heightens awareness enough to move us collectively toward an optimal approach to tackle some of the region's problems once and for all.

Finally, no discussion about ecosystem development is complete without addressing culture. As elusive and vague as the concept is, culture can be the ultimate differentiator between societies. All the capital and pro-innovation policies and initiatives in the world will not make up for the lack of a wide enough innovation-oriented culture and entrepreneurial mindset. Interestingly, the reverse is not true. You can have insufficient capital, dysfunctional regulations, and a lack of support programs in a given ecosystem and still have successful examples of entrepreneurs and startups that found workarounds in order to survive and thrive. One such entrepreneur that comes to mind is Mo Ibrahim, the Sudanese-British entrepreneur who founded Celtel, the telecom he grew magnificently throughout Africa in spite of lacking local infrastructure and other fundamental ecosystem components. Obviously, he is an outlier and by no means your typical entrepreneur. Nevertheless, his story highlights the undeniable role of mindset and culture in an ecosystem, even when only embodied by small segments in society, and even in the absence of supportive factors.

The question then becomes, what exactly is an innovation- and entrepreneurship-friendly culture and how do we go about creating and nurturing one? In this chapter, we go to great lengths to unveil some of the mystique around this intangible, yet critical and often overlooked, building block of any ecosystem. One worthwhile insight is put forth by Efosa Ojomo, Global Prosperity Lead at Clayton Christensen Institute, Co-Founder and President of Poverty Stops Here, and Co-Author of *The Prosperity Paradox*. He says, "Culture is key to developing an ecosystem. The first thing I would say about culture is that it is not static. It is dynamic. Culture changes all the time. You go back a few hundred years ago, in America, they were burning women they thought were witches. Culture is something that evolves. The idea that culture and the behavior of individuals who live in societies are fixed—that, for example, 'Some regions have an entrepreneurial culture, they're hardworking, meanwhile others are not and that's the way it is'—is just not the case."

The above observation is foundational to any society—namely, the view that culture is not deterministic, its volitional. That is, it's inherently an implicit collective choice made by each society to seek to improve, stagnate, or regress in that department. There are plenty of examples from recent history of societies that have fluctuated in either direction. This notion that culture is fixed in stone, and looking at the past as an indication of future greatness (or the impossibility thereof), is simply not true. What matters is that we live in the present and the choice is ours; hence, while we can cherish our heritage, it has no impact on where we go from here.

With respect to the MENA region, three areas have been identified as particularly important to develop the right culture in the ecosystem: (1) recognize and enforce culture's linkage to prosperity, (2) promote bias for action, risk-taking, and a "give first" mentality, and (3) encourage open communication and healthy discussion. These themes were the ones most often repeated during the dozens of interviews I conducted in regard to this topic. While they're not meant to be exhaustive by any means, I trust they provide some important clues on culture development. I encourage you, the reader, to develop your own thesis on this topic after considering the various points of view here, relying on your own experiences and learning as well.

1. Create an Attractive Environment for Talent and Investment

Enhance living and working conditions

BADR JAFAR: There are obviously certain basic requirements for people to consider a place home. On a basic level, security, access to good healthcare, and access to good education are all key components, combined with a good live, work, and play environment. These are minimum requirements because without them, people are always going to consider any posting as a hardship post, and that's not sustainable in the long haul. It's always going to be a temporary move. The other critical factor is creating a sense of belonging. We need to find a better way in our region to make people who are not from a given country really feel like they belong there.

We're doing a good job in some ways, but we can do a lot better in others. Again, I'm talking more about human needs. We need to create an environment that, on the one hand, makes people feel at home but, on the other hand, leaves them with no doubt that they are living and working in a cutting-edge, innovative, and dynamic environment.

Among other things, that requires spending more on R&D because, broadly speaking as a region, we spend far less than 1% of GDP on R&D compared to the 2-3% that you see in most OECD nations. The vast majority of our spending goes to importing foreign technology rather than creating our own. If we're going to attract people to really come and invest, not just money and time but also their energy and creativity, then they need to feel that they're part of a system that's building something—not just buying and selling, but actually creating things.

RABEA ATAYA: The UAE, and increasingly the rest of the region, has done a pretty amazing job creating a very welcoming environment throughout the last 20 years or so that I've been here. To create a welcoming and attractive environment, you need to go through the hierarchy of needs, starting with safety and security, which is naturally very important to people. The fact that I feel comfortable that my children can move around freely in Dubai, without fear, and that my house is safe, in and of itself is just an amazing asset to have, particularly in today's world.

Beyond that, there are lots of other lifestyle-related variables. People ask when making career choices, "Is the educational system good?", "Is the healthcare system good?" and "What is the cost of incorporation and doing business?" On balance, a lot of these things have been great. I would actually say, for the most part, over the last 20-something years that I've been an entrepreneur in the region, I've seen the vast majority of these livability indexes in Dubai improve. Healthcare has improved, education has improved, access to talent has improved, infrastructure has improved. In general, I think the government has done a great job of moving the needle on most of these things and attracting international talent to live, work, and invest here and start new companies.

SAMIA MELHEM: Making the region more habitable—in terms of better urban design, better infrastructure, access to electricity, access to broadband, cybersecurity, etc.—is so critical to bringing in foreign investors, as opposed to having a vibrant IT industry that is outsourcing, which is a different model. Here, we're talking about both. If you look at Morocco and Tunisia, tourism really helps them. Upper-middle class or wealthy people are coming to summer in Morocco and Tunisia, and some of these people, perhaps the head of a firm, may decide to move to Tangier Industrial Park or other areas.

Having a strong, compelling message on industrial policy, strategic direction for technology, and overall prospects in a given country can help attract FDI. Inviting investors for tours can also help familiarize them with investment opportunities available locally.

OSMAN SULTAN: First and foremost, we need to create the right ecosystem, one that will make a person with an idea or a dream say, "This is the right place for me." That's what has happened in the UAE. This is why many entrepreneurs from Lebanon, Jordan, Egypt, Syria, Tunisia, Morocco and many other countries came to the UAE; they felt that, although the ecosystem is still evolving, they had a greater chance of success there, that the environment makes it easier for them to create value and succeed.

It is not enough to create an environment from a tech, infrastructure, regulations, or funding availability point of view. You need to create a living environment that incentivizes people to come, to live, and to bring their families. It is not only, "I'm here to develop my app, build a business, and become wealthy." It is also about, "I'm bringing my family and we will enjoy living here." Other countries in the region should also be looking to take a similar approach in order to induce those changes, just like the UAE has been doing for a while.

CHRISTOPHER SCHROEDER: Talent wants to go where they can win, period. A ton of diaspora talent would flock tomorrow to a region, and broader talent would follow as well, if and only if they think the rule of law would allow them to win and that they would be surrounded by other world-class talent. To the extent that an environment that is easy to do business in is created, more and more talent, companies, and investment will be channeled to the region.

ZIAD MOKHTAR: The transparency and availability of information are key elements in creating a welcoming, inclusive, and attractive environment. Information is what any company or investor needs in order to be able to assess their risks when coming to the region: information on markets, transactions, successes, failures, local or sector data, etc. Predictability is another key component. Without being able to roughly predict policies, laws, and regulations, any risk assessment would not stand the test of time.

TON VAN 'T NOORDENDE: First and foremost, conditions of life as well as connectedness are key to creating an attractive environment for outside talent and investment. For example, I think one of the reasons that Amsterdam, for example, has done so well in developing its ecosystem has to do with the fact that it has one of the best-connected airports in the world. This made it a natural gateway to Europe. It's also a particularly friendly city to live in, in terms of quality of life and living standards. This makes it that much more likely to lure people and businesses from Europe and other parts of the world, relative to other European cities. Also, the fact that English is widely spoken and the country is quite open and stable from a political standpoint is quite helpful.

Location, access, livability, language, openness, and stability are essential ingredients to prime an ecosystem. Historically, we see a similar dynamic in such places as London and Berlin, which have been able to attract talent even from warmer climate places. More recently, Barcelona and Lisbon have also demonstrated some of this pull effect for similar reasons.

Then other variables obviously come into play, regulatory framework or policy being one. Ease and cost of doing business is another. If you look at Eastern European companies, for example, most choose to either register as a limited company in London, where they raise capital, or in places like Amsterdam, or they register in Delaware in the US instead to avoid local complications. Taxation has some effect on making a particular environment attractive or not, depending on the local taxation structure and tax-exemption policies. However, I think it's a secondary variable since it's not materially conducive or prohibitive in the presence or lack of the other, more critical, conditions.

Develop incentives to lure the right outside inflow

MAZIN AL ZAIDI: Globally, venture capital firms are key to nurturing entrepreneurship, promoting innovation, and unlocking value. With VENTURE by Invest Saudi, we are bringing this capacity to Saudi Arabia in a much bigger way. For instance, in Q1 2019, we licensed 48 startups, versus 76 throughout all of 2018. With VENTURE by Invest Saudi, the momentum is accelerating, and we have set our targets much higher for 2020.

Saudi Arabia is doing a lot to create a more attractive and favorable business environment that inspires confidence and fosters ease for international players, not just in the startup space but across the full value chain. We have identified more than 300 economic reforms and have already implemented 45% of the planned reforms. Some of these include 100% foreign ownership in a range of new sectors. Also, we are adopting faster and less complicated business registration procedures, including the issuance of business visas and business licenses in less than 24 hours.

Finally, we are improving our legal infrastructure, including implementing a new insolvency law, establishing a commercial arbitration center and specialized commercial courts, updating the

Kingdom's corporate law to increase disclosure requirements, and enhancing protections for minority shareholders.

BADR JAFAR: We can do more, not just to attract talent, but also to retain it. We are living in a time in this region where border security is critical. An unintended consequence of stricter border controls, not just in our region but everywhere around the world, is to put a dampening effect on the flow of talent. That's not a value judgment, it's just the reality. The reality is that this is a real challenge and a real economic risk, and emirates like Dubai, Abu Dhabi and others are doing their utmost to try to balance our security imperative with our economic imperative to keep the doors open to attracting the best people as part of a viable, sustainable talent model.

SANGEET PAUL CHOUDARY: Attracting talent is a multifaceted issue. There are three different levels. The first level, the most basic, is that there should be an attractive tax regulation and compensation structure that works. That element shouldn't be pegged to existing local standards, but to global standards in order to attract global talent. That is the first prerequisite, which is not a systemic approach, but nevertheless helps get talent in the door.

Second, if you want to retain talent, what's important is to have a thriving industry that allows significant mobility for the talent in the region. In order to do that, the Middle East should not just look at industries and job markets at a country level. Many Middle Eastern countries are very small on their own, so you need to look at it from a regional level perspective and ask, "How can we use the liquidity and the scale at the regional level to boost certain industries, so that talent coming in can have more options to migrate, and to scale up, across that ecosystem?"

The third piece is the ability to easily start up new companies. This is where the Middle East needs to take a closer look at the whole system, because starting and owning companies is still highly regulated in the region. As long as that continues to be the case, it will be very difficult to attract entrepreneurial talent. Deregulating that and allowing ease of business startup and business ownership will then help to attract not just workers, but also entrepreneurial talent.

KEVIN O'LEARY: The regulatory environment greatly varies in the different jurisdictions in the region, but some have the basic premise that a foreigner cannot be a majority partner in that region. This is both good and bad. It's good in the sense that it forces you to form partnerships with someone who understands the local market and local culture. Meanwhile, it's bad in the sense that you don't have full control, or at least an equal position, in deciding on capital expenditures or liquidity, or how you're going to diversify or extract capital from businesses. So, you're balancing having local partners, who could potentially help you navigate the space and make the right connections, especially on the government side, with the fact that you don't have full control on decisions and execution as you see fit. That's a big debate, with pros and cons from both sides of the table.

MOHAMMED JAFFAR: One major challenge we have in some of our countries is that only nationals can fully own companies and properties. That creates a culture where someone is there just to make money and leave. If we can instead make expats feel accepted and that this is their home too, that they are more than welcome to invest in and own hard assets for the long haul, there will be a greater impact on the country both socially and economically.

Contrast this approach with Europe, for example. If I'm an Arab person and I go to Europe, I can own my business, my house, and my real estate. Why can't a European or any foreign person similarly come to our part of the world and fully own his own business and fully own his own properties, without having to involve a local owner? Of course, some Arab countries have made reforms on this front and are reaping the benefits as a result. Still, other laggard countries need to change.

Young people now are more international and more accepting of other cultures, faiths, and backgrounds than perhaps we ever were in the past. This a very positive sign. Also, some progress has been made on the regulations side. So, in many ways, we're definitely heading down the right path. I just hope that we head there faster, so we're able to compete with the rest of the world and not stay behind. From my perspective, the question is not if we will change, but when and how fast.

ABDULAZIZ AL LOUGHANI: If we take foreign ownership in the Arab world today, for example, even with the laws that permit 100% foreign ownership, the cost of licensing is often prohibitive and poses a barrier to entry. It's also difficult for foreign companies to operate locally in terms of the work permits they need and which areas they are permitted to operate in. We still have room to improve on making foreign ownership equal to local citizens'. It's not yet equal when it comes to ease of doing business, or ease of moving people and goods, for example.

There is also a lot of room to improve on an Arab League level in terms of the connection and the standardization of trade laws and visa regulations. I think that will significantly help entrepreneurs freely maneuver and move in this part of the world and make it easier to attract talent in general. Obviously, in regard to the venture laws, there's plenty of room to improve on share classes, on preferred rights for different kind of shareholders, on shareholders' agreements, term sheets, and so on and so forth.

FOUAD JERYES: There are a lot of mental and physical barriers for international investors to come to the region, whether they're due to the general economic and media outlook or the proximity to where these investors are based. For example, it would be very rare for a US investor to be convinced to fly at least 12 hours every quarter for a board meeting. There are just too many opportunities in their own backyards for them to give our region the time of day.

Considering the proximal, cultural, and economic barriers, the regional governments have to be the catalyst for change. They need to knock on the doors of these European, US, or Asian funds and provide them with incentives, access, and perhaps even the initial funds to deploy in their respective markets. Once these seeding investments start showing promise and familiarizing these foreign funds with the landscape here, they will hopefully come back to deploy more of their own money. The most important bit would be that in doing this, we would have not only widened the availability of capital at different stages, but we would have also broadened the thesis for doing so.

MENA-BASED VS. INTERNATIONAL INVESTORS TREND

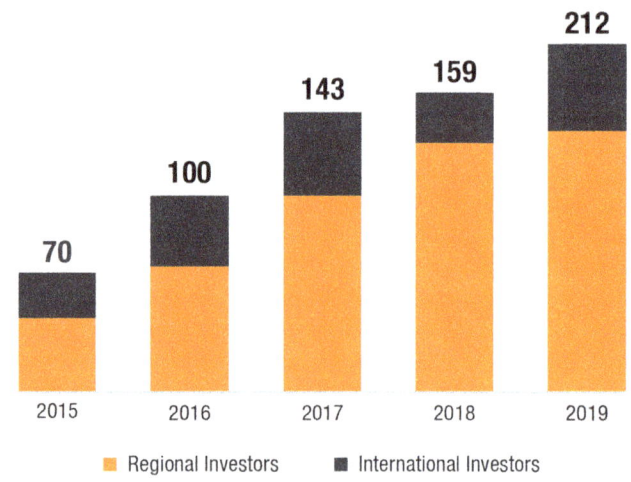

Source: MAGNiTT MENA Venture Investment Summary 2019 (www.magnitt.com)

AHMED El ALFI: Attracting the right international players to MENA is all about having free flow across the region's borders, whether that's the free flow of capital, the freedom of talent to move, or the free flow of goods and services. Investors fear they won't be able to repatriate their capital gains, and they are concerned about the inconsistent implementation of the law, the difficulty of relocating talented individuals to other MENA countries, and bringing teams together across borders.

Several European countries now offer more lenient visa and residency programs to developers, which triggered an influx of talent into those countries on top of an already healthy pipeline of developers for startups to recruit from. Meanwhile, some countries in the GCC still require 51% local ownership. The good news is that most of these requirements are increasingly being waived today, either directly or through the establishment of free zones, in order to encourage entrepreneurs and startups. It's now much easier in Egypt for 100% foreign-owned companies to operate and, in a very significant change, it's now also possible in Saudi Arabia, too. Still, investors are particularly wary of investing offshore given a lack of consistency among jurisdictions in regard to dispute resolution laws or application of the law. This still poses a perception problem for outside investors looking to invest in the region.

Overall, we can also do a better job when it comes to self-promotion. For example, certain countries in other parts of the world are perceived more positively than our countries, yet they are much more difficult to actually do business in. They are much harder to set up companies in, much more difficult when it comes to dispute resolution, and much more difficult to operate in generally. Yet, many enjoy a better international reputation than our countries simply because they do a better job of promoting themselves as a nurturing environment for startups. Perception matters, and I recommend that governments in the region do some serious evaluation and focus more on promoting the strengths and positive aspects of each ecosystem.

WALID HANNA: The UAE is a prime example of how to attract investments, talent, and successful brands to the region. Most other Arab countries have been, sadly, successful at doing the opposite, namely draining their best brains to outside the region. Long-term residency visas, better compensation packages, and employee stock ownership plans are proven ingredients to attract the right professionals.

In Abu Dhabi, Hub71 and the Ghadan initiative—backed by

Mubadala—has started to win this battle by providing all of the ingredients required to build a local tech industry. MENA's financial institutions should aid the region by participating in talent retention. One solution would be to implement grants for students excelling in secondary and higher education, thus giving them a reason to stay or to return after they leave.

YOUSEF HAMZA: Data, information, and transparency about the ecosystem are key, much like the one covered in this book, *Ecosystem Arabia*, as well as Amir Hegazi's previous book, *Startup Arabia*. Dubai does a great job of informing the world about the UAE and the great progress we are making. So I think it's about the narrative and getting ourselves out there into more countries and offering visibility and clarity on who we are and what we stand for. Despite this, I still see newspaper articles coming out of several European countries warning against doing business in Dubai due to horrible misconceptions about the legal and social environment. They miss conveying a full, accurate picture of what's happening here.

In order to attract talent, the region needs to consider different methods of longevity of status, such as longer visa periods or quasi "green cards" to attract people to build a future here for themselves and their families. That way, they will dedicate themselves to the region and choose to build their future empires from within our borders, benefiting all within. Strong talent in turn creates good investment opportunities, which are required to attract investment, followed by legislative security and clear paths to exit.

OMAR CHRISTIDIS: Many GCC countries have started to realize that they need to address the status of foreign talent in their countries. Globally, the competition between nations and economies in today's world is really a competition for talent. We're competing over talent and so we've seen both Saudi Arabia and the UAE launch these kinds of quasi-permanent residency type programs, which is a significant shift in the way they look at foreigners in the country. In effect, they are saying, "There is a place for you here in the long term."

However, freedom of movement, getting visas, and getting in and out of countries are still very difficult. If we want our countries to be more attractive to global talent, it needs to be easier to hire someone in Beirut, which it is not, or hire someone from Ukraine in Jordan. It is still difficult to hire foreign labor. I know in Lebanon, you have to show that you looked in the local market, but there are no equivalent skill sets available and there's a whole process.

We also really need to leverage the diaspora community. For me, this is another key priority point right now. There are huge diasporas all over the world, especially in Europe and North America. These guys have built very successful businesses. They've gone on to achieve great things. Amr Awadallah, for example, is Vice President at Google Cloud and was Co-Founder of Cloudera, a massive multibillion-dollar company. Similarly, many Lebanese and Arab entrepreneurs abroad have started robotics companies, hardware, and AI companies. Those guys can play a really critical role in bridging both the culture and logistical gaps between these markets and could bring some part of their value chain back to their home markets.

How do we get more of these guys who have their companies in London, Paris, New York, or San Francisco to establish a back office in Beirut, Cairo, or Amman? How do we get them to invest some of their money as angels into startups in these markets? They already have a lot of credibility in those markets where they operate, so bringing these entrepreneurs back brings a lot more credibility to the region. They have the networks. We need to look at the diaspora, engage with them, and see how they can play this bridge role.

PHILIP BAHOSHY: Cost is certainly the most prohibitive variable. I just hired someone from Egypt, the first person I had to bring to the UAE, and it proved to be more costly and complex than I had anticipated. You have to get their visa attested, there is a cost to having them go through the insurance process, and the cost of actually issuing their visa as well. These are all additional costs that I'm having to incur because I found great talent internationally that I want to bring to the UAE. These charges are definitely inhibiting the free inflow of talent to the different jurisdictions by adding an additional layer of friction. The second thing that would help is to make it easier to outsource my staff—for example, being able to employ someone in Lebanon without having to have a Lebanese entity, or to employ in Saudi Arabia out of a UAE-based license.

There are other areas of friction. Take something as simple as VoIP here in the UAE, for example. If you want to create global-minded startups and attract international investments, you need to be able to allow people to communicate freely online as is the case for the rest of the world. You do that by removing the restrictions on VoIP, which have become a pain point for cross-border communication.

Another area that needs improvement is the outdated immigration laws in many jurisdictions across the region. If you're building a tech company, for example, you'd be looking to be in that country for 10 to 15 years to be able to make a significant impact or get acquired. What rights do you have as a founder after 10 years of spending your hard-earned time in terms of becoming a national, or just getting a green card, or some kind of recognition for the work that you've done in creating an impact in that jurisdiction over the years? That's an area in serious need of reform across the region.

ANAND CHOPRA-MCGOWAN: I think the MENA region needs to think about what version of its experience can be exported and scaled, whether it's in the form of hosting more international conferences, more exchange programs, more internship programs, or more job shadowing programs. Those interaction points can help to break down some of the preconceived notions that a lot of people in the West might have about working and living in the MENA region. That's relatively simple.

The more complex issues come down to thorny areas like visa restrictions and ease of travel in the region. It also comes down to infrastructure and how simple it is for someone from a different region to visit, move to, and work out of the place. Language is also a big factor. English being the international language of business means that places where English is dominant have a much easier time accessing the global market. You see that in places like India and Singapore for example, among many others, and obviously Dubai and the UAE in the region. Those are bigger challenges to tackle.

It is also important that infrastructure and interlink points need to be made to enable more business and connections to happen between MENA and rest of the world. That said, MENA's aim should be to retain its own heritage, experience, and traditions, and bring those to big global problems and try to come up with new solutions from its own perspectives. It's not easy by any means, but it's achievable.

JOY AJLOUNY: I was recently in California and, my God, the abundance of talent there is frightening. Meanwhile, it's so hard in Dubai to find great talent. Everyone says, "You've got the greatest engineers," when the reality is that the best engineers are coming out of China, India, and Ukraine and they're wanted and hunted by every country in the world. They're wanted in Germany, they're wanted in the US, they're wanted in the UK, they're wanted by all the top companies who are searching for talent.

The talent of the best engineers is badly needed and the world's best companies constantly hunt them, companies like Google, Facebook, and Apple. Great engineers often come to the US to get their education at Stanford, Harvard, Yale, and so forth. Then, just before they graduate, Google, Facebook, and Apple are already at the table at these universities recruiting them. And what is the top incentive they offer? US residency or "green card. They're, in effect, giving them an opportunity to have a life and stability in a country where they don't have to leave.

As a local startup here in the UAE or in the region at large, how do you compete with that? How can you attract an engineer from an Indian Institute of Technology and give them an opportunity to come to Dubai or to Saudi Arabia, or anywhere in the region for that matter, without strong incentives? You're already at a disadvantage against those global markets. What are you going to offer them to outbid competing offers they're getting elsewhere—where the US, Germany, and Canada, and others are offering them residency or even citizenship, and they're offering them a permanent place to live for them and their families?

If you look at the US, for example, one of the things that made America great is it attracts talent from all over the world and give them an opportunity to go there. The US is not built on buildings; it's built on brains and people, and a strong middle class. They brought Einstein to the US, back in the day. The founders of Google are great examples as well, and the list goes on. Similarly, I strongly believe the MENA ecosystem will change dramatically if we can give people permanent residency. You can attract the brightest minds in the world if you can give them security. That's a big step for the region. Giving people a great job and a reason to leave their country, and to come and build a life with their families, I believe will be a game changer.

A big part of the challenge with resolving these issues fast enough is there's often a disconnect between the people who can help and the people who need to be helped. I believe the intention to improve things is definitely there. The gap is often as a result of not interacting enough with the young startups on the ground to fully understand their pain points and how these issues affect them and impact the ecosystem.

MOHAMED ANOUAR MAAROUF: In Tunisia, we aim to create an attractive environment to outsiders by ensuring there is an adequate legal framework. The Startup Act represents a legal framework that is open to all; we didn't specify that investors should have Tunisian nationality in the Act, in order to attract and build trust with foreign investors. Furthermore, we set up a network of ambassadors for Tunisia who can speak about the local investment opportunity for international players.

We also want to open up on the African front, given our recognition of the massive economic opportunities emerging in the continent. This is why we entered Smart Africa and established excellent relations with neighboring countries and other Arab countries in Africa.

We also have a legal structure that aligns with the European Union's. The European Union includes a large number of countries and has important exchanges with Tunisia, as well as the significant numbers of the Tunisian diaspora that are based there. We're trying to attract these people as investors in Tunisia so they can benefit from this framework.

We equally aim to attract foreigners through training, another aspect that can support the ecosystem. We are providing training to tens of thousands of foreigners, and especially Africans, at universities in Tunisia. Tunisia has a decent reputation for the quality of its higher education. This further helps Tunisia be more attractive internationally, as it becomes a place where foreigners can receive education, establish startups, invest, and succeed, and where investors can find strong talent that may be Tunisian or from other nationalities.

All in all, this delivers a positive image of Tunisia as a startup-friendly environment. This is why we also set up a program called Smart Tunisia that supports startups and ensures they don't face administrative hurdles. We find solutions to the problems startups face and support them through recruiting talent and training programs. We also provide a number of benefits and incentives for companies that aim to invest in Tunisia, which serves our objective of building an image of Tunisia as a hub for African startups.

ELISSA FREIHA: As far as attracting foreign players to do business and invest in the region, we have to speak their language back at them. We can walk the walk our way, but we have to talk the talk their way. We have to make those international players see the financial opportunities that lie within the region through hard data, showcasing the numbers, and making a convincing case for why they should focus on the region.

One of the things that gets people very excited when I go to Silicon Valley and I share information about the region is that the ARPU (average revenue per user) tends to be much higher in the GCC than in other developing markets. If you look at online video and social media consumption in Saudi Arabia, for example, you see incredible statistics with phenomenal potential for international players to really tap into. And yet we don't share enough of that data with the outside world. It's imperative to be able to communicate the real potential economic growth that the region has to offer and showcase that it presents a thriving hub in this part of the world. So we can do a lot more to promote ourselves better in the world and counter the existing narrow perception.

Leverage the power of inclusivity and diversity

MOHAMMED JAFFAR: I lived in the UK for most of my life. I was educated there as a child, and I was also educated in Kuwait in my early years, and there was a big difference between the two in terms of quality. It's not that the people are smarter in the West, it's just that they have more respect and tolerance for different cultures and personal differences in general, which is unfortunately not always the case in this part of the world, at least relatively speaking.

How can we create a more inclusive culture? It starts at the individual level. We each have to lead by example. We have to not just talk about it, we have to do it. We need to educate our young people more about that, and about accepting other people who are different from us. We have to accept other people just like we accept ourselves, regardless of how different they may be from us. We have to educate ourselves to be more accepting of other people, other faiths, other religions, and other backgrounds. I think the more we are accepting of that, the more we can work together better, and not just work with people similar to us. We have to be able to work well with people who are different from us. This is certainly not new or something I just made up myself; this is all mentioned in the teachings of Islam. Unfortunately, we don't apply it enough, or we apply what we like and omit the rest.

ELISSA FREIHA: Diversity is critical to building the ecosystem in the region, especially with respect to female inclusion. If you consider the concept of "women's empowerment," it implies that women don't have the power within themselves. That's what it suggests implicitly. I actually know a lot of women in the space who reject the word "empowerment" to begin with, but it's just an easy way to categorize. So I think it's more about female inclusion and recognition. It's about diversity first and foremost. In a region that's incredibly diverse, that's one of our strengths.

We have the opportunity to make true innovation happen, because not only do we have a diverse population, but we also face immense amounts of struggle and hardship just to live. Just our infrastructure, for example—electricity, Wi-Fi, water processing, access to food—these are real issues that affect many parts of this region. Solutions to such massive problems will naturally come from emerging markets like ours, where we not only face similar challenges, but where our experiences and perceptions are so diverse. In that sense, the region is a hotbed for innovation in such areas. You're not likely going to get the next billion-person solution for a massive emerging-market problem from five guys from Connecticut, for example. You're more likely to get it from, say, an Egyptian, a Lebanese, an Emirati, an Indian, and a Briton all working together and bringing their completely different backgrounds and perspectives to the table.

It's not just about cultural diversity, but also about religious diversity and gender diversity. As long as you're bringing different perceptions to the table, the results will be more original, more successful, more creative, and more sustainable. As such, women are one key component of that equation. Unfortunately, women's empowerment is something that, as a general rule, the Middle East is still very much behind on. It still has some of the lowest ranked countries in the world in terms of female equality and women's rights.

GENDER DISTRIBUTION AMONG FOUNDERS BY YEAR IN MENA

This figure demonstrates that the ratio of gender distribution has remained relatively consistent over the years, with female founder's ratio ranging from 12% to 19%.

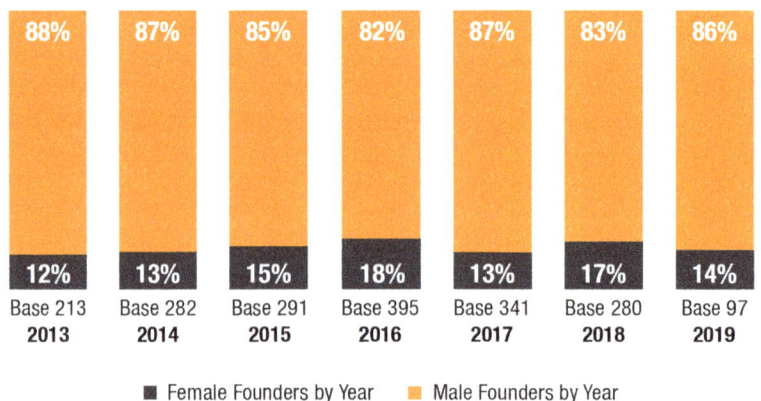

| Female Founders by Year | Male Founders by Year |

Source: ArabNet Business Intelligence Investment Report 2019 (www.arabnet.me)

I strongly believe that women-led startups are an undervalued opportunity in the region both literally and figuratively. Women-led startups tend to have lower valuations than male-led startups, yet women-led startups are 60% more likely to produce more returns with half the funding, twice as many returns with 50% of the funding, and 30% more jobs. In that sense, I see it as two-and-a-half times the opportunity. I don't want to say it's a vertical, because obviously it is sector-agnostic, but it's something that I'm excited about and continue to support and invest in as a smart investment decision, not just as a moral play.

KEVIN O'LEARY: I have personally invested in a lot of startups, over 50 of them in the last 11 years, and the majority of my returns have come from the companies run by women. This is something I started to notice seven years ago. There may be some reasons for that. Perhaps women mitigate risk very well. They are highly skilled at allocating time; that old adage, "if you want something done, give it to a busy mother," is a common trait in every culture. I have also observed in my experience that they are extremely good at keeping the mission intact in small companies and keeping companies focused.

If you look at the UAE, the government there is 50% women-staffed now. It's partly mandated, but it's also pragmatic because they're very good managers. This is an area that's challenging for Saudi Arabia. Obviously, women have not had gender equality there for a while but that's certainly changing now in the last two years. This is the right time and the right move to make, which is making Saudi Arabia increasingly interesting for investors, because you want that diversity. It's just the right thing to do from an investment point of view. So, there are plenty of economic reasons to focus on providing gender equality.

Now, while I'm a big proponent of encouraging gender equality, I wouldn't go so far as advocating for mandating female hiring quotas. Such mandates don't work from my perspective. Supporting diversity and gender equality doesn't mean you have to abandon competence. I have observed countless examples where this approach has led to disastrous outcomes. Your main criteria for hiring must be related to hiring competent men and women, and not just because of gender. They have to know what they're doing; it cannot be forced based on an artificial figure of X percentage have to be women in the workplace. This wouldn't work anymore than quotas for any particular nationality or age group. Instead, I go back to saying that when it comes specifically to hiring, competence is the greatest equalizer. You cannot overcome sexism or racism by reverting to the opposite end of the spectrum, which essentially becomes its own form of discrimination. You have to try to neutralize discrimination of any kind, whereby you provide an equal opportunity and support to all, and let individual competence be the deciding factor on who lands where, regardless of the outcome in terms of percentages of the various groups.

GENDER DISTRIBUTION AMONG FOUNDERS IN MENA

While the proportion of female founders across the MENA region has remained consistent (and low) at 14% over the years, gender diversity in local startup and tech ecosystem is increasingly becoming more of a hot topic. Local governments are pushing for greater women empowerment initiatives and increased female participation in the labor force.

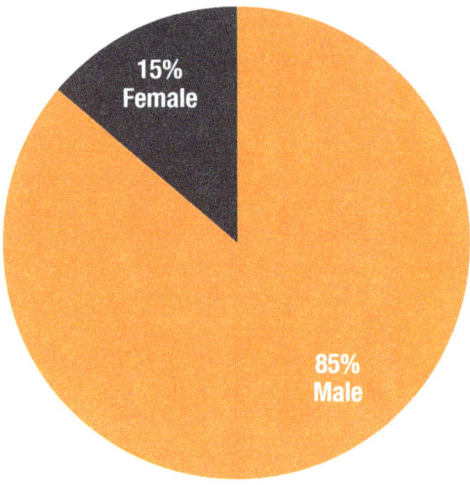

Base: 1,543

Cumulative years: 2004-2018

Source: ArabNet Business Intelligence Investment Report 2019 (www.arabnet.me)

RAMEZ SHEHADI: Diversity fosters growth, fosters creativity, fosters inclusivity and fosters positive change – more women in positions of leadership is a must.

While we have seen strides in the region in support of the empowerment of women in the workforce, much more still needs to be done. Multiple case studies show the positive impact women have when they are in organizations and institutions, and especially when they are in leadership roles, and we – the private and public sectors – need to continue to support in realizing this.

It is supremely exciting to see the big steps that are happening in nations across the region – it's encouraging to see the sea change happening in the Gulf, that perhaps has already been in motion in parts of the Levant and North Africa. A lot more across MENA can be done. The percentage of women in the labor force in the Gulf must be improved. It is absolutely within the ability of leadership, both public and private, to make that happen. It can be in a corporate environment or even in an entrepreneurial environment in the private sector.

STEVE CASE: Diversity around access to capital is paramount to an ecosystem. In the US, only 10% of venture capital goes to women and only 1% goes to African Americans. It is critical to stop the flow of capital from going to the same people, in the same places, with the same ideas. By making entrepreneurship more inclusive, we will produce a deeper and richer bench of products and services. We will also level the playing field so that more people in more communities have an onramp to economic prosperity.

JULIE LENZER: One thing that I see that doesn't work, or at least work optimally, across ecosystems is the lack of diversity. How can you drive stronger participation by underrepresented groups? True innovation is found in diversity of thought. By making sure that you're including your potential customers in your ecosystem as entrepreneurs and people who are contributing to that innovation economy, you're making sure that you're getting solutions that actually match what your customers need. This means including more women as well as other groups with different backgrounds or national origins. Without that diversity of background, thought, understanding, and insight, a lot of good businesses are going to struggle to create innovative products and services.

JONATHAN ORTMANS: A large consumer segment—women—has been an afterthought for most tech companies around the world. I would invest in companies that are offering products in markets where female tech usage and purchase decision-making are crucial to company growth. New and young firms that effectively tailor to these consumers will probably reap the rewards of tapping into that market. Thinking about diverse markets, however, always requires encouraging diverse startup teams. Succeeding in that will benefit all startups. Diverse founding teams have proven to be more successful at raising capital, among other metrics of startup success.

JOSH LERNER: Doing philanthropic activities to engage women in an ecosystem is not a mere "nice to do," it's an economic imperative. If you look at the studies around women-led companies, they are actually more capital-efficient and have better outcomes over the long haul on average than their non-diverse counterparts. I believe strongly that good ideas and opportunities are not relegated to any one gender, ethnicity, or geography. Unless and until we're able to tap into all of the good ideas of all of our people, we're risking missing out on some great innovations that could save our planet, cure cancer, or take us to the next industry, the next knowledge generation, or the next technology revolution if we don't fully engage and utilize all minds and talents in the ecosystem.

That said, I'm not a big believer in quotas and setting aside allocations saying, "Well, we have to hire or we have to fund 30% women." It's nice to have incentives but you don't want to start just investing in somebody because they're a woman, you want to invest in somebody because you believe the person is up to the task at hand. So, it's a fine line between healthy support and an artificial boost.

On a side note, as it relates to women in the Middle East, when I first came to the region to attend the MENA Business Women Summit, I was struck by how incredibly intelligent and driven the women were. That's a real asset. I was pleasantly surprised to see the caliber of top women executives and entrepreneurs there, and I was glad to see the women at the top helping lift up their sisters. I did some work with the Bahraini Women's Business Association as well and saw a similar dynamic. There's incredible potential in the region. There are incredible assets: really educated people, good flow of capital, and good ideas. I think we'll continue to see a lot of great women-led businesses and great things in general coming out of that region.

RABEA ATAYA: When it comes to diversity in the ecosystem, I'm seeing a lot of successful women entrepreneurs in the region. We also conduct women in the workplace surveys and it always impresses me that, while the assumption from outside the Middle East is that Arab women are discriminated against in the workplace, what you actually find is that most Arab women in the workplace view themselves as getting fair treatment at work. When asked about their workplace concerns, it is less about discrimination and more about what employers can provide to help them both be better with their families and at work. Things like flexible work hours and benefits that help their families, in the form of insurance, education, etc., are far more often cited as areas for improvement than any discrimination-related issues.

I also find that women are actually well represented and increasingly more broadly represented in workplaces across the region. Obviously, Saudi Arabia has made tremendous strides in this area recently. I'm always amazed these days when I visit Saudi businesses how many women are in the workplace and have prominent positions, and how much they've improved the overall work environment. A lot of positive, exciting changes are happening there on this front.

JOY AJLOUNY: One area where positive and promising reforms are taking place is with respect to female inclusion. When it comes to women's empowerment, I believe it has to be driven from women who are influencers in the region. The real change has to be organic and not always top-down. Take the women in Saudi Arabia, for example. They always struck me as smart, hungry, and driven. They want to make a difference, they want to get out of the house, they want to work and contribute, and they're conscientious. I've been very impressed with the Saudi women whom I've hired.

When you give a woman a paycheck, you give a woman her dignity and her freedom. In my view, nothing changes a woman more—not marriage, not children—than her earning a paycheck. The amount of satisfaction a woman feels in earning her own money is life-changing and enriching on a personal level, and ultimately on society as a whole.

I am optimistic. I am seeing a lot of change recently in Saudi Arabia in particular, so I think we're on the right track. I believe women are allowed to travel now without permission. If they're over 18 years of age, they don't need any permission from their family members—I think that's a great change. There are a lot more women in the workplace than ever before in Saudi Arabia who are productive and self-sufficient. All these are very encouraging signs.

HEATHER HENYON: I believe there is a significantly dispropor-tionate rate of female founders in the MENA region compared to markets like the US and Europe. Anecdotally, we believe that female founders account for 40-50% of entrepreneurs in MENA. In the UAE, more than 30% of the businesses with more than $100,000 in revenues are set up and run by women, in comparison to 13% in Silicon Valley. 60% of business leaders in Bahrain are women and 40% of business owners in Lebanon are women.

We know from studies done by groups like First Round Capital, Boston Consulting Group, McKinsey, and the World Bank that women tend to be more capital-efficient while generating more revenue, by and large, than men. Unfortunately, only 2% of venture capital in the US went to women entrepreneurs and 14% went to mixed teams in 2018.

As such, at Mindshift Capital, we created the first gender lens VC fund in the MENA region. We focus on investing in female founders as well as helping develop products or services that are created for women, by women. We also push to increase women's presence and impact in the value chain, whether as entrepreneurs, co-founders, leaders, employees, or customers. We apply a gender lens to all of our investments, ensuring that at least one female founder or co-founder is on the management team. We believe that this approach gives us a competitive advantage, as we tend to understand the founders, their products, and their customers better than other investors and we tap into opportunities often overlooked by other investors in the region.

VERA FUTORJANSKI: I have been particularly fascinated by the number of female entrepreneurs participating in our programs at 500 Startups, and with local talent in general, both female and male. Interestingly, the proportion of female graduates getting STEM degrees in the Arab world is 40%, compared to 20% in the US. In fact, in the UAE and Saudi Arabia, the number even reaches 80%, according to Gulf News.

Generally speaking, I am very impressed by Arab women, in the private as well as the public sector—women I have worked with in the Prime Minister's Office, women I came across in other government entities, and women entrepreneurs I have met across the region. I wish that the Western world knew more about their determination, resilience, and grace and changed their stereotypes of Arab women. In the Dubai government for example, almost 70% of employees are women, and 30% of ministers are women.

I consider it important to emphasize that female founders are strong globally. Boston Consulting Group ran a study called MassChallenge, concluding that startups founded or co-founded by women are more capital-efficient: they garner less in investments but generate more revenue. Women-owned startups even deliver twice as much per dollar invested than those owned by men, the study showed. Hence, it is difficult to comprehend why only 2% of all US VC dollars went to female founders in 2017, according to PitchBook. It is encouraging to see that 2018 saw an all-time high for investments in female-founded tech companies, with 17% of all venture dollars invested globally in companies with at least one female founder, according to Crunchbase. That said, there is still so much to be done for the ecosystem to be more inclusive and female-friendly, hence the reason I decided to be in the VC space. We need more women in VC globally and in MENA.

NUMBER OF FEMALE FOUNDERS BY GEOGRAPHY IN MENA

When examining the ratio of female founders by market, the data indicates that the Levant continues to exhibit the highest proportion of female founders in MENA, with Jordan and Lebanon at 20%. Tunisia and Morocco display low female to male proportions. Cultural factors seem to affect female participation in startups, such as pressure from family to find a stable job with low stress levels. Private and public sector initiatives and awareness campaigns could help boost female participation, hence decrease the disparity between male and female founders.

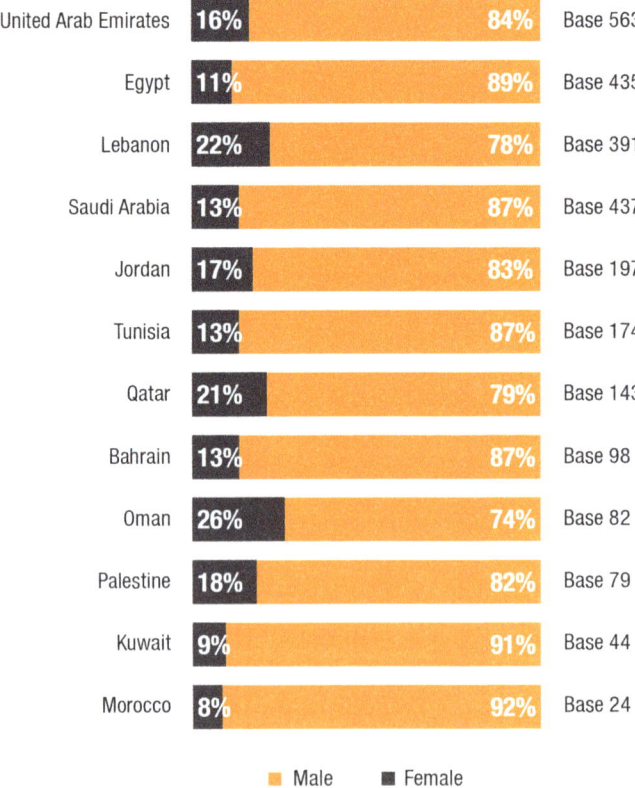

Country	Female	Male	Base
United Arab Emirates	16%	84%	Base 563
Egypt	11%	89%	Base 435
Lebanon	22%	78%	Base 391
Saudi Arabia	13%	87%	Base 437
Jordan	17%	83%	Base 197
Tunisia	13%	87%	Base 174
Qatar	21%	79%	Base 143
Bahrain	13%	87%	Base 98
Oman	26%	74%	Base 82
Palestine	18%	82%	Base 79
Kuwait	9%	91%	Base 44
Morocco	8%	92%	Base 24

■ Male ■ Female

Source: ArabNet Business Intelligence Investment Report 2019 (www.arabnet.me)

DEEMAH ALYAHYA: When it comes to women in the IT sector in Saudi Arabia, we don't have a problem attracting women to science and technology fields; the interest is certainly there. The issue then is follow-through in terms of facilitating their education and training to lead to the right employment channels. The efforts of the Ministry of Communication and IT to increase the employment of women in this sector have been quite remarkable. It's now at 13% and growing, higher than ever.

That said, focusing on promoting female talent in remote areas is very important. We tend to focus on the major cities and neglect remote areas. We need to provide women with opportunities in such places. This is a key driver in transforming our digital economy. It's critical for women to be more engaged in the ecosystem as founders and investors. Women possess empathy and care, which makes them natural nurturers and caregivers in whichever environments they operate in. This is especially important in a startup setting, where there is greater need for mentorship, care, and attention.

HISHAM ELARABY: Today in the Middle East, men are three times more likely than women to participate in the workforce. However, the tech space can be, and is becoming, an avenue to unlock the untapped potential of women in the workforce in the MENA region. Tech jobs lend themselves well to remote work and freelancing, offering women more flexibility in terms of time and mobility. Similarly, because our classes, at Udacity, are held online, students can study remotely in the privacy of their homes and determine when and where they want to study.

In Saudi Arabia, one of the largest markets in the region for Udacity, women are strong participants in our programs. Over the last couple of years, we have had more than 11,000 women apply for scholarships for the Udacity Nanodegree program, making up 48% of the total applicant pool. We have also had more than 1,500 Saudi women graduate from our Nanodegree programs, making up roughly 55% of the Nanodegree graduate pool. One example is Noora, who had recently moved to Riyadh to raise a family with her husband and signed up for Udacity's Front-End Nanodegree program. Halfway through the program, Noora discovered she was pregnant with her first child. She kept studying and is now both a mother of a baby girl and a front-end developer for Riyadh Bank. Many of our women graduates go on to become mentors for future cohorts of students; 35% of Udacity's network of mentors in Saudi Arabia are women. We hope to see this number increase over time as more and more companies in the region provide opportunities for women to take their rightful role in the local economy.

2. Foster Education for The Next Generation of Entrepreneurs

Reform outdated curriculums

HISHAM ELARABY: From an upskilling perspective, regional governments are trying to play the role of catalysts. MENA governments have traditionally been large players in education; on average MENA spends around 19% of government budgets on education, compared with a 15% global average.

While traditional education institutions in the region build fairly strong core literacies in math, for instance, a majority of surveyed CEOs see the system as failing to prepare youth for employment, and more than three-quarters of students are unhappy with the education in their country.

In recent years, governments have turned to more non-traditional models to create tech literacy and capabilities in the market. They usually come in the form of public-private partnerships with a mandate to drive talent competitiveness and address youth unemployment, which is quite high in the MENA region relative to other regions worldwide.

BADR JAFAR: I have recently been appointed to the UNESCO Futures of Education International Commission, so I have been more actively thinking about the topic of educational reforms. In general, my view is that the current education systems in place around the world are not fit for purpose. I'm also concerned that the skill sets that are being taught at schools and universities are not always relevant and well suited to the era that we're in right now, or where we're going. If you consider the World Economic Forum's projection that 80% of the jobs that people will be doing in 2030 don't even exist today, then to a degree we're shooting in the dark. The real question is how education systems can change to accommodate the fast-changing and uncertain environment that we are living in.

I was reflecting on this the other day, and I know that this is a bit "out there," but try for a moment to think about education and academic qualifications like a driver's license. To qualify for a driver's license, you need to do a certain amount of baseline learning and testing. Once you have your license, you are qualified to drive, but every five years or so in many jurisdictions you need to go back for some retesting, even if it's just to retest your eyesight. That is because they need to make sure your eyes are still working, your reflexes are still okay, and you are still equipped to drive. Additionally, the environment you drive in might have changed. The roads might be different, the regulations might be different. So, just because you qualified five years ago, it doesn't mean you're necessarily as qualified today.

Now, if we apply the same logic to education, particularly in the dynamic environment we live in today, then you would start with a baseline higher education that might only take a year or two. You would then also be required to maintain your education qualification every few years, since much of what you learned previously may have become outdated or irrelevant. Perhaps you could go back to the same institution, or another, to get a refresher and become requalified, so to speak. The cost of such a program could potentially be absorbed by your employer, which would be an investment they are making in the upskilling of their workforce. I really think something radical like this could work if we're going to make sure that we are really staying fresh, charged, and resilient, and if we are going to be able to respond to all of the changing paradigms that we're seeing across the various sectors of our economy.

Another area of education that I would like to see more emphasis on is critical thinking. I don't think we focus on these skills anywhere near as much as we should. A lot can be done to teach youth how to process and evaluate information more effectively, and to expose them more to broader areas of knowledge, particularly in the humanities, including philosophy and the arts. If you look back at every era of great transformation and advancement throughout history, including the Islamic Golden Age, you will always find it took place at the intersection of science and the humanities. Fast forward to today— we've lost that perspective. I think we're partly losing out because the arts have arguably been underappreciated and underutilized in schools compared with hard-core sciences. But for our future, the humanities and human values will be most critical in order to humanize more of what we do as opposed to just turning out and processing data.

SAMI MAHROUM: When we look at education, especially early education, we need to distinguish between private schooling and public schooling. I see private schooling adopting a lot of the latest thinking in terms of training and preparing the next generation of entrepreneurs. For instance, there's a great focus on project-based work, problem-solving, communication, time management, confidence, self-esteem, teamwork, etc. All of these are critical skills, which are now spread through the curriculum adopted in private schools.

While I cannot speak for the whole region, I know from my professional encounters during my visits to Jordan, Lebanon, and few other countries that that's not the case when it comes to public schools. Government-run schools tend to be still stuck in dated learning methods, in the old-fashioned style, both in their teaching approach and curriculum. There is too much focus on historical implants, repetition, and sentimentality. You also see an imbalanced focus in the curriculum, focusing on medieval times—medieval poets, writers, concepts, and ideas—as opposed to new skills, new technology, new concepts, new ideas, and new values in the world.

The public school system in the region tends to try to reproduce and be inspired by what they perceive to be the "Golden Age" of the region, in medieval times. Certainly, it's important to be connected to your heritage and to understand the strength of your civilization, science, arts, philosophy, history, and other subjects from the past, but we need to also equip youth with the modern tools they need to make them more effective in their future lives.

There is a clear split between the private schools and public schools from what I've seen, which might be reflected in society eventually as two separate mindsets and patterns. One is oriented toward the 21st century and the other is oriented toward medieval centuries.

ALISÉE DE TONNAC: If we look at the education system in emerging markets, including the vast majority of the MENA region, it's a very outdated industry in the sense that it's not in tune enough with the times. It's still, for the most part, trying to drill down talent using skills and competencies that are out of pace with the rapidly evolving world we live in.

The world is changing rapidly and today's youth will have to, first and foremost, reinvent and learn throughout their lives. They will have to learn to adapt to constant change. We need, above all, to groom them to be more resilient, agile, and creative. I don't see this being a focus in the more traditional education system, especially in early education where you have the greatest opportunity to seed and influence the kinds of future entrepreneurs, leaders, and innovators who can really make a difference.

RAMESH JAGANNATHAN: There is a two-part solution to education reform: access and content delivery. How could technologies like AI help education in general and, more specifically, higher education? The current education system employed throughout most of the world, including the MENA region, was created in medieval times in the West for a very small, non-diverse, and localized population. It was also set up to identify and select a group of high achievers with a particular learning style and inclination. It seems obvious that its value and relevance to supporting a diverse, 21st century, global knowledge economy and a middle class of 5.2 billion people is highly questionable at best.

We should imagine a system that is accessible and customizable to everyone in this region and on this planet, that is neutral to age, gender, learning styles, health, and economic conditions. As Regina Dugan, former head of DARPA (the Defense Advanced Research Projects Agency in the US) asks, "What would you do if you knew you couldn't fail?" There is no pass and fail in the educational process. There are no filters or gatekeepers. It is a lifelong learning process. While the traditional system cannot deliver this type of learning environment, technology embedded with AI can and is already doing it.

Let us look at access first. Professor Sebastian Thrun from Stanford founded Udacity, touted as "the 21st century university." He opened a Stanford course called "Introduction to Artificial Intelligence" to the world via the internet. The result was incredible. Instead of the usual 200 students, 160,000 registered for the class. The people came from all kinds of backgrounds including, as he put it, "businesspeople, high school kids, retired people, and people on dialysis." Students from around the world were motivated enough to translate the class themselves for free from English into 44 languages. This is a rudimentary example of "customized" individual education, the second step in 21st-century education design. The impressive fact is that the top 410 students were online students, not Stanford students.

To confirm that this amazing data is real and not a one-time wonder, let us look at another high-impact example, the Khan Academy. Its slogan is "Free World-class Education for Anyone, Anywhere." It has delivered almost one billion lessons, solved more than six billion problems, and is available in 190 countries. Around

48 million registered users access the Khan Academy in dozens of languages.

Over the last two centuries, the world went through a great expansion in learning. The global literacy rate has increased dramatically from 12% to 88%. Unfortunately, how we *teach* did not change. We therefore come to the second step in the two-step solution. This is where AI is capable of revolutionizing the way we learn and teach, using tools that can expand our horizons in ways not previously imaginable.

I recently read a compelling article by a young writer named Lucas Rizzotto, titled "The Future of Education: How A.I. and Immersive Tech Will Reshape Learning Forever." He cites a study by Dr. Judy Will, a neurologist and educator, who says, "Memories with personal meaning are most likely to become relational and long-term memories available for later retrieval." In today's brick-and-mortar education system, this would be inconceivable. With a push of a button, AI could do this in real time, at any scale and at low cost. The advent of the second machine age, driven by AI and deep learning, democratizes the education landscape for the 3 billion and rising global middle class. For the first time in history, it gives them an opportunity to compete globally on a level playing field.

RAMEZ SHEHADI: We've been applying an educational framework that is now quite dated. Content is available online. Universities have put their content up and made it available to everyone, everywhere.

We need to think about what the labor force of the future is going to look like and let that drive what we do in our schools and in our academic institutions. We need to fundamentally embrace vocational training and vocational development very differently. Coders, I would venture to say, might even be the blue-collar workers of the future. What does it mean to be a developer or a coder? That's not enough in this day and age. I read an interesting statistic not too long ago that said there are more students on the honor roll in India and China than there are students in total in North America. Think about what that means in terms of future labor force. When you look at the region, we have to ask if this is a latent advantage for the future. It is, if we are going to be able to create the jobs for them to plug into.

We have to be thinking with the end result in mind. In light of global labor forces and the impact of technology, we need to design things very differently and be innovative or "hack our way" as Facebook likes to say. You're in a constant state of problem-solving and solution development, never taking the status quo as a given, and always finding ways to improve.

We have a fundamentally important and almost existential challenge when we think about this very young population needing to enter the future labor force in light of this tsunami of labor availability. How fast must our GDP be growing to absorb the youth? I would venture to say, it would need to be significantly higher than it is, pervasively across the region. So, we need to have the end result in mind. It's easy to say, "Oh, we need to develop coders and developers." Do we? I mean, if India and China are producing the coders and the developers, do we need to do the same in the MENA region? Maybe the answer is "yes", but maybe it's something else. We need to find out and act accordingly.

DINA EL-MOFTY: Modernizing the education system and making it more open to technology are critical. We're seeing schools with computers but the computers are locked up in a storage room and not being used because they might get stolen. You see that a lot of schools in the public system are doing that—it's shocking.

A lot of rote memorization and very traditional teaching methods need to be obliterated completely. Each generation is getting more and more frustrated with dated education systems. You can't teach this generation in the 21st century in the same way that you did in the 1930s, 1940s, and 1950s. You just simply can't teach them using that same methodology. Those practices need to be overhauled; there must be complete disruption in the education system across the board within Egypt and across the region. This is the 21st century in the age of technology, the internet, and AI.

QUALITY OF MENA EDUCATION SYSTEMS

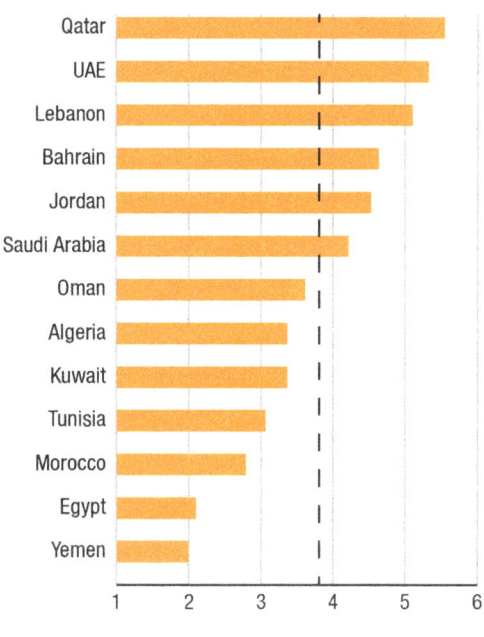

Quality rating, 1- 6 (best)

Source: World Economic Forum, Executive Opinion Survey

Emphasize practical learning

BILL AULET: Contrary to what some skeptics say, entrepreneurship can be taught. Often, people look at Steve Jobs, Bill Gates, or Mark Zuckerberg as examples of why entrepreneurship education is not needed. In every way, those examples are outliers. Entrepreneurship, like every discipline, can in fact be taught. The real question then is, "What is the most effective method for teaching entrepreneurship?" I can see how traditional methods that rely more on theory alone and outdated teaching methods can easily be dismissed as ineffective.

On the other hand, there are countless examples of very effective educational programs for teaching entrepreneurs. The data is unequivocal about that.

The first thing I would say is that entrepreneurship is not a science, nor is it an art. It's a craft and, as such, it should be taught through the apprenticeship model where theory and practice are interwoven with each other. It's also about maintaining individuality and embracing differences because entrepreneurship is about being different.

I'm a strong advocate of project-based or practical learning when it comes to entrepreneurship education. I think that is a missing piece in a lot of the programs out there and it's why they aren't as effective as they could be. Entrepreneurship cannot be taught through theory or books alone. It has to be done through the action-learning apprenticeship model. Just like sports, you can't learn by watching. You have to watch, evaluate what was done using first principles, and then do. I think that this is where the theory and practice interplay. What often happens is you have either academics or practitioners teaching entrepreneurship and neither approach alone is optimal. Academics teaching entrepreneurship by themselves apply a lot of rigor in the teaching process, but they don't have the relevance. Meanwhile, practitioners teaching entrepreneurship without academics have lots of relevance but insufficient rigor. Thus, you need a "hybrid model," if you will, that involves both practitioners and academics working together side by side.

This is not the first time we've seen this approach. In medicine, for example, researchers and doctors often collaborate in educational settings on designing curriculums and actually co-teach side by side. In practice, both academics and practitioners will be in the class making comments while the students interact with both. That way students are exposed to complementary points of view.

In terms of entrepreneurship education, however, this method is relatively new and has not yet been adopted across the board. The exceptions are places like MIT, Stanford, Harvard, University of Washington, and NYU. They have adopted this hybrid model, keeping one foot in the academic world and one foot in the practitioner world, which has proven to be the optimal method for teaching entrepreneurship. I expect the demand for such programs will really explode, given their efficacy relative to traditional methods.

When you look at a place like the Middle East with a cohort of young people coming up, new jobs will not be primarily created at established companies, no matter how big. They will be created by startups' and SMEs' innovation-driven entrepreneurs. So, I think we will see major uptake and interest in entrepreneurship and entrepreneurship education in the region.

LAMIA KAMAL-CHAOUI: Increasingly, entrepreneurship courses are part of school, college, and university curriculums. Governments have an important role in supporting this trend. Sufficient budget allocations for course development and the funding of specific activities and events (e.g., Startup Weekends) are essential. Governments need to support teachers in entrepreneurship education, including the provision of teacher training, teacher networks, best practice observatories, and learning material. Many examples of such best practices in universities are outlined in our *HEInnovate* publication series with the European Commission and in our online capacity-building tool.

All segments of our society are potential sources of the next generation of entrepreneurs and business leaders, as we stress in the OECD/European Union publication, *The Missing Entrepreneurs 2019*. More so than any other segment of society, entrepreneurial youth across the OECD have high-growth ambitions, expecting their new businesses to serve large customers segments and create new jobs. Yet their business survival rates actually tend to be low and few manage to create many jobs for others. Policy-makers could do more to help youth entrepreneurs create sustainable businesses by supporting innovative ideas, which will increase their chances of success.

In the European Union, for example, and across many geographies including MENA, women are at least half as likely as men to start and run businesses, and their businesses also tend to be smaller than those of men. As we set out in our recent *Policy Brief on Women's Entrepreneurship*, two key obstacles are: (1) culture and society are often unsupportive of women's entrepreneurship, and (2) women tend to perceive that they lack entrepreneurship skills. Across the EU, only one-third of women feel they have the skills, knowledge, and experience to start a business.

Governments everywhere are introducing a range of initiatives that can inspire others to address these issues. A common approach is to showcase specific women entrepreneur role models through ambassador programs. Entrepreneurial skills can also be developed either through dedicated women's entrepreneurship programs or increasing women's participation in general training programs. Developing women's entrepreneur mentoring relationships is another great tool. A number of countries, such as the US, Canada, Australia, and Ireland, have developed dedicated business incubators and accelerators for women. Many examples are given in the OECD/European Union webtool for inclusive entrepreneurship policy-makers.

JOY AJLOUNY: A lot of the VCs in the region don't understand how to set up precise financing structures. A lot of startups come to me and say, "I'm raising a million dollars. I'm giving 30% of my company to whomever provides this capital." My response is, "You're raising a million dollars on an idea, how are you giving away 30% of an idea?" I say, "Do a convertible note." More often than not they ask, "What's a convertible note?" They often don't even know what that is and, surprisingly, neither do many investors. There's definitely a gap there in terms of education or just basic acumen in regard to starting up, fundraising, and business in general that needs to be addressed somehow—not just with entrepreneurs, but with VCs as well.

The other issue is the level of familiarity and sophistication of VCs with the new economy. Historically, the Middle East is a real estate market, where local investors understand buildings, rent, and tangible assets. This digital world is new. I remember when I first started pitching Fetchr to investors in the region, I would explain how Fetchr could scale into a billion-dollar business and they would ask me, "Are you making money?" I would answer, "no". And they would respond by saying, "Call me when you make money." They didn't understand that startups don't work like that.

PETER COHAN: Beyond education, universities can also play a bigger role in helping develop local startups. MIT, for example, has a long history of encouraging professors to move into business and start their own companies, especially leveraging university R&D, and go back and forth between being professors and running their own companies. This began with MIT's founding in 1861. Initially, MIT couldn't afford to pay much money to its professors, so the administration encouraged and supported the professors to collaborate with local industry so they could earn side income while maintaining their teaching roles.

This runs contrary to the attitude of other universities. An extreme example: I was told that at the University of Chicago, if a professor starts or gets involved with a company, the administration pushes them out. Many universities are not that extreme, but if a professor wants tenure it is better for them to publish articles in obscure academic journals than to commercialize their intellectual property.

Essentially, in such contexts what the universities are doing is discouraging entrepreneurship, which has an adverse effect on students. Students look up to professors, and if the professors are successful entrepreneurs, then it makes students more excited about starting their own companies. At MIT and Stanford, professors are very involved with local companies and industries, which encourages students to become entrepreneurs. This practice pays off in spades. Companies started by alumni at MIT and Stanford have created trillions of dollars in economic value. Clearly, universities and universities R&D can be powerful forces in boosting a region's startup ecosystem—depending on how they are managed.

SAMI MAHROUM: In the MENA region, the public sector and the universities are light on R&D, because there hasn't been enough involvement from the government side to support them, to supply them with the resources required, and to provide needed funding to double up on long-term, strategic R&D programs. While they can train PhDs, the universities don't have the necessary equipment, laboratories, or mobility programs to utilize their expertise through R&D. You end up with PhDs who go on to become professors and train the next generations of PhDs, without practical application.

This is largely due to a lack of awareness on the part of governments in the region. They don't recognize the importance of R&D in society and its role in promoting innovation, generating startups, boosting the economy, and supporting scientific and academic institutions and societies in general.

The private sector hasn't been investing in R&D either. We know that, but then they have a very good reason not to invest in R&D, which is there is no reason for them to invest in R&D. After all, our companies and our industries are not competing at the cutting edge globally; they're merely trying to catch up. If they can buy cheaper technology from elsewhere, naturally they will. It happens constantly. You buy the technology; you deploy it. Maybe it will take you six months, a year, to really optimize its usage, train your staff on it, and observe significant savings in time, costs, or output. So, you really don't need to invest in R&D locally. You always have off-the-shelf technology you can use since you're not competing against cutting-edge, Korean, German, or American companies and don't need to use the latest and greatest technology out there.

From a business prospective, it would be a complete waste of time to spend on R&D because you may get results or you may not. There's a huge setup cost where you need to create instruments and purchase equipment, you have to have the space for it, you have to hire engineers, you have to hire full-time researchers, and they might produce something or they might not, or they might produce something too late.

On the other hand, countries where there's a high intensity of R&D tend to have economies with a high concentration of pharmaceutical research or IT, for instance, or areas where knowledge intensity is quite high. That's when you need to be really ahead and on the cutting edge, thinking about and solving problems and coming up with solutions and breakthroughs that will materialize 10 years from now.

We're not there yet, but that's the role of the government. The government should be more strategic in this regard, and it should invest in R&D. It should give the universities far more money to invest in research and other commercial-oriented and practical applications, expand research, and develop international networks, so that our researchers can go and work with researchers in Japan, Korea, Germany, and elsewhere. These are foundational steps toward developing healthy, thriving, and more sustainable economies and societies.

IDRISS AL RIFAI: Two key changes come to mind on the education side. The first is to increase the exposure of university and high school students to startups. I find it shocking that we're not bombarded with requests from schools to place some of the students in a startup environment such as ours. There is no better way to learn about being an entrepreneur or prepare for working in a startup than to have that early exposure and get some on-the-job training in such environments. I do not understand why we have not been approached by high schools or universities to have formal or informal programs or internships where the students get to experience first-hand what it's like to work in a startup. They would have the opportunity to interact with CEOs and executives and learn and develop their passion for a particular field. I sit on the board of Sharjah University and they're looking to implement this practice. I would love to see similar programs built in at high schools and universities across the region.

Second, we need to have more coding academies and stronger programs for developers in general. We have a decent education system. We have lot of universities here. Why do we not have hundreds of engineers, and good engineers, coming from those universities an annual basis? We have none or at least very few, and thus we are always dependent on foreign talent. There is a massive under-supply issue in terms of basic coding, let alone AI and deep tech and other advanced technology subjects. This is a major bottleneck on the education side in the region that needs to be addressed.

RABEA ATAYA: We need to make sure that our education system helps produce talent that thinks and acts in an entrepreneurial fashion. We must invest more in teaching about successful business practices in our educational institutions. We also need to give our youth an opportunity to have meaningful work experiences during their education.

In Europe and the United States, most people have had some sort of work experience by the time they graduate. In the Middle East, the vast majority of people have never worked a day in their life by the time they graduate at age 21 or 22. That makes them far less capable of becoming entrepreneurs or even fitting in well in any employment environment. Incorporating some kind of real-life, practical experience within the education system would be great, not just in terms of developing both technical and soft skills but also in terms of developing character and a work ethic.

In fact, the earlier someone is exposed to the workplace, the better. I was personally fortunate enough to spend a lot of time at my father's place of work as a child, which helped me decide that I wanted to be an entrepreneur. It also helped me at a very early age to decide what type of an entrepreneur I'd like to be, what type of business I'd like to run, and what type of culture I would like my business to have. The earlier you get people thinking about everything from business plans to just working as an employee, as an intern, or as a part-time worker somewhere, the better you equip them to prepare for their long-term career choices.

Universities in the region have done an increasingly better job of preparing our youth technically. From a business skills perspective, however, our business education is not yet up to global standards. I believe a lot more can be done to help young people improve both their employability skills and their entrepreneurial skills, whichever path they choose to pursue. Employability training is something that very few educational institutions cater to at present in the region. It's as basic as learning where to look for a job, how to look for one, how to apply, and how to interview.

Universities can also actively develop internship or co-op programs to help young people to better understand the demands of a workplace, develop a work ethic, and allow them to assess early on their possible career choices (which in turn may affect their education choices). I'll cite two personal examples. Up until age 19, I had always thought I wanted to work as a lawyer. I then had a summer internship while at university where I worked in a law office, and I quickly realized that that wasn't the job for me. That certainly helped me better frame which type of education I should pursue.

After graduation, the university was successful in getting me a slew of job interviews. I had the first six interviews within a few days of each other. I got rejection letters from all six of them—this in spite of the fact that I graduated with great grades from a great university, and I had never been rejected for anything before that. I quickly went into the library and studied everything I could about interviewing skills. Then I went to the career center, and they were happy to help me with mock interviews. I went to another six interviews, and this time I got all six jobs offers. Getting a job was a learned skill just like any other skill that the university was teaching me.

Finding a job is a skill, choosing the right career is also a skill, and so is entrepreneurship. Universities can help a lot in preparing people with these skills, including a whole slew of supporting skills that entrepreneurs need, such as sales, marketing, finance, some technology, etc.

HANS HENRIK CHRISTENSEN: A lot of universities in MENA offer entrepreneurship courses and degrees, and a lot of great entrepreneurship professors have been recruited to lead such programs. That is certainly a good start. These same universities need to not only run these courses, but also see if they can seed fund the best ideas and students through some kind of in-house incubation and acceleration facilities. Abu Dhabi is looking into requesting all educational institutions to set up something in this area as we speak.

We could further inspire new entrepreneurs through simply hiring aspiring entrepreneurs into existing startups so they can get field exposure and see how these entities work from the inside, and they can perhaps start their own companies once they have learned how. A kind of hiring portal exclusively for startup positions for the MENA region would therefore be a good tool, something along the lines of, say, a Monster startup talent portal that uses AI to vet and test candidates so unqualified talent can be ranked against more qualified talent. This can help close this gap, which is a big problem in the startup community since most founders often have only scant HR skills and may not be well-versed in judging the talent.

SHERIF KAMEL: Education should start with awareness and continue with lifelong learning. Investing in human capital from an early age is key for the development of the next generation of entrepreneurs who can compete on a global scale and make a concrete and sustainable difference. The entrepreneurial culture could be embedded in school curriculums in primary schools through experiential learning, role playing, gaming, and extracurricular activities. This can be complemented with university projects, internships, co-op programs, and hands-on training before graduation as an integral part of the learning process.

Being entrepreneurial does not mean that the expectation will be that every graduate will launch a startup. The objective of training the youth to be entrepreneurial and teaching entrepreneurial skills right from the outset is to prepare graduates to be agents of change, where they can always improve and be competitive, whether they work for the private sector, the public sector, or the government.

Some people believe that entrepreneurs are born not made; they would say that, "You either have it or not." Their view, in effect, is that entrepreneurship cannot be taught. My belief is that—while some people could be better gifted, more skilled, and more ready to become entrepreneurs than others—everyone has a chance to learn and improve their entrepreneurial know-how and skill set. This can be achieved in many ways, including through greater awareness, education, training, lifelong learning, exposure, proper observation, learning from one's mistakes and from others', and definitely by listening to others and learning from their experiences, successes, and failures.

In the MENA region, education and lifelong learning are key. Strategies should be devised to capitalize on global opportunities and to benefit from emerging and innovative technologies and their potential to provide universal education, knowledge, and lifelong learning across different communities. A platform, like "education 2.0" is needed. This platform can help to drastically redefine and reshape student learning and societal learning in general. It needs to focus on collaborative learning and employ experiential, hands-on learning, knowledge capture and dissemination, and working with different institutions. As such, the goal should be to position higher education institutions as innovative platforms.

Without a doubt, for the Middle East countries to cope with its growing young population and the challenges of unemployment and competition as well as the dynamics of change in the global market, both long-term strategies and short-term quick wins are needed. They need to ensure that the education process delivers when it comes to prepping students for their future careers and supporting an agile and competitive private sector in general. An important realization is that investing in human capital as part of the educational and learning ecosystem is integral to economic and social advancement.

It is necessary to stay away from focusing on pure quantity, and instead mainly address quality issues. It is necessary to reinvent education and how it is conducted in MENA—in schools, universities, and vocational training. The future of MENA depends in a special and unique way on the collective work, efforts, capacities, and skills of all stakeholders in improving the quality of education and learning, and an invaluable component of this is the quality of higher education.

Education 2.0 should be driven by promoting entrepreneurship, innovation, leadership, AI, data analytics, critical thinking, inclusive development, the shared economy, and responsible business. Investing in education helps people to unleash the creative capacities of all citizens, irrespective of their background, and effectively supports their drive to improve their lives and to build better societies. Education benefits everyone—individuals, organizations, and society—and leads to major positive transformations that could lead to further growth and development.

NABEEL KOSHAK: One challenge is that if the leaders at the universities who are handling entrepreneurship programs are conventional academics, they won't have much of an understanding or field experience of the market and innovations. A lot more practitioners and educators need to come from diverse innovative environments— including experienced professionals and entrepreneurs—in order to provide a more practical and relevant type of education for today's environment. That will also help commercialize a lot of the R&D, which has historically been for academic purposes only, into practical applications that startups can utilize and ultimately into MVPs (minimum viable products).

One way to approach this is to ensure that entrepreneurship programs are carried out by people from the industry—professionals, experts, entrepreneurs, and investors—not by academics. They should include the full innovation cycle, from inception, to ideation, to reiteration, to MVP. This trend is happening all over the world. Academics are good at teaching and doing research, but not at innovation, products, MVPs, and entrepreneurship in general.

ECONOMIC ACTIVITY, UNEMPLOYMENT AND INACITVITY AMONG MENA'S WOKRING-AGE POPULATION

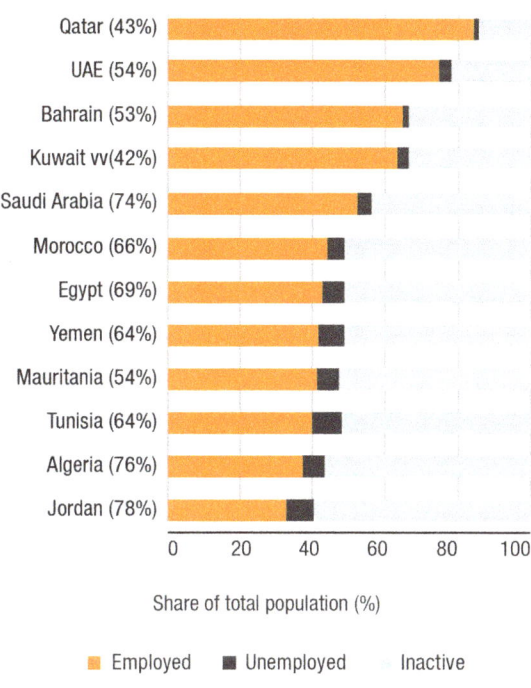

Share of total population (%)

■ Employed   ■ Unemployed   Inactive

Source: World Economic Forum, Human Capital Index 2016

OMAR CHRISTIDIS: You have to upskill so many people, including the youth who are graduating from universities today. They lack a lot of the practical skills needed to get a job in the digital domain. One issue is that we need a closer link between academia and the private sector. How do we really reflect that? We've seen in other markets the emergence of players like General Assembly, who are working on this practical reskilling.

We need more entrepreneurship development centers inside of universities. We have been working with some universities to try to help them design such programs. It can be at the level of creating awareness, like bringing in speakers who are entrepreneurs to talk to students about their experience and encourage them and inspire them. Alternatively, it can be a university incubator, where students actually pitch an idea at the beginning of the year and they get a direct salary through the incubator throughout the year.

I sit on the board of the American Community School, which is my high school here in Beirut. Every year, we do a startup assembly with them, involving the students in grades 10 through 12. We bring in six to eight entrepreneurs. Those entrepreneurs each talk about their business for a few minutes, and then at round tables the students ask them questions and really connect with these people. We try to pick startups that will resonate with the students. It's actually a highlight every year for us because we get so excited and inspired by these 16- and 17-year-olds. We need more of these kinds of activities.

I'm also working with the Prime Minister's Office on a project to connect public schools and create makerspaces in public schools in Lebanon. Curricular reform could be, in many countries, an uphill battle, because it's something that's very formalized and structured and to change it is quite a challenge, bureaucratically or otherwise. We therefore decided to try to do this as an extracurricular activity: create these centers inside the schools, train the trainers to come in, or a teacher in each school, to use the space for the students, and help them do after-school activities.

There are many examples of these kinds of programs, like Codi and Teens Who Code, that are happy to come in and do activities with these kids. We definitely need to start at the middle school level. It doesn't cost that much to have a simple makerspace, and having someone who can guide these kids would be a very powerful step and something that could be scaled to many schools. Parents are coming to me after these events saying, "My kid came home and he was so excited and inspired." It makes my day. These are the moments that remind me of why I started this business in the first place and that make us keep going.

NED JAROUDI: I've seen interesting working models around the world—for example in Finland with Aalto University—where it's all about applied learning. You have an engineering school, a business school, and a design school working together in harmony on new practical projects and creating IP that can be commercialized through a TTO (technology transfer office). Moving away from pure teaching universities to more applied research and design will go a long way to help develop the startup ecosystem locally.

Develop local success narrative

JULIE LENZER: Role models are really important, especially exposure to relatable local role models, so that someone can be inspired and learn from them and apply that learning to their current situation. I think we get starstruck with "name brand" entrepreneurs and business leaders. Sometimes, though, those people are hard to relate to, whereas there may be many local successful entrepreneurs around—people and companies you've never really heard of that can be more relevant and thus impactful. Making sure that you have that full spectrum of role models by shining the spotlight on different kinds of entrepreneurs at different stages of development is key.

Mindset is also very important as well. That happens in very early formative years with early education as well as at home. I've seen many kids who are entrepreneurial-minded and their parents are not supportive. They say, "Oh, you just need to go get a job and quit playing around", instead of exposing them to success stories and role models they can relate to, learn from, and get inspired by.

What I refer to as "possibility thinking," which focuses on looking at options and weighing out various outcomes, and problem-solving to achieve the desired result, is critical. That type of thinking has to start really early and go all the way through applied thinking, especially around STEM subjects.

ANAND CHOPRA-MCGOWAN: If you look at the most successful startups and new businesses around the world, very few of those founders have had any formal entrepreneurship training. That said, there's certainly a role to play for the education world to foster entrepreneurship. How does it actually work? I think you have to broaden the definition of what education really is. I think you have to look at it from a few different angles.

First, you have to think about education—when it comes to entrepreneurship—as perhaps being more about inspiring people and serving as role models for people than necessarily training them in exactly how to do it. The reality is that launching your own business has so many variables that the only playbook that you can learn or skills you need come from launching your own business and going through that experience first-hand. You could, however, gain insights, inspiration, and confidence from seeing people who come from your own background, region, and language who achieved remarkable success. It could give you the confidence and even the spark of an idea in the first place that you can do it as well.

I think that one of the biggest roles education has to play is to create that kind of network and to celebrate that network of success in whatever form it can take. It can be the first employee of a big tech company who happens to be from the region. It can be a startup that got launched somewhere, even if it has expanded somewhere else since then. There are lots of different versions of success, but the more those local role models' stories can be told, the better. That's a very powerful role for education to play.

LAMIA KAMAL-CHAOUI: The promotion of local role models makes entrepreneurship tangible to young people with the simple sharing of experiences through speaking at events in schools and showcasing entrepreneurs' stories in media campaigns. To appeal to youth, the role models should be wide-ranging and include relatable young entrepreneurs.

Business competitions judged by local successful entrepreneurs and business leaders can give youth a flavor of what it is like to be an entrepreneur through a short project. These competitions give young participants a business challenge and ask them to design a product to respond to it. They usually involve the young person or team in setting business objectives, developing a business plan, and presenting it to a panel of judges.

EYAD ALKASSAR: I think role models are huge—not just any role models but local ones specifically, ones that the local population can relate to and believe they can emulate. Success stories as Namshi, Souq, Snapp, and Careem are creating a pool of such role models for the region and are inspiring a new generation of entrepreneurs. Those local role models are the most convincing way to demonstrate the fact that you can build amazing multibillion-dollar companies in the Middle East, and that you don't need to be in other parts of the world. We're now seeing an exciting new phenomenon where the co-founders of Careem, Swvl, Noon, etc., are all coming from Rocket Internet or a similar environment. I'm hopeful that a lot of ex-Namshi, ex-Careem, and ex-Souq people will now go out to start their own companies, and thus seed more venture and funding back into the ecosystem.

MOHAMMED JAFFAR: Our education system doesn't focus enough on our Muslim entrepreneurs. We rarely hear about local success stories. More often than not, we only hear about stories coming from the West, which do not always resonate as well or inspire young people as much. Naturally, they will learn and get inspired more from people who share their local environment, circumstances, and challenges and managed to excel in spite of them.

Also, if we teach young people about what Islam really teaches us, and if you look at Islam, Christianity, or Judaism, they do encourage entrepreneurs. Islam does encourage putting a lot of effort into creating value and helping people. It's not all just about praying and fasting; it's also about working hard, being successful, and making an impact. It's a full lifestyle or way of living, if you will. If we focus on that and broaden our approach to be more holistic in how we practice Islam in every area of our lives, including business, we will see a lot of success happening in our part of the world. That's something I would like to see more of.

RONALDO MOUCHAWAR: Today's youth should look within themselves for inspiration. They are a brand-new generation who are coming to the table with new ideas that could potentially change the world. That is where I am looking for inspiration. Approximately 60% of the MENA population is under 30 years of age, and they have grown up with technology and innovation, so it's something that is in their DNA. That's important because innovation is now recognized as the single most important ingredient in a modern economy. It is innovation—more than the application of capital and labor—that makes the world go round.

Digital jobs are also more adaptable in the face of technological disruption, especially those related to emerging technologies. The growth of such jobs will help nationals move from largely administrative jobs in the government sector to higher-value roles in industries with future importance. A skilled digital workforce is essential to the implementation of the GCC economies' ambitious plans and the digital transformation of organizations across sectors.

The adoption of emerging digital technologies in all sectors in the GCC is limited because of an insufficient understanding of digitalization. Companies also lack the strategic direction necessary for digital transformation.

ZIAD MOKHTAR: I think the best way to educate, inspire, and empower next-generation entrepreneurs is to share stories of success—to celebrate role models and share the details of their journeys, their wins, and their losses. Little is being done to achieve that. Unfortunately, we have a culture that is somewhat secretive. It was so refreshing to see Careem's first pitch-deck shared publicly after their exit. More of that needs to be done. Local success stories have immense power to provide practical lessons learned in a way that will engrain them in the minds of those aspired for success.

ELISSA FREIHA: In terms of actual entrepreneur education, I think it's important to tailor it to the local environment. At Womentum, for example, we focus on such areas as early monetization, not depending on future rounds of funding, being very selective with investors that you bring onboard, and making sure you appreciate the complexities of building a startup and are not just looking for fast liquidity. We are educating women entrepreneurs on setting up the right company structure and legal framework when working with investors and sharing best practices on cross-border expansion across the region. We get very granular and focus on all the practical nuances of launching and scaling a startup in the region, which are otherwise largely lacking in traditional entrepreneur education programs and material from the region.

Some of these teachings fly in the face of what is being taught or accepted in Silicon Valley. For example, early monetization for startups is not being prioritized in Silicon Valley. User growth, user acquisition rate, and other growth-related metrics are more valued there. But when you're operating in a more politically and economically volatile place like MENA, you can't prioritize growth over funding. You need to make sure that you can pay yourself and your team and still operate if local funding suddenly dries up or if there's some revolution at your window. You need to be able to hold on and keep your company growing without depending on bigger investors to come in, and in the face of unforeseen circumstances that can have an adverse impact on your cash flow. Obviously, this is less of an issue in Silicon Valley; hence we need more tailored entrepreneur education in the region, which is what we've been focusing on developing at Womena.

NED JAROUDI: We need to really continue to showcase the local success stories from the region, especially those with successful exits like Maktoob, Zawya, Cobone, Talabat, Dubizzle, Souq, and Careem. Their founders are role models for budding entrepreneurs. MENA entrepreneurs can attend plenty of global events where they can see new technologies, hear inspirational speakers, and meet like-minded people in places like South by Southwest in Austin, Slush in Helsinki, and the Web Summit in Lisbon. Regionally, you have ArabNet, GITEX, STEP Conference, RiseUp Summit, etc. All of these events allow knowledge acquisition and networking, as well as a chance to vet good ideas with relevant attendees or speakers at these conferences.

ANDREW BERKOWITZ: One of the main things that helps contribute to developing that entrepreneurial mindset and inspiring folks is local success stories and especially exits. One good example is Estonia. Estonia is a very small country in Eastern Europe and very early on in the 2000s, Skype came out of Estonia. Once Skype exited to Microsoft, all of the early Skype employees and co-founders reinvested back in the local ecosystem by starting new companies in Estonia as opposed to heading to Silicon Valley. As such, they've been the most active angel investors and mentors in that ecosystem.

The best thing that can happen for the MENA region is for successful entrepreneurs, like the founders of Souq and Careem and others, to reinvest their time, money, and energy back into the ecosystem. To the extent that they do that, I almost guarantee that you'll see the next generation of entrepreneurs come up through that support system and repeat exactly what they did, and that creates positive momentum.

On the other hand, I know so many founders, particularly in sub-Saharan Africa, who taught themselves and built their companies without formal education or training, or access to local mentors or role models. With hard skills like design and engineering and development, all kinds of online resources are available for free today on YouTube and other learning platforms.

Those technical skills, in my opinion, aren't the biggest obstacle to building a company. It's more the skills of actually running a company. It's very hard, if you're not well experienced with soft skills and leadership skills, to actually scale a company. It's one thing to be coding away with just you and a couple of friends in the room; it's another to actually raise capital, have a team that scales from 10 to 15 to 20 people, and so on, and to manage and motivate people, establish a vision, develop a strategy and KPIs (key performance indicators), and lead the team. That's where local mentorship can be quite impactful in terms of helping entrepreneurs navigate those challenges.

AREIJE AL SHAKAR: Highlighting local success stories as in Amir Hegazi's book, *Startup Arabia,* and other local entrepreneurship- and business-focused publishers and publications such as Wamda, *Arabian Business, Gulf Business, Entrepreneur,* and *Forbes* magazines, is very important. After all, we're humans, and we all look up to others for education and inspiration. Being able to share those narratives, whether it's through ads, books, magazines, videos, or movies, is quite valuable.

I think that's something we need to do more of and it needs to also happen from the top. The US has entrepreneurship awards at the presidential level. In Bahrain, we award entrepreneurs through the Crown Prince Award for Entrepreneurship, which really helps bring them into the spotlight and rewards local entrepreneurs and startups. We just need to be very careful about the criteria for awarding people to ensure they in fact have actually achieved tangible, meaningful milestones.

Collaborate with world-class institutions

KEVIN O'LEARY: Traditionally, wealthy families in emerging regions, including MENA, would send their children to get educated in higher education places like London or in North America at American and Canadian universities. The mistake in that is it doesn't support institutional growth in the domestic market. It's also limited because it's accessible for only the wealthy segment for the most part and thus not accessible to everyone.

The solution is to allow world-class international educational institutions to establish campuses in Middle Eastern countries. Set up collaborations with universities like MIT, McGill, or Waterloo to open campuses in big cities, like Dubai, Riyadh, Cairo, Kuwait City, or Amman. It's a global way to think. It allows people to stay in their own culture and get educated on a global basis. It could get youth exposed to the latest and most innovative educational curriculums and methodologies from cutting-edge fields. It could also help spawn tremendous startups around engineering or AI. If they could start with, say, Engineering and Business Management, I would imagine those cohorts would be sold out immediately and profitable probably from day one.

Within a decade, you would have the spinoff: the entrepreneurs and the startups that would grow locally and decide to stay in the region and build from within. You would also have engineers and, gradually, cohorts of business managers who would also stay domestic. Ultimately, you will have many sectors and innovations that flourish across the board. There's a tremendous upside to such an approach.

In time it could also involve trying to become cooperative in the international political economy and trade with the rest of the world. China is astonishingly graduating 250,000 engineers a year now. Those kinds of disciplines establish growth in domestic markets. It starts with education. I think the Middle East has been slow to move in that direction, so there's a lot to catch up on. The good news is that it doesn't take many years before you can reap the rewards of those investments. Engineers start to train in their early 20s; they graduate four years later; they have a startup idea; and they can be funded by the government or private capital. Two or three out of 10 ideas might become companies, and on and on. That's another key initiative I think has to be focused on.

SANGEET PAUL CHOUDARY: In terms of education, to some extent this is where the Middle East will need to look at collaborations. There are already examples of schools like Cornell setting up a satellite school in Doha, and NYU in Abu Dhabi, so education is again an ecosystem issue. You cannot solve education by just building schools. You have to think about how you can collaborate with the world's best schools and have them open up campuses in the region. You also need to create rich exchange programs, so students from the Middle East can get job opportunities around the world and likewise students from around the world are sent to the Middle East. Creating those cross-border educational programs is important for the education system and the job ecosystem to be able to work together in the Middle East.

SETH LEVINE: The fastest way to enhance the local education system, as it relates to entrepreneurship, is to partner with top global educational institutions and try to encourage them to operate in your region. It's great to see this trend already happening in the Middle East. Ultimately, you want to do a combination of that and working on making your own institutions more effective. So, you're not just saying, "Hey, NYU, open a campus in Riyadh." You're saying, "Hey, NYU, let's partner with the local universities there and build a campus together."

At the end of the day, you want the local universities to also pride themselves on being at the forefront of these reforms. You don't want simply the best tech talent to be at the satellite campus of Oxford, or some university that's ultimately domiciled elsewhere. Doing a JV with those types of universities can certainly help but, ultimately, you also want to work on your own local education system.

Cultivate 21st-century skills

LAMIA KAMAL-CHAOUI: Through our analysis at OECD, we have found that ecosystems' weaknesses spread across a wide range of areas. Most notably, one widespread problem is a lack of skills for startups and scaleups, particularly digital skills, as we highlight in *OECD SME and Entrepreneurship Outlook 2019*. Entrepreneurs may have great digital skills and ideas themselves, but they quickly face problems scaling up when they seek programmers, software developers, and workers comfortable with digital technologies. Our training systems are simply not moving fast enough to meet the demand for workers with digital skills.

This important issue was at the core of the conversation among small and large business representatives, entrepreneurs, and governments at the first meeting of the OECD Digital for SMEs (D4SME) Global Initiative. This initiative promotes knowledge-sharing and learning about how different types of SMEs can seize the benefits of digitalization, and about the role of government, regulators, business sectors, and other institutions in supporting SME digitalization.

ANAND CHOPRA-MCGOWAN: We operate now in the Asia Pacific region, in Europe, and in the US. The interesting thing is that, when we think about the skills and technologies that receive the most investment and are in the highest demand in the MENA region, it really does mirror what we're seeing globally. We see cybersecurity skills as a big investment area, as well as data and AI skills. We continue to see user experience design and product management and, of course, software engineering. These are the skills that are really necessary—the skills and business opportunities and investment areas that are quite consistent around the world.

As far as skill sets needed in the region—everything from basic Excel to classroom presentations, to team collaboration is lacking. The good news, though, is that we've been able to recognize that and make some tweaks and enhancements to our syllabus, and the response rate and pickup rate on the part of students was very strong. They jump to whatever new core business skills are provided and we are able to implement that very well.

The reason we've had the opportunity to build some sense of authority and experience in the area really comes down to our partnership with the MiSK Foundation. The MiSK Foundation has been around for a few years now, but it's still relatively young. It has been a great partner for us since 2012. The partnership came about as a result of Crown Prince Mohammad bin Salman's trip to Google.

This is before he was crowned prince, actually. He was impressed with what he saw and the environment that Google had created for entrepreneurship, for innovation, and for collaboration. He became very interested in creating similar spaces to foster similar initiatives, which was the inception of many great initiatives that followed.

Today, the MiSK Foundation is very well known and is engaged in many different activities, from art to science to animation to all kinds of things. One thing that we've done with them is what we call the MiSK Academy, which is a practical skills-focused professional education institution that we launched in partnership with MiSK in April 2018. We have already graduated about 750 students, almost all of whom have new jobs as a result, and the plan is to extend that to 5,000 people by 2022. We're really investing in all of those skills that I mentioned: data science, cybersecurity, AI, software engineering, user experience design, even digital marketing, and all kinds of future-oriented and forward-thinking skills. The most important thing for us is that the students who are coming are not only expressing strong interest, but are actually completing the courses, many of which are really quite difficult. These are three-month, immersive, boot-camp style courses. Not only are they completing them but they are actually implementing those skills and getting jobs. It's been a really successful initiative for us so far.

ALEC ROSS: Two categories of skill sets are needed in the future. One is timeless skills, such as effective communication, management, and leadership skills. The other is era-specific skills, which are transitory based on the times we live in. On the latter, I think it will become increasingly important to learn a foreign, spoken language in an increasingly globalized world, as well as a coding language in an increasingly technical world. Taken together, these skills give you a much greater advantage to help you navigate this new world and mobilize geographically. Combine those two categories of skills with problem-solving and creativity skills and you enhance your position to adapt to future technological and economic changes.

Employers will play a bigger role in the future to reskill and upskill their workforce in order to remain relevant and competitive in the marketplace. They will need to make the necessary investments to drive these initiatives within their organizations, while promoting a culture of lifelong learning. Fortunately, with the advent of the internet enabling online classes and conferences, education is becoming more accessible and democratized than ever before.

ERIK BRYNJOLFSSON: First and foremost, greater investment in education across the globe is needed. Almost every country underinvests in education, especially as it relates to skills for the future. A good predictor of the future progress of a given nation is how educated the population is and how much it invests in education. It's not just how much is being invested, it's also the way it's approached in terms of focusing on creative thinking, on thinking outside the box, on problem-solving, as opposed to rote memorization.

In the 20th century, a lot of emphasis was placed on creating workers who could work alongside machines and do repetitive tasks. Now the machines are able to do almost all of the repetitive tasks. What humans need to do is focus on asking questions, identifying new problems, formulating new solutions to old problems, and being creative in general. Also, interpersonal skills and teamwork are increasingly important: persuading, leading, negotiating, etc. These are skills that become more and more important as technology automates routine jobs. Technology can also be used to help with education. For instance, online education can help provide greater access to education for larger populations.

Identifying opportunities for machine learning is an important area that every manager and entrepreneur should be thinking about. The newest wave of AI focused on machine learning is incredibly powerful. We're only in the early days of it. A tidal wave of change is coming and it's a chance for developing countries to leapfrog ahead by embracing these machine learning technologies. We need to understand that they're only useful in a relatively narrow set of categories. They can do work in vision and voice recognition and different kinds of problem-solving, but they can't do everything that humans can do.

We have a tool called the "Suitability for Machine Learning Rubric" that allows companies to identify where the opportunities are for machine learning and where they should stay away. By applying this tool, they see how they can best take advantage of machine learning and be part of this machine learning revolution. This is an example of the kind of technology that could be a real game changer going forward when it's combined with the right entrepreneurial and business efforts.

RAMI SALMAN: AI and machine learning have really become the drivers for almost every business around the world, and we really see very few people able to strategize and execute those technical tasks locally. This is the evolution of big data, but the machine learning skill set is not something routinely found in the regional toolbox. There aren't enough R&D projects in the education system or in the corporate world for some of the cutting-edge technology that exists. Whether it's machine learning, blockchain, or 3D environments, we're still going to Asia or Europe for those skills when we're starting out in the region.

Additionally, digitally focused customer acquisition and sales operations for scaling a traditional SaaS (software as a service) startup are not present either, which makes sense since so few SaaS companies have come out of the region. But as more and more businesses and startups begin operating in those spaces, we will see more and more people who have those skill sets locally.

HISHAM ELARABY: In MENA, with 60% of the region's population under 30 years of age, young people entering the workforce are already facing one of the highest youth unemployment rates globally, at around 30%. That rate has been getting worse since 2012 for some countries more than others, but particularly for young women. So, while there is a clear need for governments to play an active role in deploying tech-competitiveness initiatives, it's important for them to find a formula that delivers the right impact. The challenges with traditional offline learning models (e.g., bootcamps) are that they are not scalable, often require a full-time commitment of 12 weeks, and are costly to deliver. Conversely, the challenge with online learning is that it's difficult to create engagement and drive high completion rates. MOOCs (massive open online courses) also tend to involve watching videos passively, which does not create true, practical upskilling.

We have been working with government partners in the region like the MiSK Foundation in Saudi Arabia, the Dubai Future Foundation, and the Ministry of Communications and Information Technology of Egypt, responsible for information and communications technology (ICT), to craft programs that have the right learning product and the right delivery mechanism.

With the Egyptian Ministry of ICT, for example, we run a program called "Next Technology Leaders," which has graduated more than 3,000 learners in a variety of fields including cybersecurity and machine learning. The program enables learners to acquire industry-built and project-based skills while allowing for scale and flexibility. This is because we complement the online learning with skills application projects that are evaluated using a defined rubric, and we provide detailed, personalized feedback from Udacity reviewers within hours after a student submits a project. In this program, we have achieved a 78% graduation rate, which is much greater than graduation rates typically published by online learning platforms. Within four months of graduation, 74% of graduates report a positive career change.

Also, with Egypt's Ministry of ICT, we launched a program focused on high school students. More than 1,000 students have been enrolled in our Intro to Programming Nanodegree so far. In order to ensure engagement and high completion rates, we created a unique, gamified student journey supported by our community managers and a weekly virtual support session with our Udacity mentors. This three-month learning program is on pace to hit an 80%-plus graduation rate.

We also launched a program with the Dubai Future Foundation in early 2018 called One Million Arab Coders. The aim of the initiative is to empower Arabs with the language of the future and accelerate digital literacy by exposing learners to concepts in data science and mobile and web development. We ensure practical knowledge by having students complete "labs" embedded in their online classroom. These demonstrate their ability to write basic, functioning code to make a static website, for example. So far, more than 500,000 Arabs all over the world have enrolled in the program.

I do not believe the digital skill sets that are missing in the region are too dissimilar from elsewhere in the world. There are hot areas (e.g., AI, blockchain, and cybersecurity) and technical skills that are most in-demand in the market (e.g., cloud and distributed computing, data science, UI/UX, and SEO/SEM marketing). However, these in-demand technical skill sets, otherwise known as domain knowledge, looked rather different five years ago, and will undoubtedly evolve over the next five years. Curriculums and accrediting bodies in the MENA region are not keeping up with the pace of technological change when it comes to these skills. The rule of thumb is that if it is in a textbook, it's very likely is already outdated. Students get up-to-date exposure and knowledge through on-the-job-training and lifelong learning platforms like Udacity.

It is time for governments, education bodies, and the private sector to provide opportunities for youth to not only upgrade their domain knowledge but, more importantly, provide mentorship and space for them to develop the competencies and mindset that will help them become strong and civically engaged business leaders.

Focus on early education

JULIE LENZER: There's an opportunity to support parents to understand how they can instill curiosity, problem-solving, creative thinking, and an entrepreneurial mindset in their kids. It can be as basic as communication training. For example, kids often ask lots of questions, and parents will tell them to stop asking questions rather than encouraging them to find their own answers and solutions. That's a big piece of it—encouraging curiosity, problem-solving, and self-advocacy, like self-belief and self-confidence. That can make a big difference and leave a lasting impression on kids that influences their behavior. Encourage kids to dream and balance big picture thinking with action, their current circumstances, and their needs.

There are lots of community programs that the kids can get involved in that touch on this one way or another. It would be great, however, if there were specialized programs to train parents to prep their kids with the mindset and the character they will need to be successful in the future. The idea is obviously to help empower parents so they are better able to nurture and grow future entrepreneurs and business leaders. After all, there's no manual for parenting. There are certainly books on parenting, but I haven't seen a book or parent program for igniting creativity or an entrepreneurial mindset in your kid.

Having programs through schools would help, maybe for parents to work with the teachers to figure out how to foster that type of mindset in their kids. Maybe such a program could facilitate parents to help their kids explore the various aspects of an entrepreneurial mindset and leadership, and get the kids involved in solving problems in their communities. It might even have supportive material and games that help with the kids' development and maybe trigger an interest or even seed a lifelong passion from an early age.

A simple and beautiful book is *What Do You Do with an Idea?* by Kobi Yamada. It inspires kids to welcome ideas, learn to cultivate them, and let them grow into a world of their own, so they may even change the world. Certainly, a lot more can be done on that front to instill the right outlook, mindset, habits, and character traits that will set kids on the right track early on.

SAMIH TOUKAN: In terms of education, we need to be thinking long term. As such, governments need to invest more in early education. For example, we invested in a promising startup in Jordan called Hello World Kids, which has created a curriculum for coding for young people, starting from the age of 10 until they graduate. Now it is working with the Jordanian government and several other governments around the Arab world to make coding a compulsory part of the educational curriculum, just like learning math and English. Here's an example of a great initiative that governments have invested in to prepare their youth for the new economy. They enable candidates to enroll in four-month, intensive bootcamps to learn the latest in terms of programming languages, AI, deep tech, etc.

Today, there is a major lack of engineers in the region. We see this gap even in a small market like Jordan. When Souq started there, it needed to hire 500, 1,000, or more engineers to scale up and there was just not enough local supply. Hence, a lot of companies are resorting to India and Eastern Europe to provide that supply. Investment is needed from the government and from the private sector to increase the technical skills supply in terms of both quantity and quality, because all startups need programmers, engineers, and digital-specific expertise that our universities and our institutions are not able to create today, unfortunately.

WALID HANNA: The MENA region is currently a young region with 40% of the population under 25. Average youth unemployment across the region is at 28%, which is among the highest in the world. This is a major issue for the region, but it also represents a huge pool of startup potential. To put this youth to better use, they must gain greater access to education and an entrepreneurial risk-taking spirit must be promoted within the region. This starts with implementation in the early education curriculum and continues through to post-university programs, with more labs and R&D centers within universities and coding schools.

Meanwhile, the current education system hinders students'

ability to properly enter the competitive global tech landscape. The introduction of analytics and business intelligence (BI) is necessary in order to provide the proper base from which the required talent can grow. An added issue is that those who garner success in STEM subjects currently look outside the region for employment. With the implementation of an entrepreneurial spirit, we could see them returning to fuel MENA's growth in the fourth industrial revolution.

UNEMPLOYMENT RATE IN THE MENA REGION

MENA's average youth unemployment rate is still considered among the highest in the world with a 2% increase from last year's rate.

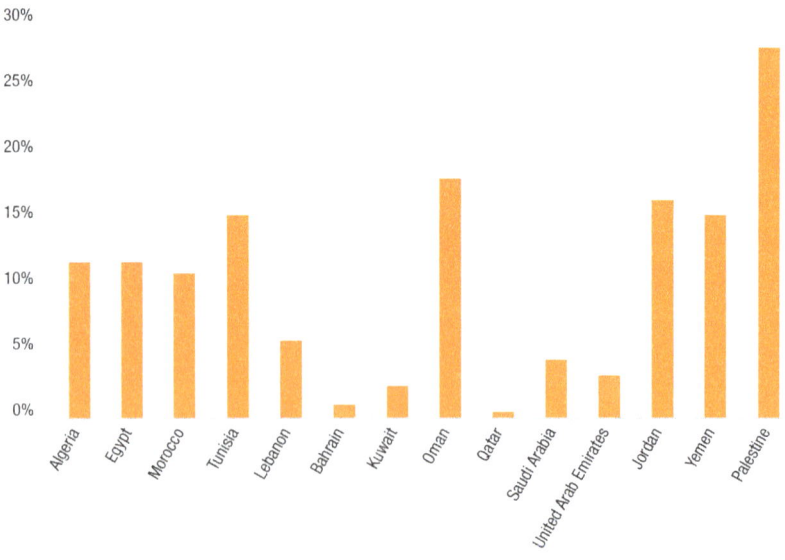

Share of unemployment rate (%)

Source: The World Bank, International Labour Organization 2017 (www.worldbank.org)

SAMIA MELHEM: The early education system needs to be rethought and modernized. The stories the kids read, the examples they get, are still sometimes from 200-300 years ago. We've had many educators on projects in MENA, and we've seen good results, but they happen in three or four schools and they're not propagated. That's why I really like the education cloud, so we don't have each school spending on content; we have good content reusable by all. Also, we should be adding new courses on computer sciences, data, programming, and other modern life-oriented education.

One of the objectives of the All Africa Digital Economy Moonshot is that kids under 15 will have know-how in using computers and be internet-savvy; that is, they will know how to search for information and data and even know how to do some coding. MENA is planning the same. In Lebanon, where I'm working right now, a law has been introduced to teach coding in public schools at age 10 or so. Dubai has already instituted AI labs and Qatar and KSA are introducing robotics training in public schools.

In countries like Senegal, which I also cover, we've had projects that help finance the students' laptops because the students cannot afford to buy a laptop on their own. We've done that by providing bank guarantees to the banks that loan money to the students to buy the laptop. These laptops come quite highly subsidized. The same concept can be adapted to higher education projects across MENA.

NED JAROUDI: When it comes to early education, look at some of the schools in the UAE: they're embedding entrepreneurship very early on into their curriculum. For example, when I was running 1776 in Dubai, we worked very closely with GEMS Education to scout startups that could help them create engaging curriculums and content for their schools. They set up the schools to be more innovative in terms of the learning environment itself, such as the classrooms and labs, as well as paying close attention to teacher education. Obviously, the more exposed teachers are to innovation and entrepreneurship, the more likely it is that they will work well with the students to bring that into the classroom.

Build youth mindset and character

WILL HERMAN: Education is the crux of everything. I think that knowledge isn't that important for entrepreneurs—it's more attitude, it's more psychological. So, yes, I think we could do substantially better at teaching entrepreneurship philosophy early on. I don't think, however, that there are many facts and figures that students need to learn that will help them become entrepreneurs. The ability to change and the acceptance of change is the single biggest factor, I believe, in a successful entrepreneur versus one who's not so successful, at least at the start.

So much of education is about fixed ways of doing things and doesn't really cover out-of-the-box thinking or dynamic thinking. Most education in the US is all about, "Here's the question and here is the answer to that question." Entrepreneurship, on the other hand, is completely open-ended, it's not multiple-choice. Rather, you have a question, and you have an infinite number of answers. That makes a lot of people uncomfortable. Also, the question itself changes rapidly. It's not like two plus two equals four; it's more like playing a chess game, except the rules keep changing and you have to keep up with the new rules and still win. I'd say we could do substantially better at preparing—not necessarily "educating"—people to be better entrepreneurs even in the earliest parts of formal education.

AMIRA RASHAD: I'll give you a little anecdote here. I didn't go through the American education system myself, so the very first time I was exposed to it was through my kids. Day one in kindergarten, I asked my son, "How was your day? What did you do? What did you learn?" He said, "I learned that I'm awesome and I can do anything that I want to do." And that never stopped. That kind of approach, that space to explore, that way of teaching things is entirely missing from our region.

You need people who literally can step out and say, "I see this; this is wrong. I see this; this is right. I have a lot of confidence in what I'm saying and here's the data, and I beg to differ." This mindset must be taught from a very early age, and we have yet to cultivate this mentality in this part of the world. At least, we don't do it early or often enough with kids at school or at home where it all starts.

We're certainly also not doing it in college because I do not see structured internship programs. I'm not seeing enough students coming from college here who actually have the ability and the confidence and empowerment to think and do things for themselves. More often than not here in the region, I see conformity as the norm, and we punish non-conformity. If you're different, we punish you, as opposed to embracing or even celebrating our individualities.

In many places across the region, being an entrepreneur is akin to being unemployed. That's how society sees you. "What do you mean you don't have a government job?" "What do you mean you don't earn a salary?" That's often seen as being the be-all and end-all of someone's work. What happens is that cultural influence on youth in this part of the world actually scares them away from entrepreneurial pursuits. This is propagated in anything and everything that you see—from media, to attitudes, to how people interact. Yet we're expected to find the best and the brightest to come to work for small startups based on a completely unknown concept called "equity," which is a bit of a stretch.

If you're looking to do something about it, you start early. You begin with seed programs where you're developing internship programs for kids in high schools or in universities where they can go out, get exposed to a business, be accountable for specific tasks over the summer or over a semester, and come back with that learning. Have that be part of structured programs within universities that they could get credit for, the equivalent of a year abroad or a year of field experience. I think that's essentially what you would learn working for a corporation, more or less. With an eye on maybe a specific task or research or whatever it is, students could bring a lot of benefits back to the organizations themselves, be they colleges, universities, or schools. But also, the experience that the student gets is priceless for them.

What the startups, or even the larger companies, that will take them in are getting is obviously having their finger on the pulse of what's going on in the youth market and having a pipeline for future talent.

NAJLA AL-MIDFA: Inspiration, education, and mentorship are vital pillars toward cultivating a future generation of change-makers. We must shift our current models of education to adapt to the needs of the market, with entrepreneurial skills embedded into the curriculum early on. Sheraa works with universities to help introduce students to these skills through classroom visits as well as community outreach workshops and events.

We have also partnered with entities such as the Sharjah Youth Council, Expo2020, ICT Fund, and IBM to teach core business skills, as well as host hackathons to encourage entrepreneurial and creative thinking. These events serve as opportunities for youth not only to be inspired toward entrepreneurship, but also to learn what it takes to become a change-maker in their own right, instilling traits such as curiosity, continuous learning, and resilience. Additionally, we recognize how important it is to have local role models to learn from, and often invite our alumni and other successful entrepreneurs to share their experiences with our community. Our annual entrepreneurship festival, SEF, is a combination of all these efforts. It brings the ecosystem together for two days of inspiration, knowledge-sharing, and networking.

Once aspiring entrepreneurs are ready to build their businesses, early-stage support is key, from idea validation through to product development and early traction. These are the key areas Sheraa's programs focus on, offering weeks of individualized mentorship, market access through our partnerships with corporate and government entities, and access to funding through equity-free grants.

OMAR AYYASH: I am a big fan of the Singaporean education model, which focuses on nurturing creativity, new teaching approaches, and innovation and entrepreneurship (I&E) across all disciplines.

It nurtures creativity as well as critical thinking. Programs have to strengthen problem-recognition and problem-solving activities and there should be spaces for creative thinking. These practices and spaces develop qualities such as creativity, confidence, and perseverance, which are essential I&E qualities.

Educational institutions' focus should not be just on the facilitation of knowledge, but more on business creation. Equipping students to apply such knowledge and abilities is a must in today's economic environment. University education should transform students into active learners by facilitating experimental and experiential environments that allow for trial and error, so that students have a diversity of I&E experiences. Therefore, lectures related to I&E should be an exception in higher education.

I&E knowledge on business creation should be provided across disciplines; I&E knowledge does not require a specific course or discipline. I&E knowledge and mindset should be embedded into every course and discipline. I&E thinking and acting are not only expected from a business founder, but also from employees and managers of established businesses as "intrapreneurs."

3. Reform and Modernize Outdated Government Legislation

Pave a clear path to win

ARUNMA OTEH: The key driver for economic development is making it easy for people to innovate, to become entrepreneurs, and to understand technology. That requires that the government provide value or simply stay out of the way when it's not bringing value. Policy-makers stand to benefit a lot by engaging with and listening to entrepreneurs, investors, and other players in the ecosystem, and intimately understanding their pain points, rather than assuming they understand what actually goes on the ground. My advice for government officials is to physically visit those startups and incubators and actively engage in the community on an ongoing basis. Always keep up on what's really happening in the ecosystem in order to create initiatives and regulations that are in sync with those realities.

The other thing governments ought to know is when to step in and when to step back. When I was the head of the Nigeria's SEC (Securities and Exchange Commission), I was on the President of Nigeria's economic management team. At each session we spent some time on every sector. We were discussing the local entertainment sector, Nollywood, and we were all making suggestions on how we could boost the industry. The President then pointed out that the Nollywood industry has grown to become the third-largest film industry in the world, after Bollywood and Hollywood, without government intervention whatsoever. He wanted us to think carefully about government intervention and when to step back and when to try to help. This has always remained with me as a real down-to-earth view and a reminder that government should basically assess whether it's bringing value or not bringing value to a given area before it goes on creating regulations and initiatives to solve everything.

JOSH LERNER: When thinking about things that are not good for governments to do, we see in many places the creation of labor laws that make it very hard to fire people and similarly costly to hire people. Now, you might say, "Why is it bad to have limits on firing people?" The main challenge is that there is a lot of uncertainty in startups. There's often one step forward and one step back, with a lot of exploration and course-correction along the way. It can be very challenging to make the process really work. In many cases, one is much better served by having more labor market flexibility rather than simply a set of rules that seemingly protects workers, but actually ends up harming them because they cannot get hired.

Similarly, consider rules around public markets. In many cases countries have created so many rules around going public that it actually discourages investors. Again, it is not bad to want to protect investors from problematic companies that want to go public and might end up shaking investor confidence. But having too many restrictions ends up actually preventing good firms from going public by just making it too onerous.

All in all, at least when it comes to entrepreneurship, I tend to take more of a hands-off approach in terms of allowing markets and industries to organically develop and mature. What is often most conducive to encouraging entrepreneurship is to let the market discover opportunities and modes itself, rather than dictating preferred industries or firms. It is not because the people within the government aren't smart or dedicated, but rather that the skill sets for running an effective government department and those involved in running a successful entrepreneurial venture are very different. Often the entrepreneurs themselves don't really know where things are heading and have to go through their own process of self-discovery to figure out where those opportunities are. Entrepreneurship is not conducive to planning things and managing top-down.

That said, it's important for governments to facilitate access to new technologies, including easing technology licensing for government-led R&D and importing regulations for machinery. Additionally, domestic labor laws play a big role in setting the stage for an ecosystem that is conducive to entrepreneurial and venture capital activities. This is not just in terms of hiring and firing, but also in the enforcement of non-compete agreements and other restrictive measures that often act as a deterrent to entrepreneurship.

In terms of attracting international investors, it's essential that tax and regulatory regimes are compatible with international standards. Even the slightest irregularities or deviations from international norms can deter investors, especially in less developed and smaller markets that lack reliable data. Investors seek environments with as little uncertainty as possible, thereby undertaking the least amount of risk.

All too often, however, gaps get overlooked or don't get enough attention. The World Bank's *Ease of Doing Business* rankings report is one such source of insight into such gaps.

One of the most important things today's policy-makers should do is continuously look into international best practices. There is a huge amount of experience with governments encouraging entrepreneurship and venture capital today around the globe. Figuring out what works and what does not work is extremely helpful. There have now been several decades of experimentation. By getting exposed to various case studies, policy-makers can distill key lessons and adapt them to their jurisdictions as needed.

SAMIH TOUKAN: Regulations are behind for the most part across the region, varying by type and degree from one country to another. We need to address the lag on a country-by-country basis. For example, in Jordan, we need to focus on reforming tax laws and bringing more stability to this area while, in the Gulf, we need to focus more on labor laws and immigration laws, and so on.

Customs remain a major bottleneck for most of the region, adversely affecting the free flow of goods in general and cross-border e-commerce most specifically. Customs regulations tend to be outdated and unpredictable. A package shipped to Egypt or Jordan, or many other places in the region, can be blocked at the border for several days or even weeks. A lot of unpredictability and friction need to be addressed once and for all.

Recently in Jordan, an issue arose related to introducing some taxes on individuals ordering via e-commerce from abroad. This significantly affected cross-border e-commerce players, such as CashBasha, to the point they had to halt their operation altogether. There was a lot of pushback on this on social media, so it seems that the government is looking to resolve this issue as we speak by trying to work with the courier companies rather than impose new taxation. I believe the procedure required the user to come in person to claim their package; it was a bit clunky from a free flow of goods perspective if we benchmark it against global standards for cross-border trade.

It just wasn't well thought out and seemed a bit reactionary and too sudden. I hope this matter is resolved by the time this book is published.

This is a small example of how unpredictable and reactionary regulations create an atmosphere of uncertainty for startups, which are already battling other forces both internally and from local and foreign competition. It is also the kind of thing that makes investors more reluctant to invest in the region—especially foreign investors who are used to more stable legal environments elsewhere and who might view the region as somewhat of a black box. This will be detrimental in the long haul beyond the immediate adverse impact.

EYAD ALKASSAR: Overall, I would say that the region has benefited significantly from a lack of regulations and red tape. On the one hand, in Europe, for example, everything is regulated to death. It's often very hard for new startups, not just because the industry is regulated, but also because the regulation is enforced. In the GCC, on the other hand, there is often a lack of regulation and more importantly a lack of immediate enforcement, which has been a blessing in disguise. For example, Careem initially operated in Saudi Arabia and the UAE in this very gray zone. If the regulators there had moved in immediately and regulated the space, you wouldn't have had this amazing company we have today.

I also think taxation is creating a big hurdle now, especially with the introduction of VAT (value-added tax) in the GCC, which adds a heavy layer of overhead. Also, now you have to basically look into a lot of tax and customs issues. Where do you sell things? Is it sold in Saudi Arabia or the UAE? What happens if we export it? This adds another layer of complexity that makes it increasingly more difficult to figure things out operationally.

SETH LEVINE: It's certainly possible that governments in the Middle East play an even bigger role than government in the US plays. One of the big challenges in the US when government gets involved is it typically wants to measure outcome in only one dimension, which is how many jobs are being created in the short term. This mentality is often influenced by politicians' motivation to get re-elected, whether or not it's actually the right priority in terms of ecosystem development for the long term. Sure, creating more jobs is good, but it's often not the best or only metric to gauge the health of an ecosystem. In fact, this approach often leads to investing in the wrong things.

Government dollars can certainly act as a propellant for a start- up ecosystem. A government-sponsored Techstars program, for example, is a great addition to a startup ecosystem that can help really coalesce many other things that need to happen to enable a startup community to thrive.

Government could also participate in and help launch different sources of capital. I'm not in favor of government as an investment vehicle though; nevertheless, I think government can play a role by investing in people who are raising funds and helping them get to a size where they can really be impactful in their local ecosystem. Government should not be the sole LP in those funds. They should be an LP, and not even a special LP, just an investor in a fund along with other individuals or other institutions. We've seen this work well in the US and other ecosystems where government dollars—as an LP—are leveraged by outside money to help funds get off the ground.

Overall, I'm not a fan of government stepping in as a controller, say, of a payment gateway or something similar. When that happens, it just promotes skepticism around whether there is a level playing field. I'm also not in favor of government picking winners and losers in any given sector. I prefer for government to play the role of an enabler rather than an operator. Thus, as a rule, I believe the government will be better off promoting entrepreneurial development in that sector rather than getting directly involved. It could certainly offer investment prizes or something like the X Prize to encourage people to work on certain types of problems. It could also set up an accelerator program focused on a certain crucial segment and support entrepreneurs working on solving particular set of problems.

Governments have ways to promote those things without saying,

"Well, we need to go create this ourselves," because more entrepreneurs, more capital, and more competition are the key drivers to solving problems. Thus, ultimately, problems are best solved through the open market, and free competition is key.

De-risk entrepreneurship and innovation

DANIEL ISENBERG: Public policy is one essential component of entrepreneurship ecosystem development but, taken by itself in isolation from the other elements, it can be anywhere from helpful, to useless, to harmful. To foster an ecosystem with the objective of more and more local firms growing more and more rapidly, you can't have policy that exists in and for itself. Policy won't make any difference unless other elements also coexist. Without a culture that supports it, the education system that creates the human capital, the talent that feeds it, the larger companies that support it, the financial institutions that fund it, and so forth, policy on its own does not foster an entrepreneurship or scaleup ecosystem.

First, just looking at the public policy angle, policy-makers need to be clear about what their objectives are and who specifically they intend their policies to target. Too often policy-makers lump microenterprise, self-employment, SMEs, innovative businesses, technology startups, and (occasionally) family businesses all together under "entrepreneurship." These are different segments that should not be grouped together since they often directly conflict with each other; that is, they are negatively correlated in reality.

Second, it's important to distinguish between what I call "hard policy" and "soft policy." Hard policy is the laws, regulations, and financial systems. They're very important. Soft policy is the roles that the policy-makers can play in convening the other stakeholders from the other sectors, aligning them, encouraging growth, celebrating growth, cheerleading when growth occurs, and recognizing it in many different ways. Soft policy also encompasses all the initiatives that governments undertake that do not have a legal dimension, but nevertheless help catalyze and facilitate more and more local firms growing more and more rapidly.

There's certainly a difference between hard and soft policy. My observation is that soft policy is much more important than hard policy when it comes to fostering entrepreneurship ecosystems. When it comes to innovation, on the other hand, hard policy is probably more important. I don't think that providing subsidized loans or other incentives on their own can be effective unless they're accompanied by a lot of other things. In fact, on their own they can be harmful because they prevent market discipline.

From a regulatory system standpoint, it's important to have an environment that makes allowances for business failure and is prepared to deal with it. I believe that failure is best treated as a byproduct of success, as far as entrepreneurship goes. There will be failures because there's an open market and that's how markets work: markets cannot function without failure (but hopefully there are more successes than failures over time). Failure is just a normal thing in any entrepreneurship ecosystem and part of its evolution. Sometimes even the largest or most promising companies fail and that's also normal.

By the way, by failure I mean significant destruction of value, usually accompanied by bankruptcy or major recapitalization. A lot of entrepreneurship experts conflate mistakes with failure. Mistakes, of course, are part of life. You can't learn without making mistakes. Failing, or what I call "catastrophic failure," is an entirely different story. That has to be offset by having a very efficient bankruptcy system, limited personal liability, and flexibility of labor.

Additionally, it's important to have a lot of opportunities for retraining people in new skills and making workforce development simple. Denmark went through a major transformation from protecting employment to flexibility in the redeployment of human resources in productive ways.

There's an important distinction between preventing unemployment or unemployment insurance and mechanisms that allow you to be re-employed easily. You want to decrease the cost for the entrepreneur of firing people, but you also want to make it very easy for those people to become productive again in other ways. This labor force mobility is essential for entrepreneurship. That's a policy issue: don't protect employment, protect employability.

EFOSA OJOMO: Many governments now appreciate innovation and are interested in it at least at face value. Professor Clayton Christensen—my Co-Author of *The Prosperity Paradox* and Author of *The Innovator's Dilemma* among a number of other popular and groundbreaking titles—always says, "Regulation and corruption are two sides of the same coin." What he means by that is when you create a new regulation—especially in a region where enforcement is lacking or there's a ton of poverty—you have just created an opportunity for corruption to thrive. What also often happens is that governments copy regulations from other places in the world; however, these copied regulations may have evolved over hundreds of years to fit the local needs of the people and environment of that region. This usually doesn't work out too well either.

Look at financial services—with respect to regulations in the banking sector and financial inclusion, for example—and ask, how do we get non-consumers of financial services into the consumption economy of financial services? A regulation in emerging markets should look entirely different from a regulation in the US or Japan or in many countries in Europe, because those are places where you already have a ton of consumption of financial services. All this comes down to freedom for the entrepreneur, not the government and the regulators, to experiment and innovate, and to find solutions to those problems.

On the other hand, basic things in terms of regulations can help pave the way toward greater innovation, such as making it easy for locals and foreigners to start businesses, not overtaxing business, incentivizing productivity not profitability, etc. For example, offer benefits for banks to give a certain number of people access to financial services. If they don't meet those numbers, then they get taxed at a different rate.

SAMI MAHROUM: One concern that comes up is IP laws, or their absence, in the MENA region, which I'm actually not too worried about. If you look at more developed, larger markets like the US, EU, Japan, and China, that's where you ought to be worried about protecting your idea against piracy or IP infringement. This is not to say that I don't encourage the local governments across the region to enforce IP laws, especially to provide incentive and protection to innovators. Still, it's not as much of an issue in this part of the world, because if you come up with an important, critical discovery or finding, your main markets will still be in North America, Europe, and Asia, and that's where your IP needs to be protected against much greater risks than here in the region. It can be a problem on the artistic scene, however. If you have a song or music developed, say, in Egypt and stolen in Lebanon, or vice versa, that's something else, but in terms of cutting-edge technology and true innovation, that is not as big of a concern.

SETH LEVINE: Legal and tax are critical issues as new markets develop, because many emerging markets don't have robust legal systems suited to startup businesses. The absence of this critical infrastructure can create a real challenge for attracting capital to those regions. In many of the markets in which I've worked in Africa and the Middle East, all of the companies are still US domiciled. That can work fine, because there's obviously a robust business law in the US that dates back for centuries, but it creates issues of money flow and tax. One of the areas in which I think regulators of those ecosystems need to look is where their local businesses are actually and legally being domiciled, and how they can work on a tax treaty of some kind with, say, the US or the UK that allows funds to flow back and forth more easily and readily.

I've found this is something that entrepreneurs in emerging

markets don't always think about because they're busy running their businesses. It can, however, create challenges when companies go to raise capital and realize that there are impediments to attracting capital simply based on the ability for investors to recognize profits without multiple taxing jurisdictions. Clearly, that's an area to examine.

A related consideration is that often the investment money is in one currency and the transactions for the underlying business are in another currency (and sometimes the payroll expenses are in a third currency). Thus, local entrepreneurs need to be thoughtful about what types of business they set up and where, where their customers reside, and how they work with the local constituency to match their dollars in and dollars out, as well as think through strategies to minimize currency fluctuation risk.

OSMAN SULTAN: The regulations in terms of risk-taking in the region remain a concern. Bankruptcy laws should be allowing some of these entrepreneurs to take risks and fail. New residency laws in the UAE coming into effect incentivize and reward entrepreneurs, so that's a great step forward in this area. It's particularly encouraging to see such initiatives at the leadership level, recognizing the positive impact, both economic and social, that entrepreneurs are having on our societies.

Earlier than any other place in the region, the UAE had, and continues to have, a forward-thinking mindset on this front. We're also starting to see this mindset in Saudi Arabia develop quite strongly more recently, and at different levels in various other parts of the region. Having said that, it's one thing to have the right intention and the right strategy, and it's another to have flawless execution and the right people in place. Perhaps that's where the gap is. There will always be some room for improvement and some fine-tuning in the execution, but I believe things are going in the right direction for the ecosystem across the board in the UAE and the whole region, whether we're taking about regulations, infrastructure, funding, or other aspects.

IDRISS AL RIFAI: The lack of proper bankruptcy and insolvency regulations across the region remains a major issue. Some positive reforms have been instigated in the UAE and a couple of other places, but all in all it's completely prohibitive for any entrepreneur or startup that is considering anything remotely risky, which is by definition all startup activities. This is a long-overdue issue across the region. It needs to be sorted out once and for all.

Protect free market, not market segments

ALEC ROSS: I have no issue with governments stepping in to help local businesses. The problem is that, in many places, governments think that the way to help local businesses is by hurting international players, such as Amazon, Uber, or others. I think it is regressive to try to keep a dominant global business out or try to slow it down in the local market in the name of protecting local companies. On the other hand, it's understandable and viable to try to lend a hand to local companies, be it helping local merchants digitize their content so they're more e-commerce ready, helping them reach new markets, or subsidizing reskilling and upskilling programs for their staff.

This is an entirely different approach focused on enabling and supporting rather than trying to keep innovation out, which comes at a heavy cost to society. This cost is ultimately borne by the local consumer. It also has an adverse impact on the local sector and economic growth in general. For example, I am a very happy Amazon Prime member. Why? Because it saves my family probably hundreds of hours over the course of a year, so we don't waste an hour going to an office supply store every time we want to buy paper, ink cartridges, or whatever. The time savings and convenience that Amazon offers, or any similar entity whether local or international, has a real impact on the quality of people's lives. If you keep people from using the efficiencies that companies like Amazon have created, instead of letting free market flow, you're ultimately keeping them in yesterday, and you're wasting their time. That's certainly the wrong orientation.

SETH LEVINE: Nationalization policies are a difficult issue. I understand why governments want to promote local economic development. I understand their concern, not the least of which is that when you hire and invest in foreigners, they have a tendency to go back to wherever they're from at some point, and that does not necessarily help develop the ecosystem they want. The US has a version of that via its program, which limits the number of foreign nationals to be hired in various sectors in the US.

There is pressure to hire locally even here in the US, so I fully get why certain governments in the Gulf are concerned about that. Having said that, and particularly in the early days of ecosystems, the more restrictions you put on the ability for companies to operate in a way that is in their best economic interest, the more you hamper the growth of the ecosystem you're purportedly trying to support. Generally speaking, I think rules that prohibit or interfere with startups operating the way they want to, within the law of course, are counterproductive.

Governments seeking to boost local employment can do so in many ways. First of all, they can focus on their education system, because the real thing that will change the trajectory of hiring over the long-term is creating a skilled labor force that has the skill set and know-how required for the new economy. The better educated the locals are, the more companies are going to hire them.

Local governments can also provide incentives to hire local citizens. (Canada has done this nationally; a number of cities in the US have done this as well.) It's not a prohibition against hiring people that are foreign or penalties for having too many foreigners, but it provides an incentive for hiring people who are local. This might take different forms—both on the employer side and the employee side—but they generally involve either lower taxes at the individual wage level or rebates for dollars spent on local workers. In my mind, programs such as these are much better than simply saying, "You have to hire X number of locals or you can't exceed X percentage of your staff being foreigners, or else we will penalize you."

ARUNMA OTEH: One interesting issue that has surfaced recently is that the world is becoming more connected and we are moving more and more into becoming a global economy. One example that comes to mind is governments' concern that Amazon will overtake the local retail market and put local merchants out of business. Do governments need to regulate these players to offset the threat?

My view on this issue is somewhat different. I would actually try to engage Amazon, while trying to understand how to support the local players to become more prepared to deal with market demands and shifts in consumer behavior. Perhaps, some kind of win-win outcome can be created where local merchants can be further incentivized to sell on Amazon or access a wider global market via Amazon's platform, versus the common knee-jerk reaction of, "let's stop Amazon from coming in" or "let's regulate." Personally, I tend to err on the side of letting free competition take its course. But I think that with some large players like Amazon, it's actually a fruitful exercise to engage with them, because they're also looking to be responsible entities and not just be branded as the bad guys.

BADR JAFAR: Another aspect, and one that I accept is complex, is the localization policies that create an imperative for government institutions to provide work, contracts, and purchase orders to local people and suppliers. At times, that can create a bit of an uneven playing field. Now, I'm a local and I completely understand the rationale for these policies, particularly when you have populations like the UAE where nationals make up a minority of the population. The state has a genuine policy interest in ensuring that local people and companies have access to opportunities.

However, it's a very delicate balance that needs to be struck because, on the one hand, there is a need to provide support systems for your citizens but, on the other hand, you don't want to create a sense of entitlement. You also don't want a sense of resentment from other members of the community who are working alongside the immediate beneficiaries of these policies, and who can be just as passionate about the success of the overall economic environment as local people are. Of course, there are many countries around the world with perks for being a national of that country, but there still has to be that sense of a level playing field, which is so important to the development of a healthy ecosystem.

WILL HERMAN: With regard to government initiatives that attempt to help protect local companies against international, dominant players, I personally don't think this has any impact on startups in general; and again, I refer to startups as scalable entities. There are no borders for startups. If an Amazon or a Walmart in the US moves into a local area, or another country for that matter, it's not going to impact local companies, with the exception of sucking up all of the potential employees. This is obviously a very big deal and can potentially raise salaries in the local environment, as was the case with Google, for example. But it's not the government's role to step in and manage the salaries companies are paying their employees.

For small businesses, though, it's a big deal. When a giant grocery chain moves into a neighborhood, it becomes much harder for them to compete. The US has laws to limit unfair competition, but this case isn't covered by such laws. Amazon can push out stores locally, say, with greater product selection, more convenience, and lower pricing.

I'm definitely a free market advocate. As long as everybody's playing by the rules, I think that this dynamic is actually good for society. The big chain store that comes in or the big e-commerce player that comes in are also supporting the local economy. They're serving customers. They're paying taxes. They're hiring people. And, in the case of Amazon—and many other third-party marketplaces such as eBay, Walmart, and Etsy—it provides a massive population of merchants an online platform for selling their goods. So, I don't see that they need to be penalized for their success.

Interfering through regulations in order to prevent local stores from closing down is not the right approach. That would be a mistake. If Amazon takes over and those stores shut down, then there's a shift in the market. There's not necessarily less value being created. On the contrary, greater value is being created, but there's a shift, so naturally there are winners and losers.

Now, I'll put something in perspective here. I live in a very small town in a very small state in the United States. In my small town, there's actually a rule—not a law—that says the town will not allow any chain restaurant, hotel, or store into the town. Defining a chain gets a little blurry, but these are basically national chains that aren't allowed into the town. The town has to approve all building permits and will not approve building permits for chains.

Does that make this town, which only has 5,000 permanent year-round residents, any better? I think some would argue that it does. I'm not one of those people. On the other hand, perhaps such a dynamic is by design; after all, nobody is going to come into a very small town if they don't think there is a large enough pool of potential customers and potential hires. A big grocery giant is not going to set up in my town, and neither would Amazon, Walmart, or Google.

Now, if you're in New York City, all those players want to come in and will naturally push out little neighborhood people unless those people can show how they add value to their customers and demonstrate some kind of personalized service or competitive advantage over their much larger competition. There are obviously ways that this can be done, so it's not a foregone conclusion that big players must necessarily eat small players. Small players can and often do out-compete big players based on their intimacy with the local market and its needs, as well as relationships they have fostered for many years with local customers and the local community. They just need to be more agile and creative to hold on to their market share in the face of fierce competition operating on, perhaps, a more efficient cost structure and/or offering customers greater value.

Overall, I think that protection policies are always going to be somewhat artificial, but I think they're reasonable for a short time. If you say that the government is going to support those with less flexibility in a way that's more educational—in terms of educating people on how to be better competitors and access resources that help them to be better competitors—that's a reasonable way of making the transition. But this is only reasonable insofar as they are implemented for a transitional period, not on an ongoing basis.

I don't believe that the taxpayers should be burdened with corporate welfare. Just because a store is underperforming doesn't mean that the taxpayers should be tapped to keep it alive. However, it's reasonable for a community's sake to have taxpayers, via the government, kick in to help train them to make the transition. I think that's a reasonable idea.

On the other hand, human nature is human nature. If you can make just as much money by not doing anything, or by doing less work, most people will choose to do it that way. Often, too much support can create an element of complacency. Having said that, I do like the idea of having money spent on people who have never had to really compete before to help them learn how to do it, but only for a limited period of time.

EYAD ALKASSAR: We have sometimes seen regulation that favors existing, established incumbents in certain markets for unknown reasons. Perhaps this entity has enjoyed a long relationship with, or is involved with, certain government agencies or initiatives, or is doing very strong lobbying work behind the scenes. Obviously, favoritism of this kind doesn't create an equal-opportunity dynamic or a level playing field and is unhealthy.

When it comes to governments stepping in to protect local players against global giants, I'm not so sure if I would support this practice because it can actually backfire and harm the very same local players that it is intended to protect. For example, Careem survived and was actually beating Uber in many markets, not because it was protected by the government or by the regulations but because it was outperforming Uber operationally and on customer acquisition. I think overprotection can be harmful because it undermines competition and thus is more likely to elicit complacency from the local companies, in effect making it worse for them. I think Careem would have been a much worse company today if it was somehow protected from Uber. It would have had much less incentive to build better algorithms, better pricing strategies, a better product, and a better overall experience for the customer.

A lot of benefit comes from having large international players enter the market, as long as they are playing fair and as long as the regulators make sure that they're playing fair. But I think all these other calls for blocking or restricting their access, and basically protecting local companies, is somewhat dangerous to the local economy.

Having said that, making funding available to local companies is very important. Obviously, the international players have a massive competitive advantage because they have access to, say, Silicon Valley money or deeper pockets in general typically from the US or China. I am a big advocate of governments encouraging investment in local companies. This can be achieved via fund-matching programs that we are seeing now in Saudi Arabia, and partially in the UAE, for example. A positive kind of favoritism for local companies through funding makes a lot of sense, whereas a negative kind of discrimination against large international companies is harmful to the ecosystem.

On the issue of nationalization policies, my belief is that it's certainly important to get the local population very involved in new companies and engaged with the new economy in general. In the beginning, a lot of people resisted such policies. I remember that Careem, Uber, and others had issues with "Saudization" initially. It was, however, probably the largest job creation in a decade. It's easy to understand where governments are coming from, and I think it's a good long-term idea. I do think, however, that it has to be implemented carefully. You can't implement this across all industries and expect equally positive results. For specific industries that require high-level or specialized kinds of talent, you should always allow inflow of foreign talent to fill key positions where local talent has yet to catch up. You should actually never restrict foreign talent coming in; those are the very same people who will come with the knowledge they acquired elsewhere and train your local population.

Certainly, universities can play a bigger role in bringing the local population up to speed. I have been a part of an amazing initiative called Qimam, founded by Dr. Annas Abedin. He basically built a scholarship system for the most talented students in Saudi Arabia, with some of the top business leaders and CEOs as mentors in the program. They are extremely selective about who they accept in the program to ensure that they graduate only the best of the best. Tens of thousands of students applied for the last admission, of which only some dozen were selected. I would like to see more programs like this that can support and feed amazing talent into the ecosystem.

ABDULAZIZ AL LOUGHANI: I certainly feel the pain and it's a very alarming trend when you look at the unemployment rate in this part of the world. In a country like Kuwait, 90% of the workforce is state-employed. I don't see that as an issue, but I would emphasize the quality of education for fresh graduates to be ready for work more than nationalizing different sectors.

I don't think mandating quotas is the fix to unemployment in the long term, but I definitely think it's the right thing to do in the short term. It is the right thing to do because corporates have very much benefited from our economies over the past 50 years with very minimal benefit for our states and our youth. Instead of paying corporate tax, corporates need to employ our graduates.

Having said that, the bigger problem is the education system. A lot of our youth are very spoiled and quite lax when it comes to their jobs and careers. You know how many people are getting paid to sit at home? A lot of people are getting paid and just sitting at home as a result of "Kuwaitization" or "Saudization" quotas. It really boils down to competency. If you and I were competent, they wouldn't pay us to sit at home. They would actually put us to good use. So, ultimately, education and skill-building are the solution.

Additionally, on the funding side, in order for us to attract the best talent and really create global franchises, I believe we need to start shifting our focus from supporting local nationals to supporting our local economy at large. We need to start funding the best founders and companies out there who are disrupting the status quo, regardless of their nationality. As long as we continue providing more focus on national funding over development money and keep chasing short-term goals, we will never create real long-term value. The focus ought to be on growing the overall economy and not elevating any one group.

SAMIH TOUKAN: I am not a big advocate of protectionism policies, as I believe they ultimately backfire. After all, we need international companies to come in. We need foreign investment. We need their knowledge. We need them to help create more local jobs. We cannot and should not try to fight them or slow them down. This is the internet. We are not China; we do not have the alternative of our own internet. Our local and regional organizations need to compete with both local and global players, as they already do.

Careem is an example of a local company that competed well with the international player, Uber, and ended up getting acquired by Uber. The same with Souq, which also competed with and ended up exiting to Amazon. Competition and exits are healthy—that's not the issue. The real issue is that we have only one type of successful outcome, which is exit to a bigger brand. There is no current clear path to an IPO in the region. Fawry is one example of a tech company that went public in Egypt recently, which is a huge milestone in the startup and tech ecosystem in and of itself. Hopefully many more will follow. The challenge is that the bar is set quite high for local startups and tech companies to get listed on those local exchanges. Ironically, the Fawry story didn't get a fraction of the PR and media coverage of Careem's acquisition by Uber being only a few months apart, nor did the significance to the ecosystem of this single event seem to have been fully appreciated.

If you look at the stock exchanges today in the Arab world, they are not really open to technology companies and startups. These are mainly tailored to banks, insurance companies, and more traditional industries. Meanwhile, in the US, the stock exchange is open to startups and tech companies to do IPOs. This is where I believe the government should focus. How do we make the regulations easier for local startups and technology companies to raise money and go public in the Arab world, and to not always have to look internationally? Careem, for example, wouldn't have qualified to go public in the region, but Lyft did in the US. When these companies can go public in the US, why are we not helping or attracting them to go public in our countries?

When this happens, there will be more exits and the ecosystem will grow much faster. Today, we are waiting for the big exits, the big foreign brands, to come and absorb the local players. But we cannot always depend on an Amazon to come and buy a local successful startup. We need to facilitate more local exits and IPOs for those companies.

PATRICK CHALHOUB: Today's world is increasingly becoming interconnected, so I'm all for open trade. This is especially the case for countries in the region, which are relatively small, unlike larger countries like China and the US, which can afford to be less open if they want to give their companies a much larger "playground," if you will. Having said that, we need to make sure that the rules of the game are the same for everyone, that there is a level playing field for all parties, whether it is a local company or an imported one. For example, if certain advantages apply to foreign companies that are not available to local ones, then that's certainly not a fair game. The basic principle is to let organic competition determine who wins and who loses, while ensuring equal opportunity for all the players.

Of course, you often end up with a dominant player in any given industry, which poses a threat to others—especially incumbents who fail to adapt to the times—by virtue of outcompeting them. That's where agility is key. Look at the success of Careem, for example. It found a key gap against Uber and just ran with it. In fact, it didn't do anything substantially different than what Uber was doing, but it was able to fill the gap of cash payments and therefore better tailor to the local market. That was its competitive advantage against a much larger player.

FOUAD JERYES: I've found that some governments are very protective of local industry and merchants, which can sometimes stunt growth, slow progress, and kill innovation. It's not because Amazon or any other e-commerce player exists, it's because the internet offered an opportunity to evolve the way retail works altogether. We see progressive governments that recognize these changes, but do not act to suddenly protect traditional retail from imminent evolution or even extinction. Some of our governments in the region, unfortunately, fear having to deal with a furor from the population coming to their doors, claiming that ministries have not done their duty in protecting them, and as a result end up acting in counterproductive ways that make the advancement of industries difficult.

On the other hand, if the governments were proactive and provided the digital channels and programs to facilitate the changes that came along, then a larger portion of local merchants, especially ones who tailor to a particular market niche and provide a so called "long tail" offering, would take advantage of what is inevitable change. The government could also claim that it played an active role in evolving the market. I'm not an economist or political scholar by any means; however, I have this burning feeling that in our very nascent new-age markets, we need to realize that we have nothing to lose and everything to gain by being proactive and enabling of these smaller, quicker, and more modern opportunities to grow into larger economic players. Not the opposite.

MOHAMMED JAFFAR: Historically speaking, well before oil, people here were entrepreneurs by nature, and they were hardworking by nature because life was very tough and they had to be to survive. With the emergence of oil, many people became complacent and we had an influx of other nationalities coming to this part of the world to perform certain jobs that many of us didn't want or know how to do.

I'm a big believer in giving equal opportunity to everyone, whether they are a national or not. We should not segregate or give or deny someone a certain job just because of their background, legally or commercially. I understand that there is a huge unemployment problem among the national population in certain countries and governments are feeling this pressure; still, I don't advocate placing restrictions on companies to make them recruit more nationals instead of foreigners. I think a more viable solution would be, looking at best practices in the developed world, to not segregate between nationalities. The best person should take the job. That creates competition between people, so it will help people to improve. This is good for business and ultimately good for the economy.

ISSA AGHABI: Generally speaking, I think imposing hiring quotas on people doesn't always work unless you have the right people and the right talent out there. As an entrepreneur, you can't be thinking about quotas and numbers and people you have to hire and by when. Rather, your focus needs to be solely on filling key roles as soon as possible with the right people. When I want to hire a CEO, I don't care about his or her race, nationality, or religion. I should care only about qualification and ability to execute.

I understand why it may be mandated in certain sectors, but in others, such as the tech and new economy sectors, it's not very efficient. It might work in government roles or more traditional industrial roles, as opposed to technology and startups, unless those local talents exist, which is not always the case. For example, I want an experienced PHP developer who is a superstar. Can I find him locally? That is the question. If so, then great. If not, I need be able to recruit from abroad.

RABEA ATAYA: I think nationalization policies are necessary in order to bridge the unemployment gap with the local population. After all, every government has a primary responsibility to take care of its population, including its nationals. If national unemployment is high, it's a primary objective of the government to mitigate that; hence, the importance of nationalization. Then the question becomes, "What's the most effective way to nationalize?" This always comes down to a combination of carrot and stick, since both can be useful. Personally-speaking, I enjoy seeing the carrot a lot more than the stick.

Leverage public-private partnerships

JOHN MACOMBER: Greater emphasis should be placed on public-private partnerships to solve infrastructure problems. For example, private companies may have solutions to big infrastructure problems. It's just a matter of governments collaborating better with them. Maybe these governments need to use open innovation competitions or platforms that bring in the right startups or companies to help fill those gaps. Where governments struggle to fill in certain big gaps, innovative companies can step up to do just that.

Everybody's preferred choice is for governments to respond to the needs of business and the people, to spend efficiently so that taxpayer money is not wasted, and to build out the physical and soft infrastructure we all need to thrive. The evidence is that very few governments are capable of doing that, or at least doing it optimally. Maybe they do in San Francisco, Boston, Singapore, and some other advanced cities, but how about the rest of the world? The question, then, is how can the private sector pick up the slack where governments fall? Governments need to be more proactive in addressing the problems of the present and future by creating the right collaborative channels with the private sector, based on the premise that the world is advancing very quickly and there are innovative solutions out there that we need to stay on top of.

For example, developing a national street address system historically has been a problem unaddressed by many governments in emerging markets and ultimately affecting the delivery of goods and services, especially in an increasingly e-commerce-oriented world.

One solution for solving the address problem is called what3words, out of the UK. It essentially takes the entire globe and divides it into a 10-meter by 10-meter grid based on GPS information. Then it assigns those GPS coordinates three random but unique words, say, "apple, ball, blue," that are not only easy to remember, but make it practical to precisely deliver goods and services to a very specific location. It thus seeks to replace the need for street addresses and for GPS coordinates and to help people figure out where they live and work and make use of a ton of other practical applications beyond deliveries. That's an example of a private sector attempt to help solve a massive, dated infrastructure problem in this region.

SAMIH TOUKAN: One example of a public-private partnership that comes to mind is an exciting startup we've invested in called ArabiaWeather. It faced regulatory challenges from day one, because essentially this company is trying to disrupt what traditionally has been handled by governments and meteorological offices. ArabiaWeather's aim is to leverage new technology and data to produce more accurate and cost-effective weather-related data and insights. It faced resistance from the existing powers early on.

Today, in the Arab world, if you want to disrupt what a government has been doing or what big banks have been doing, you're going to face some resistance and challenges there. There's no cooperation yet between government institutions and the private sector to try to solve certain key, massive problems. Uber is another example where they faced regulatory issues all over the world, not only in the Arab world.

I think there needs to be more openness from governments to collaborate with those startups, which may very well come up with solutions that can solve problems that traditional government institutions have not been able to solve. On the other hand, entrepreneurs need to show more resilience and patience, and work through the right channels and influence points in order to bring about that collaboration. That effort could take many forms, whether it's showcasing the viability of their solutions, demonstrating the merits of a new innovation, or even lobbying with other players in their space for policy change.

In the case of ArabiaWeather, Jordan's meteorological offices initially saw them as competition, but with time ArabiaWeather was able to break through and form a working relationship with them, and now it cooperates with these government offices. They figured out a model whereby they now sell their solution to the meteorological offices and they work together to sell it to other clients. It's a B2G2G (business-to-government-to-government) or B2G2B (business-to-government-to-business) models, whereby ArabiaWeather provides the solution to the metrological office and in turn the office is able to sell it to other government organizations or other big enterprises. It certainly took time and a lot of effort to come up with this model, but ultimately it was well worth it.

Both government and entrepreneurs have to work together to unblock new solutions to local problems that neither one could address on their own. Another great example of such public-private partnership is the new Careem/RTA partnership in the UAE, which just launched a new taxi service together.

One of our portfolio companies, BitOasis, is going through a similar issue and working with regulators as we speak in Abu Dhabi, where there is a sandbox for blockchain projects. Abu Dhabi's government has regulated BitOasis and other crypto exchanges. It's certainly challenging for the startup, but it comes with the territory and as an entrepreneur you ought to expect it as part of startup life and be ready to deal with it.

Naturally, if I come up with something new today that is disruptive and has not been regulated yet, regulation is not going to change just like that. Regulation is always going to be behind and it's going to take time to change. It often needs a lot of lobbying from the various stakeholders and influential figures, as well raising awareness and educating people. So, the question is to what extent is the entrepreneur and the government are proactive to accelerate that process.

BADR JAFAR: There are a number of things that governments are either too overstretched to handle, or simply not equipped to handle, because the nature of those particular problems that need solving requires nimble approaches that are more suited to small teams and small organizations. One of the most important things that governments can do in these situations is to ensure that they are incentivizing people and organizations to channel their creativity and capital into solving these challenges.

Conversely, from an entrepreneurial perspective, if you can create a business model that fundamentally addresses a systemic social challenge, and if you can demonstrate success in addressing that challenge, then you will have a phenomenal market opportunity. It's unlikely that the structural problem you are focusing on is going to completely go away anytime soon. Therefore, as well as having a positive impact, you will have built yourself a very robust, sustainable business model.

SAMIA MELHEM: In our region, governments and the private sector are very intertwined. The thing is, especially when it comes to what we call the "Mashreq" region (located in the eastern part of the Arab world, located in Western Asia and eastern North Africa, and include the GCC, the Levant, Egypt, and Sudan), government has a key role in building digital infrastructure, or broadband. Having laws that allow the telecom sector to be as open as possible to competition brings in many operators who would invest and who have incentive to invest in remote areas, say in mountains or faraway towns in the desert. Governments can offer such operators incentives. This will have a positive impact on expanding broadband coverage and reducing its cost.

MOHAMED ANOUAR MAAROUF: We are working on introducing another procedure that is relevant to the Startup Act and not currently included in it, but we're preparing for it by revising public procurement regulations. This procedure is called "Open Innovation" and it will allow the state to publicly procure innovation, which is not yet possible because we don't know how to quantify innovation. The state knows how to purchase ready-made products that are thoroughly described in calls for tender. We now want to introduce this new element to public procurement—procurement for innovation and creativity. This means that the state will be able to create challenges or incubation for startups, select the one that provides the best solutions, and then contract them based on direct negotiations instead of undergoing the complications of public procurement policies.

Implement future-proof regulations

IDRISS AL RIFAI: More often than not, good and bad regulations are related to how well the regulation itself has been able to keep up with the pace of economic and technological changes. It's natural that there would be some kind of lag with respect to regulations. However, to the extent that this lag stretches and outdated regulations are enforced on newly evolved environments that have new requirements, there will be damage.

For example, at Fetchr, we're not the only ones feeling the pain of this dynamic. You look at Careem—they got shut down because of regulations in Abu Dhabi. Careem was actually operating for years without any problems, then all of a sudden, they were forced down and had to find a new resolution. For us, it's a very similar dynamic. We keep having regulatory issues. There are a lot of gray areas, such as cross-border e-commerce withholding tax, customs clearance, B2B shipping, brand-exclusive licensing regulations, and many other vague issues. We feel like regulations are not one step behind but more like three or four steps behind. It's mind-boggling that we do not have an e-commerce playbook in this region yet.

MUHAMMED MEKKI: Whenever a new business model or technology emerges, startups are always on the front lines, often devising creative solutions to navigate an unclear regulatory environment. Regulation in the region needs to get up to speed to keep pace with innovation.

For example, Neo Technologies, a FinTech company born at AstroLabs Dubai, decided to avoid regulatory risk from the start by getting licensed as a software company that provides digital investment solutions to regulated financial institutions in the region. Most FinTech companies are taking this route, sitting under the regulatory umbrella of banks instead of attempting to get regulated directly.

BitOasis is another example. It's the region's leading cryptocurrency exchange and has been live since 2015. It took the risky approach of diving straight into an industry that was not yet regulated and worked closely with regulators to help define the rules. CEO Ola Doudin's approach has been working so far, as she was able to secure preliminary approval from UAE financial regulators in May 2019.

Sometimes, however, startups aren't as fortunate. Several years ago, a tech-enabled hourly car rental company in Dubai attempted to get licensed; however, they had to wait for the regulations to be officially released before getting the green light to proceed. They unfortunately ran out of cash and had to shut down while waiting. The regulations eventually were released, and several successful startups emerged in that space afterwards. One of them, being Udrive, which ended up being a client of ours at AstroLabs when they expanded to Saudi Arabia.

OSMAN SULTAN: We have seen, for instance, an open data law in the UAE as part of the Smart City ambition. That's a very positive move. Remember, the current global tech space has a lot of moving parts and is constantly changing, so a lot of areas have yet to be defined in terms of legal framework standards. I believe that these conversations need to and will happen between the various stakeholders on a global level.

When it comes, for instance, to AI, you see people like Bill Gates, Elon Musk, and other key figures questioning where these new technologies will take us, and whether we're ready to adjust as societies. Indeed, the pace of change is accelerating at greater speed than ever, and the full social impacts that these disruptive technologies will have are not yet entirely clear. These are complex issues that need to be addressed to reform current regulations and develop new ones that are future-ready; it's not a binary equation and the answers are very often not in "zero or one" terms.

ERIK BRYNJOLFSSON: Government has a big role to play in terms of preparing for future innovations and technologies. The main thing, however, is to make sure it doesn't entrench the incumbents. I think too much legislation is designed to try to preserve old jobs and old industries. That's the worst thing you could do. You need to embrace the new jobs and new industries.

That said, there are some real risks with these new technologies in the areas of privacy, data security, and algorithmic bias. There's also the disruption of inequality where many people are left behind. You need to do things for income support and retraining and redeploying people into new jobs as old jobs get automated. If you can manage those risks, then people will embrace the new technologies. If you ignore those risks, then there's a backlash. Many people are going to push against the adoption of new technologies and that will slow down progress.

We see something similar happening with globalization, where free trade can make the pie bigger and create wealth for a country. It also makes it very uneven, where there are winners and losers. The right policy is to make sure that the benefits are broadly shared and that people are able to transition to new jobs, as free trade creates new opportunities but also eliminates some old ones.

If a country only pushes for free trade and doesn't help with the transition, then it ends up facing a backlash and protectionist measures. We've seen that in almost every country over the past decade or so. I don't want to see the same thing happen with new technology, where people push back against the technology, because the gains are so uneven or because some people aren't sharing the prosperity that's created.

ALBERT BRAVO-BIOSCA: My view is that governments around the world need to become much more experimental. That means being more open to new programs and policy ideas from all of the different sources that they can tap into, being more willing to rigorously test them out, and being open to recognizing that they may fail. In other words, they should be constantly testing, learning, and redesigning their programs and policies rather than assuming that they are going to work, which unfortunately happens more often than it should.

This is not a radically new idea; it has been used a lot in the context of developing countries. Only a few months ago, Abhijit Banerjee, Esther Duflo, and Michael Kremer were awarded the Nobel Prize in economics for their experimental approach to alleviating global poverty. With their work, they have demonstrated the value of starting small, testing out different interventions to find out what works best, and then scaling them up. They have tested programs in the same way that we test pharmaceutical drugs, using randomized controlled trials that compare the impact of an intervention relative to the status quo. They have shown how our beliefs, hypotheses, or models can be wrong, and therefore there is no substitute for testing new programs rigorously in the real world.

Startups using lean methods often embrace a similar mindset. They set up some hypotheses, test them in the market (or online via A/B testing), see the customer response, and then decide what to do next. Similarly, for governments to become experimental, they need to turn the current model of policy-making upside-down. Despite all the unknowns, governments often act as if they have all the answers, rather than recognizing that they don't. They introduce new policies without prior small-scale testing, assuming that they have chosen the best design and hoping it will work. The alternative is to follow the example of the 2019 Nobel Prize winners: start small, trial different designs systematically, learn what works to increase impact, and scale it up.

In practice, this means that rather than starting by launching a new national program for whatever aim, with a standardized design, governments would need to pilot it first on a small scale. Can it be delivered as planned? Are their assumptions still holding? Does it appear to be working? Are there tweaks that would make it more impactful? Often minor tweaks in the design can have a larger impact. This all requires building a culture within governments and within support organizations where it's perfectly safe to try things out, where enough flexibility in the processes and systems lets people test small tweaks in addition to large-scale trials, and where failure is accepted.

NABEEL KOSHAK: Since we already have this multitude of government initiatives and government VCs, everyone is complaining about the VC fund flow. We need to enhance that flow by further creating and supporting flow-creation programs. As such, we need to provide more support to the ecosystem builders—the investor-backed accelerators and incubators—and governments should either sponsor or invest through the government VC or government funding programs. That way everyone will have skin in the game. It's important to make sure that all these programs are backed by investors, so they do not end up being just one program that is at the mercy of the sponsor, who could shut it down any time. If it's backed by investors, it's going to be more sustainable and scalable. So, we definitely need more VC-backed, investor-backed venture builder programs; that will add great value to the angel investors and accelerate the overall pace of development.

Our government operations have yet to catch up with the speed of startups and investments. We need to have more accelerated processes from the government. Some strides are being made on that front with recent startup laws and new incentive programs for entrepreneurs and investors, which is a great step. Additionally, we need to look into creating special economic zones that facilitate the creation of startups and remove pain points that entrepreneurs and investors face in setting up startups and VC funds, respectively. This will further remove unnecessary friction that those parties now experience. This is foundational to developing a thriving startup ecosystem in the future.

4. Create an Innovation- and Entrepreneurship-Friendly Culture

Recognize and enforce culture's linkage to prosperity

EFOSA OJOMO: Culture is key to developing an ecosystem. The first thing I would say about culture is that it is not static. It is dynamic. Culture changes all the time. You go back a few hundred years in America, they were burning women they thought were witches. Culture is something that evolves. The idea that the culture and behavior of individuals who live in societies are fixed—that, for example, some regions have an entrepreneurial culture, they're hardworking, meanwhile others are not and that's the way it is—is just not the case. We are merely taking a snapshot in time and we are using that snapshot to define a particular people or place in perpetuity, which is quite unfair.

Ha-Joon Chang, in his book *Bad Samaritans*, talks about a time when the Germans were considered lazy by Europeans, the Japanese were considered lazy by the Americans, the Koreans were considered lazy by the Japanese, and the Chinese were considered lazy by the Koreans. The point he was trying to make is that, while many countries in the world today are prosperous and we view their people as hardworking, at one point they were viewed as lazy by another country.

Thus, culture is very much malleable. It is a fluid process. A similar thing could be said about the culture of corruption. I just did a TED Talk where I addressed this issue of corruption and how it's really a function of scarcity versus culture. In *The Prosperity Paradox*, we talk extensively about corruption. Our view is that the most powerful mechanism to combat corruption—aside from the coercive force of a dictator indiscriminately killing or jailing corrupt people without legal due process or fair trial—is through market-creating innovations.

Only market-creating innovations can transform economies and create tangible and lasting progress, and ultimately bring down corruption and influence positive cultural change.

VICTOR HWANG: Ecosystems are about people and what makes people tick. Therefore, the attitudes, beliefs, and culture that people hold shape the ways they interact with each other (especially strangers), trust each other, share ideas together, and build companies together. Culture is the basis of everything else. And the right values you want are those that seek to catalyze irreverence, foster aspiration, connect strangers, build trust, allow experimentation, and pay it forward. Another key element is what are called in biology "keystone species." Keystones link the entire ecosystem, they cross-fertilize, they build trust, and they create energy.

JONATHAN ORTMANS: Culture impacts startup ecosystem results from many angles—from the very early decision to explore entrepreneurship as a career path to the availability of risk capital.

Some cultural barriers to entrepreneurship become apparent in the form of low levels of social trust, which inhibits networking and prevents tech talent from forming strong teams. Many people are afraid to share their business ideas due to the fear of others stealing them, in contrast to supportive cultures among founders in successful tech startup hubs.

Cultural barriers can also translate into a startup's limited growth ambitions. The lack of a global mindset, for example, prevents the rise of high-potential startups. As a result, when startups reach stability, they prefer to remain a local SME, instead of continuing to invest in innovation.

It is key to address the nuanced ways a low-trust or risk-averse culture can impact entrepreneurs across particular demographics, such as with youth and women. For example, in many cultures, parents of young graduates expect them to secure a government job.

The good news is that, while they are difficult to address, cultural barriers can be overcome. In Nordic countries, known for their innovative capacity, certain incentives have worked to overcome the risk-aversion generated by their general social welfare systems. After all, becoming an entrepreneur often means giving up the peace of mind of social insurance, a considerable deterrent for employees to decide to start their own businesses. So, these countries have done a great job helping de-risk such career path. Other solutions are even simpler, like engaging the media in disseminating information about entrepreneurial role models, which can impact the social assessment of the entrepreneurial path.

The *Startup Nations Atlas of Policies* has more ideas on how other places have worked to create awareness of entrepreneurship and to encourage a culture of self-employment and technological innovation. (Tip: filter for "cultural/mindset" under the type of barrier addressed in the search field.) MENA entries in this category range from Saudi Arabia's BADIR Technology Incubator Program to the UAE's START competition, which aimed to assist unemployed Emiratis to start their own businesses and promoted entrepreneurship as a culture and a contributor to the economy.

At Global Entrepreneurship Network, holding Global Entre-preneurship Week in all nations of the world has been an effective strategy for promoting broad acceptance of the entrepreneurial culture. While we respect some who choose to be more responsive to the geopolitical issues of the day between our nations and their governments, we have found it true, as Peter Drucker famously said, that "culture eats strategy for breakfast." Ecosystem builders need to take a long-term view and seek to build a common entrepreneurial culture among all nations regardless of the headlines about our leaders.

LINDA ROTTENBERG: The often-told founding story behind Endeavor is that I was riding in a taxi in Buenos Aires in the 1990s when I learned that the driver had an engineering degree but couldn't find any other job. He didn't want to work for the government or private sector head honchos, yet the concept of starting one's own business was outlandish at the time in Latin America. While Steve Jobs and Bill Gates were paving the way for budding entrepreneurs in the US at the time, there wasn't even a word in the Spanish lexicon for "entrepreneur."

The biggest barriers to entrepreneurship are not financial, structural, or political—they are cultural and psychological. As an entrepreneur, you have to believe in yourself and find others who believe in you. And you need role models to open up those possibilities. Most people don't give themselves permission to pursue their crazy ideas. That is why success stories matter for an economy, and that is why the most successful entrepreneurship ecosystems are anchored by entrepreneurs who have not only been able to scale, but have also dedicated themselves to reinvesting that success in their ecosystems to help others scale.

MARC NAGER: The entrepreneurship movement is a cultural movement at its core. Yes, it has a great impact on our economies, but the most fundamental and greatest thing about it is the cultural change that it can instill. Entrepreneurship can be a lens through which to view the world, and sadly it turns out that we as a society have become pretty good at suppressing it in our education and political systems.

MAX BORDERS: If we define culture as the sum of a people's attitude toward innovation and entrepreneurship, then culture is critical. For example, what is the extent to which people are generally forward- or backward-looking in some area? Is the culture one in which folks too closely guard the status quo or venerate the past? Or is enough of the population open to the kind of change that always follows innovation? Change-resistant cultures will be an impediment to the development of startup ecosystems. So culture is a huge part of the story.

The challenge is, it's very hard to plan or build culture as if it's some exogenous force. Instead, culture emerges. In my book, *The Social Singularity*, I argue that the old Marshall McLuhan maxim "We shape our tools, and then our tools shape us" has a corollary: We shape our rules and then our rules shape us. Of course, culture and rules co-evolve, but frequently good institutions are a leading indicator of an open, creative culture. If the zeitgeist in an area is one of wonder and possibility, then those forces will seek to be instantiated in new ventures. But no venture can last if the institutional substrate is inhospitable or privileges only certain industries. Not to put too fine a point on it, culture and institutions are two sides of the same coin. Getting the rules right first therefore creates a healthy context that will allow the creative class to do its thing.

OSMAN SULTAN: I don't believe that you need to force a specific artificial cultural change to create innovation. When you look at how innovation is created, you see three dimensions. First, innovation is created by necessity. Successful entrepreneurs are the ones who, when presented with a problem, keep trying different things until they find what works. Second, innovation is also created by exploration. That's how an environment like Silicon Valley flourished, where great entrepreneurs approached things differently and many were willing to try new ways. Third, innovation is created by serendipity, which is an accidental outcome. Of course, little by little, ambition grows, and other people get involved that build on the original concept. We have to play on the three components together all at once in order to maximize the prospects for innovation, notwithstanding serendipity, which is organically generated. All of the dimensions are key to a healthy, thriving ecosystem that is a fertile ground for innovation and can help startups grow.

Promote risk-taking, bias for action, and a "give first" mentality

AMR AWADALLAH: The most important ingredient of Silicon Valley's success, in my opinion, is the willingness to take risks. That characteristic is embedded in the culture of the Valley. It's okay here to walk away from a big job with a big salary and start a new venture that may or may not work, and actually more often than not will not work. You have this sense of adventure here, that people are willing to try something new.

The second ingredient, which is related to the first, is that the government needs to have rules and structures that enable risk-taking behavior to take place. California laws help a lot with that, both for the employees leaving but also for employers firing them. We don't have to wait, like in some cases in Europe, which inhibits the acceleration of startups, because when you're growing at the very early stages you're growing at a fast pace, and you need the flexibility to hire and fire fast.

By comparison, In Egypt, where I come from, our families are expecting us to finish our university education and find a job with a stable salary. If you told them, "I'm going to do a startup or work for one that might or might not work," they would be very upset at you. You might not be able to get married because the family you try to marry into might say, "We don't know if you're going to be able to provide for our daughter or not." One of the big problems in the Middle East is that our culture is not a risk-taking culture. We tend to focus more on so-called stable traditional professions: doctor, lawyer, accountant, etc. That's counter to the Silicon Valley culture.

The third ingredient is patience. Silicon Valley was not built overnight, or over five or even 10 years. It took 40-plus years, so you have to be very patient and understand that it will take time, but then when it does work, it pays off in a big way. There is no quick fix or short-term, magical program or top-down mandate that can create a world-class, innovative environment. Governments and other ecosystem builders can certainly help accelerate progress, but they must also have to have a long-term view and recognize that great ecosystems take time and effort to build over decades, not years. Those are a couple of areas I would like to see change in the region with respect to culture and outlook.

DAVE MCCLURE: Culture matters a lot in ecosystem development. In some places, a strong entrepreneurial culture plays right into innovation, while in other places that's not the case. It's interesting to look at certain cultures that are very entrepreneur-friendly. People might point to Chinese culture as having a very strong entrepreneurial tradition in spite of the fact that China might not be seen as a capitalist environment, per se. A lot of its traditions are entrepreneurial.

Meanwhile, other countries that might be closer to having a capitalist structure, like certain countries in Europe, often have a socialist bent and not as much risk-taking. Thus, you have to look at the pervasive culture, not the political system. Regional or local traditions, cultures, and systems have an impact on the ecosystem. We shouldn't forget about the academic resources and infrastructure, corporate resources and infrastructure, economic systems, securitization, and public market infrastructures as well. This makes it hard to pinpoint the exact cultural attitudes that need to be at play but, if I had to pick, it would be encouraging risk-taking, encouraging access to capital, and encouraging an equity culture.

When it comes to risk-taking, a look at the US reveals a country that's composed almost entirely of immigrants from some point in time. Meanwhile, Saudis were a Bedouin culture that were traders. I mean, a lot of the origins of Saudi or GCC culture are also merchant-focused. Again, I would point to specific things in US history that created some of that.

The MENA region is often set up to invest in companies that are already sustainable, that are already making money. A lot of investors in emerging markets say, "Well, show me your business plan, and show me your economic projections," and, "When do you get to break-even?"—and a lot of times, it's five years when you get to that. So, they don't want to take that risk and say, "Okay, well, go figure it out. You go operate in negative market economics. Then, when you're sustainable and large, I'll invest." That is exactly the opposite of what you need to build an ecosystem.

On the other hand, in the risk-taking culture of the US, there are a lot of venture capital–backed businesses, there's fast growth and negative economics in the business. I'm not suggesting that you run a business that has negative economics forever, but particularly in those first, let's say, two, three, five years, where the business is operationally negative, and maybe has negative growth for a little while.

You also had some very basic tactical elements in the US early on, like personal bankruptcy laws that encouraged a somewhat friendly approach to failure. That may not have always been easy in certain markets. Certainly, in some Arab markets, business failure has been a criminal act that can be punishable by some very severe penalties, so that may have had some impact on the local mindset. Hopefully, that will dissipate with time as proper bankruptcy laws are put in place across the region.

STEVE CASE: One of the strengths of Silicon Valley is the fearless attitude and celebration of failure. If you look at an idea, do you automatically think of how it will not work and what could go wrong, or do you think about how it can work and the possibility that it will work? Communities need a shift in mindset to think about the promise and the art of the possible. That support will be very helpful to entrepreneurs at all stages, striving to get to the next level.

AHMED EL ALFI: We need to break away from the typical, long-standing belief in our culture that pressures youth to follow a predetermined "stable" career path, such as engineering or medicine. As a society, we need to become more accepting of people venturing into non-traditional fields and embrace the notion that there are many different paths to achieving success. We must empower and encourage the next generation to take risks.

Another area that is somewhat related to culture, and which adversely impacts our productivity and economies in general, is our basic work ethic. We see it with a lack of initiative, a lack of attention to detail, and a lack of commitment and personal responsibility to follow through in the work environment. Many of the problems with the work ethic in the region are also due to the lack of correlation between performance and reward. The correlation of getting compensated for hard work has not been ingrained in our societies, historically.

The other reason for the lack of a strong work ethic in our societies relates to systems burdened by archaic regulations, which cause people to circumvent or "game" the system. This all feeds into a mindset that is oriented toward getting away with things and finding shortcuts, rather than playing by the rules and working smart and hard within the system. These are behavior patterns that are learned as a result of the surrounding environments, and eventually become ingrained in the culture, and they stem from a lack of trust in the system.

Having said that, there are two pieces of good news. This behavior is starting to change with the emergence of the new startup world, in which young entrepreneurs are filled with the drive and desire needed to succeed. Also, a hidden upside to the attitude of finding shortcuts and circumventing the system that often gets overlooked is that it breeds creativity. People are very adept at solving problems using "street smarts" honed from a young age, which can really come in handy in the startup and business world. The question becomes how to channel this in the right direction, toward complex problem-solving, dissecting each aspect of an issue, turning it upside-down, backward, sideways, and looking at it from different points of view. That's the clever mindset, or what we call "fahlawa," that we're blessed with in this part of the world, but don't fully appreciate or fully utilize.

DINA EL-MOFTY: Around 2011, we started to notice a shift toward greater interest in entrepreneurship and an appetite for risk-taking. At the time, we were reaching hundreds of schools and universities and working with hundreds of thousands of students. Then, suddenly, a lot of our graduates started taking a real interest in starting their own business. They didn't know how to start, where to go, or where to get support. In 2011, politically, Egypt was in turmoil after the revolution. The mindset shift was most felt when our graduates were no longer as interested in working in the corporate world and preferred to do their own thing instead.

That question of the timing had us perplexed over the years, as we reflected back. What was the underlying trigger? Was it really the revolution or an evolution over the years? Perhaps it might be a mix of both. A trend was happening for sure during the years leading up to the revolution. A few success stories were starting to captivate younger graduates, and they were looking up to some young entrepreneurs with great achievements. There was definitely some momentum there. Then the revolution hit and things just went into overdrive post-revolution. So, arguably, the revolution helped accelerate the process, in terms of creating an undertone of wanting to change and perhaps to control one's own destiny. It's difficult to say for sure if it was a direct effect since a lot of organic movement was already taking place. Fast forward to today and we see a much more developed entrepreneurial ecosystem and a stronger startup community in Egypt than ever.

ANDREW BERKOWITZ: I think the biggest psychological barrier in most emerging regions is just an aversion sentiment toward the idea of failure. Most startups will likely fail. That's just the reality, and the entrepreneurs who are able to start something, fail, fail, fail, fail, pivot, fail, and then find something that works are the ones who actually succeed in the end. Unfortunately, in a lot of these markets, people are too afraid to fail because of the very negative beliefs about failure.

There is no one sure-fire way to influence a positive change in a culture, but certainly mainstream media has a big effect on people's subconscious and the kind of beliefs they hold. Therefore, perhaps the best way to change the culture is through media coverage of local success stories and successful entrepreneurs, which helps inspire not only local entrepreneurs but also investors. Another way I've seen to help encourage investment is governments being more active as an LP in funds. It's much easier for an investor to put money into a fund when they know the government is going to be supporting it and backing some of the ventures that the fund is actually investing in.

OMAR AYYASH: Studies have shown that there are three startup influences: the person starting the business, their situation at the point of starting the business, and other antecedent factors. These factors could include gender, religion, family, etc. I am a strong believer that culture plays a major role in the third startup influence. In the MENA region, we still raise our kids to be highly educated. We still want our kids to be doctors, lawyers, engineers, pilots, and so on. When I was a kid, everyone wished for me to be a doctor because my father was one. We need to inspire our kids to consider entrepreneurship as a viable career option. We need a culture shift that celebrates entrepreneurship and influences our children in this direction. We need to embrace failure and view it as a learning experience and inspire our children to become entrepreneurs.

BADR JAFAR: Another gap I see is that we don't do enough to encourage our entrepreneurs to be more globally minded and to see the world as a viable marketplace for their ideas, products, and services. We need to be more ambitious when we think about how we can serve certain needs and requirements internationally.

Obviously, Careem and Souq are phenomenal regional successes, but are they global? Yes, they're global to the extent that they've raised eyebrows around the world, but the majority of their markets are in the MENA region. They are certainly remarkable success stories, but I'm also looking forward to the day when we have more global success stories, like India-based startup Oyo (being one of the fastest growing hotel chains in the world) or Netflix. But in order to do that, all of us involved in the ecosystem need to broaden our focus to be more globally oriented.

JOY AJLOUNY: We often have a notion in the Middle East at large to work in your parents' business, get a comfy government job, and get a husband, because it looks good to other people. Thus, we often have an others-orientation in the region instead of making the right choice for ourselves. We're often in fear of people's opinions. I think there's a culture—for women, especially—that has to change because they think traditionally. A lot of women are all about getting married, finding a good husband, starting a family, etc. In Dubai particularly, there's a culture shift for women. Even in the Middle East at large, I think more women are more apt to pursue a career and be self-sufficient and actually set goals and accomplish them, whatever endeavor they choose. That's a healthy trend that I'm optimistic will continue.

Another area I would like to see change in the region—especially within the business environment—is greater collaboration and accessibility. In Silicon Valley, for example, if I wanted to talk to Tim Cook, CEO of Apple, I could talk to somebody who knows somebody, and he would speak with me. I see Larry Page, founder of Google, often in shorts and flip-flops at Whole Foods in California. There's no bodyguard. I can go up to him and say, "Hey, I've got this idea. Please give me five minutes," and he will. That's just the culture of the Valley.

In Silicon Valley, everyone knows that the future will be created by the kids on the street with the ideas. The VCs in Silicon Valley make money from the successful startups they invest in and they're held accountable. It's the VCs' job to hunt talent and bring in the next billion-dollar IPO. So, they're constantly out there hunting for the next billion-dollar company. They're under the pressure of, "You better bring in the next billion-dollar IPO, or you're not going to be a venture capitalist at Sequoia Capital." As a VC in the Valley, that's how you're being evaluated, by how many IPOs or unicorns you bring in. That's why their door is open, because they're always on the lookout for opportunities. They have a FOMO (fear of missing out) mindset, so they make themselves accessible.

Contrast that with the funding environment in the Middle East, where open policies and access are much more limited, and you realize a key gap within our ecosystem. Not to mention that a lot of investment is made by employees of companies and not venture partners. The incentive is different when you get a cut of the action in Silicon Valley.

I don't think there's just one answer to creating the kind of culture that fosters growth, innovation, and job creation. It's a mix of everything. This notion that you can wear a t-shirt and flip-flops and come up with a brilliant idea and be a billionaire—that's part of the Silicon Valley culture. There's a long road between that and what we have here in the region. I think the media's role is obviously vital.

More than anything, I believe we need brutal honesty and transparency on the part of all the ecosystem players. After all, how are we ever going to change for the better if we don't take a hard, honest look at ourselves and examine our ways and resolve to fix them? How are we ever going to build trust among ourselves if we don't have openness and transparency at our core? I'm not saying there haven't been elements of progress on both fronts; unfortunately, they're not deep or wide enough if we're talking about the region as a whole.

ALISÉE DE TONNAC: A big reason why Silicon Valley has been successful over the past decades is that it has this culture where you can get on the calendar of people who are way above you in the hierarchy. You don't find that in a lot of places. Early-stage entrepreneurs can't typically get a meeting with, say, a high-level executive of a local corporate. It's because people that are kind of in tune with this whole ecosystem world understand the importance of having a sense of community, comradery, and a pay-it-forward orientation. The physical setting can help facilitate the culture, but the physical setting in and of itself can't create a thriving ecosystem with a strong startup community.

PHILIP BAHOSHY: Silicon Valley has this "coffee shop" culture where people are collaborative and generous in sharing their contacts, making introductions, and generally paying it forward. If I may be somewhat critical, we often have this defensive and ego-driven culture in the Middle East where people are protective of their network, when we actually need to be collaborative and feel comfortable sharing. That's one area I'd like to see change and I'm optimistic that it will change in due course as the ecosystem matures and so does people's behavior.

RAMI SALMAN: Places like New York or San Francisco have startup ecosystems centered around knowledge-sharing, which is really organized by the successful startups themselves. Granted, those startups hosting the event may have ulterior motives, like product placement or recruitment but, fundamentally, these sessions provide an incredible amount of community learning for aspiring entrepreneurs. I can't tell you how many meetups I've been to, hosted at swanky startup cafeterias, covering topics like sales operations, marketing analytics, hyper-scalability, and much more. Those sessions were always driven by the successful startups themselves, and they don't just promote their products or approaches, they bring in partners, mention countless tools that startups can utilize, share their learnings and failures, and provide an opportunity to network with industry peers.

By contrast, I don't see any successful startup in the MENA region really reaching out and giving back to the community. I see massive billboards for those startups that made it to hundreds of millions in valuation, but I don't see any events or startup-focused outreach for partnering or shared learning. Some VCs and angel networks organize these, but the initiative of co-learning is not commonly present in the region like you see it in the US. Our region's success stories should follow the lead of the last batch of entrepreneurs, like Fadi Ghandour, and share their success, not by boasting on stage but by investing time back into creating a stronger startup community and ecosystem.

Unfortunately, much of the culture of startups in the region is a little bit individualistic, with each one operating independently of the other. We don't see a very strong sharing and co-creation culture among startups here. I think that is something that is ingrained in the Western mentality—things like group discussions, sharing growth stories and, most of all, sharing and learning from failures. We started a startup think tank, which was just a session with four of my closest friends who were also founders of startups in different industries. The think tank includes Mahmoud Gao, Jad Halaoui and Rami Shaar from Washmen, and Anass Boumediene and Mehdi Oudghiri from Eyewa. In fact, Eyewa was just an idea when they came to their first session, and now they've gone on to raise $7.5 million in a Series A round.

We would meet on a semi-monthly basis to catch up and discuss obstacles that each of our startups were facing, looking for ways to solve them together. We would reserve four hours total: the first hour was meant to catch everyone up on the latest in more of a speed round approach, and then the remaining three hours were reserved for a deep-dive session to focus on one startup and one issue that it was facing. We would all put our minds and experience to work to see what we could do to solve that problem. It gave us different ways of looking at the same situation, and an immense amount of knowledge-sharing.

I found this to be an incredibly fulfilling and exciting routine that we all benefited from. We even started bringing in "guest startups" to sit in on the sessions and share their ideas, as well as any issues they were facing. It would be great to see more startups give back to the community in a similar fashion and build these not-for-profit, no-BS events where startups can kind of grow and cultivate their best practices. I'm optimistic that there will be a shift from what we often see as this individualistic approach to a more cooperative and collaborative one.

Open communication and healthy discussion

YOUSEF HAMZA: On the legislative level, much of the legislation in the region was made prior to the entrepreneurship explosion, especially in the tech field. It has not changed enough or fast enough to keep up with the demands of the new economy. This is not a criticism, but a reflection of the fact that the world has changed quickly in the last 20 years, and everyone is struggling to play catch-up. Globally, in terms of what's happened in tech, it is going to inevitably be hard for regulations to keep up.

Perhaps more collaboration between the public and private sectors could help. We would be best off just getting lawmakers, the tech entrepreneurs, and all vested stakeholders in a room, and openly discussing issues and what can be done to resolve them. We have moved away from our heritage and our open-discussion "Majlis" forums, which is a more personal, proactive, and inclusive way to voice concerns, debate issues, and submit requests. Instead, we've defaulted to a more standoffish approach: "Complain from a distance to your local relevant department, fill form on website, send a letter, and let's see."

TIM DRAPER: Countries that have basic freedoms (freedom of speech, freedom of religion, freedom of assembly, free markets, etc.) are the countries that seem to generate the most entrepreneurial activity. At Draper University, we promote a culture of free thinking, which seems to encourage our students to innovate. The results are extraordinary. We have had 1,200 students from 80 different countries and they have started 350 companies.

ABDULAZIZ AL LOUGHANI: We are all fortunate to be witnessing more openness of information and ease of communication globally today. It's easier for me to connect than ever before. This type of open communication and connection is certainly making a positive impact on doing business in this part of the world, as it has on the rest of the world. To the extent that we can protect this culture of openness in this region, it will continue making a positive impact on our economies and livelihood.

JOY AJLOUNY: One thing that made America as successful as it is, is its foundational tenet, freedom of speech. The system actually encourages the media and the population to provide input and debate issues. America acknowledges that there's always room for improvement, especially economically, and a healthy dose of discussion will actually push the best ideas to the surface. It does not try to project an image of perfection to the world.

Likewise, everything is not perfect in the Middle East; we also have problems, just like everything is not perfect in America. America has a homeless problem, a crime problem, a drug problem, but the best part about America is there's always an opportunity to point out what's broken and engage in a healthy debate on what the solution might be, versus trying to cover it up or shut down anyone who surfaces those issues.

The Middle East could use a greater dose of openness and transparency. I certainly see positive movement in many areas and trust it will continue moving in that direction. I point this out because I really care and because my belief is that such a cultural change will permeate its way into every facet of society, including economic development. So, there is definitely room for improvement on this front as well.

Even simple things can make a big difference in accelerating positive change. For example, enabling startups to provide feedback on a particular issue or pain point and be heard. I think that can go a long way. After all, those startups represent the pulse of the ecosystem and if they're struggling with a particular issue or policy, then it's an indication of a barrier or inefficiency that needs to be addressed. Creating those open communication channels is key.

Chapter VIII

ADDITIONAL ECOSYSTEM-RELATED TOPICS AND INSIGHTS

The following chapter touches on additional aspects of ecosystem development—namely, clusters, support, media, CSR (corporate social responsibility), community leadership, and other ecosystem-related topics. Combined, they significantly supplement some of the foundational areas covered earlier. These supplemental forces provide important support to the ecosystem at large. Much like fertilizer on already rich soil, they can improve the quality and output of the process.

Whether we're talking about clusters, innovation hubs, or free zones (also referred to as "special economic zones"), the common denominator is that they create an environment that is more focused, more specialized, and more conducive to networking, collaboration, and innovation. They also increase the probability of serendipitous interactions, or "collisions." Collisions happen when random individuals literally stumble upon each other, find common ground and common interests, and ultimately end up developing a working relationship or collaborating on a particular project. These are completely unplanned, organic encounters that would be very difficult to design or plan.

Meanwhile, matchmaking programs or specialized events can

attract like-minded people who share similar passions and interests and can be quite valuable, but those events are often occasional. The more active a location is in terms of foot traffic, and the more likely the venue is to target people with similar passions (e.g., working in a given sector, sharing interest in a particular technology, having similar backgrounds, or being entrepreneurial and aspirational in general), the more potential it has to facilitate collisions. That's the additional consolidation value that a centralized hub offers. Hence, permanent places of this kind are needed to facilitate such encounters, away from conferences and events, on an ongoing basis.

The cluster effect theory has been well documented; plenty of examples and case studies show that clustering is invaluable in accelerating ecosystem growth. One remarkable example from the region has been Dubai Internet City (DIC), established in 1999. DIC was a seminal project that developed at a key juncture in the region's development. It attracted a great deal of tech talent from both MENA and abroad, in effect leading the way as the go-to innovation hub in the region. Since then, others have followed suit, creating similar entrepreneurial spaces both in Dubai and across every major city in the region, with varying levels of success. That said, as we learn in this chapter, the views are mixed on the efficacy of such initiatives, and support programs in general, relative to their cost.

Another valuable aid to ecosystem development in the MENA region and globally—particularly in emerging markets with nascent ecosystems—has been the presence of accelerators, incubators, and other support groups and services. These organizations play an important role in ecosystem development, whether they are provided on a voluntary basis (like mentorships and CSR), on a paid basis (like events and conferences), or on an equity basis (like advisory support, in many cases). This is also true whether such programs are partly or completely government-led, or whether they are private and organic in nature, and irrespective of their setting (e.g., corporate, university, stand-alone corridors, or a host of gathering places).

The less developed a given local ecosystem is—in terms of low number and limited diversity of experienced players within it—the greater the need for hand-holding, so to speak. That's when democratized access to startup support services combined with a certain level of goodwill from industry volunteers are needed.

There is a certain ethos in these close-knit, grassroot environments: serendipitous interaction, expectation-free support, and greater realism and openness around one's challenges. This is very different from the corporate and fundraising world, where the dynamic can be more top-down, more transactional, and less personal. In the early stages of an ecosystem's development, well-recognized and well-respected entrepreneurs and industry leaders can be instrumental in promoting growth. The more local influence or "micro-celebrity" status they have within their domains or sectors, the greater the impact they can potentially make on the community. That's when big personalities, engaging events, and a certain amount of buzz are needed to break through the noise, engage people, and ultimately help build a startup community.

As the ecosystem matures and the number of participants grows, more specialized areas of support are needed. That's when you move more from, for example, general management mentorship to scaleup mentorship, and there is a greater emphasis on even more specialized mentorship in tech-oriented fields (e.g., cybersecurity, AI for financial services, etc.). It's a never-ending cycle; as the ecosystem develops, it needs to refeed itself. The very individuals who were once mentees will mature and become mentors for others, and so on. Should this cycle get short-circuited at any time for any reason, it will adversely impact the ecosystem.

What is interesting about this dynamic is that it has not been entirely digitalized yet. In an increasingly virtual world, the need for in-person interactions seems to be greater than ever. What has moved more digitally is some of the learning and mentorship around digital skills. That is partially because of the kind of individuals who are attracted to such channels in the first place—being tech-savvy individuals who are more comfortable navigating the virtual world and more inclined to use that format for learning purposes. The other reason is that educational content needs less customization than a specific business strategy issue faced by a startup. Obviously, the more unique a given context is—which is the case in more developed ecosystems with a greater need for competitive differentiation—the greater the need for one-on-one, in-person interaction.

At the opposite end of the spectrum, the media model revolves around one-to-many messaging or variations thereof. It's more mass-oriented and less personal. Hence, it's most effective as an awareness and inspirational tool, not as an educational one. Nevertheless, the power of the media to engage aspiring entrepreneurs and move hearts and minds cannot be overstated. However, to be most effective, it needs to project a combination of realism and aspiration, since lacking either will make it less engaging for a general audience.

Elissa Freiha, Founder and Director of Womena, astutely observed this phenomenon. She states, "Media coverage of the startup world in the region tends to be very matter-of-fact, with typical journalism and numbers, which is somewhat alienating to a still-nascent population who hasn't been educated in this space. It's not very inclusive. We're excited to start seeing more documentary-style coverage, longer formats, real stories that show not only successes, but also the struggles of entrepreneurs, and entertainment that's created around local role models."

As a corollary to the above, media often over-hypes funding and other success stories that are easy to capture in a headline. While success stories are certainly feel-good stories, they're not as inspirational or insightful if they are devoid of context. In other words, it's not enough to see the fruits of someone's labor; it's equally important to see their shortcomings, struggles, and even their failures. It's the two extremes—the humble beginning and the extraordinary outcome—that make a narrative simultaneously relatable and inspirational to a wide audience.

Obviously, the more local the story, with local characters and places, the more likely it will resonate with its intended audience and hit home, so to speak. Mainstream media in the region could use the production and style of short films and documentaries to present more captivating narratives than has historically been the case. They could make it more entertaining by gamifying entrepreneurship to help improve both reach and engagement. This approach is recommended for both screen and print media.

The topics in this chapter and those discussed earlier, as I mentioned, are by no means exhaustive. I have not covered some, and others may only be emerging as you read this book. Furthermore, some of the findings and recommendations presented in this book will become obsolete over time, or at least will need to be updated. Nevertheless, I hope they shed some light on, and help to advance, our understanding of what actually goes into making a robust tech and startup ecosystem in the MENA region and well beyond.

1. Clusters, Innovation Hubs, and Support Programs

PHILIP BAHOSHY: I'm a firm believer in the benefits of clustering. If you take the UAE as an example, it is not that there aren't enough incubators, accelerators, co-working spaces, VCs, investors, and service providers, but they are spread out across the whole of the UAE. That's not optimal from a clustering effect standpoint. On the other hand, when you look at Station F in Paris, incubators, accelerators, and investors were offered discounted rates to be housed there, along with major educational institutions. They created incubators such as INSEAD hub. This intellectual capital transfer that takes place there is extremely beneficial.

Another good example of this is Beirut Digital District (BDD) in the heart of the Lebanese capital. It has multiple office buildings that people are able to cluster in to network, exchange knowledge, and generally do business together. It's the government's role to create the right environment for these clusters to develop and not always force specific setups on everyone. These clusters can develop privately and organically as well.

RAMEZ SHEHADI: Special economic zones are important. There was a period where they were proliferating all across the Gulf as an interesting tool to attract leading multinational organizations into the region. Today, when you look at some of the leading special economic zones, whether it's DIFC or DIC in the UAE or Techno Valley in Saudi Arabia, or the many other equivalents that you see in Qatar and Kuwait and everywhere else in the region, they've done a great job attracting business for the most part. Perhaps, in some cases, they've remained focused on being a real estate play, and they need to offer a more compelling value-added proposition in the new economy.

TEJINDER SINGH: In Qatar, much can be improved on to further develop local ecosystem. Allowing 100% ownership to non-Qataris to start companies is an area the country has to work on. They are currently setting up free zones to resolve this issue. Qatar Science and Technology Park (QSTP) and Qatar Financial Centre (QFC) are such examples. There are other sectors that could also use special economic zones, with their own jurisdictions and setup, that allow for 100% foreign ownership for non-Qataris, expedited setup, and additional support services.

ABDULAZIZ AL LOUGHANI: I don't think that free zones are the long-term solution to creating a sustainable ecosystem. The long-term solution is opening up our economies and being a lot more liberal about foreign ownership. Currently, there is friction between geographies in terms of customs, trade, immigration, and other local and cross-border activities that are critical to certain sectors and to business in general. Plenty of verticals are monopolized or highly regulated and don't even allow for international ownership.

CHRISTOPHER ROGERS: None of what are commonly identified as critical pieces of an ecosystem—such as accelerators, incubators, and free zones—were directly responsible for the most booming ecosystem in the world, which is Silicon Valley. Thus, the cause and effect relationship is not entirely clear. At the same time, there are certainly examples where each of these initiatives has been a good way to help some entrepreneurs and startups across the board everywhere. Also, since we don't have an exact recipe to create a successful ecosystem, I think trying numerous ingredients is a very smart thing to do.

ISSA AGHABI: Clusters are very important in promoting collaboration and ecosystem development in general. The whole "cluster effect theory" is one to look at. When you put like-minded people with similar passions and ambitions together, great things will happen. That's something I'm a big believer in. Have we done it properly in the Middle East? Not always. I think Saudi Arabia is trying to do that and the UAE has done a lot in that space already, but I don't think we've cracked it just yet. Globally, if you take a look at the top startups that have succeeded, the top 50 startups globally, not many have come from accelerators and incubators. There's a question mark there: Do these programs work?

For a region like MENA, however, I'm a big proponent of support programs. Why? Because the ecosystem here is so nascent in its development, these programs add a lot of value. On the other hand, if you look at top accelerators in the US, like Y Combinator, it's not an accelerator as much as it is a networking place. I'm not undermining it by any means, it's one of the best startup support programs out there. It offers fundamental training, mentorship, and know-how, and allows you to get from point A to point B very quickly if you don't have the culture or the ability to do that otherwise.

In this region, we certainly do need that kind of hand-holding, support, access to best practices, and know-how. A lot of it is online, but spoon-feeding it is still helpful. Techstars in the UAE is doing an amazing job on that front and so is Flat6Labs, especially as it has tailored its program to each market. So, I'm a big fan of these programs despite the fact that we have yet to see unicorns come out of them.

RABEA ATAYA: I think every entrepreneur in the world needs to seek counsel, no matter how smart they are. I'm certainly a big proponent of entrepreneurs in the community seeking out each other's advice in order to improve their chances of success, and to not repeat the same mistakes that others have made.

Having said that, I'm not necessarily a firm believer in the very structured mentorship approach commonly found in the region, where someone has a preset schedule to meet the same person to discuss all sorts of business issues. I feel that an entrepreneur requires different skills and experiences from different people at different times. My take on this is that if I meet a young entrepreneur and they say, "I'd like you to be my mentor," my response usually is, "Whenever you have a question or an issue you're facing, please feel free to email me and I'll try to respond as quickly as possible. And if it's more apt for you and me to go on a call, then we'll get on a call or meet face to face and discuss it." I feel that kind of one-on-one drill-down on an as-needed basis is more valuable than a very structured "you are my mentor; we will meet monthly" approach. Not to say that the latter doesn't have value, it's just not the most efficient way.

ALISÉE DE TONNAC: All around the world, no matter where you're building a startup, you're going to face unique local challenges. Whether it's dealing with the local government or nuisances of the local culture or markets, those kinds of problems are unique to your market and geography. As such, you need local mentors who understand those problems first-hand and have "been there, done that."

I also don't think there's ever a case where it's premature to look into creating an attractive physical environment that draws the right people together to network and collaborate. Actually, it's often the first step in creating the ecosystem. If you look at most ecosystems around the world, they started from a specific incubator or hub, or one location where they started hosting events and bringing the community together. Granted, it's not the most crucial factor, but it is certainly an important one in creating a flattened-out culture and paving the way for, or accelerating the development of, a startup ecosystem.

I also think it's crucial, and certainly a catalyst for the ecosystem, to implement a successful accelerator program that's hyper-focused on a specific niche that the local city or country has differentiated assets in. One example is Chattanooga, Tennessee in the US. The city now has a VC and accelerator called Dynamo, which is a supply chain and logistics-focused accelerator program. It is certainly an outlier ecosystem for a town of its size because it went all in on the city's strength, which is supply chain and logistics. It has created numerous exits and numerous successful companies.

When you bring that approach over to MENA, a city or country needs to be asking, "What corporate, government, transportation, and other assets do we have locally that we can leverage and create an accelerator program around, and get anchor institutions to support?" This one of the best ways to facilitate startups and catalyze a local new economy.

2. Media Coverage and Startup Events

ELISSA FREIHA: Media coverage of the startup world in the region tends to be very matter-of-fact, with typical journalism and numbers, which is somewhat alienating to a still-nascent population that hasn't been educated in this space. It's not very inclusive for the most part. We're excited to start seeing more documentary-style coverage, longer formats, and real stories that show not only successes, but also the struggles of entrepreneurs. We're seeing entertainment that's created around local role models. CNN recently made a great show called *Follow That Startup*, covering the Dubai startup ecosystem, which took this approach. That was refreshing to see.

The media needs to follow not just an educational and inspirational narrative, but a realistic and entertaining one as well. It's important to highlight the opportunities and show what's possible, but equally important to show that it's not that simple and, in fact, operating a startup in this part of the world can be quite a grueling feat and take a toll on stakeholders.

For this reason, at Womena, we focus on the realities and complexities of starting a business, and the personal impact on the mental health and well-being of those who are involved and their families, which is rarely discussed. That's because entrepreneurship is very much celebrated in local media coverage. You get about two-and-a-half minutes of coverage per startup, highlighting the milestones and achievements. It doesn't shed light on the reality of startup life with all of its challenges, including the ongoing pressure to deliver results and keep up with the difficult and demanding expectations of the VC space.

Entrepreneurs are also dealing with outdated, preconceived notions of this new world in general, which is still unfamiliar in our society. We had an entrepreneur last year who is an amazing business leader, a very strong character, who is literally disrupting an industry in Jordan. She kept getting calls from the police every other month claiming that she was operating a brothel because she was doing in-home beauty services for women. She was also getting accused of tax evasion. These are some of the realities that entrepreneurs in this region have to deal with, which go well beyond business challenges.

ALISÉE DE TONNAC: The media's role in helping develop the ecosystem is very important. If you believe that you can do something, you're already halfway there. When you're young and you can look up to and learn from somebody in your part of the world whom you can relate to, somebody who just went through the process that you believe you will go through and achieved remarkable success, it's much easier to have that self-belief from the get-go. A lot of that will be driven by media shedding light on local success stories.

I don't think American or global success stories like Facebook or Google are anywhere close to sufficient examples or role models for someone sitting in Tunisia, Egypt, or Libya to emulate or get inspired by. That's also the case for mentorship. For example, if I introduce an entrepreneur who's sitting in Bahrain right now to a mentor in Silicon Valley, the value that mentor can provide to this entrepreneur only goes so far. Local problems require local experience and local solutions.

CHRISTOPHER ROGERS: The media's role is particularly important in the ecosystem, in terms of helping raise awareness and in terms of inspiration. However, where I've seen media in the Middle East fail is that it confuses funding with success. While funding certainly suggests some indication of future success, it doesn't really mean that the company is anything other than funded. It doesn't mean that its product works great. It doesn't mean that it's going to sell a lot of them. It doesn't mean it's going to have a fantastic exit. While it's completely understandable that the region has sort of taken that as a hallmark of success, because there have not been a lot of exits, I think it's important to put the narrative in the right perspective.

A similar phenomenon also happens at the numerous conferences in the region. You see many of the same companies that have achieved funding being applauded for just that, rather than for revenue or customers.

RABEA ATAYA: The media has been great at highlighting the stories of entrepreneurs in the region. I'm very encouraged by the fact that they like these stories and they're bringing them to the greater population. I see two areas for improvement, however. First, they need to be more fact-seeking in their stories. Often, the media takes the word of one person in the organization as though it were true.

As a result, many times the story being projected is actually bias or misleading, and ultimately doesn't end up really providing facts that are useful to the greater population. I think more of an investigative mindset would be useful.

Second, I would celebrate not just the exits but also the successful milestones. As important as the sale of Careem, for example, is the fact that Careem employed a very large number of people and made some pretty amazing technologies. Being able to highlight these stepping-stones is also important.

ZUBAIR NAEEM PARACHA: Media coverage is an important pillar of an ecosystem. Obviously, it has both an upside and a downside. For example, it's our job as a media outlet, at MENAbytes, to highlight the stories that could inspire others to start companies in the region and pass on accurate news; the risk, of course, is not getting the story right or not getting the full story.

We have different types of media platforms operating in this space. Some are publishing press releases and headline news of the day. Others do their own research to make sure that whatever goes on their platform is actually accurate. Those media outlets can play different roles.

Frankly, being a founder of MENAbytes, I can say that we have a lot of room for improvement. For example, if you visit the MENAbytes website you will see a lot of focus on startups that have raised funding. On the other hand, you'll see very few stories about startups that are bootstrapping their way to success. They are good enough to be profiled, but they rarely get recognized on MENAbytes, or in the media in general, because they have not raised funding, for whatever reason. This is something that I am working on changing internally while placing more emphasis on educating entrepreneurs. There's very little educational content on how to launch and operate a tech startup in the region. This is clearly a gap that the media need to step in and address.

Wamda has done some great work historically. It went quieter for

18 months or so, but it's now back and has been doing a brilliant job recently. *Entrepreneur Middle East* is another outlet that has made a great contribution. It's obviously not focused on technology, but its editorials and the quality of its content are quite good.

One challenge for all these regional media outlets and online publishers is to monetize their content, which is very limited. When I realized this at MENAbytes, we started building different products around MENAbytes that could help bring in funds. These products could focus on data, events, etc. Now that MENAbytes was recently acquired by RiseUp, those events will obviously be RiseUp events. In other parts of the world, online publishers are experimenting with subscription-based models. They are trying to earn money from every subscriber for access to their content or installing metered payrolls. For example, you have access to five stories a month and for anything beyond that, you have to become a paid subscriber. I think it's too early for this model in MENA. The market is not mature enough and the consumer is just not ready to pay for content.

3. Giving Back, CSR, and Community Leadership

BADR JAFAR: I would like to stress the importance of having a clearly defined social purpose behind any business, large or small, and creating business models that identify and address intrinsic human needs. If you can do that, then by definition you will have a fantastic commercial opportunity because you're addressing a real need and therefore providing real value.

When I am mentoring entrepreneurs, one of the first things that I try to do is help them think through whether what they're doing is really what society and the environment needs and, if necessary, help them tweak their business model to be more explicit and effective in addressing that need. This is the most powerful way to institutionalize a strong sense of purpose behind their business and business model, which in turn will generate a strong competitive advantage by building trust with both internal and external stakeholders.

YOUSEF HAMZA: I'm a big fan of CSR. I think it is critical for the growth of any economy. I have invested in business plan competitions. I have held entrepreneurship gatherings where dozens of companies join for free, and we go through legal dos and don'ts, ask questions, and openly discuss issues. I'll mentor startups without asking anything in return. However, I believe less in philanthropy and more in social enterprise or "sustainable philanthropy."

I truly believe that everyone could do more than they're currently doing in terms of CSR. All too often, we're too focused on making our business a success and postpone giving back only after that happens. Meanwhile, there's always something that we can do, no matter how little time one has. It needs to always be something on your radar, in the fabric of how you operate, to give back to the very ecosystem you are part of. Whether that takes shape in giving people advice, hosting gatherings, networking with people, bringing ideas to the table, or lobbying the government for certain reforms, it can be done. You can add value outside of your business to your environment without spending a million dollars a year. Greater attention needs to be given to this, as the old adage still holds true: "In helping others, you help yourself."

Inspirationally, I believe we have a lot of figures, and lots of events, but I feel we lack a deeper level of inspiration. I implore more people to truly dedicate time to mentoring groups or individuals on a personal level. Rather than speaking at the next generation, speak with them, on a consistent basis. This was common in the time when Majlis were more prominent, and people from different generations and from all walks of life would sit down every evening to share and inspire.

RAMEZ SHEHADI: We have tens and tens of millions of companies in our region, from self-employed individuals to global mega-organizations serving the world. They all reside here. We have the full gamut, but the percentage of these companies that are plugged into the digital economy and are actively advertising and transacting with their constituents, their audiences, and their customers online is incredibly small compared to our brothers and sisters in North America, Europe, and Southeast Asia.

We have a massive opportunity to support these companies and plug them fully into the global digital economy—whether they are micro, small, medium, or large. The call to action is for organizations like Facebook, Google, Amazon, Microsoft, Cisco, and many others to really double down on helping to unlock or empower the digital economies of this region. They can do this by instilling greater digital skills into the community and helping enterprises plug into the global economy through the digital platforms they have created. It can be as simple as creating pages—Instagram or Facebook pages—or leveraging the tools that companies like Google or Microsoft make available to the public. Local businesses can use software and platforms to help automate and streamline their operations, and make it far more efficient for these organizations to operate their businesses. This is incredibly low-hanging fruit. It is far easier to do than perhaps at any other point in history.

Now while that could fall under the remit of CSR, it could also be economic responsibility with an agenda around enabling entrepreneurship. If you are a large organization, investing in entrepreneurship is a two-way street. Historically, perhaps CSR was about giving away resources—time, money, or assets—without really expecting that it might bring back anything to your organization, and it may be important to differentiate between Corporate Social Investment and CSR. Let me be clear – the need for funding and supporting charitable causes is noble and necessary and should be acted upon by all parties. At the same time, building a true CSR framework entails looking at the core of your organization, understanding how you can, through your daily work, empower and enable further growth and opportunities. That is the essence of CSR.

KATE POPE HODEL: If you have spent any time in community organizing, you understand that you can't just go in and order people around and say, "Okay, I'm going to do this, you're going to do that, you're going to do that." You can't always be right and it can't always be your idea. A lot of the entrepreneurs are very strong in their opinions of how things should be, and sometimes that's wonderful and sometimes that is not as helpful in building a startup community.

Some of the things that we learned from all of the research that we did was this whole notion of leading from behind. When you are doing community organizing, and particularly when you're trying to build this entrepreneur infrastructure, as the organizer of it, you frequently have to be behind the scenes. You have to take every opportunity to celebrate the organizations that are part of the network and the entrepreneurs who are benefiting from the network. What you do has to be a little bit behind the scenes because if you try to make it too much about you, then everybody looks at you and says, "Well, I don't want to be part of that because you're getting all the credit." The whole notion of leading from behind is the idea that it has little to do with your title and is all about what you do and what contribution you make.

You don't have to be the czar of entrepreneurial ecosystems in any community to pull people together and get people to talk, learn, and collaborate. It's a lot about collaboration. Again, we need leaders who know how to encourage collaboration and get people to come to the table. I think it might have been Deb Markley, Co-Founder and Managing Director of the Center for Rural Entrepreneurship, who said that people come to the table based on their personal interest, and leaders have to help everybody find a common interest to stay. It's about creating a common vision for what entrepreneurship support looks like in our community and how we all play together to make that happen.

NABEEL KOSHAK: I believe that entrepreneurial programs and startup communities should be led by the private sector. If you look around, many programs started by the government did not actually develop. These innovation hubs and startup clusters can be started by government, who can create a desirable environment and perhaps provide some funding, but then they need sustainable business and financial models to grow and scale via private entities and private leadership.

We're seeing many different hubs, whether they are mega-hubs or those operating in different neighborhoods or zones. Perhaps the heavy high-tech community could be centralized into big hubs to give them easier access to markets, support, and funding, and to build the community at large. In parallel, creating smaller hubs scattered across different areas and cities would further facilitate and support startups across a much larger territory. I would also love to see a national index for universities that would measure, compare, and benchmark the outcomes of their programs in terms of commercialization, to further create competition among the different programs and encourage them to learn from each other.

Chapter IX

PROMISING OPPORTUNITIES FOR MENA STARTUPS

As the MENA region hits its stride in terms of ecosystem development, the opportunities that lie ahead are more promising than ever. Never before has there been so much potential and such a ripe environment for growth. Granted, there are some challenges, which I alluded to in earlier chapters. Nevertheless, nothing is too big for resilient entrepreneurs with solid business models, exceptional teams, and quality execution to overcome.

Some of the advances being brought to the market are long overdue; hence, the market is hungry for new solutions to persistent problems and may be less picky and more forgiving if the initially presented solution to any such problem is less than ideal. This creates a dynamic where even modestly viable new products and services can be widely accepted. That's music to local, fast-moving entrepreneurs' ears because, if their timing is right and they can provide the market with a viable—if not necessarily optimal—offering, they can win big, at least initially. Eventually, local or international competition will creep in and they will have to further enhance and differentiate their offering. Nevertheless, this early cushion of market acceptance at the start can be an advantage.

As we examine promising opportunities for MENA startups, we

can classify them into three models: copy and localize, respond to local problems, and truly innovate. Each comes with its own advantages and disadvantages, and there are plenty of success stories in each camp. One common observed trend, however, is that emerging markets typically move from the copy and localize model to the respond to local problems model, and eventually move to a true innovation model. This seems to be the natural progression, though there are plenty of exceptional cases.

Much of this is driven by the needs of the specific market and the availability of talent to provide products and services in line with those needs. As such, the copy and localize model is typically the low-hanging fruit. The most common example is the digitalization of sectors—from retail to e-commerce, from healthcare to tele-medicine, from taxi transportation to ride hailing, etc. Interestingly, both Careem and Souq, the two largest acquisition deals in the region by Uber and Amazon, respectively, followed this model.

The other large opportunity in this category is to disrupt some of the larger traditional industries in the region, such as real estate and banking. These areas will require massive investment since they are typically controlled by established large players or incumbents. Alternatively, some of those deep-pocketed, large organizations will spin off their own startups or acquire promising startups, as we've seen with the Emaar e-commerce venture, Noon, and Chalhoub Group's focus on adopting entrepreneurial technologies with its Greenhouse initiative.

With the copy and localize model, the level of adaptation to local needs varies significantly by sector and target market. For example, a service such as LinkedIn, which is geared to relatively tech-savvy, English-speaking professionals, requires less local customization than, say, a food delivery app operating in an environment where the vast majority are not English-speakers and don't own a credit card.

If there are significant local challenges and market requirements, a whole new level of innovation is needed. That could involve tweaked technology or operations (as in the case of cash-on-delivery functionality and operational processes, for example) or a new business model altogether. In both cases, an entirely new approach to execution enters the picture and will look vastly different from the original solution being copied. This a great feat in itself, in spite of the negative association where copying is assumed to be less challenging. Quite the contrary is true; it takes an astute entrepreneur to be able to combine the best of both worlds and ultimately present an offering that's fit for their local community and leverages proven technologies and business models from elsewhere. The key is to know what to replicate and what to adapt.

The second model is the respond to local problems model, where local problems are resolved using borrowed technologies but the solution itself is locally oriented. This is where the region has a strong opportunity to build the kinds of companies that can eventually expand to other markets that have more in common with MENA than, say, the US or Western Europe.

This model typically addresses large local problems. That is why it's widely accepted among the regional contributors interviewed here that FinTech is the next big frontier in the region. FinTech is viewed as the new savior in terms of providing online payment solutions for a massive population that's been largely closed off to the modern world without access to credit cards. Abdulaziz Al Loughani, CEO of Floward, Managing Partner of Faith Capital, and former Co-Founder and Managing Partner of Talabat, clearly underscores the potential of this area. He states, "The past 15 years has been focused on getting people online, where we now have 70% penetration. The next 15 years is going to be about getting people to pay online."

We also see a hybrid model of the above two opportunities. Egypt-based Swvl has taken this approach. It piggybacked on the ride-hailing concept of companies such as Uber and Lyft, but presented an entirely different customer experience. Instead of individual rides, it provides group rides with microbuses, which are more affordable locally and in line with the commuting needs of massive countries such as Egypt and many other countries in Africa. Swvl has grown by leaps and bounds since its inception. It will be interesting to see how it will scale to other, similar emerging markets and how attractive it will be as an acquisition target for some of the larger, global ride-hailing companies in spite of the variation in business model and approach. Perhaps it will continue without an acquisition, become a global player on its own, and get listed on top international exchanges. It's too early to tell, but the possibility is certainly there.

Finally, we see the emergence of new technologies, or what I refer to as the "true innovation" model, which follows global trends. This is where the foundational technology itself is new (not just the business model or execution) and presents a significantly more efficient, cost-effective, and transformative operational model or consumer offering, or both. Historically, these groundbreaking innovations have trickled in mainly from the US, and to a lesser extent from Western Europe, South Korea, Japan, and China. Examples of such innovation include the World Wide Web and smartphones.

Looking ahead, by and large, the consensus from global and regional experts is that areas such as AI, machine learning, blockchain, big data, robotics, and genomics are the next frontiers of innovative technologies. Whether the MENA region or any of its countries will emerge as active and leading players in such areas is yet to be seen. However, the time is right for MENA to participate actively as a global player in such areas and in the fourth industrial revolution.

1. Copy and Localize Model

ANDREW ROMANS: Some people think there is shame in having a copycat business model, as it was not their own unique idea. That's unfounded, since some of the best businesses, particularly in emerging markets, are copycats. That said, there is no such thing as a perfect copycat. In fact, an attempt to do so will not work locally. You cannot exactly copy something that's successful elsewhere and expect to achieve product-market fit. Careem and Souq are prime examples of taking a business model that works elsewhere and adapting it to the local environment. I don't think either would have achieved anywhere near the success they reached had they simply blindly copied Uber and Amazon, respectively, even if their execution had been great.

Additionally, those so-called copycat opportunities often represent low-hanging fruit. For one, they're often easier to raise capital for. I once heard an entrepreneur tell me he was pitching his startup to a VC. The VC asked, "Wait a minute. Who are you copying? Who else is doing this?" He responded, "No one. This is innovative." The VC shook his head and said, "We don't do that. We only back copycats here." It could be easier to raise the capital for copycats because it's easy to tell the story and sell the narrative. That can help you get going much faster and then you just need to convince local people that this will work locally. I think that the copycat model is not a bad idea, at least to get off the ground. After all, it's important for founders to try things and experiment until they find the perfect formula that works for them and their locality. They need funding to do that. It's good to experiment. If it's not working, then stop and try something else.

DAVE MCCLURE: This can be approached in three different ways. One is to look at existing consumer behaviors or business behaviors where there's already spending going on. The second is to look at which market segments have positive economics, or at least expect positive economics in the future. Then the third is what I would call breakthrough entrepreneurship.

Emerging markets do not typically start with breakthrough entrepreneurship; they start with incrementally innovative entrepreneurship. They tend to start out with e-commerce and marketplaces on the consumer side, and maybe real estate, healthcare, and education. On the business side, they typically start with FinTech and financial services.

The interest or tendency is to want to sort of copy the most innovative markets in the US, which now tend to be AI or virtual reality—things that really are very expensive to build and not necessarily obvious places to make money right away. Those are much more capital-intensive breakthrough businesses, which are tough to get off the ground globally—not necessarily because there's a lack of talent, but just because those businesses are not going to monetize right away.

I would say, for a lot of emerging markets, it's probably simpler to go after models like e-commerce or FinTech, where existing parallels are already straightforward. Jobs, education, healthcare, and travel are very straightforward parallels. That doesn't have to be where the region ends up, but those are easier places to start.

SANGEET PAUL CHOUDARY: When it comes to opportunities, sometimes there is an opportunity in copying something that has been proven elsewhere and customizing it for the local market. Sometimes there's also an opportunity in building something unique that is truly local but can also scale globally. It's somewhat difficult to say one is better than the other, although a lot of people prefer the latter approach because copying doesn't sound as innovative.

Ultimately, it comes down to where the business opportunity is. It's quite likely that all the copying that could be done in e-commerce has been done already, and therefore new local flavors would have to be created. It's also quite likely, on the other hand, that a successful shipping platform in the Baltic region can be copied in MENA and scale from there. I would not advocate one approach over the other as long as there's a clear market need and business opportunity.

Overall, there's a lot of opportunity in trade and logistics in the Middle East. A lot of technology and innovation will come into this space as trade becomes more and more digital. An equally big opportunity exists in energy since a lot of the Middle East's traditional economy has revolved around oil and gas. As we shift to other forms of energy, there are opportunities to use tech in those spaces and participate in the upside without necessarily having to rely on traditional sources of energy.

ABDULAZIZ AL LOUGHANI: The region has a $2.9 trillion economy, of which only around $28 billion is online. If you break down that $28 billion, $20 billion is within the travel industry—hotels and air tickets—and the remaining probably $8 to $9 billion is composed of fashion, food and beverage, electronics, and a mix of everything else. So, I'm bullish on consumer internet.

The past 15 years have been focused on getting people online, where we now have 70% penetration. I think that the next 15 years are going to be about getting people to pay online. The opportunity is enormous in the region for consumer internet across the board in different industries, different sectors, and different verticals. The big opportunity is in big offline industries that have yet to be converted to digital online platforms.

So many promising examples exist, some of which we have invested in, including flowers, gifts, eyewear, laundry, home appliances, classifieds, etc. The food and beverage industry has been the gazelle, the real winner, when it comes to online penetration over the past five years in the region. We will definitely see other verticals in consumer internet transform significantly over the coming years. That said, I don't believe there are enough R&D facilities or investment to enable us to make bets on new, cutting-edge technologies.

RABIH KHOURY: We focus on six sectors in our latest fund in MEVP, which correspond with where we think the hottest sectors are. One is new media, which means content and the way content is delivered. We think there is a massive opportunity for great Arabic content, which is still lagging, that people are willing to pay for.

The other promising sectors are the "e's", e-education, e-health, and e-commerce, which take traditionally inefficient industries and digitize them to provide a better delivery system. For example, governments spend a lot of money on education, health, and a host of other public services, but unfortunately the funding is not always channeled efficiently. You can do much more with this money and generate more of an impact by using technology. E-commerce is also growing quite rapidly in the region and online shopping is still a small fraction of overall retail relative to more mature e-commerce markets, so there's a massive untapped opportunity for those who are able to stand out and provide a differentiated value proposition to customers.

FinTech is quite exciting. It will play a key role in combating financial crimes, money laundering, and other fraud-related activities. We think there's going to be an explosion in FinTech. Now, FinTech is not just about hardcore FinTech services; it's also about financial inclusion and peer-to-peer lending, as well as how you can bring more people into the new economy. The Middle East has really failed when it comes to semi-lending. There is talk about it, but it really hasn't worked. There's still a huge gap, not in equity but in lending, and especially in non-recourse lending for very small enterprises. There's no real SME lending and very little microfinance. Technology can really improve many areas and help people to participate in the economy—people who are marginalized because of old laws.

SAMIH TOUKAN: The opportunities to replicate and localize across different sectors, as per Souq and Careem, are everywhere. Having said that, what interests me most, and I think this is where we will see very exciting solutions, are traditional sectors in the region, like the financial, agricultural, and real estate sectors. Technology hasn't yet moved into these very traditional sectors that are ripe for disruption, so I believe we will see more and more solutions coming up in those areas.

I also see exciting opportunities in providing solutions where governments fail. For example, in transportation—in Egypt, with buses and so on, or in Jordan, where the government has not provided proper, efficient public transportation—now startups are coming up with solutions that tackle this problem. That's an area that I am particularly passionate about—namely, providing solutions for societies in areas where governments have been in charge and not able to provide proper solutions. That's where I see massive opportunities waiting to be unlocked. I am optimistic that some of those startups will become huge companies listed on our stock exchanges in the near future.

AHMAD SUFIAN BAYRAM: For the past decade or so, I have been talking about the power of sharing and the collaborative economy as an exciting tech sector that can open up many opportunities. Although we have seen a lot of progress in this domain, a lot more can be done.

E-commerce still has a room to grow. According to a new report by McKinsey, only 8% of SMEs have an online presence, and only 1.5% of MENA's retail sales are online, despite the fact that over 90% of people in the region own a smartphone. On the other hand, blockchain technology has moved from the fringes to something that can have a real impact on all parts of our lives, and the youth of the region can lead this revolution. There's tremendous opportunity to adopt the best global innovations into the region on those fronts.

MAZIN AL ZAIDI: E-commerce is an exciting and growing sector here in Saudi Arabia and regionally. It's forecast to reach $28.5 billion by 2022. Saudi Arabia has always had a strong consumer market, with high purchasing power and demand, and internet and mobile phone penetration rates are among the highest in the world. But e-commerce is still a nascent industry with significant growth potential. The logistics sector is also primed for growth, especially given Saudi Arabia's strategic geographic position between Europe, Asia, and Africa. KSA is a natural bridge, connecting people and goods around the world.

WALID HANNA: This region has a five-year lag when compared to the West or China. In MENA, content and new media were in the headlines a decade ago, while e-commerce marketplaces and FinTech have appeared in the past five years, and SaaS and mobility in the past couple of years. Add to this more AI empowerment next year, and probably more blockchain technologies thereafter.

2. Local Problem-Response Model

JOHN MACOMBER: I see technology leapfrogging in the physical environment area. If you think about this in the Middle East, North Africa, and sub-Saharan Africa, the first technology leapfrog was mobile telephony. A lot of places in the MENA region, sub-Saharan Africa, and western and northern Asia never built a copper wire network for telephone. They went straight to mobile telephony. So, that was the first phase.

The second phase is mobile money. A lot of growing economies across South Asia, MENA, and sub-Saharan Africa have gone right to mobile money, led by telcos or other providers rather than banks. That's another leapfrog over the Western model.

The third phase—which we're in right now—is around optimization and physical infrastructure, particularly in places that have horrible traffic or horrible water shortages. As sensors and predictive analytics provide the ability to charge differential prices based on time of day, and the wealth of the user becomes more prevalent, it's possible to get a lot more throughput. I'm referring to optimizing infrastructure, where the roads and the water are exactly the same physical infrastructure. There's no need to build any more tarmac or put any more pipes in the ground, but their output is significantly greater. That's a huge opportunity that's going to be transformative.

The fourth phase will be a technology leapfrog around actual infrastructure buildout, particularly for roads and rail. It will be driven by the ubiquity of 3D printing and drones. Right now, 3D printing is a novelty for models and the desktop. Maybe some really wealthy firms can make a few metal pieces from pictures or maybe drones are delivering very lightweight things. Fast forward 10 years and think about where service is poor, notably in sub-Saharan Africa or South Asia. Rather than having to build a German or American model of eight-lane highways for hundreds of thousands of miles to accommodate deliveries of goods, you can imagine a situation where you 3D-print a particular good on the spot or nearby and don't need to have that good travel thousands of miles.

For example, to get a chair today, you often have to make the chair in China, put it in a box, place it on a ship, have it travel for months over the ocean, unload it at the port, deal with all the customs and tariffs, security, and taxes, and then put it on a road on a truck to drive it for hours or days to the destination. Now, you can imagine 3D-printing that chair in a village or a community. You don't need to build those roads for all that transport and have all those trucks on the highway. Similarly, if we're able to 3D-print a 50 kg vehicle payload, we would save hundreds of miles in last-mile delivery. That will be another technology leapfrog in a difficult physical space that will make it simple.

TIM O'REILLY: The next big set of winds are going to be in areas that are not popular today, just like the internet was not popular when we were first looking at that ecosystem grow, or open source software was not popular initially. Right now, it's most likely going to be in such areas as agriculture, energy, healthcare, and climate. These are areas where real problems need to be solved. It isn't clear yet how to make money, but the problems are real and are not going away anytime soon. If you solve them, you will make money, and that's a very different kind of uncertainty than the uncertainty about companies like Uber, where it's not clear how the economics work.

The biggest opportunities in the Middle East are to solve problems for places that don't have access to all of the technology we have today. Similarly, we're seeing the growth of electronic cash in Africa, where it jumped way out ahead of anything that was happening in the West. The main reason is that it was solving a local problem where people were unbanked and mobile infrastructure allowed them to bypass the developed world.

An example of a company that I really admire is Zipline, which is a Silicon Valley–backed company in which Goldman Sachs is an investor. They're basically using drones, not to deliver coffee or consumer goods for an affluent population, but to deliver life-saving blood and medicines to people in developing countries. Many massive opportunities such as this will exist in the developing world.

JOY AJLOUNY: Disrupting the current banking system in the region comes to mind most particularly. The banks are something that startups really struggle with. For example, for Fetchr, even after we raised $11 million, we could not get a credit card for the company. We had to have three years of accounting and operations, and be validated, in order for us to get a simple credit card. A lot of banking regulations today make it tough to accept foreign payments or transfer money and are not startup- and SME-friendly. The opportunities in that area are tremendous.

Another example is the problem with the e-commerce explosion in particular. In the region, 92% of orders are COD; there is a fear of using credit and the reverse-logistics aspect of getting a credit back to your card. In the US, if there is a discrepancy, you call the bank and it is removed immediately and the burden of proof is on the retailer, not the consumer. In the Middle East, it is up to the customer to prove that they were wronged. It goes against the "customer is always right" mentality that has caused so much e-commerce growth in the US.

A lot of things in the Middle East don't work, so naturally there are a lot of opportunities to disrupt things. In the United States, for example, it's much tougher to disrupt anything because there's so much competition. Look at Careem. One of the main reasons Careem won was because it was able to come up with something that Uber hadn't even thought of, which was paying with cash. That was a fundamental shift in how ride-hailing services operate and something more aligned with consumer behavior in the Middle East, because credit card penetration is still low and everybody pays with cash. In effect, Careem was able to speak the local language and adapt to the Arab culture, which Uber didn't understand. If you're willing and able to adapt a world-class solution to the region, you have a great chance of succeeding, either in terms of winning market share or getting acquired.

AMIRA RASHAD: The region is ripe with opportunity. It's incredible how many things in life could be made more accessible and more efficient with technology, from FinTech to e-commerce. The list goes on. The thinking is that e-commerce is a "been there, done that" type of space. If you look at the numbers, you find that the percentage of people who are actually buying online in this part of the world is minuscule compared to the US. Clearly, there is a tremendous opportunity there.

On another front, teaching a machine in this part of the world would be a completely different experience from teaching it elsewhere, yet nobody's doing that. Nobody is doing predictive analytics, the baby step of AI, around necessary daily activities in this part of the world to streamline them. Be it for traffic efficiency or for grocery purchases, personalization, or whatever, the purpose of that AI that you're developing is quite different in each region. Yet nobody is codifying that; nobody's capturing the data accurately. Data science is rare in this part of the world.

CHRISTOPHER SCHROEDER: FinTech, last-mile logistics, education, healthcare innovation, and any service that creates less friction that exists in broader infrastructure provides opportunities. One example is traffic, which can be expanded beyond the region to, say, Africa, Southeast Asia, etc. Meanwhile, the reverse can happen as well, and we might see more and more great services that succeed in those markets starting to look at MENA as an opportunity for expansion. I always look for leapfrogging opportunities—entrepreneurs not merely trying to plug and play a Western success, but highly adaptive or new-use cases for markets that wonderfully and often are starting up themselves.

MENA FUNDING SHARE BY SECTOR

Delivery & Transport still accounts for the highest amount of funding
- Delivery & Transport accounted for 19% of total funding in 2019
- EMPG's $100M fundraise largely contributed to Real Estate's ranking

MENA's Top 5 Industries by Total Funding in 2019

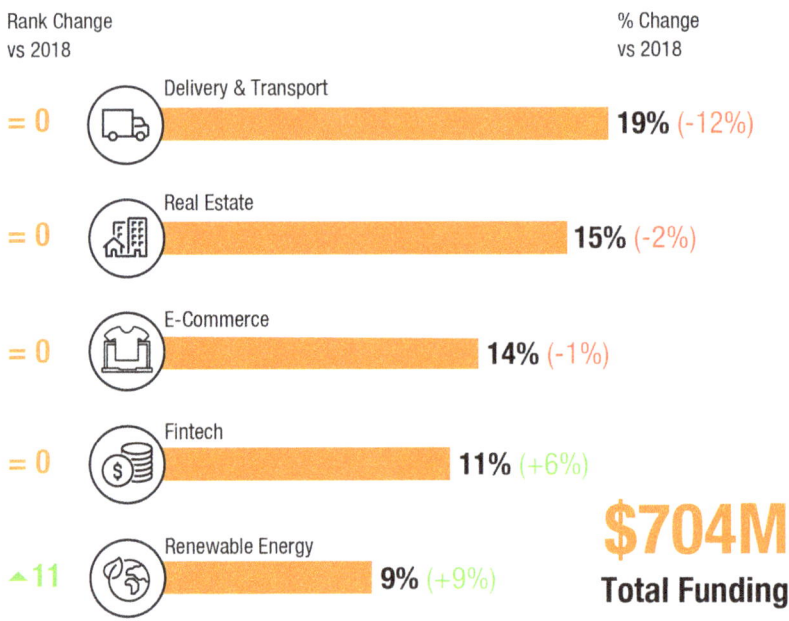

Rank Change vs 2018 / % Change vs 2018

- = 0 — Delivery & Transport — **19%** (-12%)
- = 0 — Real Estate — **15%** (-2%)
- = 0 — E-Commerce — **14%** (-1%)
- = 0 — Fintech — **11%** (+6%)
- ▲ 11 — Renewable Energy — **9%** (+9%)

$704M Total Funding

Source: MAGNiTT MENA Venture Investment Summary 2019 (www.magnitt.com)

EYAD ALKASSAR: We're looking into FinTech a lot these days. Banking is a very interesting space for us because of the large unbanked population in the region, especially outside the GCC. Payment is highly interesting for us as well because we still have a heavily cash-reliant region. I believe this will change very fast once the right products for this market are developed that allow people to move away from cash. We think consumer financing is promising as well, because historically there is a lack of consumer finance in this region. There was a lack of credit cards also, and so on. These three buckets are very important and very interesting for us: banking, payment, and financing. I believe the next big success story in this region will come out of FinTech.

I also believe that this region can be the initial incubation ground for much bigger markets than just the Middle East. One example is Swvl: it launched in Egypt and expanded massively into Africa and is dominating the market there and becoming a main transportation company. Africa is a great cross-region opportunity for Middle Eastern companies. With 1.5 billion people and geographic proximity, as well as cultural links and other environmental similarities, it's the next untapped frontier for companies in the region to scale into.

ISSA AGHABI: Right now, we're seeing a lot of promise in e-logistics —people moving food, parcels, cargo, and so on. That is a problem that's being disrupted. Companies like Swvl, Fetchr, and Careem, just to name a few, are trying to disrupt that sector across the region. Food delivery in the UAE is one the highest basket sizes in the world. That's one space that is interesting and promising and will continue to grow in the foreseeable future. This will also extend to groceries and other relevant convenience items.

FinTech is a promising space with lots of buzz, but I don't think that space has reached its potential yet. A lot more will come from that space, and as regulators start opening up and becoming a bit more flexible, we're going to see a lot more disruption from that space as well. B2B marketplaces, connecting suppliers with end corporate clients, is another space that will grow.

NED JAROUDI: There are many exciting opportunities. Blockchain is one, and we're seeing a lot of companies getting into that space. When I say blockchain, it includes blockchain and FinTech. In terms of sectors, banking and financial services are definitely a big one. Education is another huge one. E-learning or EdTech is really booming. There are some very good examples in the region, such as Lamsa. Digital health is another promising example, with doctors on call 24/7 through platforms like Vezeeta or Altibbi.

Then we have gaming. We're a young, very easily entertained population in MENA, so that's another big one that is about to take off. Overall, the creative industries are quite promising, including lifestyle content, animation, comics, digital music, etc. These are very much untapped, except for a few startup examples like 7awi, Blink Studios, and of course Anghami.

Also, very local to this region is the construction sector, which has experienced a huge boom in recent decades, creating an opportunity. Construction in general is one of the last sectors to be digitally disrupted globally, but it is now getting good traction in places like the US and Europe. Some of the local construction tech success stories include ProTenders, Handiss, and WakeCap. So that's another sector that is ripe for growth and will likely create a massive opportunity.

OMAR CHRISTIDIS: The hot thing for the last 12 or 18 months has been FinTech. Lots of countries have launched FinTech hubs. I would say that FinTech is one of those hot areas. "Smart cities" is also another really exciting space. Smart cities, IoT (internet of things), the fourth industrial revolution—governments, and large telcos are all interested in these now. There's a lot of discourse around IoT, the fourth industrial revolution, 5G, digital transformation, and ICT services. You're seeing it much more in the GCC with the UAE leading. Qatar, Oman, and others are all really investing heavily in the smart space and smart infrastructure, so that's an open space for many entrepreneurs who want to deliver services within this sector.

Property tech and real estate tech are really promising, especially because real estate development is the largest sector of the global economy and one of the largest sectors of our regional economy. Last-mile delivery is also quite promising. Whoever solves that problem will get a really big reward, whether it's the address problem or the actual last-mile delivery, because e-commerce is booming. The platform space is a red ocean with Amazon, Noon, and the big players, but support services for e-commerce is definitely a very hot space.

MENA DEAL SHARE BY SECTOR

FinTech ranks first by number of deals for the second year in a row
- FinTech accounted for 13% of all deals in 2019
- Accelerators and governments play a key role in supporting FinTech startups

MENA's Top 5 Industries by Number of Deals in 2019

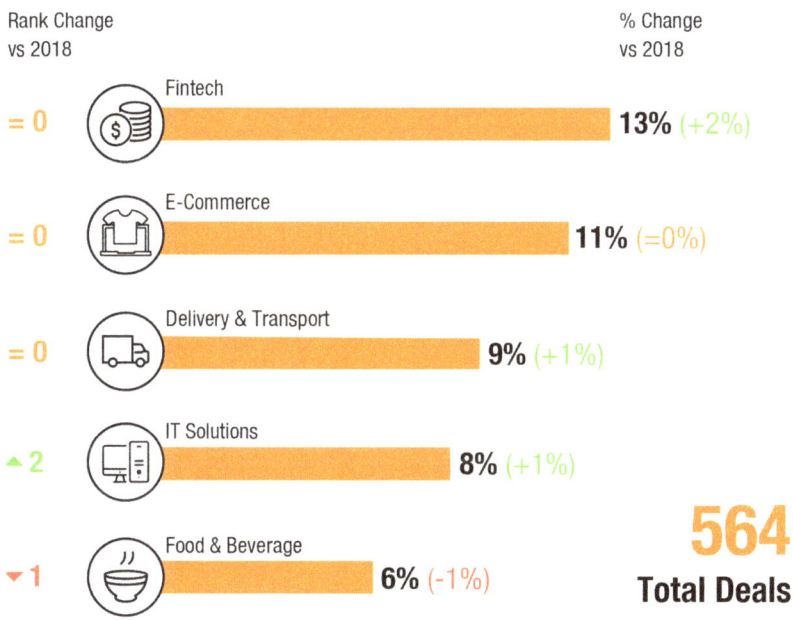

Rank Change vs 2018 | | % Change vs 2018

Rank Change vs 2018	Sector	% Change vs 2018
= 0	Fintech	**13%** (+2%)
= 0	E-Commerce	**11%** (=0%)
= 0	Delivery & Transport	**9%** (+1%)
▲ 2	IT Solutions	**8%** (+1%)
▼ 1	Food & Beverage	**6%** (-1%)

564
Total Deals

Source: MAGNiTT MENA Venture Investment Summary 2019 (www.magnitt.com)

AMMAR AL MALIK: Some of the fastest growing sectors are FinTech and e-commerce. E-commerce is still growing in the region, with the average annual online spend per capita in the UAE around $300 according to Business Monitor International (BMI). There is a lot of opportunity for growth in terms of the size of the e-commerce market. I'd like to see more companies in the region in the data science industry, including data centers, data center management, and data analytics, because that's a sector with massive growth potential.

Finally, seeing how little Arabic content is on the internet and that internet penetration is growing 15% year-on-year in the region, we need to develop more Arabic content and have companies explore and leverage relevant opportunities in this area. Social media platforms and current technologies also make it easy for people to see what opportunities exist. Considering that less than 1% of all content on the internet is Arabic, there are many opportunities for people in this region to create content and start businesses by monetizing that content. We need to educate. We need to inspire. We're on the right track, but we would like to see more and more people getting involved. The more, the merrier: the more ecosystems that are coming up across the region, the better it is for everyone, and the more success we will have across the region.

YASMEEN AL SHARAF: Open banking offers an opportunity for reforming the banking experience for customers. I certainly believe it will revolutionize the way traditional banking is being performed. I anticipate that more and more collaborations between traditional financial institutions and leading FinTech startups will take place. The main concept behind open banking is to give back to customers the control of their financial data and financial information, which is currently sitting with banks. It revolves around the notion that the data sitting with banks today belongs to the customer and not to the banks themselves. Therefore, customers have the right to have full visibility of their financial data across different banks, as well as the ability to shop around for the best offers. This in turn will stir up competition within the banking sector, leading to more innovative banking products and services, and will create huge monetization opportunities for banks.

Open banking works by traditional banks opening up and sharing customer data and information, strictly subject to authorization from customers, with third-party providers (TPPs). The TPPs are licensed and fully regulated by the Central Bank. These TPPs will then aggregate customer data across different banks, as well as financial products and services offered by existing banks to the customer, thus enhancing the financial literacy assessment. TPPs will also offer payment initiation services to customers. For example, if I'm looking to apply for a loan with a bank, I don't know if this bank is offering me the best terms available or not. By aggregating all of the banking products and services on a single app, customers can shop around for the best offers and prices. At the same time, customers will have full control and visibility of their existing financial data, helping them manage their finances more efficiently.

INDUSTRIES BREAKDOWN BY INVESTMENT DEALS IN MENA

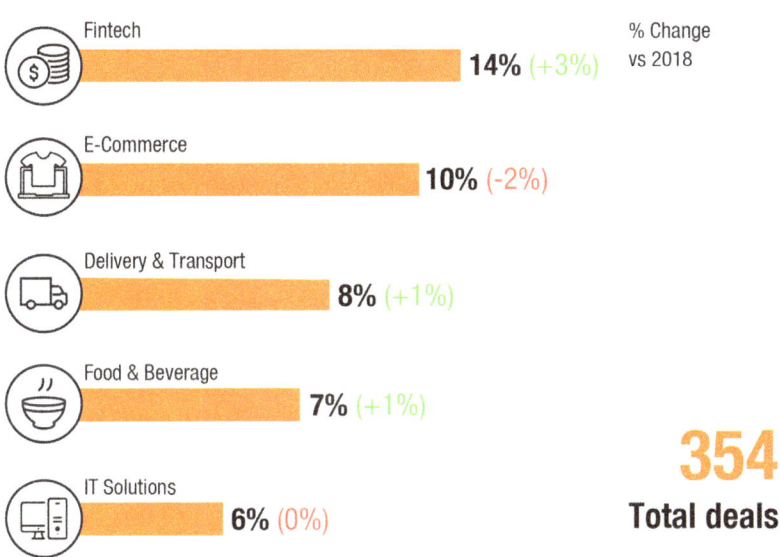

Fintech **14%** (+3%)

% Change vs 2018

E-Commerce **10%** (-2%)

Delivery & Transport **8%** (+1%)

Food & Beverage **7%** (+1%)

IT Solutions **6%** (0%)

354
Total deals

Source: MAGNiTT MENA Venture Investment Summary 2019 (www.magnitt.com)

STEVE CASE: In this new third wave of innovation, entrepreneurs all over the world are tackling real-world problems instead of creating the next photo or delivery app. I'm excited to see the solutions entrepreneurs are creating to solve problems around climate change, smart cities, better care, and lower healthcare costs. Only when we take on these major industries can we see real change in the way we live.

3. True Innovation Model

ALEC ROSS: I would categorize the game-changing industries that will shape technology and culture globally in the next two decades into five categories: robotics, genomics, big data, the codification of money (e.g., cryptocurrencies and mobile user-to-user payment systems), and the "weaponization of code" (e.g., cyberwarfare, hacking, or new forms of surveillance). Certainly, both opportunities and risks come with such great disruption; hence, our work is cut out for us in terms of the choices we make to prepare ourselves and our kids for those transformations. Just as automation is changing the nature of work today, genomics will reshape our understanding of human biology; big data will shift our relationship with information; and coding will alter everything from money to risk management.

If I were to try to predict where the next Silicon Valley will be, my view is in line with that of Mark Andreessen. He points out that the next stage of innovation will not be incubated in new Silicon Valleys, but in 50 different variations of Silicon Valley, all unique from each other and all focusing on different domains. Policy, business, and technology will have to work together to stimulate innovation. Instead of asking about the next Silicon Valley, we should be asking about the next Estonia. I use Estonia as an example because it's a small country with a mere 1.3 million people that has managed to transform its economy and create prosperity by following a disciplined, methodical approach. What Estonia has achieved in such a short period of time has been nothing short of remarkable.

ERIK BRYNJOLFSSON: In terms of technology, machine learning has to be number one. AI has been around for 50 years and people have been working on different techniques. I personally had a company that did AI as far back as the 1980s, so I'm quite familiar with the evolution. Starting around 2010, a series of breakthroughs in deep learning and using deep neural nets occurred, and these have become so powerful that people are using them to solve problems in many different categories.

Having said that, we're still in the early stages. Over the next decade, we're going to see more and more investment in this area and more and more problems solved. The bottleneck is less about where the technologies are today and more about managers being intelligent in adopting them. That's why the rubric that we developed, the Suitability of Machine Learning Rubric, is helpful in identifying the areas where opportunities are most likely to be successful.

We also have not yet fully taken advantage of all the things you can do with digitization, especially with mobile phones. A third area that is strengthening is biology and biotech. We'll see more of that area developing in spite of that fact that it requires large investments.

Additionally, a wonderful thing that happened recently is the mobile internet has connected people globally—seven billion people, actually. That doesn't simply mean that everyone has access to global information; more importantly, it means that everyone can contribute to global information. We now have billions of brains all over the world that are working on problems and can share their innovations. This means that if you're a smart person and you have access to the internet, wherever you are, you can tap into this global ecosystem and find customers, ideas, and suppliers anywhere in the world.

The smart nations are the ones that are making it easy for their citizens to be part of that global mind. Countries that block themselves and block their citizens from being part of that collective innovation are going to struggle and start falling behind. This has been one of the most wonderful things in human history, that we can all be connected and learn from each other. That's one of the reasons I'm optimistic about innovation going forward. This becomes more and more of a tool for scientific discovery and entrepreneurship.

TIM DRAPER: The MENA region has the greatest opportunity because the region is being freed up to allow open sharing of entrepreneurial energy. The region can start with opportunities that mirror the success of others, but it can quickly move into innovations that would naturally come from MENA.

Generally speaking, Bitcoin, blockchain, smart contracts, and AI have the potential to transform the world, even more so than the internet did over the last two decades. The internet transformed media, communications, information, distribution, entertainment, and many other industries in the $10-100 billion range, but Bitcoin and AI have the potential to transform trillion-dollar industries like banking, insurance, commerce, finance, healthcare, and even parts of government. We are embarking on a renaissance of enormous proportions. Entrepreneurs will thrive. Dynamic, free-flowing governments will thrive. Controlling governments will languish.

JONATHAN ORTMANS: In terms of straightforward tech sectors, the fastest growing are "deep technology" areas—those based primarily on intellectual property: advanced manufacturing and robotics, blockchain, AgriTech and new food, and AI. In blockchain, the top five ecosystems are Silicon Valley, London, New York City, Singapore, and Toronto-Waterloo. Ecosystems to watch in AI include Edmonton, Jerusalem, Montreal, and Taipei City.

Looking ahead, my favorite outlier choice would be our "astropreneurs." At GEN, we have launched GEN Space to support the 2,700 astropreneurs we have signed up who are working to leverage the emerging new space industry.

OSMAN SULTAN: The opportunities and applications around AI are quite promising, and we've yet to scratch the surface. This is the one domain, though, where we need to have the conversation about societal, cultural, and ethical implications in parallel with the technological and economic conversations.

A company like Enaible is applying AI to enhancing corporate productivity, and a company like Searchie is applying it to the fascinating area of human insights, far from the popular science fiction perception where intelligent and autonomous robots rule the world. Big data is another promising domain, specifically when more and more IoT technology will be deployed using 5G.

We are heading toward a world where we use data to create more information, then use this information to create more knowledge, and eventually use this knowledge to increase our wisdom.

RAMI SALMAN: To start, we have a proven model of appropriating existing startups that have had tremendous success internationally and adapting them for success regionally. I don't think that this is something that will go away anytime soon, so any startup that has a copy and localize approach has the potential to scale quickly in the region and establish itself as the lead player in a new and emerging space. There are countless versions of this. Entrepreneurs just need to stay tuned to up-and-comers internationally.

In general, AI and machine learning is a space that is underserved in the region, especially when you consider that data is quite specific to the region: for example, using NLP (neuro-linguistic programming) or voice recognition in the Arabic language. Localization is not limited to languages; it facilitates all kinds of specialization that only applies to local sales and usage data. Applied AI and learning is really an incredible opportunity for startups to come in and build exciting products that leverage big-data technologies to optimize business operations, customer acquisition, sales, and all kinds of funnel improvements for the market.

I also think that emerging technology, such a blockchain, has a unique place in a market like ours where the government is trying to be on the leading edge of many different technologies. If you're able to find a niche in the blockchain space that fits or solves a government need, you may find it much more exciting to work in this region versus the Western markets, where things tend to move a lot more slowly. We have some very nimble and flexible governments in some parts of the region that are able to act quickly and make major decisions, which is a great benefit. Given that, any government tech space is quite promising.

Finally, there are opportunities to serve what is working in the existing ecosystem with SaaS technologies, such as e-commerce, tourism, trade, or even oil and gas companies. These should be exciting spaces to play in, since entrepreneurs would be catering to a growing, addressable market, including mainstays in this part of the world.

FOUAD JERYES: The applications of AI and machine learning will be very transformational for how we conduct our lives or businesses but, realistically, it will take some time to evolve the "computational comprehension" required for them to be very useful and technically interesting. Very few companies (Google being one of them with their conceptual demo of Google Duplex) have enough data to "deep-fake" and add what seems to be comprehension to a computer in a way that can mimic a real human interaction. Even those few companies are still far from succeeding. Doing this in English is quite the feat, but achieving it in Arabic, considering the nuances and grammatical complexity of the language and the wide variety of accents, would be a profound achievement. The technical focus and infrastructure involved in advancing the Arabic language may even pave the way to increasing the penetration of Arabic content online.

Other exciting areas of interest are cryptocurrencies and blockchain. After AI/machine learning opportunities, they have the second-highest growth in job demand. I'm excited about this space for its ability to not just change the financial inclusion landscape and redistribute wealth, but also add more trust where trust is lacking. Transparency in the financial system as well as other industries is something that the public would like to see more of and can only be good for business. Abu Dhabi has been particularly proactive on this front and has developed a license for such ventures, so we will see whether these moves draw more companies to the space and the region.

ROBERTO CROCI: Cloud computing and AI continue to hold exciting opportunities for startups in reaching new markets, opening new revenue streams, optimizing products and services, and transforming industries. Recent research we conducted with EY found that, across the Middle East and Africa, 78% of businesses consider AI an important priority that is likely to influence their operations in the next five years; however, only 28% have early-stage AI pilots running today.

In emerging markets, cloud and AI are still gaining momentum as internet connectivity, mobile phone penetration, and digital skills increase. In the last year, Microsoft opened two new data center regions in the Middle East and Africa, together with development center sites in Kenya and Nigeria, bringing more people online and spurring local innovation. This growth in adoption means that there's still a lot of potential for startups to transform industries, like financial services or agriculture, as unbanked people or underserved farmers start coming online.

The 2019 *Digitalisation of African Agriculture Report* found that, despite some 400 solutions already in play, 90% of the market for digital services in agriculture still remains untapped—and it could be worth more than $2.26 billion. Microsoft is working with many startups in this space, and a great deal of focus is on data-driven farming and water resource management, considering the effects of climate change and the significant demand for freshwater irrigation on farms.

The UAE is already home to the largest community of FinTech startups in the MENA region, but it is poised for robust growth by 2022, particularly with the government championing blockchain policy and adoption. I believe we're still going to see a lot from blockchain and FinTech around the world, but particularly in emerging markets, which have the ability to build paperless, cashless societies and inclusive digital economies.

Chapter X

GLOBAL LESSONS FOR ECOSYSTEM DEVELOPMENT

The purpose of examining case studies and best practices in ecosystem development from around the world is not to provide a model to blindly copy; it is to learn from and apply these practices where they are relevant to one's particular ecosystem. This approach presupposes a decent level of understanding of one's own ecosystem's strengths and weakness and its needs. Only then can learning from others be a valuable tool in terms of problem-solving or filling any gaps in your ecosystem. Additionally, and just as important, the examination can provide lessons on what not to do and how to avoid common mistakes and pitfalls.

It's important to know the historical context of whichever ecosystem or model you're examining because it's unrealistic to always aim for some kind of "leapfrog effect," whereby certain stages of ecosystem evolution are skipped. Every stage of an ecosystem, whether ground-level, adolescent, mature, or advanced, will have its own needs and requirements.

That said, a number of key lessons are applicable to any ecosystem in the process of development, regardless of stage, although the ideas discussed here are not meant to be an exhaustive list, by any means. As the world becomes more complex and ecosystems mature in general, it's expected that new areas of ecosystem development will surface both as opportunities and challenges. The following areas represent perhaps a starting point for any ecosystem player to look into in order to learn from the countless examples and experiments around the world. The areas to examine include: understanding your own strengths and weaknesses, aiming to be frictionless, creating conditions to optimize capital flow, providing all-around startup support, and facilitating foreign talent and investment. Under each area, we touch on relevant international examples where a particular ecosystem has done a remarkable job in that specific area. For example, looking at ease of doing business, we highlight Singapore and the UK in terms of smart governance and seamless business setup and operational environments.

We also touch on various ecosystems making great progress in unlikely places, such as Estonia, Indonesia, and Rwanda. Additionally, we touch on the Netherlands' recent initiative with a startup visa, which enables international startups to set up and operate in the Netherlands more easily than ever before. There are many other examples of progressive and effective ecosystem development initiatives from around the world.

In some cases, we also cover a comparative analysis of two different ecosystems. Efosa Ojomo, Global Prosperity Lead at Clayton Christensen Institute, Co-Founder and President of Poverty Stops Here, and Co-Author of *The Prosperity Paradox: How Innovation Can Lift Nations Out of Poverty*, has contrasted South Korea and Mexico, which were economies of similar size 50 years ago. South Korea's GDP far exceeds that of Mexico today. He attributes the difference to a lack of disruptive innovation in Mexico.

One common mistake is attempting to blindly copy an ecosystem that one admires, with the most frequently copied ecosystem being Silicon Valley. The problem is that many people look at Silicon Valley and jump to the conclusion that they need to build a university and develop all kinds of accelerator programs and events. Certainly, any such initiatives, if executed well, could add value to an ecosystem.

The mistake here, however, is that they miss the forest for the trees. Instead of focusing on the underlying components of an ecosystem while assessing which of those areas they have gaps in, they often end up looking at byproducts of a thriving ecosystem, rather than its triggers. They also overlook the fact that Silicon Valley has evolved over decades. As such, there is no single, bulletproof shortcut to laying the right foundation for an ecosystem. One can certainly catalyze and accelerate the speed of innovation, but not indefinitely or likely via a single program or initiative. Hence, patience is needed, combined with resisting the urge to slash initiatives that don't produce immediate results. Instead, it's important to identify the reasons for their shortcomings and make a concerted effort to tweak, re-test, and fix them and stay the course. It's an iterative process, not a big bang solution.

This chapter sheds light on a wide array of international case studies and best practices that should be examined closely in order to distill the most relevant and applicable lessons for one's own ecosystem. While many lessons can be learned from the examples of both emerging ecosystems and established, successful ecosystems, the following cases offer any serious ecosystem builder great clues.

1. Understand Own Strengths and Weaknesses

RAMEZ SHEHADI: All in all, we are just scratching the surface in terms of what this region has to do vis-à-vis the digital economy. Let's take a startup, a tech startup as opposed to just startups in the internet world in general. People are always enamored by these unicorn stories, these great successes that become multibillion-dollar enterprises all around the world. You have a lot of prospectors among the startup communities, the tech startup communities, who are trying to create the next best thing out there.

While that might be the case, there is a desperate need and an opportunity for us to not reinvent the wheel. This ecosystem, this landscape, can be categorized very broadly into three buckets. There are those who are trying to create the next big innovation, the originators and inventors. Then there is another category of replicators and localizers, who look to see what is happening in other geographies, copycat that, and then nuance it to fit the local cultural and behavioral environments that apply. Then there are those who are the propagators—those who say, "I will give you an open door into my audience, my community, my segment. Let me partner with you, or let me take a piece of the pie, or let me become a business agent to you to help propagate your business in this neck of the woods." The startup community perhaps has leaned too heavily on origination and on propagation and there is fundamentally a lot more opportunity in the middle segment, which is to replicate and localize.

I would also say, overall, there isn't a strong match between where we have traditionally succeeded in a non-technical way and where technology is focusing. Clearly, there ought to be attention to those segments that bring about convenience, that bring about simplicity, that bring about comfort in people's lives. Those will always be a source of traction and benefit and opportunity—the Ubers or the Careems of this world. There is a significant opportunity for us to say we have a right to not just play in a certain segment but to win in a certain segment if we have a history and legacy of winning in that segment.

When you look at the traditional successes in this region, the match to tech investments doesn't necessarily correlate. In the Levant, for example, agriculture has been a mainstay for all of time. It's called the "fertile crescent" for a reason, but the investments in AgriTech and the productivity of AgriTech could be far more advanced. We have plenty more opportunities to leverage this energy form toward energy tech, particularly as we start to think about some of the very important aspirations coming out of the region. Whether it's Vision 2030 out of the Kingdom of Saudi Arabia or other similar national agendas from other parts of the Gulf or North Africa, the goal is to reduce hydrocarbon dependency and to become much more of a smart utility or smart energy producer. At the sovereign scale, rather than just making funds available and creating hubs and innovation centers for communities, as many governments have done, the opportunity is huge to more precisely curate the flow of these assets or the availability of these assets—physical, financial, and human— toward those segments where there is a right to win.

So we need to figure out where we have a right to play and where we have a right to win. If we were to chart out the demand and supply landscape across a digital continuum or across an industry continuum, we would find a number of areas where we are net importers and don't need to be and areas where we are exporters and therefore we can expand the value chain that enables them. That analysis would show very compelling and interesting results for North Africa and the Levant, and very different ones than in the GCC.

ADRIAN GARCIA-ARANYOS: One question that often comes up is typically, "How do we develop the next Silicon Valley?" I feel the answer to that question is that Silicon Valley is perfect where it is with all of its amazing advantages and all of its flaws.

Each city or country needs to truly embrace what they are good at and find the angle to make it work. It's crucial for governments to be aligned and recognize that any bet will normally mean disruption, and disruption needs to be tackled wisely. Some countries might be able to leverage the great quality of life, while for others it might be cheaper technical talent or stronger retention. At the end of the day, it's about building on the strengths that are already in place.

JF GAUTHIER: Every ecosystem has its own specific context and thus its own specific needs. Those needs evolve over time as the ecosystem itself evolves from one phase to another. A common problem we see around the world is trying to copy, rather than learn from, other successful ecosystems. You can't just look at London and try to replicate it in Dubai, Riyadh, or Cairo and expect it's going to work in the same fashion. In fact, copying London's policy of the last three years will be very damaging and a huge waste of time and resources in the Middle East. Similarly, what Singapore has been doing in the past five years will not apply to the region. You need to look specifically at your own circumstances and the stage of development of your ecosystem to determine the strategies that address your most pressing needs. In short, study the case studies but avoid copying blindly.

You might even have to rewind back and see, for example, what Singapore did in the mid-1990s to understand what worked and what didn't work if your ecosystem resembles that of Singapore in the mid-1990s rather than today. Going back to history is a very useful exercise because the only way to see what worked and what didn't in a startup ecosystem is to have a 5-10-year horizon. When you see new policies that were enacted two years ago, copying them is dangerous because you really don't know if they are going to be successful and what the issues associated with those policies are.

SAMI MAHROUM: You have to emulate in line with your own understanding of your strengths and weaknesses, as opposed to copying blindly. You also have to work with your strengths first, as opposed to working only on your weaknesses. We don't need to spend the next 30 years complaining about regulations, complaining about infrastructure, complaining about corruption, or whatever. It doesn't help.

If the guys at Careem, Namshi, or Souq managed to do it, that means it's doable and that's all that matters. If Instabug or someone else out of Egypt manages to build a successful tech startup, it means it is doable, and so on in every country across the region. Let's focus on how these people managed to create this success, and study their strategy and their execution methods, and try to replicate them, to magnify them, to amplify them, and to learn from those lessons at home. That's more important than looking to the east and west.

Of course, we can learn about experiences in Silicon Valley. We can look at Finland. We can look at the Netherlands. But even countries like the Netherlands and others in Europe see themselves as lagging behind in terms of entrepreneurship, and that's just because of how things are. The grass looks quite green in places like Europe from the outside, but it's not always as rosy and easy as it may seem. Entrepreneurs still have to go through taxation, regulation, and red tape challenges.

I don't see any one place as a model that we need to emulate in the region. We can be inspired by and learn from certain policy instruments or programs coming from various parts of the world, and we're doing more and more of that. We now have all these great matchmaking initiatives; we have created hubs, oases, parks, valleys, and whatever. We'll be training young people on how to pitch a business idea, business canvasses, design-thinking, etc. But beyond that I don't see any really great use of emulating a system or copying a system. Apparently, you can set up a successful company anywhere in the world. It could be in Somalia. It could be in Siberia. It could be anywhere, really. What we have to do is to look at the individual level and study the local entrepreneurs and learn how they did it, rather than to always look for a magic solution at the macro level.

SANGEET PAUL CHOUDARY: Singapore has deregulated a lot of industries to attract IP. It has deregulated financial services and attracted some of the best FinTech firms to Singapore. It has deregulated autonomous driving and attracted a lot of driverless technology to Singapore. It's doing the same thing with trade and maritime technologies. The Singapore model, essentially, is to deregulate, attract IP, and enable a very good innovation ecosystem, not just with startups, but also between startups and large companies.

The Monetary Authority of Singapore has deregulated financial services to the extent where banks can share their data and startups can come and work with the banks. That's the third model, where you attract IP and then you get the ecosystem going. MENA trying to copy the Silicon Valley model would be a loser's game. The model that MENA should emulate is the Singapore model.

Trying to copy Silicon Valley simply has not worked. There's not a single example of a successful Silicon Valley copycat anywhere. There are examples of a few developed startup hubs that have been influenced by Silicon Valley—for example, Berlin, East London, and Amsterdam. But they all grew around some level of deregulation and attractive immigration status; none really grew organically the way Silicon Valley has grown. The way to kickstart tech ecosystems is to do it through some form of deregulation, which helps attract talent. The less sustainable way of doing it is by offering some tax advantage, while the most sustainable way of doing it is deregulating and attracting IP.

In short, abundance of capital and government funding alone cannot build an ecosystem; countless examples of failed case studies demonstrate that such attempts led nowhere. You simply cannot buy a thriving ecosystem, so to speak. You need all the key pieces in place.

TIM O'REILLY: If I were sitting in the Middle East and thinking about my ecosystem, I would ask, "Who can I learn from?" I would imagine learning from China would probably be more relevant—in terms of similarities of contexts, strengths, and weakness—and more valuable than what can be learned from Silicon Valley. Granted, Silicon Valley has been more studied and more in the spotlight than just about any other ecosystem in the world. On the other hand, China may seem like somewhat of a black box. Nevertheless, China has managed to build a very competitive ecosystem in a relatively short time. I highly recommend the book by Kai-Fu Lee, *AI Superpowers: China, Silicon Valley, and the New World Order*, in which he compares and contrasts the startup scenes in Silicon Valley and China.

VICTOR HWANG: No single case study covers all ecosystem development, just like no single artwork can teach people how to paint. But we can point to lessons that elevate certain aspects of ecosystem development. For growing a capital industry to invest in startups, look at the much-publicized Yozma Fund, for example, for its use of a fund of funds mechanism to anchor and seed the formation of new funds. Look at the Kauffman Fellows program for how to build leadership capacity, peer networks, and cross-boundary networks in capital formation. For how to engage large corporations with startups, look at Cintrifuse in Ohio for its work in engaging corporate executives in mentoring local startups, or the Larta Institute for how it brings in leading sector experts to mentor science-based startups and create partnership opportunities. For how to coordinate regional economic development strategies to foster startups, some exciting work is happening now in Minneapolis. For examples of accelerators and co-working spaces that serve as the hub of their communities, not just to help their client companies, look at Plexpod in Kansas City, Galvanize in Phoenix, and 1871 in Chicago.

AHMED EL ALFI: This is not like mathematics, where you layer on top of developed formulas. Each country is different and you can learn from everyone. See how people are being creative in all fields, and add your own touch based on local talent and experiences and aimed at your audience, ecosystem, or target market.

I don't particularly like the concept of blindly copying international best practices. I prefer a more intuitive learning method, based on the concept of building and making sure that each year you're improving, and making meaningful progress. If you get better every year, it doesn't matter if the other guys get farther ahead or fall behind. Our goal should be to be better than the year before in every aspect, as a country, as a region, and as individuals. Our journey will be more meaningful if it's focused on agility and achieving excellence in what we do. Opportunities to learn are lost when we benchmark ourselves against other people. We need to put ego aside, stop comparing for the sake of comparison, and just build and improve.

ISSA AGHABI: When we benchmark the region against international best practices, we are better off looking at more relevant markets. Historically, we compare ourselves to Silicon Valley, which is the gold standard for a startup ecosystem. That's not a good comparable.

What we should be looking at is other countries that have similar demographics and similar fundamentals to those we have. For example, if you're a Cairo entrepreneur or a Cairo fund, compare yourself to what's happening in Africa, in Pakistan, or in India, because they have the same emerging market problems that we have in Egypt. Meanwhile, a country such as the UAE should maybe be looking at Singapore. The UAE is similar to Singapore in that both are hubs, so maybe we can learn from what the government has done there.

NAJLA AL-MIDFA: On a recent fellowship in the United States, while I was exploring how cities outside of Silicon Valley have established themselves as hubs for entrepreneurship, it was interesting to see the different approaches each had taken. For some, it was a top-down approach: a big PR campaign to brand the city as a leading startup hub, along with incentives such as tax exemptions, subsidized housing, and a big pool of public and private capital that attracts successful startups.

For others it was a bottom-up, grassroots approach: cultivating the right mindset and culture, developing local talent, and supporting this talent with the skills and mentorship required to build great startups. While it is a slower, more long-term strategy, it does subsequently attract investment, influence entrepreneur-friendly policies, and eventually lead to the city's crowning as a successful startup hub. It has the potential to be a more sustainable method.

There is nothing wrong with either approach—one could argue that they are both necessary for the development of a healthy entrepreneurship ecosystem. The UAE government has been spot on with its top-down strategy, especially as evidenced by the recent policy changes regarding permanent residency. However, we tend to forget the importance of also working bottom-up. We have to find the approach that works best for us.

DAVE MCCLURE: Looking back at how the US startup ecosystem got started, a number of different factors led to the creation of the venture capital ecosystem. It initially got started with research agencies providing R&D dollars that ultimately created products that were commercialized by private companies. You had public programs like the Small Business Investment Act and Small Business Investment Company (SBIC) structures. I think the primary thing that really kicked off a lot of that ecosystem development in the late 1970s and early 1980s were significant reductions in US capital gains taxes, several notable tech company IPOs like Microsoft and Apple, and, even more importantly, changes to investment regulations that enabled pension funds to invest in VC funds. This led to an explosion of VC funds and capital in the '80s and '90s. Subsequent to that, you had success with the IPO market in the US. It boiled down to establishing a more institutional structure for investors in VC funds through pensions, endowments, foundations, mutual funds, and so on. Then came the success of that capital allocation through the public market in the US that led to further expansion, but much of that initial structure came from the SBIC programs.

Having large institutional investment in VC funds probably helped the structures put in place. Parallels to that exist in China, that probably started 20 years ago, although some were more governmental. More recently, Singapore has been quite successful in getting off the ground. It didn't just happen accidentally. Usually, both governmental and private institutional and structural capital sources have fostered the creation of other VC firms. These really make a big difference in getting those programs off the ground. Again, people tend to moan and complain about entrepreneurial expertise, training and programs, and the lack of human capital, but I don't really see that as big of a deal. It's usually solved by the access to capital. Had people tended to look at the investor structures as being critical, those ecosystems would have gotten off the ground.

Many emerging markets try to copy Silicon Valley but end up copying the wrong things. They tend to copy the current things they think are generating that success, like accelerator programs and education programs. I'm not saying these programs are not useful or important, because they certainly can be. The problem arises when they focus solely on such programs and miss the historical evidence of the need of larger governmental and larger institutional participation in the creation of the ecosystem, and overlook the key metrics, such as the number of VC firms per million people, or millions of dollars of VC capital per million people. That's where the main focus ought to be from my perspective.

Silicon Valley wasn't built overnight, it was 30, 40, 50 years in the making. The infrastructure-building was in a lot of different areas: the academic infrastructure, corporate structure, securities and public market infrastructure, accounting, and so forth.

ABDULAZIZ AL LOUGHANI: So many international examples can be applied in this part of the world, looking toward Chile, Spain, Singapore, or the UK. There are also great case studies in the US, for example how the SBA (Small Business Administration) really started investing in fund of funds and great managers.

When it comes to education, I firmly believe that Northern European countries, places like Finland and Sweden, for example, have really mastered that domain and we can learn from them. Another example is how the US has commercialized a lot of its IP. The US is a great model when it comes to business laws and legal practices to open up an economy in general.

Certainly, from a legal framework design perspective, I feel that the European commercial laws are very appropriate to our region, mainly because each country has its own jurisdiction yet all are part of the European Union. When we look at the ecosystem, we also need to look at the full supply chain: early education, schooling to undergrad, grad school, and R&D facilities and labs that are in universities, developing real IP protection laws rather than just focusing on copyright laws, and commercializing a lot of IP, all the way to funding and building a global franchise. On the other hand, I would love to see more proactive entrepreneurs. An entrepreneur should never wait for governments to lead change; they should lead their communities and make change happen.

KEVIN O'LEARY: When it comes to global models of successful ecosystems the region can learn from, why go far when there's one next door? I would give the UAE the highest marks in terms of transforming itself over the last 25 years into a highly investible economy. It checked the boxes on all the conditions that matter to institutional investors. It's a shining example of what has to happen in the Middle East in terms of attracting capital because most of the capital from other jurisdictions there comes from the sovereign funds that are being petitioned by European and North American managers to extract capital, particularly the cash flows in energy in Saudi Arabia, for example.

My advice to all governments in the region is to look first and foremost at that transformation. Look at what the UAE has done over the last 25 years and basically follow suit. It's not that hard to do from an investment point of view. I'm not talking about cultural issues, which vary from country to country. I'm referring to laying down the financial infrastructure that will be required to make the rest of the region investible. This is why everyone is going there now. This November, where will the G20 be? In the UAE. Where will the Global Government Summit be? In the UAE. Where is Expo 2020 going to be from October for six months? Right there in the UAE. It's spending billions of dollars to make it a destination and it's starting to compete with New York and London in terms of where capital goes. I have no choice but to get on a flight and go there. The UAE has done the right thing and it is now world-class in terms of attracting capital, ideas, technology, and startups. Saudi Arabia and other countries in the region just have to do exactly what the UAE did, in their own style, and they would attract billions in capital, including their own.

2. Aim to Be Frictionless

STEVE CASE: All around the world, nations are working to replicate the conditions necessary for a vibrant entrepreneurial environment. Many more nations are encouraging entrepreneurship, making it easier to start and run a business, increasing access to capital, and creating the support networks needed to better position their citizen entrepreneurs—and those they can attract to their shores—for success. Canada implemented a startup visa program, offering permanent residency to entrepreneurs willing to move to Canada and start a business or relocate their current one. In Chile, the government launched a flagship seed accelerator program called Startup Chile to change the nation's attitude toward entrepreneurship and to position Chile as a hub of innovation in Latin America. Nigeria and Kenya are emerging as hotbeds of entrepreneurial innovation in Africa.

ALEC ROSS: Everyone knows that Silicon Valley has the highest number of unicorns and billion-dollar startups on a per capita basis in the world, but very few people know that number two is Stockholm, Sweden. Stockholm has managed to create a remarkable ecosystem that combines a creative element with a deeply technical element, especially in such areas as mobile and cryptocurrencies. The access to capital and openness attract technical talent from all across Europe.

I'm also really excited by some of what is coming out of Cambridge, England right now. A lot of people talk about tech transfer and about the necessity of connecting university research institutions and making them more entrepreneurial. People always point to Stanford, while Cambridge often gets overlooked. Cambridge University has done an amazing job of helping to create an ecosystem there that, when you actually look at the verticals, is principally rooted in data analytics in the life sciences,

Another one I would point to is Jakarta, Indonesia, which has managed to transform into a vibrant entrepreneurial ecosystem recently. Some people in the United States might think that there's something about being Muslim that constrains entrepreneurship, which I believe is false. Jakarta is a great example that debunks this misconception, since Indonesia is one of the largest majority Muslim countries in the world. When you visit Jakarta, you realize that it has a spectacular ecosystem in gaming, mobile, and social media. It has Muslim CEOs, Muslim founders, and Muslim workforces. You see women wearing hijabs, working shoulder to shoulder with male engineers. When people ask, "What Muslim majority country would you point to that has an entrepreneurial culture?" I often point to Indonesia, and to Jakarta specifically. Other interesting examples exist out there as well.

JONATHAN ORTMANS: Healthy startup ecosystems can ultimately only be led by their actual entrepreneurs, but government sets the rules and incentives and plays an increasingly important role in removing barriers. Especially in an age when digital disruption is reinventing the business models of practically every industry and field on the planet, we need a new generation of startup-savvy public sector officials.

Better practices from public officials are emerging in terms of listening more to their entrepreneurs in an attempt to avoid the backlash against technology disruption often brought by startups' innovative products and services. This is seen perhaps most notably with the likes of Uber. For example, some governments have established "sandboxes" where companies in initial stages of development can test prototypes without the normal regulatory requirements in place. Sandbox-type approaches facilitate government collaboration with entrepreneurs, and vice versa. Take, for example, the Accelerate Estonia government program, which aims to provide a test bed for projects in highly regulated industries, which are naturally challenging environments for startups. At GEN, we have started to document some of these in our *Startup Nations Atlas of Policies*, in the category filter for "disruption dialogue/sandboxes."

We are also seeing more global policy hacks. Policy-makers know that national boundaries are porous to innovation, and they are keen to learn from their peers who have tested policies in other nations to address a current challenge. Governments can share successes and, more importantly, failures with policy experiments and interventions. For example, more than 30 nations now have startup visas, and they are learning from each other how to fine-tune newly rolled out policies to be more effective.

SAMIA MELHEM: At the World Bank, we are trying to support digital government by helping governments provide services online, so citizens are further incentivized to access broadband and to use it on a regular basis. All of this has helped offload many government services. People don't have to line up in front of a government clerk when the same services can be made available online more seamlessly and more efficiently. This also helps eliminate corruption and bribes because all of the transactions happen virtually. In addition, users of online services can provide feedback on the quality of service and suggest improvements.

eParticipation, one of the three indicators measured by the UN in its eGovernment development index (EGDI), is a concept directly derived from the adoption of digital government. Another key aspect is digital payments enabling businesses and people to pay electronically. That is the change most requested by businesses and SMEs from government, to facilitate faster payments of taxes, social security, licenses, or insurance for their employees. It's also key for the payment of utilities, school fees, fines, or obligations.

PHILIP BAHOSHY: Singapore is a good case study, and very similar to Dubai in particular, in terms of being a regional hub for entrepreneurs to help them scale into other Southeast Asian markets. Singapore has a remarkable education system, a regulatory system that's quite conducive to startups, and an entrepreneur-friendly environment in general.

Other examples are the UK's very successful SEIS (Seed Enterprise Investment Scheme) and EIS (Enterprise Investment Scheme) models.

These are basically tax incentives for angel investors to invest in early-stage startups, whereby the programs provide capital guarantees as well as the ability to offset investors' investments against their own income tax. These have spurred early-stage startups. The challenge in duplicating this model in the Middle East is obviously that many Middle Eastern countries don't have tax to be offset. On the other hand, startups incur upfront and ongoing charges (licenses, utility bills, etc.) that could be discounted or waived as further incentives for people to take the risk of investing in early-stage startups.

FOUAD JERYES: Estonia has done a phenomenal job of creating a transformative model to supercharge its ecosystem and bring the world to it. If all of your papers are together, you can register a company completely electronically from anywhere in about 17 minutes. You can apply for e-residency and collect it in one of a number of EU countries. This way of getting set up is fully self-serve, online, paperless, and cost-effective. The system has built obtaining a business banking account right into the process. This type of national strategy has led to 99.6% of transactions in the country being made electronically and has elevated the country to the top spot in SME competitiveness in the EU, with the most startups per capita as well. In our region, it might take 6-10 weeks to get a bank account for your business, for example.

RABEA ATAYA: Great examples of successful models are available all over the world when it comes to ease of doing business. The fact that I was able to incorporate a company in the UK within a few hours by going online and paying something like £40 is a great best practice. You would hope that it is doable in the UAE and across the region, which would obviously significantly reduce operating costs.

The fact that in most countries in the world incorporation does not require the rental of office space is also valuable. You hear about entrepreneurs all over the world who start companies from their garages; facilitating that in this region would be tremendously helpful.

The ability to incorporate or license once and tackle a massive market is also a great global best practice. In the United States, if, for example, you incorporate in Delaware, you can tackle what is today perhaps the largest market in the world, which is over 300 million people, with that single incorporation. That's another best practice that I would love to see adopted in this part of the world. The list goes on, but these are the basic ones that I think would have a tremendous impact.

SAMIH TOUKAN: London has a good sandbox model for financial regulations, where startups apply to the sandbox, get accepted, and develop their solution close to the regulators, who provide them with support. It's a great approach. That approach works very well in many parts of the world and has been adopted by Abu Dhabi and Bahrain. Also, the UK has certain investor programs that offer investors tax incentives for funding startups. Maybe a similar approach can be adapted to this part of the world to encourage local and regional investors to invest more in the region, especially in startups. Such programs offer a lot to look at and learn from, whether entrepreneur incentives or investor incentives.

CHRISTOPHER SCHROEDER: Look beyond the obvious examples of the US. Look to rising markets that get some things right—assuming that it lasts, of course. Brazil and Indonesia have been very forward-leaning in FinTech legislation, really encouraging innovation on that front given its impact on financial inclusion. It's part of an attempt to offer more transparency, combat corruption, and raise tax revenue. Brazil has increased the requirements for digitizing data—every receipt is digitized, for example—which has helped not only FinTech but the services sector as well.

PETER COHAN: An example of positive government regulations that comes to mind is a city in Tennessee called Chattanooga. Its electric utility industry was essentially bankrupt. The government put money into turning the rights of way for this electric utility into a high-speed fiber optic network that was made available to companies in Chattanooga. This gave local companies access to very high-speed bandwidth at a very low cost. Entrepreneurs from the southeastern US moved there and some became quite successful, including one that was acquired for over $1 billion. By providing entrepreneurs with this very valuable resource, the government paved the way for great local success.

Another interesting example in rural Washington State is Wenatchee. It has the lowest-cost source of continuous hydroelectric power in the United States. When Bitcoin mining became a big thing, Bitcoin miners moved to Wenatchee. Very cheap hydroelectric power ran their computers 24/7 to solve the math problems that create more Bitcoin.

Obviously, the government in Wenatchee did not create the dam with the expectation that Bitcoin miners would want to locate there. But this story highlights the idea that if a region wants to attract entrepreneurship, it must have a world-class resource that is both valuable to founders and regionally superior. Just because a city sets up a local incubator and gives startups money and mentoring, it doesn't mean that entrepreneurs are going to flock to that city. To achieve that outcome, local leaders must figure out what resources the region has that are both valuable to entrepreneurs in specific industries and superior to other regions.

ANDREW ROMANS: In the United States, I can go online, go to legalzoom.com and establish an LLC on the spot; I can file a couple of forms with the Securities and Exchange Commission online; then I can file a form with the IRS and get a tax number. I can take those documents to a bank and open a bank account and then I've got my documents to start taking in money for a VC fund. It is incredibly easy to do that in California, whereas I have a feeling it's not so easy to do that across the Middle East, although it has improved significantly recently in a couple of places.

ANDREW BERKOWITZ: What Rwanda has done recently is nothing short of amazing. It is certainly an outlier in Africa and a prime example of an emerging market that is starting to develop into a mature environment that attracts private capital. There are three key pieces to that transformation, which other markets can learn from. The first piece is that the rule of law must exist equally for everybody. That means that whether it's an international investor coming in, a local partner, or the tax collector, everybody must be equal under the law. The second piece is no corruption and, in Africa and emerging markets in general, some countries are certainly better at this than others. But the more you can bring that down, the more capital will want to come in. And then the third piece that I touched on before is a mature tax and regulatory policy.

Combining all three pieces and showing that you are committed to implementing them will attract more capital, and Rwanda has done an exceptional job at this in the past few years. No leader is perfect, but Paul Kagame is certainly an example of a benevolent leader and an inspiration for all of Africa. A lot of emerging markets should look to Rwanda as a case study and implement some of its initiatives.

OMAR CHRISTIDIS: Asia and Africa have seen a boom in mobile payments. while, in the Middle East, this is still stifled by regulatory challenges. It's only just starting to pick up in Saudi Arabia with STC Pay, ApplePay, Halala, etc. All of these companies launched in the last 6-12 months. This is an interesting area that's facing regulatory hurdles. We could capture this market and look to other markets for how to do this.

Definitely, many of the markets are still lagging in open banking and FinTech innovation. Open data, overall, is a regulatory area that we need to work on. In Europe, through PSD2 (Payment Services Directive), the EU pushed all banks to open their data, which will now allow a huge boom in FinTech through APIs and the ability to build on data that customers have at their banks. This doesn't exist today in the Middle East. A lot of these FinTech companies cannot access any data from the banks. For open data, we can look to Europe for that interesting PSD2 regulation initiative.

Right now, the fund of funds structures in the region are the biggest initiatives. They're everywhere. How the fund of funds gets implemented, regulated, and governed will really affect the success of these programs.

ALBERT BRAVO-BIOSCA: A policy challenge that the UK has in common with many other countries is the widening divide between the top-performing businesses and all the rest. The UK government is investigating how best to close that gap. To find out, it has launched a new program to fund different types of interventions to increase the adoption of technologies and management best practices by UK SMEs.

How the government is doing that is interesting. Instead of launching a new national program and hoping that it will work, it has taken the different approach of "letting a hundred flowers bloom." It decided to create a pot of money and fund a bunch of pilot experiments proposed by organizations across the ecosystem— universities, transfer offices, chambers of commerce, private companies, etc. Anyone who has a good idea for an intervention to support tech adoption can offer it and be funded to create a prototype and test it on the ground. In exchange, the approach demands the idea be evaluated very thoroughly through a randomized controlled trial or equivalent rigorous methodology.

This same approach (setting up an experimentation fund) could also be applied to address many of the challenges of ecosystem building. How do you connect universities and knowledge providers with startups? How do you encourage academic entrepreneurship? How do you facilitate innovation collaborations?

Innovation in how we use public funding through experimentation is necessary, but not sufficient. We also need to innovate through the second lever that policy-makers have at their disposal to support innovation: regulation. How do you create regulatory frameworks that are much more flexible, anticipatory, and dynamic?

A challenges with regulation is that it will always going to be based on the present and the past. Thus, innovation may be hampered by the unintended consequences of outdated regulations drafted many years ago. For instance, a FinTech startup may want to try something doesn't fit well with the existing regulatory regime. This is not because the regulators don't want it to happen but because no one naturally anticipated that particular business model emerging when the regulations were drafted 5, 10, or 15 years ago. The question then becomes how to make sure the regulatory framework is kept up to date. It's possible to regularly keep writing and rewriting the rules—that needs to be done on a regular basis—but it's not possible to have permanent uncertainty on what the rules will be. The regulatory sandbox model is one approach that keeps some regulatory certainty and at the same time creates a space for new innovation.

The sandbox model was pioneered in the UK by the Financial Conduct Authority, who stated: "If you are a company with a new FinTech business model and you want to try it out in the real world, come to us and we'll look at your idea. We'll look at the risks and we'll basically let you test your idea in the real market for a limited period of time with us. That's a way you can validate the business model. Then, after some time, a year or two, we'll basically look at what has happened and we'll decide what needs to be done next." It could be that a company tries an idea in the market and it doesn't really work, so maybe there's no need to touch the regulation. It could be that the idea really works in the market and it's feasible to make it fit with existing rules, in which case the company has to comply with them. Alternatively, the conclusion might be that this new idea works, but it doesn't really fit with the existing regulatory regime, so it's time to change the rules to allow this activity to happen because there's no reason it shouldn't. What's interesting with this model is that while the technology and business model are being tested in the real world, the regulator may actually waive some of the rules that otherwise would stop the startup from trying it. This model has now been replicated, I think, by over 100 regulators worldwide across many sectors. It's part of a much wider trend of rethinking regulation so that it becomes much more anticipatory, flexible, and supportive of innovation.

TIM DRAPER: It is interesting that small countries like Malta, Gibraltar, Switzerland, Estonia, and a few large ones like Japan, have embraced these technologies. Japan made Bitcoin a national currency, for example. Some of the larger countries are trying too hard to control the actions of entrepreneurs.

ERIK STAM: From a policy point of view, the Global Entrepreneurship Monitor, the World Bank, the OECD, the Kauffman Foundation, and the Aspen Institute are great resources for providing insights into ecosystems around the world. Some also do diagnostic work that can be valuable to learn from, especially for emerging markets. These are great resources for ecosystem builders, governments, or anyone interested in learning from other ecosystems' experiences and trials and possibly adapting them to their own city, country, or region. Obviously, this book, *Ecosystem Arabia*, is a great resource in terms of providing a comprehensive and deep perspective on diverse topics related to ecosystem development, especially as it relates to the MENA region and emerging markets, from a diverse group of local and regional ecosystem experts and players.

3. Create Conditions to Optimize Capital Flow

JOSH LERNER: Looking at government funding globally, shows that what's most important is using matching funds. This allows the market to figure out what areas are likely to be the most attractive. In an ideal world, the returns on the government funds will be capped so much of the upside will go to the investors. The basic idea is that matching funds encourages knowledgeable people to put money in, and gives them a little bit of added return.

Also—contrary to common recommendations advocated by local

entrepreneurs, consultants, and investors—sovereign funds should not be mandated to deploy their funds locally. This is counterintuitive from a local-orientation perspective; nevertheless, the evidence suggests that, often, sovereign funds allocated locally end up falling into local startups that are not poised for success. Thus, it is better for sovereign funds to have more of an international orientation and allocate capital to the most promising investments globally. Additionally, deploying sovereign funds domestically poses the risk of flooding the market, which hurts rather than helps the ecosystem.

ANDREW ROMANS: Around the globe, investment dollars follow the perception of opportunity. You see that everywhere, and plenty of examples and case studies illustrate this point. Money from outside the region will only come in if the perception is of a significant local investment opportunity. And it will only come in based on a track record. International money therefore typically follows exits or success stories in general.

A lot of emerging markets, including the Middle East, suffer from a lack of access to sufficient capital because of the lack of a track record. That said, the government can help facilitate more capital and thus accelerate the evolution of the startup ecosystem. For example, governments in the Middle East should strongly communicate to large family office conglomerates and large corporations that their participation in the high-tech scene is no longer optional—they now have to. They should make it clear that they need to invest some of their capital into VC funds and/or startups.

Governments can also invest in some VC funds first, and then start cherry-picking and make direct investments alongside the general partners at those VC funds. If they start by making direct investments, they will go through a very painful, expensive, and time-consuming disaster of a learning experience. If they invest in a couple of VC funds, on the other hand, then they're investing in a fund that will be open and share information with them, and even teach and mentor them. Then things will eventually start coming together. That's a much less risky way to go.

Singapore is certainly a great example among actual case studies. It tried a number of different policies; many were initially unsuccessful and gradually refined over time. Most of the policies implemented to promote venture capital weren't terribly successful initially. Having staying power in terms of your approach is important. Don't expect the first things to necessarily work, but don't be discouraged by the fact that they don't work. Policy-makers need to learn what works and what doesn't and fine-tune the approach accordingly.

Another thing is not being afraid to get outside investors and capital as well. The Singaporeans have very much encouraged foreign venture groups to be active in their markets, and they have benefited from these groups' involvement. Even though policy-makers in these nations may have wanted a domestic industry, they saw that local entrepreneurs and venture capitalists could learn a lot from the way the foreign groups act. In any case, the foreign groups hire local people who develop skills and then go off and raise their own funds.

One interesting recent example has been New Zealand. New Zealand is very small and remote, but it has built quite an interesting venture environment through good policies. It's definitely one that is worth looking at. The Kiwis had a lot of obstacles and yet they've had a fair amount of success. It was a real effort to try to educate the local venture community and to work with groups to bring them up to speed. But New Zealand's policy-makers have been very patient and steady, putting in thoughtful effort over time.

DAVID SHELTERS: Case studies are helpful tools for understanding the cause-and-effect relationship of various variables within ecosystems. As such, I like to draw a comparison between pursuing a top-down approach of ecosystem development as opposed to a bottom-up approach. To illustrate, I'll compare two startup ecosystems that took these two completely different approaches—Singapore and Thailand.

Singapore is rightly considered one of the most successful startup ecosystems in the world. However, to close observers, Singapore began the development of its startup ecosystem very inefficiently. Its innovation inputs far exceeded the innovation outputs in the early days. The lead driver was the Singapore government. Flush with public funding administered by a staggering number of government agencies, the standing joke was, "All you needed was a pulse to secure public funding." The result was the funding of a large number of startups that should not have received funding, which prevented market forces from truly determining the rightful victors in several startup sectors. Later the lead driver for this top-down approach was the Singaporean corporate community. This resulted in a massive proliferation of corporate incubators and accelerators. At this point, the running joke was, "There were more corporate incubator and accelerator programs than investment-grade startups."

To their credit, Singapore recognized their faults and decisively changed their focus to creating a more favorable business environment for tech startups by leveraging, extending, and then promoting their strong rule of law. Singapore was a leader in implementing a suite of highly favorable regulations in the areas of digital economy and governance that established it as a leading FinTech center, where digital assets are protected and laws governing such digital transactions are unambiguous.

In contrast, Thailand took a radically different, bottom-up approach. At the dawn of the Thai startup ecosystem, there was simply no money to be had. This forced startups to pursue true product-solution fit and market validation. In a short period of time, Thai startups would prove to be some of the most successful in Southeast Asia, winning an impressive streak of regional competitions. It was more of a grind, but eventually Thailand began to attract the attention and resources of foreign stakeholders.

In 2016, with the emergence of the FinTech craze, Thailand took an increasingly top-down approach as larger corporations and government agencies assumed leadership of the Thai startup community. A great opportunity was lost. By the end of 2015, there were many Thai-based startups poised to expand regionally. These opportunities remained wide open at this point in time. Greater corporate engagement was called for. However, the increased corporate engagement did not take the form of the much-needed partnerships with local startups to permit them to scale and attract the later-stage funding needed for regional expansion. Instead corporate engagement took the form of a proliferation of corporate venture capital arms and accelerator programs.

Now venture funding in Thailand is dominated by corporate VCs. The combination of this and the rapid emergence of startup ecosystems in neighboring countries compelled many regional investors to leave Thailand. The relocation of the later-stage startups to neighboring countries also contributed to this widening funding gap at every funding stage. Many Thai-based startups have used the numerous corporate accelerator programs as a safety net, going from one program to another to stay alive. Fortunately, Thailand has begun to change its focus as corporations increasingly pursue more strategic partnerships with local startups, particularly large industrial conglomerates that perceive startups as less of a threat.

Another best practice is the success story of the regulatory guillotine in South Korea. A regulatory guillotine is a program in which an entity within a government reviews or oversees the review of each law currently on the books across the various departments. Laws that are antiquated or unenforceable are cut and necessary updates are made to others. Following the implementation of this program, South Korea enjoyed a substantial boost in its GDP and ease of doing business numbers, which made it a far more attractive place for local startups. Both Singapore and South Korea offer perfect examples of how governments can make a large contribution by getting out of the way and reducing regulatory risks and costs.

KEVIN O'LEARY: Hundreds of thousands of global fund managers are making decisions every day about where to pour capital. It would be such an attractive proposition if somebody were to say to me, "There's a telco bond being issued out of Riyadh for $2 billion and instead of just funding it themselves, they're letting international investors get a piece of it." I mean, Riyadh wants to diversify its economy. It wants to move away from depending on just energy over the next 20 years. Saudi Arabia obviously has the most lucrative returns in energy of any country on earth, but it's smart enough to want to diversify. But, instead of just hoarding all the investment opportunity, it has to attract other capital. By sharing the opportunity, it actually gets more. When one fund goes in with, say, half a billion dollars and succeeds, it attracts many others to follow suit.

That's the opportunity—to let other investors invest in the transformation of the region into a more thoroughly diverse economy. The way to do that is to provide political stability, IP protection, and access to the ports and the local jurisdictions; make it easy to understand how to play by the rules there; and make a special effort to educate global players on the region and learn to speak and communicate in their language, literally and figuratively.

If Saudi Arabia and other countries in the region can do just that and build a similar financial infrastructure to the UAE, they will attract billions of dollars and employ hundreds of thousands of people. They have high unemployment there because they are based on one sector—energy. That has to change and, because the world works at a 5% return and so many VCs are trying to get that 5% return, this is probably one of the most interesting times ever for globalization. The governments that makes it attractive to provide a 5% return will have unlimited capital available globally.

HEATHER HENYON: I would like to see an emerging manager program for new venture capital funds. We need new VC players and models in the region. This would consist of both capital and a grant facility. Fundraising is incredibly time consuming and it takes emerging managers 18-24 months to get their first fund off of the ground.

For example, new funds in the US can access these kinds of support programs from the government—some of the funds receive grants of $250,000-$300,000 to cover fundraising costs, legal expenses, and hiring. Some of the governments are offering matching VC fund programs, but none are actual emerging manager programs.

It is very difficult for a first-time fund manager to raise institutional capital because of the risk perception. One possibility is to offer a first loss guarantee from the governments for the fund manager. In this case, investors would be guaranteed the return of their principal commitment, which would hopefully get more of them to invest in VC since they would at least get their capital back. Many of the investors in the region are slow, uneducated, and risk adverse—they are interested in investing in real estate and brick-and-mortar businesses that they understand. Technology and venture capital are new to them; therefore, they need a subsidy to lower their perception of the risk.

BADR JAFAR: In terms of the state of capital and funding in the region, one thing I would very much like to see more often is private capital and public capital working alongside the missing "P," which is philanthropic capital, toward the achievement of common goals or a defined social purpose.

For example, take the eradication of greenhouse gas emissions. Emissions are a major global threat that affects everyone, and many governments are putting money into addressing it. In addition, a lot of private capital is trying to identify new energy solutions, both upstream and downstream. Philanthropic capital could also contribute in this area in a big way. Obviously, the nature of this kind of capital is that it doesn't necessarily demand a financial return on capital, but it certainly demands—and increasingly expects—a measurable return on capital generally in the form of a clear social return or impact.

To give you another example, take Islamic philanthropic capital, through which up to a trillion dollars a year is donated by two billion Muslims around the world. The natural question is, where is this money going? Well, of course it's all supposed to be going to do good. That's its purpose. But without the right transparent and accountable mechanisms for deployment, some of it—even despite the best intentions—will inevitably find its way into the wrong hands.

Now, imagine we're able to align and combine these huge sums, or even just a small fraction of those funds, to invest in entrepreneurial, nonprofit solutions that are dedicated to solving societal problems. That could mean billions every year finding its way into a philanthropic startup ecosystem that is specifically earmarked to make a positive difference in people's lives. Can you imagine how much difference that could make? Sure, it's risk capital, but the same is true when you donate to a nonprofit, an NGO (non-governmental organization), or a charity. It's rarely clear how much of that capital is being allocated to the right channels, let alone what the return on that capital is in terms of social impact. On the other hand, the returns on capital invested in viable startups that seek to solve social problems would be designed to be more measurable.

To be clear, I'm obviously not criticizing the concept of charity, or charities themselves. I'm just saying that there can be different ways to support the same objectives.

What I would like to see is the creation of a local incubator for what I call "philanthro-entrepreneurs"—tailored to entrepreneurs who have a very defined philanthropic goal. This is different concept than social entrepreneurs, because here I'm referring to entrepreneurs who set up a nonprofit philanthropic institution while using principles of entrepreneurship. Thus, they will be relying on best-in-class innovation, use lean startup methodology, release minimum viable products or services initially, bootstrap when they need to, and adopt all of the other common best practices for startups.

What this incubator would do is give these types of startups the best chance of creating investible organizations—not from the traditional financial institutions, but from philanthropic capital, whether it's family offices, companies, or individuals who want to deploy their capital to support certain causes. I would be happy to work with others to co-fund an incubator of this type. This is definitely a missed opportunity.

Another opportunity would be to give people more choice in how their charitable donations are allocated, in part or in full, in order to support particular causes or initiatives. If I were given two options: going and throwing a bunch of cash in a collection box in the mosque or putting this money into a tried and tested philanthropic platform that has the potential to generate a particular impact, which I could scrutinize just like a financial investor would and be able to track the impact generated, I would without a doubt take the second option.

ARUNMA OTEH: One of my favorite books is *Start-Up Nation*, which makes a strong case that innovation can spring up in the least likely places—even disadvantaged ones that lack natural resources, are undergoing geopolitical issues, or have other challenges. Moreover, it makes the case that innovation-focused environments do not have to look and feel like Silicon Valley to be impactful; they can develop in their own unique way based on their circumstances. Overall, the book does a great job of distilling some of the key elements and lessons that ecosystem builders anywhere can learn from.

DANY FARHA: In the words of the great Charlie Munger of Berkshire Hathaway, "Show me the incentive and I'll show you the outcome." We need more governments and sovereign wealth funds to step up and invest in this sector. This funding must be phased across all the different stages.

Matching programs that invest in startups that get funded by reputable angel groups will create the pipeline for early-stage venture funds. Then move on to investing in early-stage funds through loan guarantees, where the government will invest $2 for every $1 raised from accredited investors, for example. And then provide seed funding for growth investors to ensure funding across the cycle of stages. An investment of $10 million per year in angel matching programs for five years could create 200 startups per year, while $50 million per year for four years invested in three reputable early-stage venture funds per country would then create the pipeline to fund another Careem-sized outcome every year for this four-year period. The governments and sovereign funds would only have to be the catalyst for a short, seven-year period, after which investors would see the exits and massive returns and want to participate in this asset class. Governments can help turn venture into an asset class in the region.

EYAD LATIF: The Nordic countries are the best comparables to learn from. What they did in terms of institutional government support for funding, for ease of doing business, for cost of living, is what we're seeing take place in certain areas in the Middle East.

The other best practice is adopting investment documents in the Middle East similar to NVCA or BVCA (National Venture Capital Association or British Private Equity & Venture Capital Association) like Singapore has done recently. If you speak with any investor or entrepreneur in the region, the legal documents for financings have been a nightmare for a lot of people. The international best practice that we can implement is having consistent, commoditized, model standard venture capital investment documents that everybody can use across the ecosystem.

The other important aspect is negotiating and executing transactions in accordance with international standard market practice. If we can implement these two best practices, it will be a game changer for the Middle East.

Many clients we work with, whether entrepreneurs or investors, are starting to implement holding company structures that are consistent with international best practices, like those in the US, and they're starting to consistently adopt international standard market VC terms. Everyone always looks at Careem, a major startup in the region that was able to raise hundreds of millions of dollars in a relatively short period of time, as the exception to the rule. Careem had an international holding company and it had international standard market venture capital financing documents. However, many of our startup clients are now starting to raise tens of millions of dollars in just weeks from investors based in Silicon Valley, Europe, Asia, and the Middle East by following international standard market practice. That's a great sign of what's to come. We encourage everyone in the ecosystem to follow those examples.

RAMEZ SHEHADI: Certainly, the Canadian model is quite remarkable. The beauty of this model, in light of what has proven to be a very successful organic experience in the US, is predicated on access to sophisticated funding and smart money that doesn't hobble the investment by trying to take on too much or to direct too much. Unfortunately, that's uncharacteristic of the region and the quality of the entrepreneurs in terms of their digital skills.

You have layers and layers of tech innovation in the US. It has produced fantastic talent with access to a lot. The Canadians said, "We don't have the time or the privilege to try to only grow organically, so how can we curate success?" They have determined a few key sectors to double down on, which they're going to invest in and direct support to. They won't necessarily refuse other things, but they will give priority to these areas of historical or traditional success. It's yielding incredible results in Canada; whether it's in nanotechnology, HealthTech, or at the periphery of HealthTech or AI, it is absolutely world-class and world-leading. And it goes on and on in Canada around a few key, prioritized, select areas.

This presents the kind of template we should consider at the sovereign scales all across the region, where governments consider first what areas traditionally we have a right to play in and ultimately where we have a right to win. On this basis, they would direct their support and guide their priorities. So there is this additional step that governments can consider in terms of creating the right ecosystem for the digital startup space to really, really thrive.

The Singapore model is also quite impressive. Lee Kuan Yew looked at what his country has to offer and recognized that Singapore cannot necessarily become another Malaysia or Indonesia. Singapore doesn't have the human assets to be able to play that game, so it won't have a compelling value proposition compared with those countries. Instead, he focused on creating a knowledge economy and driving margins north to create a premium in terms of the labor environment. He's been able to trigger a tremendous amount of good in Singapore.

As a key driver in his agenda, he investigated what could be done to make the country attractive on many levels. One solution was creating a premium labor force. The other was to focus on making the country beautiful and sustainable at the same time, right from the beginning. He personally put attention into figuring out what plants should be grown and how they should be irrigated, and using the weather to advantage in curating a beautiful place to live.

These are all important factors to think about. How do you bring people into your country and let them contribute willingly and sustainably over time? We can all benefit across the board, from North Africa to the Levant to the GCC, from bringing in smart people who want to become a part of the evolution of your story and your nation. Whether you're a government or a business, the question is how to get people to buy in and to want to be a part of it, not just as a transaction but over the long term.

Canada offers a great story, Singapore offers a great story, and so does Norway, which is another geography that is massively invested in the hydrocarbon economy. But at the same time, Norway has been able to use that wealth to create other sectors and to promote new sectors in a way that, again, is curated and highly successful. Estonia has figured out that big success stories create an awakening, if you will, and that one or two key success stories can have a multiplier effect. Many more case studies can be drawn upon from all around the world to figure out what works but, ultimately, it's not just about best practices, it's about relevant practices. We don't all face the same circumstances, so there isn't only one way to succeed.

TAMMER QADDUMI: From a funding standpoint, I fundamentally believe that the GP/LP structure of managing venture capital, which is the traditional venture capital business model, doesn't work well in this part of the world. The US is a massive pool. It has institutional pools of money that have been collected over time. Individuals are taxed 25-35%. That money is collected and used to fund the government budget or it sits in a massive pool called social security. The large insurance companies are sitting on massive premiums, and the structural institutional pools of capital need to be managed. The most efficient way to manage those is to give them to independent managers. Those independent managers should be incentivized to outperform, and so the result is this "2 and 20" venture capital model in which a manager raises money from these structural pools and competes with other managers to outperform them.

In the Middle East, the same type of formula doesn't exist. That capital is really distributed widely. It sits within the government to a certain extent and is used primarily to manage the budget. But much of the pool of money sits with individual families, and those individual families have operated businesses that have generated trans-generational wealth. Those families have different prerogatives, so they don't—nor do they have a desire or need to—just give the money to someone else to manage for them. They all see themselves as strategic. The idea that they would give money to someone else and say, "Manage it for me" is, therefore, not the right formula. Every individual group wants to become its own venture capital firm for structural uses. In addition, there are ego-related or emotional reasons to maintain control. The feeling is, "I want my name to be in front of whatever is happening. I want to build my own brand equity."

There's substantial capital in this region, but a set of people who need the capital act as though there should be a whole class of venture capital funds: some to do seed, some to do Series A, and some to do Series B. Then, a whole class of venture capital firms are saying to themselves, "Well, where are my LPs? They should all just be writing me checks so that I can manage for them."

That's not how it works here. Here it's much more like a blended, nebulous collection of people who have capital and people who need capital, but it's not segmented into the same roles as in other parts of the world. That makes it very difficult. Approaching it with the wrong expectations actually makes funding very difficult. People should recognize and admit to the reality that funding will be done in a very different way here. That's what the real challenge in funding is. It's really a fundamental challenge. So, it's not that there's a gap in

Series A funding, or there's a shortfall in Series B funding, or there's no one who specializes in deep tech. That's a misdiagnosis of the current funding issues in the region.

RABIH KHOURY: One thing that has negatively affected the funding environment is the whole issue with Abraaj, which has tainted the entire industry. It's a shame what happened. The Middle East has some reasonable laws, but they tend not to be applied correctly. That created the gap for Abraaj. At the end of the day, who uncovered the last fraud in Abraaj? The LPs, the World Bank, and the Gates Foundation.

LPs have to be very diligent. They have to ask the right questions. If there's an impact on the PPM (private placement memorandum), if a quarterly meeting is missed, they have to raise concerns and a flag: they have to double-check and do their own diligence. They have to check with the independent fund administrator and check with their attorneys. They have to have their own people because LPs, if they are reasonably enlightened and disciplined, can find these things very early.

Sometimes people get enamored by perceived high multiples, that everyone's going to make money, but as the adage says, "If it sounds too good to be true, it probably is." There should be more engagement among the LP community; then fiascos like Abraaj will never happen again. As such, it would be worthwhile to examine more mature funding environments and distill some lessons around putting the right legal mechanisms and safeguards in place to prevent such disasters.

ZUBAIR NAEEM PARACHA: One of the things that bothers me in the ecosystem in this region is the prevalence of VCs and parties who take advantage of inexperienced entrepreneurs. There are plenty of great VCs and other players who are well intentioned and fair, but unfortunately, there are others who give the category a bad rap and damage the ecosystem at large.

Obviously, if a founder accepts unfair terms put forth by a VC, the

VC cannot be blamed entirely. At the end of the day, it's a negotiation exercise. Nevertheless, I would argue that it is the responsibility of the VC to be reasonable and not exploit legal loopholes or any naivete or desperation on the part of the founder. Doing so not only hurts the entrepreneur's prospects, but ultimately the company's chances of success as well. When I see an accelerator, for example, offering a startup $10,000 in exchange for 25% equity, it saddens me. The founder has been diluted, and as soon as they graduate from the accelerator they will need more money and will end up getting further diluted by, say, an additional 40% just to raise another $100,000 from a seed investor.

The investors should know that being greedy is not only bad for founders, it's also not going to help the investors themselves. At the end of the day, if the product fails because the founders were not able to commit to the startup, after giving up a large portion of direct equity and losing motivation in the absence of a solid incentive, the venture will all come crashing down on everyone. My hope is that the region can live up to higher global standards in this area in the future.

4. Provide All-Around Startup Support

SANGEET PAUL CHOUDARY: Regarding regulations to further support tech startups, it's important to look broadly at what has worked and what has not worked globally. A good example is what's happening in Europe and the deregulation of the financial services industry with the Payment Services Directive, PSD2. PSD2 essentially requires banks to open up their data and allow startups to directly access that data, with customer consent of course, to grow their business. That is a step in the right direction. Having said that, the best way for regulation to catalyze innovation is not by doing it at the cost of one party, in this case at the cost of the banking system.

The best way for regulation to help catalyze innovation is by creating collaboration models. Singapore, for example, created a FinTech regulatory sandbox where banks can share data and startups can come and work with that data, but the startups cannot just take off and work off and work on a business on their own. They still need the banks to continue partnering with them, even after the innovation has been created within the sandbox. That creates more of a sustainable partnership between the larger incumbents and smaller companies. This encourages the incumbents to participate and open up their data but also ensures that they do not miss out on the advantages of the innovation.

That is where you can really have sustainable innovation and create a truly innovative ecosystem, not just from startups but also from leveraging the assets that the incumbents have in a given geography. This is particularly important in a geography like the Middle East, where you don't need to build an entire tech ecosystem from scratch and create, say, a new Facebook, Amazon, and Alibaba of the Middle East. You can actually focus on developing new businesses that work with the big traditional industries in that region, whether it's oil and gas, logistics, or real estate, and focus on building a startup ecosystem around those core industries. That's where the Singapore model would apply as being most relevant to the Middle East.

Digital regulation has three aspects. One is regulation based on metrics of economic development. The key question to ask here is whether economic development is being helped or harmed. That's how you should measure whether something should be regulated or not, rather than on the basis of the business model itself.

The second piece is that regulation should look at creating standards. Without standards, it becomes difficult for industries to be developed and for the companies to come and build these standards themselves. Singapore has developed a lot of standards around trade. Implementing those standards helps to create a lot of compatibility between different companies that need to work together.

The third piece, seen in the example of IndiaStack, is to build the public digital infrastructure on which private innovation can happen. Generally speaking, these are the three things that regulations should be addressing. Within them might be specific elements around regulating financial services, cybersecurity, identity, consent, etc.

ANAND CHOPRA-MCGOWAN: I can give three examples of some very interesting developments we're seeing in terms of providing government support for promoting education, and they are very much part of a larger trend. The first is from about 18 months ago. The newish French government under Emmanuel Macron put forward a new set of flexible learning accounts for French citizens. It recognized that when it comes to fostering an entrepreneurial ecosystem, when it comes to fostering a tech ecosystem, one of the critical inputs is talent. That talent may already be in the marketplace: working people who don't really have the skills to participate in this new and exciting area.

To address this, the government launched a portal that French citizens can access, with a certain amount of funding every year. The government essentially subsidizes continuous learning. It also made it cumulative, so if a citizen doesn't use it one year, they can apply a credit to the next year. That is allowing a lot more people access to a host of new educational opportunities. That's one thing we've seen, with flexibility that is key.

We've also seen a very similar initiative that has had more years of success in a very different part of the world: Singapore. Every Singaporean citizen receives a significant tuition credit or reimbursement for any course they take with General Assembly. That's an extraordinary investment in people and, obviously, speaks to the kind of economy and workforce that Singapore intends to build.

Those are two examples from government and regional standpoints, but a lot of companies are also beginning to take the lead in fostering the talent pipeline they need for their own businesses; they also see it as their role in benefiting society at large. For example, in 2018 the Walt Disney Company made a big investment in a program called "CODE: Rosie," which is dedicated to getting more women into software engineering roles. Disney did this by releasing a skill-assessment program across the company. It effectively allowed any female worker, even those in non-technical roles, to apply to become a software engineer. If they were selected, the company would not only pay for the course but would also put them through six months of internal apprenticeship to give them on-the-job training. They would then have a job waiting for them at the end. Finally, to make this as risk-proof as possible for the participants, it allows the women to go back to their original jobs if they complete the program and, for whatever reason, decide that these tech jobs actually don't work for them.

The amazing thing is that there have been something like 300 applications. Around 40 participants have been selected, and almost everyone has graduated and is now working in technology roles at Disney. This is an example of a company really taking the investment initiative into their own hands and recognizing that, to build up the technology workforce they need, they have to do it themselves.

AHMAD SUFIAN BAYRAM: The UK government has created what is known as the Catapult Programme, a network of world-leading technology and innovation centers designed to transform the UK's capability for innovation in specific areas and help drive future economic growth. What is good about this initiative is that it aspires to bridge the gap between research already taking place in universities and businesses. This leads to additional financial benefit from academic research. It is an excellent example of a program helping founders to access and build on cutting-edge research and ideas generated by universities and other businesses.

SAMIA MELHEM: The countries that have succeeded and are a shining example have been doing it for a while. It takes a long time to transform a country, and digital transformation is complicated because it requires people to be educated, to be literate, and to be connected. It requires a lot of prerequisites. It's possible to advance a lot and then become static, while other countries make greater progress. Sustained leadership and smart investments are key. We all know the great examples of Estonia, South Korea, and Singapore, all of which transformed their economies to digital ones.

In Africa, I've worked with countries that you wouldn't have believed 15 years ago would be where they are now. It's because their governments made technology a priority 15 or 20 years ago. My best three examples are Ghana, Kenya, and Rwanda. I worked with all of them. All three had a head of state who, some 15 years ago or so, said, "Digital is going to be very important for the future. Let's prepare for it. Let's connect our people and let's use it to leapfrog. Let's create right away all the laws that allow for it."

Countries like Rwanda and Kenya have had digital ID for online authentication for a while now, which is helpful for transactions with banks, access to subsidies, and post transfers. Our big example in Latin America is Peru. Ten years ago, Peru's government started to register all of its population, granting everyone registered a digital ID. India's implementation of the Aadhaar unique ID number, providing 1.3 billion people with a unique ID linked to access to services, is the most striking example of a successful transformation on a massive scale.

Central Asia has some of the highest ranked countries in the world on the Ease of Doing Business Index. Those countries are reforming the fastest by simplifying procedures and making it easy and seamless to interface with the government.

At the end of the day, it's up to the government to make those reforms and make them fast enough. Government officials can learn about all those great case studies, travel all over the world, and get exposed to all those great success stories. But unless they actually implement those changes in their countries, none of this learning will materialize into impact. If a critical digital economy-related law, for example, sits in parliament for 10 years and is not passed, a thriving digital economy will never emerge. That's why it's crucial to have a top-level champion, like a president or a prime minister, who sets the tone from the top, monitors, and pushes those government bodies to perform and gets them to change fast. Trickling this approach down to individual ministries is very important.

LAMIA KAMAL CHAOUI: In Canada, the five federal regional development agencies and FedNor play a critical role in the local tailoring of federal small business and entrepreneurship policies to make sure that local intelligence is used to create adapted policies. They provide locally tailored support in areas including access to finance (e.g., interest-free repayable contributions), support for innovation (e.g., product development and commercialization and SME-university collaborations), and the provision of management training to small businesses, as discussed in the OECD report *SME and Entrepreneurship Policy in Canada.*

In Germany, several branches of the German Chambers of Commerce and Industry have developed checklists, training seminars, and online support materials to help local governments create a business-friendly environment for entrepreneurs and SMEs in their community, city, or region. The checklists include questions on whether one-stop shops have been enacted locally, how they have secured high quality and transparency in service provision to businesses, and what online services have been established.

Ireland established a system of Regional Enterprise Plans (REPs) early last year to complement national enterprise policy with bottom-up initiatives. Each region has a steering committee composed of representatives from the private sector, local authorities, enterprise agencies, and other public bodies. Each REP contains a small number of high-level strategic objectives and sets out priority actions under each of the objectives to strengthen the ecosystem for enterprise development. More details are in the OECD report *SME and Entrepreneurship Policy in Ireland.*

KATE POPE HODEL: NetWork Kansas built a statewide network of resources for entrepreneurs, then organized individual E-Communities in small, rural areas. In addition to identifying resources to help local entrepreneurs start or grow a business, NetWork Kansas works with community partners to establish locally administered loan funds. From 2007-2017, a total of $12.71 million in E-Community loans were awarded to 424 businesses. That funding leveraged an additional $63.5 million.

The City of Albuquerque had a vision to become the most entrepreneur-friendly city in the nation. Through the Molino project, Albuquerque identified the region's entrepreneurial strengths and resource gaps. It then engaged a number of business support agencies to streamline the process for starting or growing a business, with a focus on immigrant and low-income entrepreneurs. Part of the research phase involved going door to door to ask entrepreneurs about the challenges they faced in starting or scaling.

Colmena66 is a regional referral network (built on SourceLink technology) that links Puerto Rico–based entrepreneurs and business owners with more than 100 local and regional resource partners, such as nonprofit organizations, academia, and government agencies that provide services to help businesses grow and prosper. After Hurricane Maria tore through the island in 2017, Colmena66 led the effort to launch Shop and Hire PR to make it easier for shoppers to connect with Puerto Rican goods and services in order to help rebuild local businesses.

ALI ABUKUMAIL: Cluj in Romania and Chattanooga in the US are two very small cities, both under the radar, that provide great case studies. What they have done over the last five to seven years is quite remarkable. First, they built strong broadband networks in their cities. Then they built additional support infrastructure relevant to parks or some co-working spaces. Then they created some incentive programs for entrepreneurs to come in, along with tax incentives. They also boosted the university programs to provide add-on training to individuals so they become fit for the market. The totality of support that they offered had a transformative effect on their ecosystems.

In Europe, Cluj is now well known as an emerging spot in Romania. Meanwhile, Chattanooga, Tennessee is an interesting case because it has similar services to Silicon Valley, but at less than half the price. There have been numerous exits of billions of dollars in the last

10 years there. That's much bigger than everything MENA has done, just from one very small, relatively unknown city in the US.

ABDUL BASET AL JANAHI: In recent years, Russia has been making significant advances in the SME sphere through exemplary initiatives. The Russian Small and Medium Business Corporation, for example, provides comprehensive business startup support and information as part of their SME Business Navigator tool. It provides assistance with supply and demand statistics, company registration, statutory requirements regarding various types of activity, as well as financial support of SMEs and business training. Companies also receive advice on various forms of subsidies, occupational safety requirements for enterprises, and opportunities for promoting goods and services in regional and global markets. An online service that will help business owners choose the best tax plan is another attraction.

VERA SONGWE: Kenya is one of the best examples when it comes to international best practices in ecosystem development, especially in emerging markets. It has been able to create an environment that drives innovation in spite of a host of local challenges. With regard to innovation, Kenya introduced M-Pesa, which led to 50% of Kenya's GDP now moving through cashless systems. The product converted even the most basic cell phones into bank accounts and secure money-transfer devices without a large expansion of banking infrastructure. This shows that innovation can happen practically anywhere, even in the least likely places. Kenya is also a clear example of what can happen when proper focus on ecosystem development is undertaken by top leadership as a national priority, and the right strategies and resources are used to drive entrepreneurship and innovation.

5. Facilitate Foreign Talent and Investment

TON VAN 'T NOORDENDE: One big step the Netherlands took recently was to introduce a startup visa, which enables international startups to set up and operate in the Netherlands more easily than ever before. The government essentially helped companies to fast-track their market entry through this program and have a so-called soft landing. The program was initiated and implemented by the government as well as semi-governmental organizations. In effect, they created a checklist that makes it seamless for founders to get at least a temporary visa to operate in the country. They simply need to provide some personal information and the method of operation of the business and present their business plan. While the program represents one key piece in further unlocking the potential of the local ecosystem, it's no longer unique as other places in Europe and globally have adopted similar initiatives.

ALEC ROSS: Soon after the dissolution of the Soviet Union and the re-established independence of Estonia, the country embraced an open economy and enabled technological innovation (Skype is the most notable example). It did so while rolling out a number of extraordinary initiatives, including enacting a flat tax rate, achieving the world's fastest internet speed, adopting a universal health record system, pioneering the use of online voting, breaking down barriers to residency, and achieving 100% school enrollment and literacy rates. Additionally, it reduced trade tariffs and ended all export restrictions, turning the small country into a trading hub.

The government also reached out to foreign investors. The citizenship law was amended to provide equal civil protection to resident aliens. Estonia passed laws to ensure that foreigners could purchase land. All special privileges for existing investors were abolished to ensure a level playing field for new investors. As a result, Estonia has achieved a standard of living far beyond that of 20 years ago and has quickly become a center for global investment.

Estonia made yet another bold move, offering what it calls "e-residency" to any person in the world. As the country put more of its government services online, from incorporating a company (which happens at a world-leading speed, estimated at five minutes) to authenticating electronic signatures, it has seized the opportunity to position itself as a hub for digital government services. To become an e-resident of Estonia, a person needs to make one trip to the country to submit their biometrics and other personal data for verification. They pay the registration fee and receive a secure chip-enabled identity card. They can then use their Estonian e-residency for a variety of things, such as doing business throughout the EU and leveraging its online-only programs for contracting and tax filing. It's a way to bypass other countries' more expensive and less efficient systems. There's no more paperwork, lower taxes and, for business owners, it provides all the freedom that comes with being an incorporated business in the EU.

In a similar way to how other countries have created tax havens to benefit from large deposits in their banks, Estonia has established itself as an efficiency haven. The country is a great example and inspiration to many nations around the world for how to create innovation in the industries of the future. It's a way to not just generate wealth and employment opportunities but to enhance civic and political life as well. In this respect, we should stop asking about the next Silicon Valley and start asking about the next Estonia.

EFOSA OJOMO: Singapore is a very good example. It's small but the history of how it developed reveals that it really tried to focus on innovation. People might characterize Singapore's economy as an export-based economy. This is understandable because its exports-to-GDP ratio is almost 2:1. However, what Singapore was exporting 50 years ago is quite different from what it's exporting today. It actually continues to increase exports. If you look at the critical unit of analysis, though, it's innovation.

How did Singapore do it? It set up an Economic Development

Board. The focus of that board was to attract money to the country, to attract investments that would create jobs for local Singaporeans, and so on. It didn't stop there. It invested in education, it invested in infrastructure and healthcare, and it supported the growth of the new economy. Having a holistic approach to development is key—recognizing that it's not just education, not just healthcare, not just roads—it's how all these pieces work together.

In contrast, Mexico has historically invested quite a bit in efficiency innovations, a thriving petroleum sector, and a thriving manufacturing sector, but those investments have not created the kind of prosperity hoped for. That is largely because it has not focused on converting non-consumers to consumers. Meanwhile, South Korea was able to do that, and the difference there can be seen in terms of phenomenal GDP growth over the past 50 years. For us, when we think about innovation and economy, we think of the process by which I take a non-consumer of something—whether it's mobility, e-commerce, or other innovative products or services—and turn that person into an active consumer. That's where the bulk of focus and investment should go.

Chapter XI

FINAL THOUGHTS ON ECOSYSTEM DEVELOPMENT

Cultivating entrepreneurship and entrepreneurial ecosystems is one of the central issues of our time. It's a foundational tenet for any society that seeks to thrive and prosper. No society can reach its full potential without mobilizing its main economic engine: entrepreneurs, startups, and SMEs. Not only does this segment have the potential to create local and global innovations and solutions that can transform our lives, it has the power to provide wide economic participation in the form of creating jobs and providing livelihoods to massive populations.

Unemployment is an epidemic that is haunting the MENA region. With the majority of its population under the age of 30, the prospect of mass youth unemployment looms closer than ever, exacerbated by an economy that is unable to absorb this massive segment coming of age at once. There are simply not enough jobs available in the region to provide for tens of millions of youth, possibly up to 100 million. It's what is commonly referred to as the "youth bulge." So far, entrepreneurship and mobilizing these masses to start their own businesses and employ others represents the only viable option put forward to resolve this issue.

Granted, entrepreneurship is not a guaranteed formula for success. A large proportion of startups fail, even in the most vibrant ecosystems and economies. Nevertheless, such failures are not necessarily a loss to the overall ecosystem since many of the same founders go on to learn from their failures and achieve success in subsequent attempts. Furthermore, startups act as training grounds in terms of job skills and career experience that can also be leveraged by unsuccessful entrepreneurs into future jobs. All in all, a valuable element of recycling within the ecosystem, which cannot be overlooked, goes into effect as a result of failed companies. Hence, even with a high percentage of failure among startups, the ecosystem stands to gain in the long haul from new entrepreneurial ventures.

Additionally, entrepreneurship holds the key to solving massive societal problems that are either unrecognized or incapable of being solved by large organizations. By design, startups can be more agile and faster in utilizing new technologies and exploiting new opportunities. A greater number of entrepreneurs are acknowledging the role they play in society and ensuring that they have a social purpose in society beyond personal wealth. Similarly, it's important for all stakeholders to strive for shared prosperity, as Erik Brynjolfsson, Director of the MIT Initiative on Digital Economy and Co-Author of *The Second Machine Age: Work, Progress and Prosperity in a Time of Brilliant Technologies* describes in this chapter. To do so, more collaboration is needed on the part of entrepreneurs and all ecosystem builders, as Steve Case, Chairman and CEO of Revolution LLC, Chairman of Case Foundation, Co-Founder of AOL, and Author of *The Third Wave* also emphasizes here.

We discuss how to lay the foundation for a startup community from the ground up and the importance of having an initial group of like-minded, committed, and passionate entrepreneurs who are both experienced and credible to lead that movement. They may also be joined by non-entrepreneurs who share similar attributes and goals, since inclusivity is paramount in such an environment. This group, in effect, acts as a catalyst to spark a startup movement that attracts others to join it.

To follow such an approach, one must take a long-term view. There are no shortcuts to launching a robust startup community. Rome wasn't built in a day. Similarly, Silicon Valley was built in over half a century or so. Thus, any attempt to find shortcuts and not take the time to build the right foundation or seed the right relationships will ultimately backfire and undermine the potential of the environment.

Finally, as the fourth industrial revolution—a concept popularized by Klaus Schwab, Founder and Executive Chairman of the World Economic Forum and Author of *The Fourth Industrial Revolution*—dawns upon us, the study of ecosystem development takes center stage. None of the innovations society needs can be expected to emerge without a conducive environment for creativity and imagination that draws holistically on both our individual best and our collective best. As Klaus Schwab eloquently describes, "The fourth industrial revolution may be driving disruption, but the challenges it presents are of our own making. It is thus in our power to address them and enact the changes and policies needed to adapt and flourish in our emerging new environment. We can only meaningfully address these challenges if we mobilize the collective wisdom of our minds, hearts, and souls."

1. An Economic and Nation-Building Imperative

ARUNMA OTEH: Entrepreneurship and promoting entrepreneurship, especially in developing nations, is extremely important because we must broaden economic participation in those societies. We need to create jobs. The best way to create jobs is to encourage people to start their own businesses; startups, entrepreneurship, and innovation are absolutely essential ingredients. That's where the greatest opportunity for growth lies in such places. Around 90% of the businesses in Africa, for example, are SMEs according to the London Stock Exchange. If we're going to tackle the challenges of struggling economies in emerging markets, such as North Africa or the Middle East, it's absolutely crucial to create an ecosystem that supports people to become entrepreneurs because jobs are created through businesses. Therefore, we must promote startups, in spite of the fact that the odds are stacked against them, because even if they fail, new ideas and lessons are birthed and recycled back into the ecosystem. They also keep some of the large companies and incumbents on their toes, so they're constantly innovating and not becoming too complacent.

ERIK BRYNJOLFSSON: Digital technologies create tremendous opportunities to improve productivity, create wealth, and improve health and other metrics of living standards. The barrier these days is not so much in the technology itself, but in organizations' ability to apply those technologies to problems. That requires a lot of reorganization of companies, of industries, even of whole societies.

The role of the entrepreneur is essential in driving that kind of change. In the United States and other countries, we haven't seen as much dynamism and entrepreneurship as we did in past decades, which is a global challenge. This is especially challenging for developing countries. If they're looking to reach the living standards of more developed countries, then they not only have to apply the technology but have to spur innovation through more entrepreneurship.

I'm very optimistic about the technologies that we have, but I'm concerned that our governments and our organizations aren't taking full advantage of these technologies. The real gap now is on the organizational side of human capital. Humans change much more slowly than technologies, so we aren't keeping up. In particular, one of the challenges is that while we are making the economic pie bigger and productivity and overall levels of wealth are higher than they've ever been in history—we have more millionaires and billionaires than ever—we aren't creating the shared prosperity that we should be. Many people are being left behind. We need to think hard, not only about how to use the technologies to create wealth, but how to use them to create shared prosperity. At MIT, we have something called the Inclusive Innovation Challenge, which we recognizes and rewards organizations that are using technologies to create benefits for the many, not just the few.

I encourage everyone to think about how we can use technologies in these ways. Ultimately, I'm optimistic if we make those kinds of broad investments and the technology can potentially be wildly beneficial. However, there's nothing automatic about that happening. It won't happen unless we actively try to work toward creating shared prosperity. As people make these investments, I encourage them to think not only about productivity and growth, but also about shared prosperity and inclusive innovation.

JONATHAN ORTMANS: Part of the reason I do this work is to make it possible for anyone, anywhere not just to start but also to scale a business. It is one way we all fight for more economic equality and, ultimately, economic development. As the GSER report outlines, it is no longer about the next Silicon Valley; we already have the next 30 Silicon Valleys. Across the world, 25 startup ecosystems have an ecosystem value above $10 billion each, and an additional 54 that have an ecosystem value of between $1 billion and $10 billion. Together, they create thousands of jobs and billions in economic productivity.

To help ecosystem leaders look beyond Silicon Valley and unicorns, I float an approach proposed in GEN's global national benchmarking tool—the Index of Dynamic Entrepreneurship (IDE). The metaphorical concepts of unicorns or gazelles can lead us to have an oversimplified understanding of the complex nature of entrepreneurial dynamics. The concept of "dynamic entrepreneurship" includes unicorns and gazelles, but also encompasses a broader subset of diverse and heterogeneous new and young firms, and accepts instability in the companies' growth trajectory.

In the annual IDE report, we explore systemic conditions for dynamic entrepreneurship in 65 countries. The creation of new companies is the result of a process that is shaped by diverse social, cultural, political, and economic factors. The IDE research team, based in the PRODEM think tank, considers 10 key social, cultural, economic, and political dimensions that have an impact on the quantity and quality of the emerging companies. These dimensions are measured using a combination of more than 40 variables from globally recognized sources of secondary data. It's an analysis worth leveraging when running an ecosystem diagnostic.

Entrepreneurship has always been tied to job creation and economic growth. Now it is also about healthier and more inclusive ecosystems that level the playing field and democratize entrepreneurship so that it can include all those in our communities who dream about the possibility of human endeavor for the benefit of all.

2. Entrepreneurs are Prime Movers

DANIEL ISENBERG: With respect to the Arab world, I've actually spent time in the region, especially the Gulf, and the entrepreneurial legacy there is quite deep. People in MENA often downplay, belittle, or devalue the history of entrepreneurship in the region—the long tradition of, for example, trading networks or the tremendous business innovations that are part of its history.

Recognizing this legacy is an important part of inculcating a culture of entrepreneurship. To say "We've never had entrepreneurship" is just inaccurate. The region has never developed computer chips, perhaps. Nevertheless, all kinds of entrepreneurial activity have taken place for thousands of years in the region. That fact should be celebrated and used to inspire.

SAMI MAHROUM: An ecosystem is not something you build and people then populate. It is something that people generate. It's the entrepreneurs that create the system, ultimately. Even regulation, even government policy, initiatives, etc., are not the fundamental catalyst for change. It's really the entrepreneurs who work hard to change the system, to lobby for reform, to point out its weaknesses so that eventually a more friendly, conducive ecosystem emerges.

To be an entrepreneur is to be resilient and to succeed where most would fail, often in spite of less-than-favorable conditions. Having said that, we should be careful not to pitch or present entrepreneurs or entrepreneurship as something easy that everyone can do and suggest that we should all do it. There will always be a minority of us who are entrepreneurs, and among this minority there will be an even smaller minority who will be successful entrepreneurs, who get the prestige and the media spotlight.

Culturally, in this region we support and reward that type of success. In our region, you are admired for standing out and excelling, which is good. Individualism is supported, but the individualism in our region is not a selfish one. A successful individual will still take care of their family and their friends and their network. It's a unique form of individualism that characterizes our region. It's not the same type of individualism that you might find in the West, for instance. It's also not all community-based, but it's different nevertheless from, say, individualism that characterizes the Netherlands or Scandinavia. In the Netherlands they say the sky is low, which means don't aim too high or you will lose your head. There's always pressure not to stand out and to conform to the community at large.

As I illustrated in my book *Black Swan Start-ups*, the ecosystem is generated by the individual, the entrepreneur, and an individual entrepreneur can succeed within their own micro-ecosystem. They work to amplify and leverage the advantages, the surpluses that exist in their locality. It could be the low cost of talent or office space, for example. It could also be being close to a big airport or a big port. It could be the language.

It may be necessary to mitigate or offset local shortcomings by extending their networks elsewhere, connecting with the other hubs or resources that are missing locally. If you need to raise money, you've got to run to people in New York, or you go to Dubai. No one is stopping you from moving there. If you have a very good idea, you may need to pitch it in London, and you may get funded there. No one is stopping you. As an entrepreneur you must do what you have to and go where you have to in order to make your idea a reality.

In the 11 cases I featured in the book, none of those startups were supposed to succeed. The odds were well stacked against each, yet none of their entrepreneurs let their circumstances get in the way of their dreams. There's the story of a company called Sofizar, launched by a Lahore entrepreneur, with all of its disadvantages. He developed algorithms that work on top of Google, customizing markets and different segments, selling advertising to different companies. All he needed was a server and a power generator, and cheap engineers to work on the algorithms with him, and that's all he had. He didn't need an airport, a road system, an infrastructure. The regulations were certainly not favorable to startups, nor was he offered special funding or mentorship, or an accelerator program. He didn't have access to startup events or media coverage. None of that. He had to rely on ingenuity and good, old fashioned hard work.

I came to realize after writing this book that stories like these are not the rare exception. They're common in the least likely of places. There are a ton of remarkable stories everywhere around the world, where resilient entrepreneurs find their way to success without all the bells and whistles, and without any glimpse of an ecosystem. A great, thriving startup environment certainly helps a great deal, but that does not mean its shortfalls or absence should be a deterrent by any means. There is a lot that we can learn from those stories.

STEVE CASE: We are entering a new era of the internet that I call the "third wave," where entrepreneurs have an opportunity to change the way we live, work, and interact. The first wave occurred when AOL and other companies laid the foundation for consumers to connect to the internet. The second wave saw companies like Google and Facebook build on top of the internet to create search and social networking capabilities, and apps like Instagram leverage the smartphone revolution. Now we're entering the third wave, a period in which entrepreneurs will vastly transform major "real-world" sectors like health, education, transportation, energy, and food—and in the process they will change the way we live our daily lives. Much of that industry knowledge will exist outside of the coastal tech hubs. Building companies in this new era will require a new mindset and a new playbook. It will require what I refer to as the three Ps: partnerships, policy, and perseverance.

Entrepreneurs will need to focus on building constructive partnerships. I like to quote an African proverb, "If you want to go fast, go alone; if you want to go far, go together." Companies will need to create relationships with organizations and individuals that understand the industry they are trying to disrupt. Otherwise, those same organizations and individuals will be the barrier to entry. If you want to change healthcare, you will need to partner with hospitals, doctors, insurance companies, and nurses to succeed. The landscape of education cannot change without buy-in from teachers, school systems, and parents.

In the third wave, the industries being transformed are highly regulated. They don't like to hear this, but entrepreneurs will have to work with policy-makers and government. The era of "ask for forgiveness" is over.

Finally, entrepreneurs will need perseverance in this new age. When tackling complicated industries, you will need the patience to work through the many roadblocks and hurdles. Overnight successes will be very rare. I'm excited and optimistic about the third wave and look forward to seeing the products and services that entrepreneurs create to change and enhance the way we live.

3. Getting Your Local Startup Community Going

BRAD FELD: Generally speaking, you don't need all the entrepreneurs to catalyze or be the "leaders" of the startup community, but you certainly need a critical mass of like-minded, passionate, and committed individuals. That critical mass doesn't have to be a huge number; it could literally be half a dozen like-minded, passionate people. You also don't need or want entrepreneurs to be spending 100% of their time on the startup community because, of course, what you want them to be doing is building companies. After all, this is the whole reason that a startup community exists in the first place: to help support the creation of startups, and to help support entrepreneurs to build over time—from the startup community—a very vibrant and healthy entrepreneurial ecosystem.

The interesting thing that happens in a startup community, if you look at the range of entrepreneurs, is the tendency to have a spectrum from very experienced, successful entrepreneurs at one end who have started multiple companies, and aspiring and first-time entrepreneurs at the other end. The other thing that you tend to have on that dimension is people who focus differently on their businesses at different points in time.

There are phases in which, as a founder or a leader of a company, you have no ability to think about anything other than your company, in the context of your work activity. Then there are plenty of phases during which you might not be focused to that extent, including shortly after you sell your company, when you transition out, after your company has failed, or when you've just hired a CEO to run the business and you're playing a different role. Time, focus, and priorities shift depending on the particular phase.

In addition, most enlightened entrepreneurs recognize that having a healthier local startup community actually helps their business. The most obvious element is recruiting. If you're visible as a company and you're participating in the startup community as a leader, you'll attract more talent to your business. It will actually make recruiting and hiring easier. Most companies that grow and are successful are beneficiaries of their local startup communities, so you get real value from what's going on in the startup community beyond recruitment. Again, entrepreneurs who have a long-term view tend to want to invest back into their startup community some of the benefits and rewards that they have had, rather than having a take-only attitude where they're building their business but ignoring their local community.

Most entrepreneurs I know understand that a part of their own journey is continual learning and growth. They also recognize that, in many cases, that learning and growth come from other entrepreneurs. There is a lot of incentive for an entrepreneur to invest in relationships with other entrepreneurs, including peers, mentors, and mentees.

Many people also have very deep affection for the place they call home, or what is referred to as "topophilia," which means "love of place." If you love the place you are living in and you're building a company or investing in that place as part of your overall activity, that can be incredibly rewarding.

An extremely busy entrepreneur can do lots of tactical things to engage with the startup community. Most entrepreneurs recognize at some level that they can incorporate the activities of participating in their startup community and leading their startup community into the growth, health, and development of their own company

Since I published *Startup Communities* in 2012, as I've watched startup communities develop globally, I have started to understand more clearly the nature and essence of the evolution of the startup community. In a new book I'm writing, called *The Startup Community Way*, I use the metaphor or the construct of a complex adaptive system, where we show the complex, underlying system for how a startup community operates and evolves.

We've also segmented and separated a startup community from an entrepreneurial ecosystem. That's another phenomenon that is often conflated.

Another concept that I've developed a lot over the last five years, in conjunction with Techstars, is the concept of "give first," which is now a mantra of Techstars. It's the idea of putting energy into a system without expecting something back in return. It's not altruism, since you do expect to eventually get something back—you just don't know when, from whom, what consideration, over what time frame, and at what magnitude. If you can get people around a startup community to give first—that is, to put energy into the system without defining transactionally what they're going to get out of it—you can generate this intense flywheel effect. This, in turn, creates lots and lots of momentum and positive outcomes over time that are very powerful for the system.

"Give first" is related to "pay it forward"; you can call it a cousin. However, "pay it forward" has an obligatory characteristic associated with it, namely this notion that, "Somebody once did something for me, therefore I must pay it forward." It's a nice concept, but I don't think it's the right one. It's one with a requirement to pay it forward as a result of an action that's happened to you in the past. With "give first", you're not doing it because of something somebody else has done for you. It's because of the operating philosophy you have.

JF GAUTHIER: The best way to build a startup community from scratch is to start small and from the inside. You need a nucleus that essentially acts as a catalyst. The initial focus should be directed at creating a core group of young entrepreneurs who help each other in a no-hierarchy atmosphere in which everybody works together, shares best practices, and helps each other. What we see a lot of countries trying to do is educate and inspire, and ultimately influence a mass population of millions to become entrepreneurs and have an entrepreneurial mindset. It's much easier to start small, from a core group of 50 key individuals, then to double from 100 to 200 to 400 people in that community and grow from there. If you look at Silicon Valley has around 13,000 startups—that's just 39,000 or so entrepreneurs out of 7 million people. That's a fraction of 1%. Therefore, in the beginning, it's better to focus on creating a small, strong community that can be influential in attracting others, and ultimately help grow the ecosystem overall.

BALA KAMALLAKHARAN: Brad Feld's book *Startup Communities*, in my opinion, is by far the most comprehensive in terms of describing what's really needed to develop a thriving ecosystem. He is spot on when he stresses the importance of having an inclusive environment with the kind of openness where everyone feels welcome to come and participate. Also, I like his emphasis on the need to have a long-term view and to make sure that the community is led by entrepreneurs, as opposed to governments or institutions.

We actually implemented his "Boulder thesis" here in Iceland, which in turn provides a great case study for the implementation of those ideas and the actual "proof of concept," if you will. The number of successful companies built and the amount of money raised in Iceland per capita in the last decade are remarkable and actually dwarf a lot of the bigger ecosystems.

JOSH LERNER: Ecosystem development, especially when you're starting from scratch in a particular community or city, is not a short-term endeavor. There are no quick fixes; you must have patience to build it from the ground up. You also have to look for early signs of success and leverage those while learning from missteps and dead ends. You really need entrepreneurs involved in building ecosystems because they are credible and have what we call "street cred." It helps to have people who have been there and done that, helping to build these ecosystems, but how do you get those people? It's a cart before the horse thing. How do you get successful entrepreneurs if you don't have the ecosystem? Sometimes, they go away and come back. Reaching out to folks who have some type of affinity for a community, a university, or a town, and bringing them back to help build and mentor is really important in terms of knowledge-transfer and community-building.

KATE POPE HODEL: Building an entrepreneurial community has to be entrepreneur-centric and entrepreneur focused, since it cannot always be entrepreneur led. Entrepreneurs are typically too busy building their companies, so what is needed is someone who is focused and passionate about building the startup community.

At SourceLink, we've come up with a short list of things that anyone can do to help the emerging businesses in their neighborhoods. First, know what the startup process looks like in your community and who can help. Then make the appropriate referrals. Introduce new businesses to customers, investors, or mentors. Mingle with leaders of emerging businesses at events, and if no networking event exists in your community, start one. Finally, celebrate entrepreneurs at every opportunity. Tell their stories and showcase their successes.

Overall, start with what you have and what is unique to your community, your arena. Don't try to replicate specific programs that work in another region. Understand your community's strengths and challenges, and then figure out how you can build on the strengths and fill the gaps in what your entrepreneurs need to start and grow successful companies.

RUBEN NIEUWENHUIS: My advice to anyone who's trying to kickstart their ecosystem in their respective city or country is to really focus on the basics. Too often, ecosystem builders try to get fancy before they have the fundamentals in place. There's a lot to be said for executing the ordinary exceptionally well and quickly versus spending too much time trying to be unique at the expense of getting the foundational building blocks right. That's the base from which you can differentiate or get creative later.

Once the foundation is in place, you can start specializing and, say, decide to focus on blockchain, AI, or FinTech. Initially, you need to provide a soft landing to outside companies entering your market so they can be up and running as seamlessly as possible, and focus on making sure your local events grow strong. Also, start implementing entrepreneurial programs within universities and startup-in-residence programs to help engage private academies that are bringing tech skills like coding, growth hacking, and data analysis into the ecosystem.

Execution and speed are critical. Don't spend too much time in planning and analysis or figuring out more complex issues like how governance should work, for example. A lot of time can be lost in structuring governance. Instead, just set up a temporary organization and say, "Let's make it work for one year and we will figure out later how we put governance together." We did a few of these things in Amsterdam, which turned out quite well. We had our action plan after just six weeks, and after two months we were up and running. We had the website up along with the story and the narrative. We were super focused on our planning and super-fast in implementation. My other advice would be to not try to take either an entrepreneurs-only approach or a public-only approach to your ecosystem. Taking a private-public approach and being inclusive is really important.

Finally, as your ecosystem grows, you can focus more on how to connect and grow together with other ecosystems. In Amsterdam, we made sure that our efforts to develop and support local AI companies were not made in a silo. We had the wider European context and collaboration in mind. Another example is our startup-in-residence program, where we took an open source approach and created a platform that is available for other cities around the world, thereby helping startups to grow city-to-city globally by taking this approach.

TIM DRAPER: It takes a long time (half a century or more) to fully develop a Silicon Valley like ecosystem. Governments and leaders should create an open platform for innovation and have patience. There is an old expression, "Rome wasn't built in a day." It means that leaders should build foundations for the decades ahead when drones will deliver goods to us in minutes, when digital currencies will make political currencies obsolete, when borders will become less and less relevant, when space exploration will be commonplace, when data will give us better medical diagnoses than doctors alone, when therapeutics will be built specifically for the patient's DNA and situation, and where anything is possible.

TIM O'REILLY: Almost all of the really interesting technology movements start in areas that are too small to even be thinking about regulation. The personal computer was dismissed by all the titans of the industry. They initially thought "This is a toy. This isn't a real business." Steve Wozniak created the first prototype of the Apple I in a wood shop. They were just kids who thought, "So cool! We can have our own computer." Similarly, the internet was initially non-commercial by law when people started building the first commercial websites. Then there was open source software, which Linus Torvalds pioneered, as captured by the title of his book, *Just for Fun*.

This whole idea that you can put together some magical set of top-down regulations that will spark a startup revolution is unrealistic, no matter how much money you throw at it, without the pioneering inventors and entrepreneurs needed to catalyze change. Governments can be helpful in growing an ecosystem, but when you look at startup ecosystems that have developed, especially in their early stages, nobody was there to support them. We keep modeling the late or mid-stage of these ecosystems and forgetting the early stage.

The other big role of government is to make sure that the leading companies don't suck all the air out of the system. It's critical that there always be room for new innovations and disruptions to take hold without the incumbents interfering in any given industry. This is key for innovation to flourish across the ecosystem.

4. Ecosystem Development as the Next Frontier

WILL HERMAN: Entrepreneurship is the next great movement in social justice. I believe that cities, states, and nations are looking for a better way to run their economies, empower people, and give them the opportunity to grow and live fulfilling lives. The economic consensus of the last 50 years has favored large, established businesses over small, new businesses. That doesn't work well because it leads to greater inequality and a feeling of loss of control by individuals over their own lives. Now economic priorities are starting to change.

The future is about making entrepreneurship a top strategic priority for economic growth, which is already happening across the globe. I personally engage with many leaders, including leaders at the United Nations, and the common theme I hear is that entrepreneurship has become a top priority in global development strategy.

We also see similar sentiment with governments and policy-makers around the world. For instance, the new President of Colombia was elected on a pro-entrepreneurship platform, with the underlying premise that entrepreneurship is key to economic equality. Meanwhile, the EU is pushing entrepreneurship as a means to offset social unrest in Europe. The message I hear repeatedly is that nations and leaders are aiming to convert job seekers into job creators.

Countless other examples from across the globe signify positive change. India announced a new law that exempts startups from paying income tax for their first three years of operation. In parts of Argentina, the registration process for a new company has been cut from eight months to just 15 minutes. Malaysia is consolidating its government structure so that startups and SMEs, which historically have been regulated by 60 agencies, are now regulated by just one agency.

I'm bullish on ecosystem development around the world. We're experiencing a mindset shift in how nations view and prioritize entrepreneurship as it relates to their economic development agenda. In doing so, discussions and initiatives around entrepreneurial ecosystem development have moved to the forefront. Contrast this with past approaches, just a few years back, when the focus was on top-down initiatives. Today, it's about empowering and connecting local entrepreneurs. We're seeing a lot more governments working closely with entrepreneurs on solving their challenges, unblocking barriers, and facilitating their companies' growth beyond just offering subsidies. All in all, there is much to be excited about in many parts of the world. Hopefully many of those changes will manifest positive examples that permeate throughout the globe.

ALEC ROSS: Looking back at the last 25 years of digitalization, from 1994 to 2019, reveals that most of the wealth created came from places like Silicon Valley and Seattle, Washington, which is home to Microsoft and Amazon. My prediction is that between 2020 to 2035, geographic spread will increase across the world. I think there will really be 10-12 of what I call "alpha cities" or "alpha regions" that have a very high concentration of headquarters and wealth creation through entrepreneurship. Meanwhile, I think there will be another 30-40 "beta cities," which will be quite vibrant as well, but will not have as many headquarters as alpha cities. They will be an essential part of the global supply chain, nevertheless. As a result, wealth distribution will be more broadly created than historically has been the case.

EFOSA OJOMO: In our book, *The Prosperity Paradox*, the message we espouse is one of hope. It's one of hope because what I see when I look at a country with a militaristic government, a ton of corruption, unimaginable poverty, or any dysfunction in general, is a baseline. That is where it is today. That does not mean that's where it will be tomorrow. With what I've learned and the little that I know about innovation and economic prosperity, I can see a clear and predictable path that will help transform such a country from intense poverty to lasting prosperity.

This path will not be easy. It's incredibly difficult. Innovation is blood, sweat, and tears. It's not something that grows by throwing money at it or something you develop just by putting up a modern incubator with Wi-Fi and co-working space. That's not innovation. Innovation is blood, sweat, and tears. It is going against everything in society to say, "I'm going to create a new, disruptive value." That's incredibly difficult, but that has tremendous impact on society.

When I think about the ideas we've introduced in *The Prosperity Paradox*—much like Amir Hegazi is attempting to do with *Ecosystem Arabia*—they are about really trying to change the rhetoric and introduce a new language and a new mindset for innovation, ecosystems, and entrepreneurship. We're really helping to raise awareness and accelerate change. That makes me quite optimistic, because it's pointing to a world where the message and mechanism that can help us to prosper are becoming more and more widespread, which is wonderful.

BILL AULET: I am a strong believer that entrepreneurship is part of the answer to many of the world's greatest problems. On an individual level, entrepreneurship offers people hope in their lives; it gives them pride, meaning, rigor, and discipline. And when you give people all those great things, they become more constructive citizens.

Imagine a hypothetical world where we could train everyone in the Middle East to be an entrepreneur or at least entrepreneurial in how they think and approach problems. I strongly believe that would be transformational because people would then be more proactive in finding opportunities and making positive changes, instead of always relying on their families or their governments to fix things. They would, in effect, become more active participants in their own ecosystem development.

If you find a way to direct and unleash that untapped capacity through entrepreneurship and entrepreneurship education, I believe that not only will more of them have jobs, they will have more dignity, and society at large will be more empowered. And if we do that, we will have a much more harmonious society and we will be able to solve some of these seemingly intractable problems like climate change, education, healthcare, and poverty, as opposed to engaging in civil unrest and other destructive behavior. That's my sincere hope for the region and for the world, and that's what gets me fired up every day in what I do.

EPILOGUE

An Open Call to Action to Ecosystem Builders

"It is not the most intellectual or the strongest of the species that survives, but the one that is able to adapt and adjust to its changing environment. Similarly, the civilization that survives is the one that is able to adapt to its changing physical, social, political, moral, and spiritual environment."

—**CHARLES DARWIN**, *Origin of Species*

We're moving into an entirely transformative world, and with transformation comes numerous new challenges and disruptions. The great news is that this new world holds the potential to significantly enhance our lives in every way possible, despite the difficulties and risks involved. We have a much greater and more powerful selection of tools and innovations in our arsenal than ever before. As such, we need not only new policies and initiatives, but a new "upgraded" collective mindset.

In essence, what we need is a new shared mindset of growth—one that is cognizant of our potential and always seeking to expand and learn, but humble enough to know that our past thinking will no longer lead to the future results we want, and thus change is needed.

Part of this new mindset involves embracing individual humility regardless of one's title, pedigree, wealth, or ranking in society's implicit hierarchy. After all, we cannot expect the world to change if we cannot change ourselves and, more importantly, deal with and leverage that change to our advantage.

We're dealing with a world that is far more complex than anything we've experienced in the past, and that will continue to become even more complex over time. Hence, there is no longer a single, dependable authority or school of thought that we can rely on to navigate this infinitely complex and dynamic world. We need to be less attached than ever to specific practices, especially outdated methods that have run their full course and are no longer applicable. We can continue to hold on to our core aspirations and ideals, since they are by definition infinitely applicable and timeless; our methods of achieving them, however, must be more flexible than ever.

Furthermore, we will need to be more experimental and analytical, trying out all kinds of methods and programs and keeping only what works. We must let the positive results of these experiments (or lack thereof) guide our subsequent decisions rather than remain fixated on our own past biased beliefs and behavior. This approach is what is demanded by the times and required to carry us into the future and unlock its promise, irrespective of one's role or domain.

We don't have enough time and resources to test everything ourselves, so we must be active, lifelong global learners, seeking to constantly understand from the experience of others. After all, as the world is becoming more globalized, humanity has more in common than ever before. Hence, what happens in the world is more relevant to us than ever before. I'm certainly not advocating blind copying; instead, we should look beyond our geographical and mental boundaries and consider the world itself as one big laboratory from which we can learn, and then apply those lessons within our own local scope.

Both the potential challenges and rewards ahead are immense. To succeed, a much more connected and collaborative approach is needed. Silo groups, closed networks, and shut societies are dead, or soon will be. They can no longer survive the global economy, so it's important to embrace those titanic shifts and work together as individuals, organizations, and societies at large.

For our ecosystem to develop and our economies to flourish, whether we're referring to the MENA region or anywhere else—be it Nairobi, Bangalore, Montevideo, Lisbon, or Boise, Idaho—the ingredients of success are the same: openness, proactiveness, humility, and collaboration. The more these ideas are reflected in our decision-making, our work ethic, our follow-through, and our general approach, the better the results.

These are obviously general principles or guidelines, and a great deal of effort must be made to infuse them into our everyday lives, thoughts, words, and actions. Nevertheless, if we do, I wager to say that great rewards await us.

Finally, we will need one additional virtue, without which none of the ones mentioned can be optimized—namely, courage: the courage to break away from what is holding us back and the courage to reinvent ourselves and, in effect, change ourselves. Change is good and changing to keep up with the times is critical. The world is changing faster than ever and we must do the same by calling on every tool we have at our disposal to be the change we seek. The above is true for all stakeholders playing a role in ecosystem building, including entrepreneurs, investors, service providers, and policy-makers.

Whoever you are, wherever you are—in the MENA region or elsewhere—and regardless of why you've selected this book to read, what you have in your hands are some of the best and latest thoughts and examples of ecosystem development from among the world's most brilliant minds and the region's most impactful individuals in this field. It's full of big ideas, yet it's up to you to utilize them to shape your own thinking and views on the topic, and to decide how to articulate them to educate and inspire others. And, ultimately, you and others must put those ideas into action and help to build your own local ecosystem your way.

CONTRIBUTOR PROFILES

ALI ABUKUMAIL
Senior Private Sector Specialistat the World Bank
www.worldbank.org

In 2012, Ali AbuKumail joined the World Bank, where he led projects in MENA that focused on the development of SMEs, entrepreneurship ecosystems, trail-based adventure tourism, and business environment reforms. Prior, he worked as a Private Sector Development Adviser to the Quartet Representative in 2009-2011, where he led policy dialogue and provided advice on private-sector development issues in Palestine. AbuKumail holds an MPA from the Harvard Kennedy School of Government and a BSc in Architectural Engineering from the Islamic University.

MAHMOUD ADI
Founding CEO of Hub71
www.hub71.com

Mahmoud Adi served as the Founding CEO of Hub71, which launched in March 2019, a one billion-dirham initiative driven by Mubadala and supported by the Abu Dhabi Government. Prior, Adi was Vice President of the Mubadala Technology, Manufacturing, and Mining (TM&M) platform, including at GLOBALFOUNDRIES, a semi-conductor Mubadala company, Mahmoud has extensive experience in major technology projects. He has designed strategic M&A deals and successfully delivered corporate venture programs. Mahmoud holds an MBA from Stanford Graduate School of Business and a BSc in Mechanical Engineering from the Petroleum Institute in Abu Dhabi with Honor and Distinction.

ISSA AGHABI
Investment Officer of IFC (International Finance Corporation), MENA and Pakistan
www.ifc.org/vc

Issa Aghabi has been in the finance and investment industry for over 15 years, with a focus on VC in the wider TMT (telecommunications, media, and technology) space. He has successfully closed 50-plus direct and indirect investment deals (ranging from $100,000 to $25 million per transaction), managed over $150 million in emerging market venture funds, and served as a board member for a number of companies. In, 2015 he led the exit of twofour54's two largest investments. In 2017, he led the exit of IFC's largest MENA direct deal, Souq. He also led the creation and launch of a leading accelerator in the MENA region. He currently heads IFC MENAP venture investments both from a direct (early-stage and growth capital) and indirect (accelerators and fund of funds) perspective. Issa holds an MBA with focus on strategy, entrepreneurship, M&A, and corporate finance from Cass Business School (City University of London) and a bachelor's degree in Commerce from Concordia University.

JOY AJLOUNY
Co-Founder of Fetchr
www.fetchr.us

Joy Ajlouny is the Co-Founder of Fetchr, a Silicon Valley–backed technology company based in Dubai that aims to solve the "no address" problem hindering e-commerce growth in emerging markets, especially in the Middle East. Joy was a key driver in facilitating $11 million in initial investment in Fetchr, as well as $41 million in a Series B round in 2017. Having raised over $72 million, the company now operates in five markets and was dubbed the number one startup in the Middle East by *Forbes* magazine. Prior to founding Fetchr, Joy launched and ran the e-commerce luxury fashion platform, Bonfaire. Bonfaire was acquired in 2013 by Moda Operandi, a fashion e-commerce giant owned by LVMH and Condé Nast. Joy is passionate about encouraging and investing knowledge in the young women of tomorrow. She is regularly invited to speak at forums and events across the world and most recently took the stage at the World Economic Forum in Jordan and BoF VOICES in the UK. Joy was born and raised in California.

ABDUL BASET AL JANAHI

CEO of Mohammed Bin Rashid Establishment for SMEs Development (Dubai SME)
www.sme.ae

Abdul Baset Al Janahi is currently the CEO of the Mohammed bin Rashid Establishment for SMEs development, an agency of the Department of Economic Development. He has become renowned for his support of aspiring entrepreneurs in the UAE, and for developing the SME ecosystem in Dubai. To date, under Al Janahi's leadership, more than 13,000 entrepreneurs have been assisted, of which about 1,200 are active members of the Establishment. As the CEO of Dubai SME, Al Janahi's main responsibilities are to formulate the long-term plan, strategies, and policy frameworks for SME development, and to execute strategic initiatives for the Dubai SME sector and entrepreneurs. Al Janahi is also the Vice Chairman and Managing Director of the Mohammad Bin Rashid Fund for SMEs, a member of the Board of Directors of Cooch4good in Dubai, and a member of Board of Directors of Tejuri.com (LLC).

ABDULAZIZ AL LOUGHANI

CEO of Floward, Managing Partner of Faith Capital, and former Co-Founder and Managing Partner of Talabat
www.floward.com; www.faithcapital.com; www.talabat.com

Abdulaziz Al Loughani is Co-Founder and CEO of Floward, a full-fledged flowers and gifts e-commerce platform. He is the Co-Founder and Managing Partner of Faith Capital, a venture capital practice that is focused on the GCC. Previously, Abdulaziz was the founding Executive Vice Chairman of the Kuwait National Fund for SMEs Development (2013-2017), a $7 billion independent public institution responsible for developing the entrepreneurial ecosystem in Kuwait. He was a Co-Founder and Managing Partner of Talabat.com until 2010, and since then he has been investing and involved in technology startups. Abdulaziz also previously served as Director at Global Capital Management, the alternative investments arm of Global Investment House "Global." Abdulaziz has served as an executive and board member on a number of companies across various sectors. Abdulaziz holds a bachelor's degree with a double major in Information Systems and E-Commerce from University of Toledo, and an MBA from London Business School.

AMMAR AL MALIK

Managing Director of Dubai Internet City and Dubai Outsource City, and Tech Lead at in5
www.dic.ae; www.dubaioutsourcecity.ae; www.infive.ae

Ammar Al Malik was appointed Managing Director of Dubai Internet City and Dubai Outsource City in 2016, following a successful stint as Business Development Director at the same organizations. Focused on strengthening the role of TECOM Group's ICT communities in enabling Dubai's growth, Ammar has been instrumental in shaping the development of a community in which Fortune 500 businesses, innovative entrepreneurs, and startups continue to thrive. With the convergence of ICT in business services, Ammar has helped nurture Dubai Outsource City to become equipped to respond to the evolving needs of global outsourcing firms. By leading the delivery of TECOM Group's innovation strategy across both communities, Ammar plays a crucial role in nurturing the next generation of home-grown enterprises led by forward-thinking and innovative tech entrepreneurs, primarily through the TECOM in5 innovation center. He holds an MBA in Business from Kwansei Gakuin University in Japan, a leading private institution renowned for producing highly influential leaders.

IDRISS AL RIFAI

Co-Founder and CEO of Fetchr
www.fetchr.us

In 2012, Idriss Al Rifai co-founded Fetchr, a Silicon Valley–backed technology company based in Dubai that aims to solve the "no address" problem hindering e-commerce growth in emerging markets, especially in the Middle East and North Africa region (MENA). Fetchr helps local merchants and global brands build, launch, and grow profitable e-commerce businesses. With easy-to-use, proprietary shipping, the Fetchr app and pick up and delivery software takes the hassle out of online shopping. Before founding Fetchr, Idriss was Director of Operations of MarkaVIP and a consultant with the Boston Consulting Group (BCG). He earned his master's degree at Institut d'Etudes Politiques de Paris and his MBA at the University of Chicago, Booth School of Business.

AREIJE AL SHAKAR

Senior Vice President of Bahrain Development Bank and
Director of Al Waha Venture Capital Fund of Funds
www.bdb-bh.com; www.alwahafund.com

Areije Al Shakar has 15 years of experience in banking and entrepreneurship. In her current role at Bahrain Development Bank (BDB), she is she is Senior Vice President of the Development Services Division. Her role and involvement at the bank include coaching, mentorship, startup seed funding, and entrepreneur development. She played a key role in establishing BDB's Rowad Program, a holistic entrepreneur support platform, and the SeedFuel-Rowad startup funding program, which is managed and run out of Development Services and is part of the Global Accelerator Network. She has worked in reputable organizations such as Investcorp, Citibank, BNP Paribas, and Lehman Brothers in the treasury, investment management, and advisory areas. She holds a MSc in Public Policy and Management from the School of Oriental and African Studies (SOAS), University of London, a Bachelor of Commerce in Finance from the John Molson School of Business, Concordia University, and is a Certified Business Coach and Mentor through the Chartered Management Institute, UK.

YASMEEN AL SHARAF

Head of the FinTech and Innovation Unit at Central Bank of
Bahrain (CBB)
www.cbb.gov.bh

Yasmeen Al Sharaf is Heading the FinTech and Innovation Unit at the Central Bank of Bahrain (CBB), tasked with setting up a conducive ecosystem to facilitate a robust regulatory framework that fosters innovation within the financial services sector. Yasmeen has been working with the CBB for 14 years, and has held the post of Superintendent, Licensing Research and Development in the Licensing Directorate at the CBB for 7 years. Prior, she was a Senior Analyst in the same directorate. During her time at the Licensing Directorate, Yasmeen got to work closely with banks, investment companies, insurance companies, financing companies, and ancillary service providers, both local and international. She gained insight and a thorough understanding of Bahrain's regulatory framework governing all sectors in the financial services industry. Prior to joining CBB, Yasmeen worked briefly in the banking sector. Yasmeen also sits on multiple committees handling different key initiatives that revolve around FinTech and innovation, including as Vice Chair of the Regulatory Sandbox Applications Committee at the CBB. She has also been selected as one of the Top 100 Women in FinTech 2019 by Lattice80 Hub in collaboration with Miss Kaya. Yasmeen holds a BSc in Banking and Finance from the University of Bahrain.

MAZIN ALZAIDI
Director of Innovation of Entrepreneurship of Saudi Arabian General Investment Authority (SAGIA)
www.sagia.gov.sa

Dr. Mazin AlZaidi is currently part of the Investment Attraction and Development team at the Saudi Arabian General Investment Authority (SAGIA), specializing in venture investment development. A key focus of his work is the continuous attraction of startups and VCs to support the development of the startup ecosystem in the Kingdom. Prior, Dr. AlZaidi worked as a consultant at EY Advisory Services in Riyadh. As an entrepreneur, Dr. AlZaidi spent eight years in the startup tech and innovation ecosystem in London. He launched his own business during his postgraduate studies in the UK. He has led the design and delivery of entrepreneurship development programs for Saudi entrepreneurs in London, Tokyo, and San Francisco. Dr. AlZaidi holds a bachelor's degree in Computer Engineering, two master's degrees, and a PhD in Cyber Security. He conducted his PhD research at the Cyber Security Center in the International Digital Lab (IDL) at the University of Warwick, UK. Dr. AlZaidi's research in cybersecurity focuses on the protection of intellectual assets within agile dynamic business environments in large corporates. He is also a guest lecturer on corporate innovation at the University of Warwick.

EYAD ALKASSAR
CEO of Rocket Internet ME
www.rocket-internet.com

Eyad Alkassar holds a PhD Summa Cum Laude in Computer Science from Saarland University. During his studies he was a fellow of the German National Academic Foundation. Since he joined Rocket Internet as CEO, Middle East, Eyad has co-founded and run over a dozen companies, which raised hundreds of millions of dollars in funding. Some of them are now among the largest tech companies in the Middle East, fulfilling millions of orders daily. Among others, Eyad is a Co-Founder of Snapp (one of the largest internet companies in the Middle East) and Namshi.com. In 2018, he was honored as a Young Global Leader by the World Economic Forum.

OMAR ALMAJDOUIE

Founding Partner of Raed Ventures
www.raed.vc

Omar Almajdouie is the Founding Partner and CEO of Raed Ventures, a Saudi venture capital firm owned by Almajdouie Holding, which invests in seed and early-stage startups in the MENA region. He is the former CEO of Almajdouie Manufacturing LLC and has over 17 years of enriched experience in various managerial and executive positions. As an investor and entrepreneur, Omar founded Raed Ventures in 2016 as part of Almajdouie Holding's diversification strategy. Omar is the Vice Chairman of the Saudi Venture Capital and Private Equity Association, and a board member of several leading tech companies.

MARYAM EID ALMHEIRI

Vice-Chair of twofour54
www.twofour54.com

Her Excellency Maryam Eid AlMheiri was appointed Vice-Chair to the Board of Directors of twofour54 Abu Dhabi in June 2019, after leading the Media Zone Authority and twofour54 as Chief Executive Officer. H.E. Maryam Eid AlMheiri is also the Director-General of the Abu Dhabi Government Media Office, and the Chairwoman of Bidaya Media, a leading edutainment company. Her Excellency holds a TRIUM Global Executive MBA jointly issued by New York University Stern School of Business, London School of Economics and Political Science, and HEC Paris School of Management. She also holds a master's in Strategy and National Security Studies, issued by the National Defense College in Abu Dhabi. H.E. Maryam completed her undergraduate studies in Accounting and Business Administration with distinction and honors at the UAE's Higher Colleges of Technology.

NAJLA AL-MIDFA

CEO of Sharjah Entrepreneurship Center (Sheraa)
www.sheraa.ae

Najla Al-Midfa is CEO of the Sharjah Entrepreneurship Center (Sheraa), a government-supported entity launched in 2016, with a mandate to build the entrepreneurial ecosystem in Sharjah and support entrepreneurs as they build and grow innovative startups that will contribute positively to the region's economy. To date, Sheraa has built a portfolio of over 70 startups, which have raised over $37 million, created more than 500 jobs, and generated over $24 million in cumulative revenue. Sheraa also hosts the annual Sharjah Entrepreneurship Festival (SharjahEF), a gathering of more than 3,000 entrepreneurs, investors, mentors, and ecosystem supporters. Prior to leading Sheraa, Najla was Senior Manager at Khalifa Fund for Enterprise Development. Prior, Najla was a Senior Associate at McKinsey and Company's New York office. Her experience also includes roles at PWC and Shell. Najla is the Founder of Khayarat, a platform that empowers young, high-potential Emiratis to make informed career choices. Najla is a board member of United Arab Bank, Vice Chairperson of Young Arab Leaders, and a board member of Endeavor UAE. She is also a fellow of the Aspen Institute's Middle East Leadership Initiative. In 2019, she was selected to be an Eisenhower Global Fellow. Najla holds an MBA from Stanford University.

DEEMAH ALYAHYA

Founder of WomenSpark
@dalyahya

Deemah Alyahya is a tech pioneer. At Microsoft, where she led Developer Experience and Digital Innovation, she was the first Saudi female to be appointed as an Executive Director. She was a consultant for various government and private organizations in the fields of innovation and digital economy and led Saudi Arabia's national digital transformation strategy. With a commitment to support Saudi females, Deemah has launched and led several initiatives that focus on enabling women in the IT Industry and enhancing their skills to meet the highest standards of the Saudi labor markets. This led her to establish the WomenSpark Initiative. Deemah Alyahya seeks to move Saudi youth to the forefront of digital nations by developing a technical ecosystem built primarily around Saudi talents.

RABEA ATAYA

Co-Founder and CEO of Bayt.com
www.bayt.com

Rabea Ataya is focused on providing employment opportunities for Middle Eastern youth by helping to develop both the internet and SME sectors in the region. Rabea is the Co-Founder and CEO of Bayt.com, the Middle East's leading job site, which now serves more than 36.5 million professionals and 40,000 employers from its 12 regional offices. He co-founded Gonabit.com, the region's first group purchasing site; InfoFort, the Middle East's first and leading records management company; and he serves on the boards of several Middle Eastern technology companies. Rabea also served on the board of the Queen Rania Foundation, which is focused on empowering youth through education in the region. Rabea is a graduate of Stanford University with a BSc in Electrical Engineering and an MSc in Engineering Economic Systems.

DAVID AUDRETSCH

Distinguished Professor Ameritech Chair of Economic Development at Indiana University and Co-Author of *Entrepreneurial Ecosystems*
https://oneill.indiana.edu/

David Audretsch is a Distinguished Professor and Ameritech Chair of Economic Development at Indiana University, where he also serves as Director of the Institute for Development Strategies. Audretsch's research is focused on the links between entrepreneurship, government policy, innovation, economic development, and global competitiveness. He is also Co-Author of *The Seven Secrets of Germany* (Oxford University Press). He is Co-Founder and Editor-in-Chief of *Small Business Economics: An Entrepreneurship Journal*. He was awarded the Global Award for Entrepreneurship Research by the Swedish Foundation for Entrepreneurship. He has received honorary doctorates from the University of Augsburg, Jonköping University, and the University of Siegen, among others. Audretsch is member of the Advisory Board of the American Center for Entrepreneurship in Washington, DC and others.

BILL AULET

Managing Director of the Martin Trust Center for MIT Entrepreneurship and Author of *Disciplined Entrepreneurship: 24 Steps to a Successful Startup*
www.d-eship.com

Bill Aulet is changing the way entrepreneurship is understood, taught, and practiced around the world. He is an award-winning educator and author whose current work is built on the foundation of his successful 25-year business career, first at IBM and then as a three-time serial entrepreneur. During this time, he directly raised over $100 million and created hundreds of millions of dollars of shareholder value through his companies. Since 2009, he has been responsible for leading the development of entrepreneurship education across MIT at the Trust Center. Bill's first book, Disciplined Entrepreneurship, released in 2013, has been translated into more than 20 languages and has provided the content for three online edX courses, which have been taken by hundreds of thousands of people in 199 different countries. The accompanying follow-up book, Disciplined Entrepreneurship Workbook was released in 2017. He is widely published and many of his articles can be found at www.d-eship.com. He has degrees from Harvard and MIT and is a board member of public and private companies. On 2017, Bill was named a Professor of the Practice at MIT Sloan.

AMR AWADALAH

Vice President of Developer Relations at Google Cloud and former Co-Founder and Global CTO of Cloudera
www.linkedin.com/in/awadallah

Amr Awadallah (@awadallah) is the Vice President of Developer Relations at Google Cloud. Prior, Amr was the Co-Founder and Global CTO of Cloudera. Before co-founding Cloudera, Amr was an entrepreneur-in-residence at Accel Partners. He served as Vice President of Product Intelligence Engineering at Yahoo! and ran one of the very first organizations to use Hadoop for data analysis and business intelligence. Amr joined Yahoo! after they acquired his first startup, VivaSmart, in July 2000. Amr holds a bachelor's and master's degree in Electrical Engineering from Cairo University, Egypt, and a doctorate in Electrical Engineering from Stanford University.

OMAR AYYASH

Ambassador of the UAE Innovation and Entrepreneurship
Program at Higher Colleges of Technology
www.hct.ac.ae

Omar Ayyash currently leads many of the innovation and entrepreneurship initiatives for a UAE-based educational institution and is a program ambassador for the Ministry of Education / Stanford University innovation and entrepreneurship initiative focused on entrepreneurship curriculum and ecosystem development. His areas of expertise are entrepreneurship, globalization, and business ethics. He has helped several students take part in national and international competitions such as the CERT/Wharton Entrepreneurial Planning and Innovation competition. He has launched several successful annual events promoting entrepreneurship, including celebrating Global Entrepreneurship Week, a worldwide initiative hosted by over 80 countries, and LEQA—Learning from Entrepreneurs through Questions and Answers. Omar holds a bachelor's degree in Business Administration with an emphasis in Marketing from the University of Kentucky. He also earned an MBA with a concentration in Entrepreneurial Studies from the University of Louisville in 2000. He is finalizing his Doctorate in Business Administration with a focus on how MENA technology entrepreneurs successfully manage working capital.

BIJAN AZAD

Director of Center for Innovation Management and
Entrepreneurship at the American University of Beirut (AUB)
www.aub.edu.lb

Dr. Bijan Azad teaches in Suliman S. Olayan School of Business Executive MBA, Executive Education, and MBA programs. Dr. Azad pioneered the popular experiential Startup Acceleration Practicum graduate course at AUB (modeled after Steve Blank's Lean LaunchPad), a critical ingredient for developing an investible startup. In 2016, he designed AUB's Growth Readiness Program, supported in part by USAID, which focuses on overcoming scaleup challenges for companies wanting to exceed $5 million in revenue. He is also very active in the startup ecosystem, serving as a boot camp mentor/instructor at Flat6Labs and SPEED accelerator, and as a mentor at the IM-Capital MIT Venture Mentoring Service. In 1988, Dr. Azad was Co-Founder of GIS/Trans, a successful map technology startup in Cambridge, Massachusetts, which was acquired later by Google

Maps. In 2001, he co-founded another successful map technology startup, International Land Information Systems (acquired by ARCADIS in 2003) in Arnhem, Netherlands. Dr. Azad holds PhD and master's degrees from Massachusetts Institute of Technology.

PHILIP BAHOSHY
Founder and CEO of MAGNiTT
www.magnitt.com

Philip Bahoshy is the Founder and CEO of MAGNiTT, the largest investment data platform in the MENA startup ecosystem; it includes investors, entrepreneurs, and corporates. Raised in the UK with Iraqi origins, Philip obtained an MBA from INSEAD in 2013 and a BSc in Economics from the London School of Economics. Philip worked at Oliver Wyman in the Financial Services practice for three years, followed by three years at Barclays Wealth as Chief of Staff to the CEO, where he advised on strategic initiatives. Philip has lived in the UAE for more than 12 years and is passionate about developing the MENA startup ecosystem.

SHADI BANNA
Founder and CEO of Potential.com
www.potential.com

Shadi Banna is the Founder and CEO of Potential.com, a pioneer in EdTech and a leading provider of blended learning solutions across emerging markets. By developing innovative learning solutions to fuel the world's ambition, Potential.com empowers millions of individuals and companies from over 30 different countries to perform at their very best. Shadi works closely with several startups, incubators, and business schools to provide strategic mentoring and coaching support. Prior to founding Potential.com, Shadi held several leadership roles within the ICT sector, including at SafeNet (Gemalto), HP, and NCR. Shadi is an MBA graduate from Heriot-Watt University and also has a bachelor's degree in Computer and Communications Engineering from the American University of Beirut. In 2008, he completed the Executive Entrepreneurship program at the Carnegie Mellon University.

AMIR BARSOUM

Co-Founder and CEO of Vezeeta
www.vezeeta.com

Amir Barsoum is the Co-Founder and CEO of Vezeeta.com, the first digital healthcare booking platform in MENA, launched in late 2012. Vezeeta is an innovative platform in the healthcare industry that's focused on solving numerous challenges in healthcare. Amir is also an Endeavor Entrepreneur, on the Board of Directors of Endeavor Egypt, and a board member of the Entrepreneurs' Organization. He holds an MBA from the American University in Cairo, a Bachelor of Pharmacy from Ain Shams University, and an Executive Education Certificate about scaling startups from Harvard Business School.

AHMAD SUFIAN BAYRAM

Regional Manager of Techstars, MENA and SSA (sub-Saharan Africa)
www.techstars.com

Ahmad Sufian Bayram is a social entrepreneur, author, and strategy and creative leader in technology. Ahmad is the Regional Manager of Techstars in Middle East and North Africa (MENA) and Sub-Saharan Africa (SSA), a worldwide network that helps entrepreneurs succeed, which operates in 150 countries with a portfolio of over 1,500 companies, which operate in 150 countries. Since 2012, Ahmad has been supporting hundreds of Syrians to gain access to entrepreneurship opportunities and build a supportive environment. Ahmad is also a Jusoor's entrepreneurship program manager, an adviser in the Techfugee Board, and Entrepreneur in Residence at Aliqtsadi. Ahmad published the book *Entrepreneurship in Conflict Zones*, highlighting the experiences and needs of Syrian entrepreneurs in the country during the conflict, and a second book, *Entrepreneurship in Exile*, which provides insights into Syrian refugees' startups in host countries. Ahmad has also appeared in top-tier publications such as the *World Economic Forum*, *Forbes*, *The Guardian*, *Financial Times*, *The Wall Street Journal*, *The Huffington Post*, and many others. He has presented on top stages including the EU Parliament, the World Bank, Wilton Park, the Goethe Institut, Google, SPARK Ignite, Techfugees Summit, Startup Istanbul, and others.

ANDREW BERKOWITZ

Founder and CEO of Global Startup Media
www.globalstartupmedia.com

Andrew Berkowitz is the Founder and CEO of Global Startup Media, a podcast media company creating highly produced, award-winning podcasts, syndicated op-eds, omnichannel media projects, and in-depth fringe insights. It also produces branded podcasts for companies, governments, and conferences. Global Startup Media has done work with brands worldwide including Web Summit, the iHub, MEST Africa, and Collision Conference. Andrew hosts the "Global Startup Movement" podcast, an iTunes #1 New and Noteworthy Technology podcast, on which he covers emerging and frontier market startup ecosystems. Andrew is also the Director and Host of Global Startup Media's portfolio of shows including The Global Startup Movement. Andrew attended Virginia Tech and currently resides in the Washington, DC Metro Area.

MAX BORDERS

Executive Director at Social Evolution and Author of *The Social Singularity*
www.linkedin.com/in/maxborders

Max Borders is Author of *The Social Singularity: A Decentralist Manifesto*. Max is Founder of Social Evolution, Inc., a company dedicated to creating a world of mutual benefit and "liberating humanity through innovation." Max is also Founder of its nonprofit sibling, Social Evolution Foundation. He is a widely published writer and Co-Founder of the event experience Future Frontiers.

ALBERT BRAVO-BIOSCA

Director of Innovation Growth Lab at Nesta
www.nesta.org.uk

Albert Bravo-Biosca is the Founding Director of the Innovation Growth Lab (IGL), a global partnership based at Nesta that brings together governments, foundations, and researchers to develop and test new approaches to increase innovation, support high-growth entrepreneurship, and accelerate business growth. IGL aims to make innovation and growth policy more experimental and evidence-based, in order to improve the design of the programs and institutions. Among other subjects, his research has looked at the drivers of venture capital performance, the linkages between financial institutions and innovative performance, and the effectiveness of innovation policy. Albert holds a PhD and MA in Economics from Harvard University, an MSc in Economics from the London School of Economics, and a BA in Economics from Universitat Pompeu Fabra. He has also been a visiting economist at the OECD and a consultant for the World Bank.

ERIK BRYNJOLFSSON

Director of the MIT Initiative on Digital Economy, Professor at MIT Sloan School, and Co-Author of *The Second Machine Age*
http://digital.mit.edu/erik/

Erik Brynjolfsson is Director of the MIT Initiative on the Digital Economy, Professor at MIT Sloan School, and Research Associate at NBER. His research examines the effects of information technologies on business strategy, productivity and performance, digital commerce, and intangible assets. At MIT, he teaches courses on the Economics of Information and the Analytics Lab. He is the Author or Co-Author of several books including, with Co-Author Andrew McAfee, *Machine Platform Crowd: Harnessing our Digital Future* (2017) and the New York Times bestseller *The Second Machine Age: Work, Progress and Prosperity in a Time of Brilliant Technologies* (2014). Brynjolfsson is also editor of SSRN's Information System Network and has served on the editorial boards of numerous academic journals.

STEVE CASE

Chairman and CEO of Revolution LLC, Chairman of the Case Foundation, Co-Founder of AOL, and Author of *The Third Wave*
www.revolution.com; www.casefoundation.com; www.aol.com

Steve Case is one of America's best-known and most accomplished entrepreneurs and philanthropists, and a pioneer in making the internet part of everyday life. Case co-founded AOL in 1985. Under his leadership and vision, AOL became the world's largest and most valuable internet company, driving the worldwide adoption of the internet. As Chairman and CEO of Revolution LLC, a Washington, DC–based investment firm, Case launched the Rise of the Rest, a platform to shine a spotlight on entrepreneurs outside of Silicon Valley, New York, and Boston. He was the founding Chair of the Startup America Partnership—an effort launched at the White House to accelerate high-growth entrepreneurship throughout the nation—and a member of President Obama's Council on Jobs and Competitiveness, where he chaired the subcommittee on entrepreneurship. Case serves as Chairman of the Case Foundation. He is also the Author of the New York Times bestselling book, The Third Wave: An Entrepreneur's Vision of the Future.

PATRICK CHALHOUB
CEO of the Chalhoub Group
www.chalhoubgroup.com

Patrick Chalhoub is the CEO of the Chalhoub Group, a leading partner for luxury across the Middle East. The Group manages over 700 retail outlets and has been a member of the United Nations Global Compact Community since 2014. It is also a signatory of the Women's Empowerment Principles (WEP). Initially joining the Group in 1979. Named retailer of the year at the 2011 CEO Middle East Awards, Patrick Chalhoub plays a prominent role in promoting the Group's rich legacy through active involvement in the French Business Council in Dubai, and has set up various scholarship funds in Lebanon. He was also awarded the Chevalier de l'Ordre National du Mérite by the French Government and has been a Chevalier de l'Ordre National de la Légion d'Honneur since January 2016. In June 2018, the United Nations Secretary-General appointed Chalhoub to the Board of the UN Global Compact.

ANAND CHOPRA-MCGOWAN
Vice President and Managing Director of General Assembly, Europe, Middle East, and Asia Pacific
www.generalassemb.ly

Anand Chopra-McGowan leads General Assembly's (GA's) enterprise business in the Europe, Middle East, and Asia Pacific regions. General Assembly is a global education startup focused on helping individuals and large companies build the skills they need to succeed in the digital age. GA operates in 25 cities around the world and online, has graduated over 70,000 individuals, and works with over 350 large companies including Walmart,

GE, Visa, L'Oréal, Lloyds Banking Group, and more. General Assembly was named the most innovative education company in the world by *Fast Company* magazine. In November 2017, GA was named as one of the 25 most disruptive startups by LinkedIn. Anand has been with the company since its founding in 2011, filling various roles over the past seven years. He is also responsible for GA's work with consumer products companies globally. He manages teams in London, Sydney, and New York City. Anand is a member of GA's global leadership team.

SANGEET PAUL CHOUDARY

Founder of Platformation Labs and Co-Author of *Platform Revolution and Platform Scale*
www.platformthinkinglabs.com

Sangeet Paul Choudary, the bestselling Author of *Platform Revolution* and *Platform Scale*, has advised the leadership of 25 Fortune 500 firms and has been selected as a Young Global Leader by the World Economic Forum. His work on platforms was selected by *Harvard Business Review* as one of the top 10 business ideas for 2017. He is a frequent keynote speaker at leading global forums including the G20 Summit, the World50 Summit, the United Nations, and the World Economic Forum. Sangeet's work has been selected as one of the top 10 articles on business model innovation ever published in the *Harvard Business Review*.

HANS HENRIK CHRISTENSEN

Vice President of Dubai Technology Entrepreneur Campus (Dtec), a department of Dubai Silicon Oasis Authority (DSOA)
www.dtec.ae

Hans Henrik Christensen holds a BA in Finance, a degree from Bentley, an MBA from Hult, and is a PhD candidate at Tübingen. Hans also earned certificates from Oxford and MIT in Blockchain and AI. For the past seven years, he has led Dtec, the largest tech hub in MENA with more than 800 startups from 71 nations. Dtec has helped create 3,000 jobs and brought $300 million into the local economy. Dtec excels in providing co-working spaces, acceleration, incubation, labs, events, learning, venture capital, and corporate innovation. Hans founded and ran several startups and departments at multinationals on different continents, including the first incubator at Siemens. Hans also serves as a Board Director and adviser for startups and universities. Dtec has won nine awards under Hans's leadership.

OMAR CHRISTIDIS
Founder and CEO of ArabNet
www.arabnet.me

Omar Christidis is an entrepreneur and ecosystem builder who has built deep expertise on digital disruption across sectors. He holds multiple positions, including Founder and CEO of ArabNet, which produces leading events, insights, and innovation programs focused on the technology and innovation industry in the MENA region, and Partner and Board Member at Lebanon Seed Fund, a $20 million early-stage fund aimed at supporting 100 Lebanese startups. The fund has invested in 33 startups to date. Omar is actively involved in advising government leaders on digital innovation. He is a founding Board Member of IDEAS, a nonprofit association supported by the Prime Minister of Lebanon that focuses on developing public-private partnerships to enable the innovation ecosystem in Lebanon. He also serves on the Private Sector Advisory Group for the Lebanese Minister of Technology and Investment. Omar holds a BA and an MBA from Yale University and is the Co-Founder of the Yale Arab Alumni Association.

PETER COHAN
Lecturer of Strategy at Babson College and Author of *Startup Cities*
www.babson.edu

Peter Cohan is Lecturer of Strategy at Babson College, teaching strategy and entrepreneurship to undergraduate and MBA students. He is the Founding Principal of Peter S Cohan and Associates, a management consulting and venture capital firm. He has completed over 150 growth-strategy consulting projects for global technology companies and invested in seven startups, three of which were sold for over $2 billion. Peter has written 14 books and writes columns on entrepreneurship for *Forbes* and *Inc*. He also appeared in the film, *We the People: The Market Basket Effect*. Prior to starting his firm, he worked as a case team leader for Harvard Business School professor Michael Porter's consulting firm and taught at MIT, Stanford, and the University of Hong Kong. Peter earned an MBA from Wharton, did graduate work in computer science at MIT, and holds a BSc in Electrical Engineering from Swarthmore College.

ROBERTO CROCI

Managing Director of Microsoft for Startups, MEA (Middle East and Africa)
www.microsoft.com

As the Managing Director at Microsoft for Startups MEA, Roberto Croci is passionate about empowering startups achieve their goals by promoting their tech solutions and enabling them to unlock the right opportunities for growth. Roberto joined the Microsoft for Startups team with a wide range of knowledge, having previously worked as the Regional Head for Google's EMEA Emerging Markets. In that role, he helped businesses by building and mentoring teams that could successfully penetrate new markets and ensure sustainable revenue growth. He has specialized in leadership development as a Harvard Business School graduate with a proven track-record of creating successful teams and growing businesses in unpredictable environments.

TIM DRAPER

Founder of Draper Associates, DFJ, and Draper University; and Author of *The Startup Hero:*
www.draper.vc; www.dfj.com; www.draperuniversity.com

Tim Draper is a top global venture capitalist and Founder of Draper Associates, DFJ, and the Draper Venture Network, a global network of venture capital funds. The firms' investments include Coinbase, Skype, Tesla, Baidu, Hotmail, SolarCity, SpaceX, and many others. He is a leading spokesperson for Bitcoin, blockchain, ICOs, and cryptocurrencies. He created viral marketing. He is regularly featured on all major networks and has received various awards and honors including the World Entrepreneurship Forum's Entrepreneur of the World. He is listed among top 100 most powerful people in finance by *Worth Magazine*, the top 20 most influential people in crypto by *CryptoWeekly*, most networked VC by *AlwaysOn*, number seven on the *Forbes* Midas List, and number 48 among most influential Harvard alumni. He created Draper University of Heroes and authored a popular entrepreneur's textbook called *How to be The Startup Hero*. He created a crowdsourced TV series with Sony Network called *Meet The Drapers*. He started Innovate Your State. He served on the California State Board of Education. Tim Draper received a Bachelor of Science from Stanford University and an MBA from the Harvard Business School.

AHMED EL ALFI

Chairman of Sawari Ventures, Founder and Chairman of the GrEEK Campus, and Co-Founder of Flat6Labs
www.sawariventures.com; www.thegreekcampus.com; www.flat6labs.com

Ahmed El Alfi is the Co-Founder and Chairman of Sawari Ventures, a leading venture capital firm based in Cairo; Founder and Chairman of The Greek Campus, a startup innovation hub; and Co-Founder of Flat6Labs, the largest accelerator in MENA. Named as one of the most creative people in the world by Fast Company magazine, Alfi has been an investor for the past 25 years and has extensive experience in funding and supporting the growth of early-stage companies. He grew up in California and relocated to Egypt in 2006 as the CEO of EFG-Hermes Private Equity. Prior, he co-founded Hybrid Capital Partners, a private investment partnership. Alfi is passionate about building a venture capital industry with an ethos that centers around enabling young people to realize their innovative ideas and solve societal challenges using technology, and one that changes perceptions about the opportunities the startup ecosystem in the MENA region presents. In 2011, Sawari created and funded Flat6Labs, its own startup accelerator. Flat6Labs has since grown to become the region's premier startup accelerator with operations in five countries.

HISHAM ELARABY

Regional Director of Udacity, MENA
www.udacity.com

Hisham Elaraby is the Regional Director for MENA at Udacity, a Silicon Valley–based online education platform with a mission to power careers through tech education. Hisham joined Udacity in 2017 to lead the establishment and expansion of Udacity in the MENA region. Before joining Udacity, Hisham was the Industry Head of Automotive and Mobile at Google MENA. In that role, he led the execution of Google's largest ecosystem investment in the region, the Mobile App Launchpad, in partnership with Egypt's Ministry of Information Technology (MCIT) and Udacity. Hisham has a background in consulting with McKinsey and Company. Prior to that, he obtained his MBA from INSEAD and his undergraduate degree in Economics from the American University in Cairo.

DINA EL-MOFTY

CEO of Injaz Egypt
www.injaz-egypt.org

Dina El-Mofty is the Founder and CEO of Injaz Egypt, an organization with a strong educational focus on entrepreneurship and work readiness. It is part of the Junior Achievement worldwide network. Injaz works in partnership with schools and universities across Egypt, and has helped more than half a million young people through its entrepreneurial and work readiness programs. The organization also supports young entrepreneurs through its startup incubator and helps them launch and accelerate their businesses. Injaz has seed funded and supported more than 60 successful startup businesses. Nominated as one of the world's most influential Arabs under 40 by Arabian Business, she received their Young Achiever of the Year award for 2016. She was also the recipient of the Women's Top 50 Award for top-performing women in Egypt for 2016. She served as a judge on the popular TV show on CBC, *Hona Al Shabab*. Dina holds a graduate degree from the Fletcher School at Tufts University, pursued undergraduate studies at Georgetown University, and graduated from the American University in Cairo. She also holds professional degrees from Penn State, INSEAD, and Harvard.

DANY FARHA

Co-Founder and Managing Partner of BECO Capital
www.becocapital.com

Dany Farha is the Co-Founder and Managing Partner of BECO Capital, a venture capital firm that provides early-stage growth capital and hands-on operational support for technology companies in the MENA region, with a focus on the GCC. Farha has a 20-year track record in the region as a successful serial entrepreneur and investor. Prior to co-founding BECO Capital, Farha co-founded and exited Bayt.com, Butlers (the UAE's largest commercial laundry company), and Intercat (one of the largest catering companies in the UAE). He was also a seed investor in Gonabit, a Middle East-focused daily deal website that was acquired by Living Social in 2011. A graduate of UCL (University College London) in Management Sciences and Finance, he currently sits on the boards of Property Finder and other portfolio companies.

BRAD FELD

Co-Founder of Foundry Group and Techstars, and Author of *Startup Communities: Building an Entrepreneurial Ecosystem in Your City*
www.foundrygroup.com; www.techstars.com

Brad Feld has been an early-stage investor and entrepreneur since 1987. Prior to co-founding Foundry Group, he co-founded Mobius Venture Capital and, prior to that, founded Intensity Ventures. Brad is also a Co-Founder of Techstars. Brad is a writer and speaker on the topics of venture capital investment and entrepreneurship. He has written a number of books as part of the *Startup Revolution* series. Most notably, he authored *Startup Communities: Building an Entrepreneurial Ecosystem in Your City* in 2012. The book was ground-breaking in distilling the key pillars of ecosystem development. Other titles, Brad wrote, include *Venture Deals, Startup Boards, Do More Faster, Startup Opportunities, Startup Life*, and others. He also writes the blogs "Feld Thoughts" and "Venture Deals." Feld holds Bachelor of Science and Master of Science degrees in Management Science from the Massachusetts Institute of Technology.

ELISSA FREIHA

Founder and Director of Womena
www.womena.com

Elissa Freiha is an angel investor, motivational speaker, and Founder of Womena, a Dubai-based angel investment platform. Womena focuses on empowering women to invest in MENA tech startups. Womena has simplified the investment process by managing deals, from sourcing and vetting through diligence and portfolio management. As an active angel with over 40 investments, she has won numerous awards, including being the first female recipient of Investor of the Year at the StartUp Awards. She is frequently listed by media outlets, most notably by the BBC, as one of their 30 Women Under 30, and by *Arabian Business* as one of the 100 most influential Arabs. Elissa received her Bachelor of Arts in Global Communications from the American University of Paris. She is a strong advocate for equal rights and women's rights, with a focus on the MENA region. Her passions for entrepreneurship and gender diversity have given her opportunity to speak at events around the world.

VERA FUTORJANSKI
Innovation Director at 500 Startups
www.500.co

Vera Futorjanski is in charge of Innovation for the Middle East region and Russia for the global venture capital firm 500 Startups. She advises corporates and governments on innovation and helps them build thriving ecosystems. Vera is also a strong female empowerment supporter and a social impact advocate. Vera serves as a Global Ambassador and mentor for Vital Voices, an NGO led by Hillary Clinton and Madeleine Albright that works with women leaders. She is a founding member of the Dubai Future Accelerators, an initiative of the Dubai Government to accelerate innovation. Prior, Vera was the Founder of a tech startup in MENA. Before that Vera ran the global communications for Rocket Internet during its IPO—the largest tech IPO in Germany in a decade. Before her career in the tech and innovation world, Vera completed her MSc at the London School of Economics and worked as a political consultant at the European Union in Brussels.

ADRIAN GARCIA-ARANYOS
President of Endeavor
www.endeavor.org

Adrian Garcia-Aranyos is the President of Endeavor Global, a not-for-profit focused on scaling high-impact entrepreneurs. He was previously the Founding Managing Director at Endeavor Spain, Vice President of Media Relations for Latin America at JP Morgan Chase and Co, Americas Marketing Director and Latin America Co-Head for The Economist Newspaper Group, Foreign Trade Manager at the Spain-US Chamber of Commerce, and Foreign Exchange and Money Markets Broker at CM Capital Markets in Madrid. Since 2004, Mr. Garcia-Aranyos serves as board member at Thune Eureka. He obtained a BA in Political Science from Universidad Complutense de Madrid (2000); a Banking and Finance Certificate at IEB Madrid (2001); a master's in Trade and Commerce at CECO Madrid (2003-04); a Marketing Certificate at Kellogg Chicago (2010); an SEP at IESE NY/Miami (2013-14); and a Scaling Entrepreneurial Ventures Certificate at Harvard Business School (2015).

JF GAUTHIER
Founder and CEO of Startup Genome
www.startupgenome.com

JF Gauthier is a Silicon Valley serial entrepreneur and Founder and CEO of Startup Genome. He advises more than 30 governments across 25 countries on how to accelerate the growth of their entrepreneurial ecosystems through evidence-based policy-making. He is also an active angel investor and startup adviser and the Co-Founder of Exit Reality, a fast-growing VR startup. Based on the input of more than 10,000 entrepreneurs and 300 local partner organizations in more than 50 cities across 28 countries, Startup Genome has built the largest body of knowledge on what fuels the performance of startups and their ecosystems. Based in Silicon Valley for 20 years, JF has founded and played pivotal roles in numerous companies in the tech, life sciences, and clean tech sectors. He has also led several exits and acquisitions on both sides of the table. He has an MBA from Harvard Business School.

YOUSEF HAMZA
Partner at V7 Group
www.v7group.com

Yousef Hamza was educated in Kuwait and the UAE, then earned a law degree from the University of Cardiff in the UK. Having worked as a lawyer for two years, Yousef then moved to Envestors, one of the first angel networks in the Middle East, assisting in legal, strategic, and developmental aspects. His current scope of practice falls under one umbrella, V7 Group. This includes four pillars: legal, accounting, capital, and digital services for entrepreneurs and startups. Having invested in multiple startups, and with a portfolio of successful SMEs in the region, he sets up and manages funds for his own capital, his family, and other family offices.

WALID HANNA

Co-Founder and CEO of Middle East Venture Partners (MEVP)
www.mevp.com

Walid Hanna has been active in venture capital and new venture development for the past 19 years, with more than 50 VC investments executed since 2010 and numerous exits. He is the CEO of MEVP, a Middle East–focused venture capital firm that invests in the early and growth stages of innovative companies. With over $260 million in assets under management (AUM), it is the largest and most established VC firm in the region. The funds are technology focused and are managed by a team of 20 investment professionals in MEVP's offices in Dubai, Beirut, Riyadh, and Bahrain. Prior to founding MEVP and growing its AUM to $260 million, Walid was the CEO of Dubai International Capital's venture arm, the Arab Business Angels Network (ABAN), which managed a regional seed venture fund and was the first business angel network in the Arab world. In 2017, Mr. Mohamed Alabbar acquired a non-controlling stake in MEVP. Walid has received a bachelor's degree in Economics from McGill University (Canada), and a master's in Finance from HEC (France).

OSSAMA HASSANEIN

Chairman of Rising Tide Fund and TechWadi, and Board Adviser to the Mohammed bin Rashid Innovation Fund (MBRIF)
www.rtf.vc; www.techwadi.org; www.mbrif.ae

Dr. Ossama Hassanein is an entrepreneur, mentor, and venture capitalist based in Silicon Valley. Over the last 35 years, he has managed over $1 billion of international technology funds in diverse leadership roles including Executive Vice President (EVP) of Berkeley International in San Francisco, Chairman of Technocom Ventures in Paris, and Chair of the Rising Tide Fund in Silicon Valley. In the 1980s, he led the mezzanine financing of more than 80 Silicon Valley–based IT companies with a combined market value today exceeding $200 billion. Dr. Hassanein was Chairman or Co-Founder of seven leading-edge technology startups in the US, the UK, France, and Switzerland. Currently, he is Director of Bank of the West in San Francisco and the Mohammed Bin Rashid Innovation Fund in Dubai. He is also a President's Cabinet member at the University of British Columbia (UBC), where he also serves on the Dean of Applied Sciences Board of Advisers. He has served on the Board of Advisers of Harvard University Center for Middle Eastern

Studies. He also served as Chairman of TechWadi, focusing on mentoring, financing, and business acceleration of leading MENA entrepreneurs

HEATHER HENYON
Founding General Partner of Mindshift Capital
www.mindshiftcapital.com

Heather Henyon is Founding Partner of Mindshift Capital, a global venture fund investing in women-led technology startup companies. She is Founder of the Women's Angel Investor Network (WAIN), the first and largest women's angel group in the Middle East. An active venture investor with a passion for FinTech, Heather has over 100 direct and fund investments in the US, Europe, and the Middle East. She started her career on Wall Street and has almost 20 years of experience in finance, strategy, and technology in emerging markets. Heather is a member of the Investment Committee of Dubai Angel Investors and the US-based Next Wave Impact Fund. She serves on the Board of Directors of the Sekem Holding Group in Egypt and several tech startups' boards and advisory boards. Heather was nominated as Investor of the Year by *Arabian Business* in 2016 and 2017. She holds an MBA from the Johnson School at Cornell University and a BA from Oberlin College. Heather lives in Dubai, UAE.

WILL HERMAN
Startup Mentor and Co-Author of *The Startup Playbook: Founder-to-Founder Advice on How to Create and Build Your Startup*
www.linkedin.com/in/willherman

Will Herman is an entrepreneur, active angel investor, corporate director, startup mentor, and Author of *The Startup Playbook: Founder-to-Founder Advice on How to Create and Build Your Startup.* He was previously a serial entrepreneur, having started and managed five venture-backed companies, resulting in two IPOs and two corporate sales. In a series of transactions, including multiple IPOs, acquisitions, and management buyouts, Will created almost $4 billion in value for his investors. Will is currently a Fund Adviser at the venture capital firm, Bolt, a mentor at Techstars and is a frequent speaker at startup accelerators. As an angel investor, Will has invested in over 80 startups and actively advises 10 of those companies. He sits on the boards of JumpCloud and Concrete Sensors.

KATE POPE HODEL

Co-Author of *Beyond Collisions: How to Build Your Entrepreneurial Infrastructure*
www.linkedin.com/in/katepopehodel

Kate Pope Hodel has had a front-row seat for the entrepreneurial revolution in the US, having joined the Ewing Marion Kauffman Foundation in 1991. She directed the Kauffman Foundation's efforts to develop a national reputation around entrepreneurship, working with organizations such as NPR, the national Entrepreneur of the Year awards, and the international board for the Young Entrepreneurs Organization. She is the Co-Author of *Beyond Collisions: How to Build Your Entrepreneurial Infrastructure*. Kate is also Chair of NetWork Kansas, a SourceLink affiliate, and serves on their Startup Kansas Loan and Capital Multiplier Venture Fund committees. Her efforts to support entrepreneurship have been recognized by the SBA and the White House. She holds a bachelor's degree in journalism from the University of Missouri, Columbia and an MBA from Rockhurst University.

VICTOR HWANG

Vice President of Entrepreneurship at the Kauffman Foundation and Co-Author of *The Rainforest: The Secret to Building the Next Silicon Valley*
www.kauffman.org

Victor Hwang is Vice President of Entrepreneurship at the Ewing Marion Kauffman Foundation. The Foundation supports entrepreneurs starting and building businesses, leaders seeking guidance in the innovation economy, and cities and communities growing competitive jobs and sustained business creation. Prior, Hwang was Co-Founder and CEO of Liquidity. He was also CEO and Co-Founder of T2 Venture Creation, a venture firm that built startup companies and designed ecosystems that foster entrepreneurial innovation in dozens of countries and cities. In addition, Hwang was Executive Director of the Global Innovation Summit, a conference focused on building innovative ecosystems globally. Hwang is an alumnus of the Kauffman Fellows, a leadership society for venture investors. He is Co-Author of *The Rainforest: The Secret to Building the Next Silicon Valley*. The book was awarded Book of the Year, Gold Medal, by *ForeWord Reviews*. He also wrote the follow-up book, *The Rainforest Blueprint*, a practical design guide for innovation ecosystems. He has been a contributing columnist to *Forbes, The Wall Street Journal, TechCrunch*, and *Entrepreneur* and has been cited in *The New York Times, The Wall Street Journal, and The Los Angeles Times*, among others. Hwang is a graduate of Harvard University and the University of Chicago Law School.

DANIEL ISENBERG

Professor of Entrepreneurship Practice at Babson College Executive Education and Author of *Worthless, Impossible, and Stupid*
www.linkedin.com/in/disenberg

Daniel Isenberg is founding Executive Director of the Babson Entrepreneurship Ecosystem Platform, Adjunct Professor at Columbia Business School, and for two years was an Associate at the Harvard Kennedy School of Government. Daniel authored *Worthless, Impossible and Stupid: How Contrarian Entrepreneurs Create and Capture Extraordinary Value* (Harvard Business Review Press, 2013), published more than 30 articles on entrepreneurship in the *Harvard Business Review*, and has been featured in *The Economist, Forbes, The Wall Street Journal*, and on NPR, Bloomberg, and others. Daniel is a pioneer of the conception and development of entrepreneurship ecosystems and scaleup concepts and methodologies. Daniel was an active member in the World Economic Forum and conducted Forum events in Davos, Africa, Europe, and China. In 2012, Mikhail Gorbachev awarded Daniel the Pio Manzu Award for Innovations in Economic Development. At Babson Executive Education, Daniel created and directs the three-day open program, Driving Economic Growth Through Entrepreneurship Ecosystems. He holds a PhD in Social Psychology from Harvard University, received under the mentorship of Robert Freed Bales.

BADR JAFAR

CEO of Crescent Enterprises and President of Crescent Petroleum
www.crescent.ae

Badr Jafar is Chief Executive Officer of Crescent Enterprises and President of Crescent Petroleum. Badr serves as Chairman of Gas Cities LLC, a joint venture between Crescent Petroleum and Dana Gas PJSC, and as Chairman of Pearl Petroleum, a partnership between Crescent Petroleum, Dana Gas, OMV of Austria, MOL of Hungary and RWE of Germany. Additionally, Badr is active in a variety of other industries including ports and logistics, serving as Chair of the Executive Board of Gulftainer (the world's largest private container port operator). In 2010, Badr founded the Pearl Initiative, a non-profit organization in cooperation with the United Nations Office for Partnerships to promote a corporate culture of transparency and accountability across the Gulf Region of the Middle East. As part of his efforts advocating social entrepreneurship, he is Chairman of Endeavor UAE; an initiative encouraging high-impact entrepreneurship, is a member of the Synergos Arab World Social Innovators (AWSI) Program Board of Governors and serves on the Board of Advisers for the Sharjah Entrepreneurship Centre (Sheraa) and Gaza Sky Geeks. Badr is active with higher education institutions, serving as a member of the Advisory Boards of Cambridge University Judge Business School, American University of Beirut and American University of Sharjah. In September 2019, Badr was appointed to UNESCO's Future of Education International Commission, which aims to re-examine and reimagine how knowledge and learning can contribute to the global common good. Badr attended Eton College and studied Engineering in Cambridge University (Churchill College) graduating with a master's degree. He also holds an MST from Cambridge University's Judge Business School.

MOHAMMED JAFFAR

CEO of JustClean, Deputy Chairman, and CEO of Faith Capital Holding
https://justclean.com; www.faithcapital.com

Mohammed Jaffar is the CEO of JustClean, a Kuwait-based company and the GCC's leading laundry technology company. He is also the Deputy Chairman and CEO of Faith Capital Holding, a venture capital fund that focuses on e-commerce businesses that have high growth potential for the future. Prior to these roles, Mohammed was CEO of Talabat.com, an online food delivery platform acquired in 2010 for approximately $170 million by Rocket Internet. Under his leadership the company became a market leader throughout the GCC, which was successfully sold in 2015 to Rocket Internet. Mohammed is currently the Vice-President of The Kuwait Olympic Committee and is also a board member of both Injaz-Kuwait and Nexgen Group Company. He previously held the position of Deputy Chairman of Danah Al Safat Foodstuff Company and was a board member of Al Safat Dhiafa Company, Kuwait National Fund for SMEs Development, Tujjar Events Management and Execution Company, and Azzad Trading Group Company, and was an executive committee member of Noon.com.

RAMESH JAGANNATHAN
Managing Director of New York University, Abu Dhabi (startAD)
https://sites.nyuad.nyu.edu/nyuadstartad

Ramesh Jagannathan is currently the Vice President for Innovation and Entrepreneurship and Managing Director of startAD, the global accelerator at NYU Abu Dhabi. Since 2010, Ramesh has led the focus on innovation and entrepreneurship at NYU Abu Dhabi. Before that, Ramesh spent 30 years at Eastman Kodak in the US and the UK, which culminated in a prestigious appointment as Research Fellow at Kodak Research Labs. He also received the Kodak Distinguished Inventor Award. A gold medalist from the University of Madras, where he received his BTech degree, Ramesh went on to complete his PhD at Clarkson University and sat on the Cambridge University Mentor Panel. Ramesh holds 43 US patents and has written 31 peer-reviewed articles in journals such as *Nature Scientific Reports* and *Advanced Functional Materials*, including "Organic Nanoparticles: Preparation, Self-Assembly, and Novel Properties," one of the most accessed papers of 2006 in *Advanced Functional Materials*.

NED JAROUDI
Startup Business Development Lead at Amazon Web Services, MENA
www.linkedin.com/in/nedjaroudi

Ned Jaroudi is a seasoned executive with more than 25 years' unique experience in successfully setting up and managing new divisions/functions for multinationals (Amazon, Intel, CA, Raytheon), startups (1776, Zawya), family firms (National Holding), and government (UAE Prime Minister's Office, Expo 2020) in the US, Europe, and MEA. Ned is currently leading startup programs for Amazon Web Services in MENA. He previously launched and led 1776 Dubai, the first international tech incubator in the Middle East, in partnership with the Dubai Future Foundation. He has also driven impactful development programs in the Arab world, such as Intel® Teach for K-12 teachers, and hosted the "Internet Education" radio show in Dubai. Ned also gives back to the community by mentoring high-impact startups and SMEs and has served as Executive Board Member, United Nations ICT Arab Task Force; Board Member, Young Arab Leaders; Founding President, Stanford UAE Alumni Club; and Steering Committee Member, in5 Tech Innovation Centre. He holds an MSc from Stanford University, a BSc from Northeastern University, and a management certificate from INSEAD. He is a frequently requested industry speaker and media authority.

FOUAD JERYES
Co-Founder of Alpha Apps Inc.
www.alphaappsinc.com

Fouad Jeryes is the Co-Founder of Alpha Apps Inc., a venture focused on the e-commerce space. Fouad has served as a partner and manager at a number of forward-thinking ventures between the United States and the MENA region, particularly in Jordan, including Open Insights, BlueKangaroo, Oasis 500, and d1g.com. He has also offered and led technical and data strategy consulting for top-tier telecom, software, and internet companies such as Google, Microsoft, Yahoo!, and Verizon. He graduated with a Bachelor of Science from University of Massachusetts, Dartmouth.

AIMAN KABLI
Co-Founder and COO of eleva8or
www.eleva8or.com

Aiman Kabli holds an engineering degree, an MBA, and is currently pursuing a Professional Certificate in Innovation and Entrepreneurship from Stanford University. He has worked with such notable organizations as Unilever, the International Monetary Fund, and Emirates Airline. Currently, he is a serial entrepreneur and investor with a diversified portfolio of technology startups including innovative web platforms and mobile apps. Aiman has co-founded the platform eleva8or.com, which offers many investment preparation tools and connections for startups. The platform acts as a virtual accelerator for startups at the funding stage. It helps them to prepare for fundraising and negotiate and communicate with investors efficiently by polishing the documentation necessary to be considered for investment from around the world. eleva8or supports the ecosystem by helping to educate the startups and bring them up to the right level, and also by facilitating the flow between different countries and regions. The platform covers more than 40 countries across emerging markets, primarily in MENA. It assists companies to move back and forth, enter different markets, and grow and expand globally.

LAMIA KAMAL-CHAOUI

Director of the Centre for Entrepreneurship, SMEs, Regions and Cities at the Organisation for Economic Co-operation and Development (OECD)
www.oecd.org

As a key member of the OECD's Senior Management team, Ms. Kamal-Chaoui supports the Secretary-General in achieving the OECD's mission to advance economic growth and social progress as well as contributing to other global agendas such as the G20, the Paris Agreement on Climate Change, and the implementation of the United Nations Sustainable Development Goals. Ms. Kamal-Chaoui has held several senior positions at the OECD since 1998, including Senior Adviser to the OECD Secretary-General. In this role, she supported the Secretary-General's strategic agenda and led the OECD Inclusive Growth initiative, the Knowledge-Sharing Alliance program, the development of the Global Deal, and the implementation of the OECD Strategy on Development. Ms. Kamal-Chaoui is a French and Moroccan national. She holds a master's degree in Macroeconomics from the University of Paris Dauphine and a master's degree in Foreign Languages and History from the University of Paris, Diderot. She recently received the Women of the Decade in Enterprise and Leadership Award from the Women's Economic Forum.

BALA KAMALLAKHARAN

Founder of Startup Iceland and Co-Founder and Managing Director of Iceland Venture Studio
www.startupiceland.com; www.icelandventurestudio.com

Bala Kamallakharan is the Founder of Startup Iceland, a grassroots initiative to build sustainable startup ecosystems in Iceland. Bala is also Co-Founder of Dattaca Labs and Iceland Venture Studio. Bala has served as an Executive Board Member for Guide to Iceland and TravelShift. Bala has invested in, mentored, and was the Chairman of the Board at CLARA (Resonata), an Icelandic Community Analytics company that was acquired by Jive Software in 2013. CLARA was the first Icelandic company to be acquired into Silicon Valley. Bala has done various early-stage investments like Buuteeq (acquired by Priceline.com; NASDAQ:PCLN) and GreenQloud (acquired by NetApp; NASDAQ:NTAP). He holds master's degrees in Economics and Information Systems and Decision Science from Louisiana State University, Baton Rouge. Bala passed the PhD qualifying examination in Economics.

SHERIF KAMEL

Dean, School of Business at the American University in Cairo (AUC)
www.business.aucegypt.edu

Sherif Kamel is Professor of Management and Dean of the School of Business at the American University in Cairo (AUC) and president of the American Chamber of Commerce in Egypt. Before joining the university, he was Director of the Regional IT Institute. Prior, he managed the training department of the Cabinet of Egypt Information and Decision Support Center. His research and teaching interests include management of information technology, information technology transfer to developing nations, organizational transformation, electronic business, decision support systems, and entrepreneurship. His work has been broadly published in over 200 articles, chapters, and cases in information systems and management journals and books. He holds a PhD in Information Systems from London School of Economics and Political Science as well as an MBA, a BA in Business Administration, and an MA in Islamic Art and Architecture from the American University in Cairo. He is an Eisenhower Fellow and sits on the board of several private enterprises and NGOs in Egypt and the US.

RABIH KHOURY

Partner and Chief Exit Officer of Middle East Venture Partners (MEVP)
www.mevp.com

Rabih Khoury is Partner & Chief Exit Officer of Middle East Venture Partners ("MEVP"), the leading Technology Venture Capital firm in MENA. Mr. Khoury is also the Managing Partner of Melwood Capital, a Merchant Bank that specializes in structuring private investments in MENA and Turkey. Mr. Khoury has extensive experience in Private Equity, Financial Advisory and Mergers & Acquisitions, having executed more than US$5 billion in transactions and raised more than US$2 billion in capital. Previously, Mr. Khoury was the Chief Executive Officer of DIC Emerging Markets, in charge of Dubai International Capital's ("DIC") investment portfolio in Emerging Markets (including MENA, Turkey, Asia and Latin America). DIC is the international investment arm of the Dubai–based conglomerate Dubai Holding. At DIC, Mr. Khoury had overall responsibility for transaction origination and execution, portfolio company management and exits across Emerging Markets. In addition, Mr. Khoury was a member of DIC's

Executive Management Committee. Mr. Khoury also represented DIC on the investment committees of Dubai Aerospace Enterprise (as Chairman), Jordan Dubai Capital, and the MENA Infrastructure Fund. Mr. Khoury is a founding member of the Dubai Chapter of LIFE ("Lebanese International Finance Executives") and was the President of the New York Alumni Association Chapter of the American University of Beirut. He was also a member of the Arab Bankers Association of North America ("ABANA"). Mr. Khoury received his MBA in Finance from Columbia University and his MSc from the University of California, Berkeley. He also received a Bachelor of Engineering with Distinction from AUB and graduated with Honors from Lebanon's International College.

NABEEL KOSHAK

CEO of Saudi Venture Capital Company (SVC)
www.svc.com.sa

H.E. Dr. Nabeel Koshak is the CEO of Saudi Venture Capital Company (SVC). Koshak is also the Founder and Chairman of Athaal (Angel Investors Group) and the former Founding Dean of Prince Mohammad Bin Salman College (MBSC) of Business and Entrepreneurship at King Abdullah Economic City. He is the Co-Founder and Vice Chairman of the Board of Directors of Wadi Makkah Company (seed fund, startup accelerator, and venture capital). He is a Board Member of King Abdulaziz and His Companions Foundation for Giftedness and Innovation (Mawhiba). Koshak is also a Member of the Executive Committee of the King Faisal International Prize, a Board Member of Oqal (Angel Investors Network) Jeddah branch, and a mentor at Flat6Labs Jeddah Startup Accelerator and Endeavor Saudi Arabia. He is the former Co-Founder of King Abdulaziz City for Science and Technology (KACST) GIS Technology Innovation Center. Nabeel received an Executive Education from Harvard University in Venture Capital and Private Equity in 2019, an Executive Education from Massachusetts Institute of Technology (MIT) in its Regional Entrepreneurship Acceleration Program and Management, Innovation, Technology in 2017, a PhD in Design Computing from Carnegie Mellon University in 2002, and a Master of Architecture (Computing in Design and Planning) from the University of Colorado in 1997.

EYAD LATIF

Counsel of Emerging Companies, Latham and Watkins,
Middle East
www.lw.com/offices/dubai

Eyad Latif, Counsel in the Dubai office of Latham and Watkins, is a member of the Corporate Department and the Mergers and Acquisitions and Emerging Companies Practices. He represents emerging-growth companies, both public and private, and their funding sources, including VC and PE firms. He also advises international and MENA-based emerging-growth companies and VC and PE firms in transactions across a wide range of industries. Eyad has extensive experience advising on some of the largest VC financings and exits in the region, including Careem's acquisition by Uber; Mohamed Alabbar and the PIF on the launch of the $1 billion Noon.com; STV, the largest VC in the Middle East; BECO Capital, as co-investor with General Atlantic, on the $120 million Series B financing for Property Finder; Yahoo! on its acquisition of Maktoob.com; and Symphony Investments, an entity controlled by Mohamed Alabbar, on its €100 million purchase of a minority interest in Yoox Net-a-Porter Group. He worked with Standard Chartered Bank on its $50 million investment (as part of a $275 million consortium) in Souq.com, MENA's largest online marketplace, and the sale of Souq.com to Amazon. Eyad regularly provides private briefings and training sessions to major Middle East–based corporates on venture capital matters and is a mentor for a number of incubators and accelerators in MENA.

JULIE LENZER

Chief Innovation Officer, University of Maryland, Board
Member for the Center for American Entrepreneurship,
and Author of *ParentPreneur Edge*
www.linkedin.com/in/julielenzer

Julie Lenzer is currently Chief Innovation Officer at the University of Maryland. Prior to that, Julie was appointed by US Secretary of Commerce Penny Pritzker to lead the Office of Innovation and Entrepreneurship (OIE). Prior to that appointment, Julie was the Executive Director of the Maryland Center for Entrepreneurship (MCE) in Columbia, MD. She is also the Co-Founder of Startup Maryland and former CEO of the Path Forward Center for Innovation and Entrepreneurship, a nonprofit that helped women expand their economic opportunities by starting and building growth-oriented businesses. An award-winning serial entrepreneur, Julie founded her first company, Applied Creative Technologies, Inc. (ACT), in 1995 as an IT solutions firm focusing on manufacturing operations and inventory control. With Fortune 500 clients, she grew the company to multimillion-dollar revenues, winning several national awards for workplace excellence. Julie was named one of Maryland's Top 100 Women in 2005, 2008, and 2014, at which time she joined the Circle of Excellence for sustained service to the community.

JOSH LERNER

Chairman of the Entrepreneurial Management Unit at Harvard Business School and Author of *Boulevard of Broken Dreams*
www.hbs.edu

Josh Lerner is the Jacob H. Schiff Professor of Investment Banking at Harvard Business School, with a joint appointment in the Finance and Entrepreneurial Management Units. He graduated from Yale College with a Special Divisional in physics and technology. He worked extensively on technological innovation and public policy issues, and earned a PhD from Harvard's Economics department. Much of his research focuses on the structure and role of venture capital and private equity organizations. (This research is collected in his books: *The Venture Capital Cycle*, *The Money of Invention*, *Patient Capital*, and *Boulevard of Broken Dreams*.) He also examines policies about innovation and how they impact firm strategies. He co-directs the National Bureau of Economic Research's Productivity, Research, and Innovation Program and serves as Co-Editor of their publication, *Innovation Policy and the Economy*. He founded and currently runs the Private Capital Research Institute, a nonprofit devoted to encouraging access to data and research about venture capital and private equity. He is the winner of the Swedish government's 2010 Global Entrepreneurship Research Award.

SETH LEVINE

Co-Founder and Partner at Foundry Group, Founder of Pledge 1%, and Trustee of Macalester College
www.foundrygroup.com; www.macalester.edu; www.sethlevine.com

Seth Levine is Co-Founder and Partner at Boulder-based Foundry Group, focusing on making early-stage technology investments and identifying and supporting the next generation of venture fund managers in markets in the US. With nearly $3 billion under management, Foundry investments include companies such as Rover, Admeld, and Fitbit. Seth is also active around the world in the entrepreneurial community. He was a founding board member of The Unreasonable Institute and an adviser to the Palestinian venture fund, Sadara, and other venture funds in the US, Africa, and the Middle East. In 2016, Seth co-founded Pledge 1%, an international organization that encourages startups to give back to their local communities through gifts of equity, profit, product, and time. Pledge has over 6,000 members across the globe. Seth is an adviser to the Greater Colorado Venture Fund, a fund set up to invest in rural Colorado. He is also the Co-Chair of StartupColorado. He is a summa cum laude graduate of Macalester College, where he is currently serves as a member of the Board of Trustees. You can find him on Twitter at @sether or online at www.sethlevine.com.

MOHAMED ANOUAR MAAROUF

Minister of Communication Technologies and Digital Economy, Tunisia
www.mtcen.gov.tn

H.E. Mohamed Anouar Maarouf holds a doctorate in Mathematics, a master's degree in Telecommunications, and a professional master's degree in organizational change. In 2012, he was adviser to Mongi Marzouk, Minister of Information of Technology and Communications, a position he held until 2013. He then became Chairman of the Board of Directors of Dar Assabah and Director of Telecoms and Media at El Karama Holding. In 2016, he was appointed Minister of Information Technology and Digital Economy in the government of Youssef Chahed.

JOHN MACOMBER

Senior Lecturer in the Finance Unit at Harvard Business School
www.linkedin.com/in/john-d-macomber

John Macomber is a Senior Lecturer in the Finance unit at Harvard Business School. His professional background includes leadership of real estate, construction, and information technology businesses. At HBS, Mr. Macomber's work focuses on the future of cities, particularly as aided by private financing and delivery of public infrastructure projects in both the developed and emerging worlds. His teaching combines infrastructure finance (including public-private partnerships), investing in resilience (notably in response to sea rise in some areas and drought in others), economic development, and the impact of new technologies on delivering new infrastructure and making old infrastructure more efficient. Mr. Macomber is the Faculty Chair of the HBS Africa Research Center. He is also engaged in the Business and Environment Initiative and Social Enterprise Initiative at HBS and is a member of the Executive Committee of the Harvard University Center for African Studies. He teaches Finance, Real Estate, Urbanization, and Entrepreneurship. Mr. Macomber is the former Chairman and CEO of the George B H Macomber Company. He serves or has served on the boards of Young Presidents Organization International (YPO), Boston Private Bank, Mount Auburn Hospital, and the WGBH Educational Foundation.

SAMI MAHROUM

Professor at the Faculty of Social Sciences and Solvay Business School, VUB (Brussels) and Author of *Black Swan Start-ups*
www.vub.be

Dr. Sami Mahroum is Professor at the Faculty of Social Sciences and Solvay Business School, VUB (Brussels). His experience in the UAE includes providing scientific directorship to the Dubai Future Labs at the Dubai Future Foundation and founding and managing INSEAD's Innovation and Policy Initiative in Abu Dhabi. Professor Mahroum was also a Senior Lecturer at INSEAD in Abu Dhabi. He has worked as a researcher and an academic, and has been a policy analyst and an adviser on innovation policy in Austria (Austrian Institute of Technology), Canada (Ontario Government), France (OECD), Holland (TNO and RAND), Spain (European Commission think-tank), and the UK (University of Manchester and NESTA). He is an alumnus of the d-School, Stanford, and Author of *Black Swan Start-ups: Understanding the Rise of Successful Technology Business in Unlikely Places* (Palgrave).

MUHAMMAD MANSOUR

Co-Founder of RiseUp Summit
www.riseupsummit.com

Muhammad Mansour is the Co-Founder of RiseUp Summit, which he co-founded in 2013. After attending SXSW for the first time, he was inspired to co-create RiseUp Summit. It grew to become an annual technology and entrepreneurship conference with over 5,000 attendees from 50 countries, and speakers from Microsoft, MIT, Tech Crunch, Google, and Facebook, among others. Muhammad previously worked in the startup ecosystem in various roles in such organizations as Startup Genome, Mercy Corps, Starappz, and N2V.

WALID MANSOUR

Managing Partner of Middle East Venture Partners (MEVP)
www.mevp.com

Walid Mansour has more than 15 years of experience in venture capital, strategy, corporate finance, and engineering within the digital, telecom, software, and new media industries. Prior to joining MEVP in 2010, Walid was a Lead Associate at Roland Berger Strategy Consultants, and before that he worked as a strategy manager at the UAE's Prime Ministry Executive Office focusing on public policy initiatives. During his stay in Dubai, he worked on setting up entrepreneurship-related programs and developing incubation in the Arab world through several Dubai-based initiatives, such as the Mohammed Bin Rashid Foundation. Walid holds an Industrial and Urban Planning Engineering degree from Institut National des Science Appliquées de Lyon (INSA de Lyon) and an MBA in Finance from the Wharton School at the University of Pennsylvania.

DAVE MCCLURE

Founder of 500 Startups and Practical Venture Capital
www.500.co

Dave McClure has been an investor and entrepreneur in Silicon Valley for over 25 years. He was the Founding Partner of 500 Startups, a global VC firm and startup accelerator with over $500 million in assets under management. Dave has invested in hundreds of companies around the world, including more than 10 unicorns and five IPOs: Twilio (NYSE: TWLO), SendGrid (NYSE: SEND), Lyft (NASDAQ: LYFT), The RealReal (NASDAQ: REAL), and Life 360 (ASX:360). He was named by *Forbes* as one of the top VCs in the world in 2016 and 2017 (*Forbes* Midas List). Before 500 Startups, Dave worked at Founders Fund and PayPal, and he graduated from Johns Hopkins University in 1988 with a BSc in Engineering and Applied Mathematics.

MUHAMMED MEKKI
Founding Partner of AstroLabs
www.astrolabs.com

Muhammed Mekki is a Founding Partner at AstroLabs, an organization dedicated to accelerating the Middle East and North Africa region's digital economy. AstroLabs has graduated over 3,000 alumni from its capability-building Academy and has enabled hundreds of tech companies to set up in the United Arab Emirates and Saudi Arabia at its network of collaborative co-working communities. AstroLabs mission is to enable tech entrepreneurs & startups through its coworking space tech hubs and via its high impact workshops and events. Prior, he co-founded Dubai-based Namshi, which is now one of the largest e-commerce players in the region, specialized in fashion and lifestyle. Namshi was recently acquired by Emaar Malls. Muhammed received an MBA from the Stanford University Graduate School of Business as a Mohammed bin Rashid Al Maktoum Fellow. He earned a BSc in Economics from the Wharton School and a BA in International Studies and Political Science from the University of Pennsylvania.

SAMIA MELHEM
Lead Digital Development Policy Specialist at the World Bank
www.worldbank.org

Samia Melhem is a Lead Policy Officer in the World Bank's Digital Development Global Practice. She has recently been selected as the World Bank's Global Lead on Digital Capabilities. Her current operational responsibilities include lending and technical assistance to the World Bank's client countries to harness digital technologies for development. Samia has in-depth expertise in the digital economy, digital infrastructure, GovTech, innovation, and private sector development. Samia held several Regional Coordinator positions, such as for Africa, the Middle East, and North Africa. She has been Strategy and Policy Officer in corporate functions and done project management for investment operations. She has authored several publications, research notes, working papers, case studies, and policy notes. She holds degrees in Electrical Engineering (BSc), Computer Sciences (MSc), and Finance (MBA).

ZIAD MOKHTAR
Managing Partner of Algebra Ventures
www.algebraventures.com

Ziad Mokhtar is Managing Partner at Algebra Ventures, Egypt's leading VC firm. Ziad is also Managing Partner at Ideavelopers and has been an active VC investor since 2010. He has invested in many transformative technology companies in Egypt and the Middle East, including Siware, Vezeeta, Fawry, Elmenus, Trella, Dsquares, and Posrocket. Before becoming a venture investor, Ziad served as a consultant at McKinsey and Company where he worked in areas of economic development, healthcare reform, and education. Prior to McKinsey, he co-founded eSpace in 2000 and served as its Chief Executive Officer until 2006. While at eSpace, he led the development of the number one mobile salesforce solution in the Middle East and spearheaded eSpace's international services. Ziad holds an MBA from Stanford Graduate School of Business and a bachelor's degree in Computer Science and Engineering from Alexandria University.

RONALDO MOUCHAWAR
Co-Founder and CEO of Souq.com and Vice President of Amazon, MENA
www.souq.com; www.amazon.ae

In 2005, Ronaldo Mouchawar co-founded Souq, which went on to become the Middle East's largest e-commerce retailer. In 2017, Amazon acquired Souq in a landmark acquisition for e-commerce in the region. Souq was active in three countries—UAE, Saudi Arabia, and Egypt—and was built on the Amazon model including retail, fulfillment, and marketplace, with more than 50 million active users monthly across the Middle East (including cross-border trade into neighboring countries). The acquisition was headline news across all major news platforms in the region, as well as receiving international coverage. In March 2015, Mouchawar received an award from His Highness Sheikh Mohammed bin Rashid Al Maktoum, Vice President and Prime Minister of the UAE and Ruler of Dubai, in recognition of Souq's digital influence in the UAE. He was also awarded the prestigious Retail Business Leader of the Year and Entrepreneur of the Year awards by *Gulf Business* (Motivate Publishing). Mouchawar holds a master's degree in Digital Communications and a bachelor's degree in Electrical and Computer Engineering from Northeastern University in Boston, MA.

MUHAMMAD NABIL

Partner and Startup Strategy Lead at Microsoft 4Afrika
www.microsoft.com

Muhammad Nabil has over 15 years' experience in information communication technology, engineering, and business development. Muhammad is the Partner and Startup Strategy Lead for Microsoft's 4Afrika Initiative, the tech giant's market and economic development program in Africa. 4Afrika seeks to enhance affordable access to the internet, digital skills, and opportunities for cloud-based innovation. His role focuses on building a self-sustainable ecosystem for partners and startups with innovative business models, and supporting them in integrating technology to take their ventures to the next level. Prior to joining Microsoft in 2010, he worked as a senior analyst for such companies as IBM and Google. Muhammad holds a BSc in Computer Science, a master's in Information Systems, and a diploma in Cognitive Psychology. He is particularly passionate about digital solutions in healthcare, agriculture, education, and finance, due to their long-term social impact.

MARC NAGER

Fund Director of the Greater Colorado Venture Fund and former CEO of Startup Weekend
www.greatercolorado.vc; www.startupweekend.org

Marc Nager is the Managing Partner at the Greater Colorado Venture Fund, focused on seed-stage investing in rural Colorado. He was the Co-Founder of Startup Weekend and CEO of UP Global after it merged with Startup America. He has traveled to nearly 50 countries around the world helping to guide strategies for building startup ecosystems. After selling UP Global to Techstars, he spent a year as their Chief Community Officer. Marc currently sits on the Board of Advisers for both GAN and Startups.com, as well as several startups. Marc is currently focused on helping to prove models for venture capital for small and rural communities around the world. He is on a mission to help find new ways for venture capital and accelerator programs to support founders that don't fit the traditional VC profile. You can find more about his work on social media: @marcnager. Marc holds a BSc in International Business from Chapman University.

RUBEN NIEUWENHUIS

Managing Director of TechConnect, Managing Partner of TechGrounds, and Co-Author of *StartupCity*
www.techgrounds.nl; www.techconnect.city

Ruben Nieuwenhuis is an entrepreneur, and now an entrepreneur-in-residence, acting as the Managing Director of TechConnect, a program spearheaded by the Amsterdam Economic Board. He was the Managing Director of StartupAmsterdam, helping to connect top Dutch startup initiatives and tech clusters in a catalyst program: StartupDelta. Ruben's roles include Managing Director of TechConnect, a tech talent program to activate, reskill, upskill, and attract 50,000 tech talents to the Amsterdam Metropolitan area, and Educating Cities, which aims to grow Amsterdam as a Tech hub. Nieuwenhuis was also involved in various startups and innovation projects: DutchBasecamp (Founder), CodeUur, now FutureNL (Co-Founder), FellowForce (Co-Founder and CEO), StBC (Founder and CEO), Amsterdam Capital Week, and others. He is the Author of *StartupCity*, which is designed to provide civil servants and public-private initiatives with guidance on how they can think and work as a startup. It's a comprehensive look at how the public sector can boost the startup ecosystem and nurture the city as a breeding ground for innovation and job growth.

TON VAN 'T NOORDENDE

Founder of PHX
www.thephx.co

Ton van 'T Noordende is the Founder of PHX, a yearly conference taking place on an island near Amsterdam, bringing together the world's most original thinkers, scientists, creatives and artists, top-tier investors, founders, and ultra-high net worth individuals from Europe and the US. He is also the Investor-in-Residence at Techleap, working closely together with HRH Prince Constantijn of Oranje. Additionally, Ton is the Founder and former Partner at deeptech venture capital firm 01Ventures. He has also worked for leading global brands like Samsung, Sony Mobile, Saatchi & Saatchi, and Leo Burnett. He has created brand campaigns for and with top media agencies like GroupM, Mindshare, MEC Global, and Starcom. In his previous role as CMO for Capitalonstage.com, Ton has evaluated over 200+ VC's reverse-pitch on stage.

KEVIN O'LEARY

Chairman of O'Shares Investments and television star at *Shark Tank*
www.kevinoleary.com

Kevin O'Leary comes from Lebanese heritage. As the son of a United Nations ILO official, he had the opportunity to live and be educated in Cambodia, Cyprus, Tunisia, Ethiopia, France and Switzerland. He attended the University of Waterloo, where he received an honors bachelor's degree in Environmental Studies and Psychology. He attended the Ivey Business School where he received his MBA in 1980. Kevin co-founded SoftKey Software in 1986, which grew quickly and was acquired by Mattel Toy Company for $4.2 billion. In 2003, Kevin also became a co-investor and Director in Storage Now, a leading developer of climate-controlled storage facilities. Through a series of development projects and acquisitions, Storage Now was acquired by the In Storage REIT in March 2007 for $110 million. Kevin is the Chairman of O'Leary Funds Management LP and O'Shares ETF Investments. He is a contributor to Fox News, CNBC, ABC News, and Good Morning America and an entrepreneur/investor co-host for the Discovery Channel's "Project Earth" series, which explores innovative ways to reverse global warming. He is also an investor/host of ABC's four-time Emmy Award–winning venture capital reality programs *Shark Tank* and *Beyond The Tank*, produced by Mark Burnett/Sony/ABC. Kevin is also the Author of three #1 bestselling books: *Cold Hard Truth*; *Men, Women and Money*; and *Family, Kids and Money*.

TIM O'REILLY

Founder and CEO of O'Reilly Media and Author of *What is Web 2.0* and *WTF?: What's the Future and Why It's Up to Us*
www.oreilly.com

Tim O'Reilly is the Founder, CEO, and Chairman of O'Reilly Media, the company that has been providing the picks and shovels of learning to the Silicon Valley gold rush for the past 35 years. The company delivers online learning, publishes books, and runs conferences about cutting-edge technology. If you've heard the term "open source software," "web 2.0," "the Maker movement," "government as a platform," or "the WTF economy," he's had a hand in framing each of those big ideas. Tim is also a partner at early-stage venture firm O'Reilly AlphaTech Ventures (OATV), and sits on the boards of Code for America, PeerJ, Civis Analytics, and PopVox. He is the Author of many technical books published by O'Reilly Media, including most recently, *WTF? What's the Future and Why It's Up to Us* (Harper Business, 2017). He is working on a new book about why we need to rethink antitrust in the era of internet-scale platforms.

EFOSA OJOMO

Global Prosperity Lead at Clayton Christensen Institute,
Co-Founder and President of Poverty Stops Here, and
Co-Author of *The Prosperity Paradox*
www.christenseninstitute.org

Efosa Ojomo researches and writes about how innovation can transform organizations and create inclusive prosperity for many. In January 2019, alongside Harvard Business School professor Clayton Christensen, he published the book, *The Prosperity Paradox: How Innovation Can Lift Nations Out of Poverty*. Efosa leads the Global Prosperity Research Group at the Clayton Christensen Institute for Disruptive Innovation, an innovation-focused think-tank based in Boston and Silicon Valley. His work has been published and covered by *The Wall Street Journal, Harvard Business Review, The Guardian, Quartz, Forbes, Fortune*, the World Bank, NPR, and several other media outlets. He speaks regularly and has presented his work at TED, the Aspen Ideas Festival, the World Bank, Harvard, Yale, Oxford, and several other conferences and institutions. Efosa has a degree in computer engineering from Vanderbilt University and an MBA from Harvard Business School.

JONATHAN ORTMANS

President of Global Entrepreneurship Network (GEN)
www.genglobal.org

Jonathan Ortmans is Founder and President of the Global Entrepreneurship Network (GEN), a Washington, DC–based organization operating programs and chapters in 170 nations to support entrepreneurs and foster healthier entrepreneurial ecosystems. Ortmans launched GEN's cornerstone initiative, Global Entrepreneurship Week (GEW), in 2008 with the Ewing Marion Kauffman Foundation. Each November, millions of people explore their potential as entrepreneurs through thousands of local GEW events in nearly 200 countries. Ortmans also chairs the Global Entrepreneurship Congress (GEC), which gathers thousands of leaders each April to collaborate on effective approaches to advancing entrepreneurial growth. After launching the GEC at the Kauffman Foundation in Kansas City, he chaired the event in following years in Dubai, Shanghai, Liverpool, Rio de Janeiro, Moscow, Milan, Medellin, Johannesburg, Istanbul, and Bahrain. Ortmans has long been involved in policy development on many issues. This has influenced his development of Startup Nations, GEN's policy-focused initiative that drives scholarship, policy hacks, and knowledge-sharing across borders between governments and advisers. He has served as a longtime adviser to the Kauffman Foundation and currently serves on the board of the Center for American Entrepreneurship in Washington, DC. Outside the United States, he chairs the boards of dozens of GEN affiliates and the Center for Entrepreneurship in Moscow.

ARUNMA OTEH

Academic Scholar at Oxford University and former Vice President and Treasurer of the World Bank
www.worldbank.org

Arunma Oteh is the former Treasurer of the World Bank, where she led a team that managed a $200 billion debt portfolio for 65 internal and external clients including the World Bank Group, central banks, sovereign wealth funds, and other official institutions. They also leveraged a derivatives portfolio of more than $600 billion for risk management and process annual cashflows of more than $7 trillion. Arunma served as Director General of the Securities and Exchange Commission in Nigeria. She has served on the boards of the International Organization of Securities Commissions, the World Economic Forum Agenda Council on Institutional Governance, and the Africa Advisory Council for World Women's Banking. She holds an MBA from Harvard Business School. Arunma was named the Africa Investor Capital Market Personality of the Year as well as AI Global Institutional Investment Personality of the Year.

ZUBAIR NAEEM PARACHA

Founder of MENAbytes and Qraar
www.menabytes.com; @qraarhq

Zubair Naeem Parachi is a tech and startup enthusiast and the Founder of MENAbytes, one of the leading media platforms that covers startups and technology in the MENA region, with around 300,000-500,000 page views and 80,000-120,000 unique visits per month. MENAbytes aims to become the go-to platform for startups and for all-things startups and technology-related across emerging markets. MENAbytes was acquired by RiseUp in 2019; Zubair continues at the helm of MENAbytes following the acquisition. Zubair has also built Qraar, a career discovery and development platform for millennials in MENA.

TAMMER QADDUMI
Founding Partner of VentureSouq
www.venturesouq.com

Tammer Qaddumi is a Founding Partner of VentureSouq. Previously, he was Vice President of Private Equity at Waha Capital, a diversified investment company based in Abu Dhabi with assets of $3 billion. Prior to joining Waha, Tammer worked with UBS and HSBC in New York and Dubai, respectively. He served as a Fulbright Scholar in Damascus, Syria and worked with the Office of Presidential Personnel at the White House in Washington, DC. Tammer holds a BA from Yale University and serves on the Board of Directors of Addax Bank in Bahrain and of the Yale Arab Alumni Association.

AMIRA RASHAD
Founder and CEO of BulkWhiz
www.bulkwhiz.com

Amira Rashad is the Founder and CEO of BulkWhiz, the Middle East's first e-commerce platform for ordering groceries in bulk. Amira gained 25 years of experience in leadership, strategy, operations, and marketing in the corporate world at PepsiCo, Booz Allen, Yahoo!, and Facebook before embarking on her entrepreneurial journey. Amira holds a BA in Economics from the University of Cairo, a Master of Science in International Marketing Management from the University of Salford, and an MBA from Harvard Business School.

CHRISTOPHER ROGERS

Partner at Lumia Capital and Co-Founder of Nextel
Communications
www.lumiacapital.com

Christopher Rogers, JD, is a Partner at Lumia Capital, a San Francisco–based venture capital firm that invests in US category leaders pursuing international markets and local leaders dominating the fastest growing global markets. Before joining Lumia, Chris was the Co-Founder of Nextel Communications, which he grew to $13 billion in sales and 19,000 employees before it was acquired by Sprint for $35 billion. Prior, Chris helped spearhead the roll-up of local carriers that transformed Nextel into a major national operator. Chris was responsible for negotiations with regulators, investors, and carriers in Saudi Arabia, Jordan, Pakistan, India, and China, among other countries.

ANDREW ROMANS

CEO and General Partner of 7BC Venture Capital, General Partner at Rubicon Venture Capital, and Author of *Masters of Corporate Venture Capital*
www.7bc.vc

Andrew Romans is a successful VC; a VC-backed entrepreneur; the Author of *Masters of Corporate Venture Capital*, *Masters of Blockchain*, and *The Entrepreneurial Bible to Venture Capital: Inside Secrets from the Leaders in the Startup Game*; a former tech VC and M&A investment banker; Co-Founder of an angel group; CEO and General Partner of the AI, FinTech, and blockchain–focused VC 7BC; and Venture Capital and General Partner of tech VC Rubicon Venture Capital. By the age of 28, Romans had raised over $48 million for tech startups he founded. Romans founded and raised VC funding for numerous companies and led startups to exits including The Founders Club (a VC secondaries and equity exchange fund backed by 42 VCs), Sentito Networks ($58 million in VC funding; acquired by Verso Technologies), The Global TeleExchange (raised $50 million) and Motive Communications (enterprise sales in Europe; NASDAQ IPO). He is fluent in English, French, and German and has an MBA from Georgetown University completed on scholarship.

ALEC ROSS

Former Senior Adviser for Innovation to the US Secretary of State and Author of *The Industries of the Future*
www.alecross.com

Alec Ross is a Visiting Professor at King's College London and his book, *The Industries of the Future*, has been translated into 24 languages and been a bestseller on four continents. He is a Board Partner at Amplo, a global venture capital firm. He has served as a Distinguished Senior Fellow at Johns Hopkins University and the Columbia University School of International and Public Affairs. During the Obama Administration, he served as Senior Adviser for Innovation to the Secretary of State to help modernize the practice of diplomacy and use innovative solutions to advance America's foreign policy interests. Alec served as the Convener for the Technology and Media Policy Committee on Barack Obama's 2008 presidential campaign. Prior to this, he co-founded a technology-focused social enterprise serving millions of low-income people globally. Alec has been recognized as one of the Top 100 Global Thinkers by *Foreign Policy Magazine* and *Huffington Post*'s 10 Game Changers in Politics. He has received the US Department of State Distinguished Honor Award, Oxford University Internet and Society Award, and Tribeca Film Festival Disruptive Innovation Award.

LINDA ROTTENBERG

Co-Founder and CEO of Endeavor
www.endeavor.org

As Co-Founder and CEO of Endeavor, Linda Rottenberg has been a leader of the global entrepreneurship movement since 1997. With 60 offices spanning the world, Endeavor's team of more than 500 people and its international mentor network rigorously identify, select, and scale up the most promising entrepreneurs in emerging and underserved markets, including secondary US cities. The 2,000 selected Endeavor Entrepreneurs now generate over $20 billion in annual revenues and have created more than 3 million jobs. Linda also oversees the Endeavor Catalyst LP Fund with over $200 million in assets under management, which co-invests in top Endeavor Entrepreneurs raising equity capital. She is the Author of *Crazy Is A Compliment: The Power of Zigging When Everyone Else Zags*, which became an instant *New York Times* bestseller. Her other recognition includes: Global Leader for Tomorrow/ Young Global Leader (World Economic Forum); 2017 Visionary Award

(Silicon Valley Forum); Honorary Doctorate of Humane Letters (Babson College); and the 2018 Heinz Award in Technology, the Economy and Employment. She is a graduate of Harvard College and Yale Law School.

ASHRAF SABRY
Founder and CEO of Fawry
www.fawry.com

Ashraf Sabry serves as the Chief Executive Officer of Fawry, an electronic bill payment and presentment (EBPP) company. Ashraf gained experience in information and communication technology during his time at IBM, where he spent 10 years in sales and marketing. He is also the Founder of Oratech, Raya Telecom, and Raya Contact Centre. Ashraf has been one of Raya's key players: he led several businesses to success, managed to establish several companies, and drove the expansion of Raya into MENA. He was also responsible for Raya's IPO and, as the Vice Chairman and COO of Raya Holding, he drove its revenue growth to 2 billion Egyptian pounds. Sabry holds an MBA from Leeds University in the UK.

RAMI SALMAN
Founder and CEO of Wrappup and Vice President of Growth at Voicea
www.wrappup.co; www.voicea.com

Rami Salman is the Vice President of Growth at Voicea. Prior to joining the team, he was the Founder and CEO of Wrappup in Dubai, a company acquired by Silicon Valley-based Voicea. Within 18 months of the Wrappup acquisition, Voicea itself was acquired by Cisco. After graduating as a Mechanical Engineer from the University of Maryland, he built his business foundations in the world of management consulting at Bain and Company, working on high-profile projects for technology, retail, finance, telecom, and oil and gas clients across the GCC. He came up with the idea for a voice-based meeting summarization app and took the idea to a hackathon, where he was lucky to meet his brainy technical co-founders. Their award-winning prototype was built in 24 hours and went on to win the $10,000 prize at Global Demo Day in San Francisco. The Wrappup team went on to raise a seed round of funding led by BECO Capital and 500 Startups.

CHRISTOPHER SCHROEDER

Global Venture Investor, Tech Media CEO, and Author of
*Startup Rising: The Entrepreneurial Revolution Remaking
the Middle East*
www.startuprisingbook.com

Christopher Schroeder is an American entrepreneur, adviser, and global investor in interactive technologies and social media. He was the CEO and Publisher of *Washington Post Newsweek* interactive. He is also Co-Founder of the Silicon Valley venture capital–backed startup HealthCentral.com. He is an investor in many disruptive enterprises. He is also an LP in leading Silicon Valley venture capital funds and on the advisory committees of top funds in the Middle East. He is Author of the bestseller *Startup Rising: The Entrepreneurial Revolution Remaking the Middle East*, the first book on startups in the Arab world. He co-led the Economic Recovery and Revitalization working group of the Atlantic Council's Middle East Strategy Task Force, co-chaired by Madeleine Albright and Steve Hadley. Schroeder serves on the boards of advisers of American University School of International Service, Endeavor Global, 500 Startups in emerging markets, GEN, 1776 fund, and the American University of Beirut. He has written and speaks extensively on startups and innovation in the Middle East, and he has been featured regularly on leading news shows. He was named in LinkedIn's Top 50 Influencers. He graduated from Harvard College and Harvard Business School.

RAMEZ SHEHADI

Managing Director of Facebook, MENA
www.facebook.com

Ramez Shehadi is an internationally seasoned transformational leader, industry and technology strategist, thought leader, venture capitalist, and community builder. As the Managing Director of Facebook for MENA, he leads the operational and commercial growth of Facebook and its expanding portfolio of apps, services, and platforms (Instagram, WhatsApp, Facebook, Messenger, Oculus, Workplace, etc.). Ramez was formerly Senior Partner, Executive Vice President, and Managing Director of Booz Allen Hamilton. He is also the Co-Founder and Senior Director of Product Development at eBreviate, a billion-dollar online e-sourcing solutions platform in San Francisco. He is a frequent speaker and presenter at regional and international conferences, forums, and media outlets on a wide variety of digital innovation and regional development topics. Ramez is a member of the Board of Directors of Aramex and MMA (Mobile Marketing Association) in MENA; a former member of the Board of Directors of Young Arab Leaders; an Endeavor Mentor; and remains an active YPO Member in both the Emirates and Lebanon chapters. Ramez is a Fellow of the Aspen Institute's Middle East Leadership Initiative and the Aspen Global Leadership Network. Ramez holds a BEng in Mechanical Engineering from Rutgers University and an MASc in Industrial Engineering from the University of Toronto. He has enjoyed continuing education programs at Oxford, INSEAD, and the University of St. Gallen.

MUDASSIR SHEIKHA
Co-Founder and CEO of Careem
www.careem.com

Mudassir Sheikha co-founded Careem Networks in 2012 and serves as its CEO. Prior to that, Mudassir served as the Vice President of Solutions at Keynote DeviceAnywhere. He was responsible for the solutions organization, managing all aspects of delivery of products to customers. Before that, he spent two years in Karachi, Pakistan, where he established and headed Mobile Complete's offshore development center. He also founded Solerent and served as its Director. Earlier, he was part of the Venture Finance group at Garage Technology Ventures, where he worked with seed-stage companies in the software and consumer internet industry. Before Garage, he held various technical positions at Brience and Trilogy Software, and he started his career as a consultant at Ernst and Young. Mudassir holds a master's in Computer Science from Stanford University and a bachelor's in Computer Science and Economics from the University of Southern California.

DAVID SHELTERS
Author of *Building Startup Ecosystems: Introducing the Vibrancy Rating*
www.linkedin.com/in/dmshelters

David Shelters has over 25 years of entrepreneurial experience as a Founder, Co-Founder, CFO, Board Adviser, and mentor to numerous tech startups in both America and Asia. He served as a member of several committees of the

Joint Foreign Chambers of Commerce Thailand. David is also the Founding Editor of "Thailand Startup Review" (TSR), a leading blog focused on the local startup community. He has written extensively on tech entrepreneurship and building startup ecosystems. David is a John Wiley–published author of three full-length books in addition to several annual *Thailand Startup Funding Reports*. His latest book is *Building Startup Ecosystems*. David has published over 100 articles appearing in numerous online tech media outlets as well as his two previous blogs, "Finance for Geeks" and TSR. He is considered to be an expert on the topic of startup and tech ecosystems.

TEJINDER SINGH
Founder and CEO of Q-Tickets
www.q-tickets.com

Tejinder Singh is a serial entrepreneur who has been the major driving force behind the emanation and turnaround of many ventures for over 25 years in the areas of entertainment, ticketing, internet, tech, e-commerce, back-office in voice and non-voice, digital media and marketing, ITES, B2C, and others. His visionary businesses have changed the business landscape and provided employment to over 20,000 people. Tejinder grew four successful startups in India before moving to MENA, including the first onshore BPO for India, named Sparsh—the first ever to be listed on stock market and the first ever to get acquired in the domestic BPO space. He founded BPO+, which is recognized today as one of the largest and fastest growing BPO providers in the Middle East, with a headcount of more than 1,500. Tejinder is one of the most influential voices in the startup community across India and Middle East for his active participation in mentoring, advising, and investing in startups. He chairs the Board of the Entrepreneurs' Organization (EO) and IBPN Board (Indian Embassy). *Forbes* has listed him as a Business Leader in the Middle East for five consecutive years. Tejinder also founded and ran Q-Tickets, one of the largest e-ticketing platforms in the Middle East with presence in multiple regions, and the e-commerce platform QTSouq, with more than 25 million page views per month. Tejinder was awarded Person of the Year in 2018 by *Asia One Magazine*, BPO Entrepreneur of the Year by the Asia Outsourcing Congress and Awards in 2016, and Innovative Leader Award 2015 as CEO of the Year by Asian Knowledge Management Leadership Awards, Dubai.

VERA SONGWE

Executive Secretary of United Nations Economic Commission on Africa
www.uneca.org/executive-secretary

Dr. Vera Songwe is the United Nations Under-Secretary-General and the Executive Secretary of the Economic Commission for Africa (ECA). Following her appointment, she became the first woman to lead the institution in the organization's 60-year history and the highest-ranking United Nations regional official. As Executive Secretary, Songwe focuses on "ideas for a prosperous Africa." Her organizational reforms have addressed macroeconomic stability, development finance, growth and the private sector, poverty and inequality, the digital transformation and data, and trade and competitiveness. She was named among the 100 Most Influential Africans by *Jeune Afrique* in 2019 and the 100 Most Influential Africans by *New African Magazine* in 2017. In 2018, she was chosen by the Institut Choiseul pour la politique internationale et la géoéconomie (France) as one of its African Leaders of Tomorrow, and she was included in the Top 10 Female Business Leaders in Africa by the *African Business Review* in 2014. In 2015, she was listed as one of the 25 Africans to Watch by the *Financial Times*. Prior to joining the UN, Songwe held a number of leading roles at the World Bank and the IFC. Songwe serves as a Nonresident Senior Fellow at the Brookings Institution. She is also a member of the African Union Institutional Reform team under the direction of the President of Rwanda, Paul Kagame, and an Advisory Board Member of the African Leadership Network and the Mo Ibrahim Foundation.

ERIK STAM

Professor and Dean of the Utrecht University School of Economics and Co-Author of *Entrepreneurial Ecosystems: Place-Based Transformations and Transitions*
www.uu.nl/staff/FCStam

Erik Stam is Professor at the Utrecht University School of Economics, where he holds the Chair of Entrepreneurship and Innovation. He was Co-Founder and Academic Director of the Utrecht Center for Entrepreneurship and leader of the Innovation and Welfare research area of the Utrecht University Strategic Research Theme Institutions. He held positions at Erasmus University Rotterdam, the University of Cambridge, the Max Planck Institute of Economics (Jena, Germany), and the Netherlands Scientific Council for Government Policy (WRR). In 2007, he was awarded the Herbert Simon Prize by the European Association for Evolutionary Political Economy. He is currently Associate Editor of *Small Business Economics*. His research focuses on institutions, entrepreneurship, innovation, and their relationships with economic development at the micro and macro levels. He has co-authored seven books (including *Micro-Foundations for Innovation Policy and Ambitious Entrepreneurship*) and over 80 book chapters and articles in journals including *Economic Geography*, *Industrial and Corporate Change*, *Journal of Evolutionary Economics*, *Regional Studies*, and *Small Business Economics*. In addition to his scientific work, he is often consulted by local, regional, national (Netherlands, Belgium, UK, US), and supranational (World Bank, OECD, EU) policy-makers and private sector organizations about innovation and entrepreneurship.

OSMAN SULTAN

Founding CEO of Emirates Integrated Telecommunication Company PJSC (du)
www.du.ae

Osman Sultan is the founding CEO of Emirates Integrated Telecommunications Company PJSC-du. Sultan joined the company in January 2006. Under his guidance and leadership, and continues to grow today as one of the top telecoms in the GCC. Sultan has enjoyed a successful career for over 30 years, spanning Europe, North America, and the MENA region. Prior, Sultan was the founding CEO of another successful Middle Eastern operator, Mobinil in Egypt, which he set up in 1998. A notable public speaker, Sultan often shares his knowledge and experience at industry lectures on the subjects of digital society, the internet, telecommunications, and information technology. He has also mentored a generation of key telecom sector players who have gone on to occupy leadership roles, many of them as CEOs across the world. As one of the most influential figures in the region in the telecommunications field, Sultan's drive and acute business acumen has earned him several industry accolades, including being selected as one of the 100 most powerful executives in the telecoms industry in the world on the GTB Power 100 List in 2010 and 2011.

NOOR SWEID
Founder of Global Ventures
www.global.vc

Noor Sweid is the Founder of Global Ventures, a Dubai-based, growth-stage venture capital firm focusing on investing in emerging markets. Noor was also the Chief Investment Officer at The Dubai Future Foundation and a Managing Partner at Leap Ventures. She also helped scale and led the IPO of Depa, the world's largest interior contractor, on the NASDAQ Dubai and the LSE. Noor is Chairperson of the Middle East Venture Capital Association, was on the Founding Board of Endeavor UAE, and serves as a Director for MIT Sloan, TechWadi, The Grooming Company, the Collegiate American School in Dubai, and the portfolio companies of Global Ventures. In 2018, Noor was named as one of the World's Top 50 Women in Tech by *Forbes*, and received the Arab Woman Award for Finance. Noor has also been named on the *Arabian Business* 100 Most Powerful Arab Women list three. Noor holds bachelors' degrees in Finance and Economics from Boston College as well as an MBA from MIT Sloan.

KHALDOON TABAZA
Founder and Managing Director of iMENA Group
www.imena.com

Dr. Khaldoon Tabaza is the Founder and Managing Director of iMENA Group, which portfolio includes OpenSooq, SellAnyCar, and others. He has over 25 years of experience founding, investing, managing, and advising many successful online, technology, and media companies in the MENA region. This includes the first venture-backed online business in the Arab world, Arabia.com, which he founded in 1995. In 2005, Khaldoon founded Riyada Ventures, a venture capital firm that was acquired in 2009 by the Abraaj Group. Khaldoon was recognized by the World Economic Forum as a Young Global Leader. He is also a Kauffman Venture Fellow and a member of the Young Presidents Organization (YPO). He holds a Bachelor of Medicine and Surgery from The University of Jordan and has completed the Young Global Leaders Leadership and Policy program at Harvard University's Kennedy School, and YPO education programs at Stanford, Harvard Business School, and London Business School.

ALISÉE DE TONNAC

Co-Founder and CEO of Seedstars World
www.seedstars.com

Alisée de Tonnac set up the first edition of the Seedstars World startup competition in 2013 and is now managing the company. The competition is now present in more than 85 cities, and by next year the Seedstars Group will be launching 15 strategic hubs (Seedspace co-working activities, acceleration programs, and academy centers). Alisée is a board member of the School of Management of Fribourg and a member of the Swiss National Innovation Council. She was nominated as Social Entrepreneur by *Forbes* 30 Under 30, Innovation Fellow by Wired UK, 50: Europe's most influential women in the startup and venture capital space, and the 29 Powerful Women by Refinery29. Seedstars has been quite present and active in the MENA region, hosting various kinds of startup competitions, educational programs for entrepreneurs and investors, and a host of other activities geared to supporting local entrepreneurs and startup ecosystems.

SAMIH TOUKAN

Chairman of Jabbar Internet Group and Co-Founder of
Souq.com and Maktoob Group
www.jabbar.com; www.souq.com; www.maktoob.com

Samih Toukan is the Founder and Chairman of Jabbar Internet Group. In 2000, Samih founded and became the CEO of Maktoob.com, the world's first Arabic email service and largest Arab online community, with more than 16 million users. Maktoob.com was acquired by Yahoo! in 2009 for $164 million. He is the Co-Founder of Souq, the largest e-commerce platform in the Arab world, which was recently acquired by Amazon.com for about $600 million. In 2009, Samih received the Al Hussein Medal for Distinguished Performance of the First Order from His Majesty King Abdullah II in recognition of his contribution to the IT and telecommunications sector in Jordan and the region. From 2003 to 2005, he was appointed by the Jordanian government as a Member of the Board of the Social Security Investment Fund (a fund of several billion dollars). He is also an active angel investor, backing several startups in the region, and he acts as a mentor to several entrepreneurs. He holds a bachelor's degree in Electrical Engineering from the University of London and a master's in Management and International Business from HEC University in France.

ECOSYSTEM ARABIA

AN EXCERPT FROM
STARTUP ARABIA

MUDASSIR SHEIKHA
Co-Founder and CEO of Careem
www.careem.com

Founded in July 2012 as a website-based service for corporate car bookings, Careem evolved to become the leading ride-hailing provider in MENA. It is currently in the process of expanding its services across its platform to include mass transportation, delivery and payments. Careem operates in 120 cities across 15 countries and has created more than one million employment opportunities in the region. Careem was acquired by Uber in March, 2019 for $3.1 million, which marks the largest acquisition for MENA tech startup in the region to date.

Tell us a little about your background.

I was born in Karachi, Pakistan. I'm the eldest of three siblings. I have two younger sisters. I come from a relatively middle-class family. My parents did not have the opportunity to go to college, so they had a deep desire to give us an education. They sent me and my sisters to English-medium schools so that we could acquire the education that they were not able to get.

My dad came from a business-oriented family. He had worked in the rice trading family business from the time he was a teenager, and that became his life. He still works there today and managed to raise us and give us an education.

My mom was a very good student in school. She was one of the very top students in high school. In Pakistan, they had these annual rankings. She was number three in the entire city of Karachi the year she graduated. She was also quite ambitious, but like what happens with most women in Pakistan, she got married quite early, started having kids and was not able to pursue a career and realize her potential. So, from the very beginning, my mom's untapped ambition and her unrealized potential became a part of our lives. We had to be at the top of our class, and nothing less was good enough. She would work extremely hard with us to make sure that we were doing our homework and that we were working hard on a daily basis. We were always getting 200% of her attention and focus.

My dad, on the other hand, was not able to get much education, but he was a hard-working individual who would focus on something and do it really well. If anything had to be done, you called my dad, and he would take care of it. The entire family would call him for fixing their houses, fixing relationships, fixing whatever. He was the youngest of seven siblings and was known to be the guy that would go out and fix things for everyone.

I grew up in a joint family household, so my uncles were living in the same household with us. It was a very interesting upbringing. It was very much influenced by the ambition of my mom and the humility of my dad. Growing up in this environment, I always had lots of people around me, so I thrive on and get energy from having people around me.

I did my schooling in Pakistan and ended up getting the highest GPA in all of Pakistan when I graduated from high school. I wanted to go to college in the US and hoped to get a scholarship because my family did not have money to pay for it. I applied to a bunch of schools. My grades were awesome, so I naturally expected I would get into a good school and get a full ride. As it turned out, for some reason, I got lots of rejections. I eventually got into a big college in Los Angeles, USC (University of Southern California), with a full scholarship.

I initially started studying economics at USC in '95-'96 when dot-coms were about to happen. Technology was a big topic in California then. I always enjoyed physics and math, so I found myself gravitating toward computer science. Since I loved both majors, I decided to pursue both and graduated in three-and-a-half years from USC.

What was your first business experience like?

In 1999, California was at the height of the dot-com boom. I graduated, and I didn't want to do anything but a startup. I really wanted to be in the San Francisco Bay area, where this whole, exciting technology thing was happening. Since I had a computer science degree, it was relatively easy to get a job straight out of college. After a few months, I found myself at another company working at a very early-stage startup in San Francisco. The startup was an exciting and foundational experience for me, because up until now I was the nerd. I was the one that was working hard and getting the best grades in school, and that was the only thing that mattered in life. Then, all of a sudden, here I am in Silicon Valley, working at a startup that has raised a ton of money. They had raised more than $200 million in the first round of funding. Even by Silicon Valley standards, that was by far the best ever investment round, the best ever series of investment rounds, for any startup. The objective was to bring this thing up quickly and go public in nine months.

When I joined this startup in March 2000, the objective was to go public in December 2000, in nine months, hopefully make a ton of money, and not have to work for the rest of our lives. That's how the pitch was sold to us. There's a lot of things I ended up learning not to do as a result of that experience. This was a very artificial build-to-flip mindset: let's build something extremely quickly that we don't care if the foundations are solid enough or not, but we just need to build it quickly. We need to go public. We need to make a lot of money and then we'll go and do the next thing if that day comes.

That was the mindset, and a lot of things were done that were not right, but we were getting short-term gains for long-term liability. In spite of the shortcomings, what I did get out of that experience was the ability to dream. In a way, we were trying to achieve the impossible. The founders of the business said we would do it. They actually showed us by doing whatever it took to make it a reality. Ambition within the company was through the roof.

I also learned how to work extremely fast, because this company wanted it not only for the business, but also to go public in nine months. So, literally in three months, we had hired almost three or four hundred people in Silicon Valley. That was incredible, because at that time, it was literally impossible to hire people with so much competition from other startups. We acquired a company in Florida and Armenia. We had already acquired a whole bunch of customers. This is all from the start of the business to the six-month mark.

Then, of course, there was a small correction of the markets. We had already filed our S-1 to go public. We felt this was just a correction, that the markets would come back. They came back and then they went down again, and then down again, and then we realized that this was the new reality and eventually accepted that this IPO wouldn't happen after all and that was the end of that.

I did that for about three years, which is around the time that I got my Green Card as well, and in time I became a US citizen. I went to Stanford and did my master's in computer science. I came out with the aspiration to return to Pakistan. I felt I had spent enough time in California and in the US, and it was time to head back home. I'm the only son, so I felt it would be good to be close to my parents. So, I moved back to Pakistan in 2003 to be with my parents.

Once I was in Pakistan, I started a small IT business there and met up with some friends from the last startup I was at. They were starting a business called DeviceAnywhere. It was a startup that I eventually joined as a third Co-Founder. I was responsible for the operations in Pakistan initially and then, as fate had it, had to move again to the US, where I looked after professional services out of the US.

I did that until 2008, and then felt that I had to move back once again to Pakistan because my parents were all by themselves. At the time, things were quite unstable in Pakistan. I decided to move to Dubai to be near my parents and basically park myself there until things got better in Pakistan and then move back. I joined McKinsey Management Consulting's Dubai office and did that for four years. All the while, the aspiration had always been to either go back to Pakistan or do something entrepreneurial.

How did your experience at McKinsey prepare you to become an entrepreneur?

McKinsey was the best way for me to get a business education, because I was an engineer all along, and I hadn't really done business. In the startups that I worked at I felt a void of business education. I would do things and would not have the confidence that these were the right things to do because I was not trained in them. McKinsey was amazing in building that confidence. I learned to look at business problems and solve them. I also learned how to communicate with top executives. I would present to them, and it really built confidence in my ability to solve problems the right way and articulate my message the right way.

When did Careem enter the picture?

In 2012, the startup that I left in 2008, which I had shares in, was acquired. I made some money and felt that now was the time to move and do something on my own. Around the same time, I was starting to feel that I should do something else, and as part of that thinking, I joined a group of Pakistanis in the McKinsey office in Dubai. They were working on opening an office in Pakistan. Since I was thinking of leaving anyway or going to Pakistan, I felt this was the perfect opportunity to be a part of that initiative. I joined that team and did the due diligence to make the Pakistan office happen. I had to make a list of all the companies that McKinsey could serve in Pakistan.

We started making a list of the largest companies in Pakistan. We ranked them in order of size, and the results of that exercise were quite shocking to me. Guess how many billion-dollar businesses were in Pakistan at that time, in 2011? There was only one business that was worth a billion dollars plus. This does not include the oil and gas industry; that tends to be a bit larger. It was a nation of 200 million people, and we, unfortunately, had produced only one billion-dollar business. I didn't care about the billion-dollar number so much, but the fact that we, as such a large nation, had only built one large corporate institution, I felt, was really embarrassing.

I would often joke around with Magnus, who later became my Co-Founder at Careem, that Sweden, where Magnus comes from, is a nation of nine to ten million people, and they have produced IKEA, Volvo, Erikson, Spotify—there's so much that has come out of that country. Even in the time that I spent in the Silicon Valley, every 300 meters there were large corporate institutions, and for some reason in Pakistan we had hardly built one that was big enough.

The story is not different from other parts of the Middle East. That is why I associate myself with the region, with the Muslim identity. I felt that it was more than just a Pakistan issue, that this is a region-wide problem. This is where I was coming from as I was thinking of leaving, and there was a deep desire to build something big in the region for the region. So that was my thinking then, which really planted the seed for Careem.

How did you and Magnus start working together on Careem?

I first met Magnus at McKinsey. We were the only two people at McKinsey in the Middle East who were working in technology. He similarly had a background in computer science. He also had been at some startups before, hence both of us were assigned to anything that was closely tied to technology in some shape or form at McKinsey.

I ran into Magnus again in 2012. He had just had a life-changing event where he was diagnosed with bleeding in the brain and was told that he may not survive. He had to go through a brain surgery and resolved to himself that if he survived, he would pursue becoming what he called "Magnus 2.0." Fortunately, the surgery was successful and he was healthy again. Through this experience, however, he realized that his true calling in life was to build something big and meaningful. That would be his legacy in the world. We were both coming from a place of yearning to build something big and really make an impact.

Magnus is married to a Palestinian. He was also connected to the region as I was. We decided to partner up and said, "Let's figure out what to do." At that time, we didn't have an idea. We just said, "Whatever we do has to be massively impactful over time, and it has to be meaningful. It's not about making money. Money is going to come. It's only the byproduct. It's really about improving the lives of people, making an impact and ultimately building something that will be our legacy in the world."

How did you become interested in transportation?

We looked at opportunities that could be impactful in the region. We started looking at impactful sectors like education and healthcare, looking for something that could become massive. We knew of the opportunity in transportation from our days as consultants, because every time we would travel the region, we would struggle to find reliable and convenient transportation.

As consultants, we would often spend most of our days on the road. There was always trouble finding someone to pick you up from the airport in Riyadh, then take you to your business meetings. They would not always know the directions to the place that you needed to go, and you had to pay them in cash, which you would not always have. You had to go to the ATM. It was a quite cumbersome process, and what we ended up doing, for the most part, was for every city that we would have to go to, we kept the phone number of one or two drivers that we would typically call when we land in those cities, so that worked. The problem was that the minute those drivers were not available, we would be without reliable options, and it would be quite a pain to get around.

We knew there was this opportunity. We weren't sure how big it could be or if this was meaningful enough. What's meaningful about providing a taxi service for people? This is essentially what we would be doing. When we started digging deeper, we realized that ground transportation is quite broken and in many of our cities is nonexistent, so it was a huge opportunity to come and fill this gap.

When we spoke to some of the drivers that were servicing us, we realized that their lives were quite challenging. They were working long hours. Most of them in Dubai or Pakistan were working 16-hour days. They would save 90% of the money they would make to send back home to their families to educate their kids and to keep up their families. They were living in very challenging conditions. Literally, in one room there would be four beds, and in four beds these people would sleep in shifts. We really saw this opportunity as a way to improve their lives, and we found that if we could build this thing, we could end up creating a lot of jobs, and this would then make it especially meaningful.

So that's why we took this opportunity a bit more seriously. Our first stop was McKinsey, the consulting company that we had worked with. We asked them if they would come on board as a client. There was a small pilot period after which they joined, and that's really how we got started. It was just our own pain as consultants traveling the region and finding this as a potentially big opportunity and one that would allow us to create a lot of jobs and improve the lives of drivers, or "captains," as we call them now.

What did you initially imagine Careem to be?

We started in 2012, and I remember on the first day, I took a bus from Dubai to Abu Dhabi, where Magnus lived. We met in his study, and the first thing that we did was we put in order the five values to which we would guide Careem. We had selected the name "Careem" already. Careem means generous in Arabic, and we felt this was a strong value from the region, generosity. We said we wanted to be generous on three dimensions.

We wanted to be generous to our customers, meaning that we would provide exceptionally outstanding customer service, something that you don't see much of in the region. We said we wanted to be generous to our captains. This means that we would look after them, not just by giving them work, but look after them holistically. We would be looking after their health, looking after their families and everything else they would need help with.

Finally, we would also be generous to our colleagues, the people at Careem. We would make sure that they became partners in our success and that we looked after their professional development. We would pay, for example, to have stock options in Careem. They have been very well rewarded since then as a result of Careem's growth.

We found the name Careem and the value that it represented as a way for us to be generous to customers, captains, and colleagues. That became a central value at Careem, and this is something that we decided very early on in the life of this business.

Initially, we were building a B2B service for large companies. We didn't have a consumer app. We didn't have an on-demand service. We basically had a web-based service that we would target to large companies. We understood the pain points first-hand.

When you're servicing large companies, you are as good as your "last screwup," so to speak. You have to be very particular about the call to your service. You may have delivered a thousand trips really well, but if one trip went wrong with the wrong person, it would completely destroy that relationship for you. So, we had to build a service that was very reliable. We wanted to offer very high levels of customer service, so if things went wrong, which they often and inevitably do in this business, we would respond very professionally through customer service. We would do things even before people would complain, just wow them with our customer service. We built very strong capabilities in delivering a reliable service and exceptional, high-quality customer service.

How did you deal with outside competition entering the market?

In 2013, nine months after we had started, someone sent me a job description from Uber looking for a general manager for Dubai. We didn't know much about Uber at that time because we were delivering a corporate service and we weren't doing app-based on-demand service. We saw our future on the consumer front to be an app, to be on-demand. When we heard that they were coming to the region, we naturally felt quite concerned; maybe there's a risk that we will remain corporate-focused and they will take the big consumer market opportunity right from underneath us. Uber had already raised a lot of money by then. They had an app, and it was undeniably very slick. We had no app. We had no on-demand service. We didn't even have our first round of funding closed.

It was frankly a very high-stress time for us, but there's nothing like competition to get you running really, really fast. Instead of sleeping six hours a day, we started sleeping three hours a day. We said, we have to launch an app, and we have to have it up and running before they come to the market. And we did just that. We were live on the app store a matter of weeks before Uber came to town. Very much a basic app, but we were up and running. Uber hit Dubai with their much more advanced app and serious financial backing that affords them to do whatever it takes to land-grab. Not only did this offer them more marketing opportunities; they used their buying power to try and get our captains to exclusively work for them with huge incentive schemes. What happened next was interesting. Since the Middle East tends to be somewhat challenging from an infrastructure standpoint, the maps in the region were not accurate, and a lot of these captains are not as educated as drivers that Uber may have worked with in the US. It resulted in a lot of behaviors that were unexpected for them.

When Uber first came to Dubai and launched the service, the service was quite unreliable. Even though they were giving people extreme discounts, free trips, and they were paying drivers a lot of money, they were not able to deliver a reliable service. What would happen was, you ordered a ride and would expect a car to come, and the driver would not be able to get to you reliably because he didn't have your accurate location. Other times, he would be coming to you, but on the way, he gets a call from his other client and then he cancels the booking and goes on to his other client. Something or another like that would happen because they did not build their service based on this environment, so they weren't familiar and ready with the reality of this region.

Whereas our service, even though we had a very basic app, we were totally reliable. When we said we would get you a car, we would get you a car. It would come to your exact location. It would take you where you needed to go, and when things didn't go well, we would compensate you with amazing customer service.

So, in the first year of competition, we were winning because of our reliability and because of our customer service. We figured we got another year on them because they were still learning the region. By the time they had learned, we would be able to raise some more money as well, and we would be able to compete a bit more equally. Today, we have raised much, much less money than they have raised, so we still have to be very scrappy. We really had to fight a guerrilla war and very creatively to compete with them.

How did you go about raising those funds?

Along the way we found some very strong supporters. The first round of funding was with Saudi Telecom Ventures, who were very helpful when we launched in Saudi. Then we got Al Tayyar Group on board as a second-round investor. Again, a very strong family group in Saudi that was able to support us and help us develop that market. The first round was Saudi-led, because that's where the battle was being fought.

Then after we had captured Saudi, we wanted to expand a bit broader in the region. We wanted to go to North Africa, Egypt in particular. We wanted to go to the Levant. We wanted to go to Pakistan. At that point, Abraaj Capital, the private equity group in Dubai, saw an opportunity to help us expand to those markets. They came on board as an investor, and they were instrumental in us going into North Africa and Pakistan. Then we became big enough that we were able to attract international investors' interest. Up until then we were so small, and the region was such a low priority for the global investor, that every time you would talk to global investors, they would not show interest. They were like, "You guys are small, and your region is small."

Around 2016, we became quite sizable. We were mostly growing 20-30% month on month, and at some point, the scaling charts slid up, and we became big by global standards. Not only did Careem as a platform become interesting for global investors, but they also started realizing the opportunities in the region, in overlooked places like Egypt. They started thinking that if a Careem could come out of the region, this meant that the regional investment opportunity was not to be dismissed. That's when Rakuten, the Japanese e-commerce company, came on board as a lead investor for our last round. Since then we have received investment from Daimler, the car maker, and from many other global investors. During the last 12 months, the profile of the business changed from being completely regionally owned to now having an A-list of global investors, and we continue to grow rapidly.

What do you feel was Careem's greatest differentiator against Uber?

I think that growth has happened despite competition as a result of us being hyper-local. We understand the region better than the competition, and we prioritize the needs of the region. When we go to Saudi and find out that most people in Saudi don't have a credit card, we are very quick to launch a cash-favored option, and that gives us a big edge of nine or ten months that the competition doesn't see. When we find out that women in the region would not like their phone numbers to be shared with strange male captains, we launch a feature that hides the phone number of these women from captains in order to protect their identity. The competition doesn't do that, and since they don't pick up on that, they are not able to prioritize it along with many other requests that are unique to local consumers.

It's really been a story of us being closer to the needs of the market and prioritizing those needs before the competition can catch up. Sure, they learn, and they copy, but typically with everything that we do, we get a three- to six-month leap, which always keeps us as a better overall product in the region. That allows us to compete with them with even less money. If they sold $100 million in the market, we're able to compete with them with just $20-30 million, because our product is just a better fit for the market, and its more mass-oriented than their product. That's where we are today, and I think in total we are now in 13 countries.

Our last market very proudly was Palestine, so we are really excited to be in Ramallah and making it in that part of the region, which is very close to our heart. We are in 80 cities, and hopefully we'll continue to grow 20-30% month on month. We have almost half a million captains that are working with us, and we feel quite responsible for providing them a living and their families a decent quality of life. We have almost 16 million users or customers that have signed up to use the service.

Luckily, all this has grown much faster than we ever imagined. We are grateful to have been in the right place at the right time.

We are grateful for competition, which fueled us to become more aggressive and more ambitious. We are very grateful for the support that everyone in the region has given Careem, with all the support that came from our investors who believed in us and saw opportunity in the region. We are very grateful to our captains who supported us because of being local. We are very grateful to our customers who continue to support us because we are local and they find the story inspiring. It's really a blessing to have come this far with that kind of support. We're quite grateful.

What's your advice to aspiring entrepreneurs?

I think the first advice is finding the right partner. It's a tough journey, and it has its trials and heartbreaks. I think it would have been extremely difficult to do it alone. My first advice to entrepreneurs is to really find someone who they're aligned with on the vision, mission, and whom they get along with socially to do this with. Find someone whom you have some common history with, ideally, who would complement you in some way, who is aligned with you on values. Look up into your past and search for people who might be looking to do something similar. Don't do it just by yourself.

Another piece of advice: I think sometimes we are quite obsessed with what is happening in other markets, and we think that this is working in Germany, this is working in the US, what can we bring into the region that's going to work? Often, what happens when we try to bring those ideas to the region, we find out that the region may not be ready for them yet. I strongly advise entrepreneurs not to think that way.

If your focus is on understanding and solving local problems, then you can feel free to get inspiration and learning from solutions that might be applicable that may have worked in other markets, but don't make those solutions your focus. Even in the case of Careem, even though we may look similar to Uber or other foreign solutions, if we had obsessed over bringing, let's say, our competition to the Middle

East or that exact solution to the Middle East, we would have been wiped out after the first year of business.

The only way we were able to really compete successfully was because we had the focus on understanding the local problems. We had solved mapping. We had solved privacy. We had solved driver education. We had solved customer service. All of these things that we had solved to deliver a reliable service that is tailored to the region were the real reasons we survived. If we had just blindly copied and pasted foreign solutions, we would have been out of the market by the second year.

So, talk to customers. Talk to other stakeholders, not just at the beginning, but as a continuous process. Constantly understand the problems at hand. Constantly learn how your product is doing or not doing, and everything about the experience. Make sure that it's a realistic, good experience, and make it fit the needs of your customers.

The third piece of advice, which is not region-specific and is more general on how you build startups and technology: Sometimes what we used to do before is we would have an idea. We would then take six or twelve months to build a product and then go to market. Unfortunately, that's how many people still approach product development today.

When we were starting Careem, fortunately, we had read this book called *The Lean Startup*, which also reflected some of the recent methods of early startups in the Valley. The idea was you go to the market with what they call an "MVP" (minimum viable product), which is basically a working prototype that you could develop very quickly that would add some small value to some customers, launch it as soon as possible, and use the feedback that you get from customers to learn from and tweak the product.

That book was quite valuable for us, because when we launched, we said, let's do an MVP. We gave ourselves only six weeks from the day we started to do the first trip. You can only develop so many things in six weeks. We had to go to market with something very basic. There were many things that we wanted to build, but we just didn't have time to build, because we gave ourselves a time deadline of just six weeks to launch it, and it's been five years since that launch.

There are some cool features that were on our wish list that we still haven't implemented, because when we went to the market and launched the service, people started asking for different things than the ones that we felt the market needed. The third piece of advice is to be quick to market and use feedback to refine the product and keep learning and refining until you hit what they call "product-market fit." You will know you've hit product-market fit, because things will click and you will start growing automatically without you doing a lot of hard work.

The fourth piece of advice is about the team: It's quite difficult in the beginning to hire people, because you don't have the money to pay them well, and good people are generally employed at good places and paid well. Also, in the region, we don't have a culture of inkling to work at startups. In Silicon Valley, on the other hand, everyone wants to work at a startup. In fact, the better you are there, the more you want to launch your own startup or work at a startup. Whereas here, many people still want to work at multinational companies, and if they don't want to work at multinational companies, their families want them to work at multinational companies. It becomes quite difficult to attract top talent at startups in the region. Hence, we had to do a few things differently to get people on board.

First, we decided we wanted to attract the best people we could find. Given the experience we had at McKinsey and other places, we felt that with our profile, we should be able to attract top talent. It wasn't easy, though; in fact, what we realized very soon was that we would not be able to hire employees, or at least the caliber we were after. We stopped looking to hire "employees" and started looking for "business partners." This was our recruitment pitch in the early days. We said, "Look, I don't want you to come in and work for us. I want you to come in and become a partner in this business. We'll give you equity. This is your company just like it's ours. Just come in, and let's build this thing together."

So, first, focus on top talent, because in a startup you don't have a lot of cross-functional systems, so smart people can really make or break your business. Second, use equity and an open approach to attract top talent. Third, don't give up. Sure, it's going to take time to onboard top talent, but when you find someone that you think will make a big difference in the trajectory of your startup, please don't give up on them. Knock on their door 10 times until that person stops answering your phone calls and make sure one way or another that you get that person on board. For example, Abdulla Elyas, who is our third Co-Founder, rejected us at least three or four times before we got him on board. So, if you feel that someone is going to add value, you owe it to yourself and to your startup to keep trying. Having said that, a lot of our leads came through referrals, people who we knew directly or indirectly who came on board, which was quite helpful.

How is the work dynamic between you and Magnus?

Magnus is such an amazing guy that it's very easy to work with him. I think what has really worked for us, and I suppose there are two things that have made it easy—I think the first thing is mutual trust. We trust each other blindly. There was trust before we started Careem. It has just become even stronger since then. We don't second-guess each other. Even though we have divided things between us, with Magnus focusing on technology, operations, and experience, whereas I'm on commercial, marketing, branding, business development, and fundraising, we jointly discuss many topics that are important for the business overall. There is a very healthy problem-solving dynamic between us. We like to find solutions together. When we disagree, the person that owns that topic tends to decide what to do.

We also go to each other with quite regular feedback, and this is something that we learned at McKinsey. It had a very strong feedback culture. So, from time to time there are things that I might do, or that Magnus might do, that don't seem right. It creates some emotions, and then we try to make sure that we don't let that linger. We let all things out and get constructive feedback so that we can re-address those things. It's always a team effort. We especially help each other out when we are down. We are brothers before we are partners at this point.

One thing that has really helped us is discovering the purpose behind Careem. As much as we came from different places, we were aligned on the big picture. We both were striving to create a big impact, though we didn't articulate it in the very beginning. Though everyone that has interacted with us would know in loose terms what our purpose was, it wasn't until the second year when we realized we were growing rapidly that we undertook an exercise to discover the essence of that purpose and figure out how to articulate it well.

How would you describe the mission of Careem?

The mission of Careem is to simplify the lives of people in the region and build an awesome organization that inspires. There are two parts of the mission. There's the simplifying of lives, and this is based on the premise that living in the region is difficult. You know we all lived in many parts of the world, and there is just more friction in daily life here than elsewhere. Friction basically is a lot of overhead and wasted energy that pushes people down and does not allow them to realize their full potential. We wanted to simplify people's lives so that they can actually focus on things that really matter and realize their full potential.

The second part of the mission is to build an awesome organization that inspires. Here, it's coming from the perspective that the region hasn't had huge successes. We believe that if the region gets to building great big companies, it will lead to many more. So, we would love to become one of the few companies in the region that becomes so awesome that it inspires the entire ecosystem of entrepreneurship in the region. It also means that we do things in a way that inspires.

I truly believe that the mission of Careem is the real differentiator. It has attracted people who are aligned with this mission, who are passionate about this mission, to come and work with us even though they might be earning 30 to 50% less money than they would working elsewhere. It really gets the best out of them, because they're not doing this for money; sure, they will make a lot of money over time, but they're doing this for the wider purpose of improving the region.

Everyone will have their own reasons for creating a startup. If you, an entrepreneur or founder, can figure out its purpose and articulate it well, it will be a motivator when things become challenging. It will attract like-minded people to support the mission, and it will manifest itself much more easily than it would have otherwise. I truly believe that this has been the "secret sauce" behind Careem's success.

Any resources you recommend for entrepreneurs to continue learning?

If you're an entrepreneur and your business begins to do well, it really needs you to play different roles at different stages, and it is critical for you to develop with the startup. I remember listening to the Founder of Dropbox speak, and he basically said, "The things that you do really well in one phase of a startup are the things that become your biggest handicap in the next phase." He gave the example of himself, where he was an amazing coder at the beginning. He did the initial source code version of Dropbox and did really well. As the company grew and he was entering the second phase of the startup, he realized that he was such a good coder that it actually became a huge handicap, because no one could code as well as him. He would literally be micromanaging everyone who was developing code for Dropbox. Whereas when he was in the second phase, he had to step up and provide leadership, especially tech leadership, to the people who were writing the code, versus micromanaging them at that level. I think the same is true for other areas as well.

As an entrepreneur, if you want to continue growing with the business, you need to focus on your own personal development as well. What I do, personally, is listen to a lot of podcasts. So, every time I'm traveling or on the road driving, I'm typically listening to podcasts. The ones that I listen to are more tech-oriented, like "*Masters of Scale*" with Reid Hoffman, the Founder of LinkedIn. Andreessen

Horowitz also has a good podcast, and it's keenly insightful. *Harvard Business Review*'s podcasts are quite interesting as well. "McKinsey Quarterly" I also listen to from time to time.

You also have to read. I try to focus on biographies and autobiographies of entrepreneurs. The one I've read and really liked is *Made in America* by Sam Walton, which is an incredible story of this entrepreneur from the middle of nowhere in the US starting with such humble roots and creating a global retail empire. It's quite inspiring. More recently, I read the book about Amazon, *The Everything Store* by Brad Stone. There are a few more insightful ones like this that are in the pipeline. The advice here is, as an entrepreneur, you never should stop learning.

What's working across the different components of the ecosystem?

Let's start with what's working. Dubai itself is a huge success story, because up until recently we had a brain drain from the region, where a lot of the top talent from the region would go abroad to the West. I think Dubai has created a valuable position that is enabling a bit of a reverse brain drain and is attracting talent from within the region as well as global talent. Dubai is really the best of both east and west for many people like me. It has a very solid and a very compelling social and physical infrastructure. I'm very excited about what Dubai has done and continues to do for the region as a whole.

The second thing that is working is that the collaborative spirit of the ecosystem is quite amazing. Even though we're a small ecosystem, everyone is aligned in that they want to make something happen and they share the sense that if you promote entrepreneurship, this will lead to incredible things from the region. From Fadi Ghandour, to Dany Farha , to Mohamed Alabbar, everyone is excited to put entrepreneurship on the map for the region.

The third thing that is working, and it's ironic, is that there are a lot of problems to solve in the region. You have the fact that there are problems, and this means that things are not working, but these problems are also opportunities. The bigger the problems, the bigger the opportunities. There are all sorts of opportunities in the region, which is exciting. You find an industry, you find an area, and you will see that things are not working as seamlessly, as efficiently, as effectively as they can, and that presents an opportunity to improve things. So, in some weird, twisted way, this is also working.

What areas need more attention in the regional ecosystem?

Now, things that are not working so well: The fragmentation of the region is not helping. The region is unlike the US. In the US, you have 300 million people that live in one geographic boundary. When you register a company or open a bank in California, you can immediately target the entire United States of 300 million people's purchasing power. It's quite remarkable. That's not the case in the region. There are 22 countries that make up the region, and these countries are quite different when it comes to their stages of development. They have different currencies. They have different laws. They have different border patrols and different frameworks. The challenge then for a technology business is how do you scale across an entire region when the investment that's required to build some of those smaller or less developed markets cannot be justified. The enormous complexity that you have to tackle to operate in the region as a whole makes things quite tough.

In many parts of the region, except for maybe the UAE and to some extent the Gulf, we don't have a lot of the required infrastructure to build these internet businesses. For Careem, our business requires accurate maps for us to operate, and I remember in 2011, 2012, when we were developing the first version of our app, we realized that Google Maps in the region is neither always accurate nor complete. Many locations don't exist, and some locations are purely incorrect. We had to build our own maps for the region.

We also recognized that many people in the region don't have credit cards. We had to figure out a way to work with cash. Similarly, we realized that there are no messaging services in common in two different markets, so we had to build our own similar services, migrating with telecom operators throughout the region. Unlike in the West, these things don't exist consistently in the region, and as a result, a lot more time, money, and effort need to go into development just to build the base infrastructure that is taken for granted, say, in the US or Europe.

The second thing that's not working, though is changing rapidly, is the lack of funding for startups. There is no shortage of money in the region. As a region, we are a net exporter of capital to the rest of the world, but that capital from the region does not always flow into the local startups. The big money in the region is being invested abroad away from the region. A lot of our entrepreneurs and startups in the region don't make it just because they aren't able to raise money. You know there's not enough money to go around in the ideas that are being developed, and it's a little bit torturous, a vicious cycle. Since there is not enough money, there are not enough successes, and since there aren't enough successes, a lot of top talent that'll do startups seek refuge in working at multinationals to have a good career and to do well for themselves. We really need to solve the funding issue.

The last thing that's not working is talent. I mean, to build internet businesses, you need a lot of technical talent, and unfortunately, we still don't have enough amazing engineering colleges and universities that are producing strong engineering and computer science graduates, and it's a very big issue. Not only do we not have enough, the people who come out of our colleges, after spending a few years working in the region, the best ones also get offers from Microsoft, Google, and Facebook, and they end up moving away from the region.

Now, for Careem, we are enabling a little bit of reverse brain drain of this tech talent as well, where we are actively doing recruiting road- shows in the US, looking for people from the region who may be working at good companies in the US and would like to move back to the region. It's actually going well. Our head of engineering is ex-Facebook. Our head of product is a Y Combinator executive. There are many other people who have joined Careem from companies like Google, Facebook, and others who have moved to Dubai with their families and are now developing the business.

What's your future vision for Careem?

We are the largest internet business in the region today, and the internet in the region is quite small. Less than 2% of what consumers spend goes through the internet. That number in places like China is almost 30%. There is going to be a huge shift from traditional retail to the internet in the region over the next five to ten years, and we want to make sure that as the largest internet platform in the region today, we are able to enable the region's move to the internet. What we have done over the last five years is build a lot of the building blocks that are required to build an internet business in the region, and we would like to prototype these building blocks and enable others to scale much faster to all parts of the region.

Imagine you can create a business in Casablanca, Morocco— without having to register 20 legal entities, 20 bank accounts, 20 offices, and God knows how many integrations with favored plat- forms and otherwise—with just one legal entity, with just one integration with Careem. We should be able to enable you to operate in the entire region, just like you're able to operate from one legal entity in California to the entire US. We literally want to build the United States of Middle East as far as enabling the internet for the ecosystem is concerned. In the next 10 years, Careem should be the dominant internet platform in the region that has played a key role in moving the region to the internet. Of course, ride hailing and mobility will be a big part of our business, but the business will be a broader internet business than just the ride-hailing business. That's the hope and the broader vision.

At Careem, our vision is, first and foremost, to build a lasting institution that impacts the lives of everyone in the region. So, we should, over time, impact the life of every single person in the region. There are 400 million people in the region, and God willing, we will impact each and every person's life. Second, we should be building amazing products and services versus substandard or non-world-class products and services. Third, we should be doing things in a socially meaningful way, not just focus on profits, but focus on social good. Last, we eventually become the leadership factory for the region so people who work at Careem learn things from us and then they go out and do their own startups or assume other leadership positions in the region. So just like places like PayPal had this PayPal mafia and a lot of entrepreneurs and leaders in California come out of places like Google, we would love to be the leadership factory for the region. We have a functional vision, which is to hopefully develop an internet platform in the region, but on the more organizational part, we would love to build a lasting institution for the region that does these four things. We want it to be a part of the region for centuries to come, even after we are gone, and be a source of welfare and prosperity for the region.

Full e-book available for free download on
www.StartupArabiaBook.com

ACKNOWLEDGMENTS

This book was a collective effort in every sense of the word. As such, I'm very grateful to the hundreds of people who were involved in various capacities and who, in effect, helped bring this book to life. Without them, this project would have never gotten off the ground.

First and foremost, thank you Brad Feld and Ramez Shehadi for your invaluable inspiration and guidance, most particularly with structuring this work and overall framework. I would also like to acknowledge Rachel Meier and Peter Birkeland for their astute and timely input—your feedback and suggestions proved to be spot on.

To Professor Klaus Schwab, it's an honor to gain your endorsement. It means a lot to me, as I continue to work diligently to live up to your confidence in me and my work.

I want to extend special thanks and deep gratitude to Ned Jaroudi for his invaluable feedback and for being the bedrock of this project from day one. Much gratitude also goes out to Joy Ajlouny and Muhammed Mekki. To Philip Bahoshy, Sietse van de Kerkhof, Noor Salama, and Roy Korkomaz, and MAGNiTT team; and Omar Christidis and Azza Yehia, and ArabNet team: thank you very much for all your support and generosity and your continued contribution to the MENA ecosystem. Additional thanks to Lara Fakih at Wamda and Ray Dargham at Step Conference for their generosity sharing reports material.

I would also like to personally acknowledge Fadi Ghandour, Samih Toukan, Ronaldo Mouchawar, and Christopher Schroeder for their great contribution and relentlessness over the years, championing entrepreneurship and ecosystem-building in the region. I would also like to acknowledge the countless other contributors to the regional ecosystem, too many to name individually here.

I am grateful for the opportunity to interview and feature the following individuals, who have been very generous and supportive. I would like to extend special thanks to those exceptional individuals for their remarkable contributions—you were chosen for a reason and you certainly lived up to it. I look forward to continuing our discussion and collaboration:

Abdul Baset Al Janahi, Abdulaziz Al Loughani, Adrian Garcia-Aranyos, Ahmad Sufian Bayram, Ahmed El Alfi, Aiman Kabli, Albert Bravo-Biosca, Alec Ross, Ali Abukumail, Alisée De Tonnac, Amir Barsoum, Amira Rashad, Ammar Al Malik, Amr Awadallah, Anand Chopra-Mcgowan, Andrew Berkowitz, Andrew Romans, Areije Al Shakar, Arunma Oteh, Ashraf Sabry, Badr Jafar, Bala Kamallakharan, Bijan Azad, Bill Aulet, Brad Feld, Christopher Rogers, Christopher Schroeder, Daniel Isenberg, Dany Farha, Dave Mcclure, David Audretsch, David Shelters, Deemah Alyahya, Dina El-Mofty, Efosa Ojomo, Elissa Freiha, Erik Brynjolfsson, Erik Stam, Eyad Alkassar, Eyad Latif, Fouad Jeryes, Hans Henrik Christensen, Heather Henyon, Hisham Elaraby, Idriss Al Rifai, Issa Aghabi, JF Gauthier, John Macomber, Jonathan Ortmans, Josh Lerner, Joy Ajlouny, Julie Lenzer, Kate Pope Hodel, Kevin O'Leary, Khaldoon Tabaza, Lamia Kamal-Chaou, Linda Rottenberg, Mahmoud Adi, Marc Nager, Maryam Eid AlMheiri, Max Borders, Mazin Al Zaidi, Mohamed Anouar Maarouf, Mohammed Jaffar, Mudassir Sheikha, Muhammad Mansour, Muhammad Nabil, Muhammed Mekki, Nabeel Koshak, Najla Al-Midfa, Ned Jaroudi, Noor Sweid, Omar Almajdouie, Omar Ayyash, Omar Christidis, Osman Sultan, Ossama Hassanein, Patrick Chalhoub, Peter Cohan, Philip Bahoshy, Rabea Ataya, Rabih Khoury, Ramesh Jagannathan, Ramez Shehadi, Rami Salman, Roberto Croci, Ronaldo Mouchawar, Ruben Nieuwenhuis, Sami Mahroum, Samia Melhem, Samih Toukan, Sangeet Paul Choudary, Seth Levine, Shadi Banna, Sherif Kamel, Steve Case, Tammer Qaddumi, Tejinder Singh,

Tim Draper, Tim O'Reilly, Ton Van 't Noordende, Vera Futorjanski, Vera Songwe, Victor Hwang, Walid Hanna, Walid Mansour, Will Herman, Yasmeen Al Sharaf, Yousef Hamza, Ziad Mokhtar, and Zubair Naeem Paracha.

Additional thanks to the following individuals for their great input and support to the project: Magnus Olsson, Dani Abu Ghaida, Abdelhameed Sharara, Gemma McKeown, Randa Helmy Khouzam, Mahmoud Fansa, Abdulwahab Alessa, Amr Shady, Alexandra Talty, Amal Dokhan, Aya Sadder, Fadi Tadros, Fahad AlSharekh, Ihsan Jawad, Jon Richards, Khaloud Talhouni, Mutaz Ghuni, Nicolas Rouhana, Omar Gabr, Osama Alraee, Osama Ashri, Raf Fatani, Ramez El-Sherafy, Ray Dargham, Riad Hartani, Sharif Badawi, Wael El-Desouki, Ziad Matar, Amjad Ahmed, Emile Cubeisy, Fawaz Zu'bi, Ali Mnif, Karim Jouini, Norris Krueger, Haythem Mehouachi, and Elaine Aboud.

To my great editorial and publishing superhero team, Fabienne Stassen, Michelle Waitzman, Carol Reed, and Aisha Meddeb: thank you very much for all your diligence and efforts bridging what this book could be ultimately into what it is today. I trust you'd be proud of the final product, which is very much your creation as well.

To Andy Meaden, Seham Sayed, Nanne, Kristin Muller, Rebekah Berger, Chris Kridler, Moustafa Abou El Ela, Karim Abou El Ela, Jamie Dempsey, Paco Salgado, and Ivan Bernal—for all your invaluable and timely help and patience, as well as to Terkwaz and Zanetti Photography.

To Erika Vericima and Aysha Espada—for your wonderful support and great encouragement every step of this journey with all of its ups and downs.

To Nash Salah, Claudia Bueno, Bernadette Valdivia, Amr Belal, Dean Adams, Dorian Yates, Gal Yates, Yana Kiselyunas, Lauren Marke, Sila Celik, Brian Hollowaty, and Samantha Cook—for your priceless friendship and encouragement in this project and over the years.

To Rawia Helmy, Omar Soudodi, Ahmed Soudodi, Reem Soudodi, Mostafa Hegazi, Rimy Allam, Amal Elsayed, Maryam Allam, Liala El

Edwy, and Moustafa El Edwy—for being a family in every sense of the world and for all your encouragement and care over the years.

To my mother and my father, may they rest in peace—beyond any gratitude or words can express, I owe my best to you.

Special thanks and appreciation to everyone else who helped me in this journey, even if you're not mentioned here by name. My sincere apologies for not being able to feature the countless individuals making a great impact on the startup and tech ecosystem in the Arab world—many of whom I actually interviewed—but was unable to feature given space and editorial constrains, and who are every bit worthy of praise and acknowledgment here.

INDEX

ECOSYSTEM ARABIA

"I'm an optimist about the region's prospects. I want to make this very clear from the outset. I am in this region because I believe in it and its promise. I'm convinced that people like you, like me, like so many others, have to be agents of positive change. Our region deserves it. It needs it. We must become a source of great stories, of great outcomes, of amazing contributions—not just for ourselves and the neighborhoods that we're in, but for the world. While the region has historically seen its fair share of negative attention, our role is to support in changing that, building a framework that allows for positivity to flourish. If people like us don't do it, then who will? If not now, then when? I'm an optimist by intention. It's very easy to be a pessimist, but you don't get very far being one. We must continue looking at the horizon and striving to better ourselves every day in every way."

—**RAMEZ SHEHADI**, Managing Director of Facebook, MENA

ABOUT THE AUTHOR

Amir Hegazi is a lifelong entrepreneur, with over 20 years of startup, tech, e-commerce, and digital media experience. He is the Managing Partner of intoMENA Group, a consulting firm that helps international companies do business into the MENA region. Amir was previously the Director of Marketplace at Souq.com, the region's largest e-commerce platform (recently acquired by Amazon.com). He helped build Souq.com's marketplace from the ground up to account for a sizable portion of overall sales volume. He is also one of the early pioneers of digital media in the region, having launched the largest online TV network in the Arab world at such companies as JumpTV and Talfazat. He is also an adviser on tech startups, entrepreneurial ecosystems, and go-to-market and e-commerce strategies for ministers, policy-makers, CEOs, and entrepreneurs. Hegazi is the Author of Amazon.com bestseller *Startup Arabia*, which was recognized as one of the top global startup books of 2019. Amir is Egyptian-American. He grew up in California and has been living and working in MENA since 2005.

CPSIA information can be obtained
at www.ICGtesting.com
Printed in the USA
LVHW072043060420
652404LV00008B/12/J